Education Law in Canada

A Guide for Teachers and Administrators

EDUCATION LAW IN CANADA

A Guide for Teachers and Administrators

Edited by David C. Young

Education Law in Canada: A Guide for Teachers and Administrators
© Irwin Law Inc., 2017

Published in 2017 by

Irwin Law Inc.
14 Duncan Street
Suite 206
Toronto, ON
M5H 3G8

www.irwinlaw.com

ISBN: 978-1-55221-442-8
e-book ISBN: 978-1-55221-443-5

Library and Archives Canada Cataloguing in Publication

Education law in Canada (2017)
    Education law in Canada : a guide for teachers and administrators / edited by David Young.

Includes bibliographical references and index.
Issued in print and electronic formats.
ISBN 978-1-55221-442-8 (softcover).—ISBN 978-1-55221-443-5 (PDF)

    1. Educational law and legislation—Canada. I. Young, David C., 1971–, editor II. Title. III. Title: Education law in Canada (2017)

KE3805 E39 2017   344.71'07   C2017-905958-0
KF4119 E39 2017   C2017-905959-9

Printed and bound in Canada.

1 2 3 4 5   21 20 19 18 17

Contents

Preface

When I enrolled in university several years ago, my thoughts at the time were, upon completion of my bachelor of arts degree, to attend law school, with the ultimate goal of becoming a practising lawyer. However, as is often the case in life, the path towards a career is seldom linear, and my experience is not an exception to this norm. Early in my first degree, I realized I had a love of teaching, and instead of becoming a lawyer, I opted to pursue a career in public education. The pull towards law was never far from the surface, though, and in both my master of education and doctor of philosophy degrees, I completed, respectively, a thesis and a dissertation dealing with the intersection of law and education. I was extremely fortunate in both of these degrees to have received excellent mentorship and support from Lawrence Bezeau at the MEd level and Gregory Dickinson during my PhD studies. Both of these individuals truly opened my eyes to the many issues pertaining to education law, and for this I am eternally grateful.

Although my career as a public school educator is now behind me, I am fortunate to teach in a post-secondary institution where I routinely offer both preservice and graduate courses in education law. Although I admit that I am extremely biased towards my education law courses, I truly believe that they are among, if not the most valuable courses offered. I fundamentally believe that all educators need an understanding and appreciation of the profound impact law has on the teaching profession, which then brings me to the genesis for this particular book. Throughout my post-secondary teaching career, I have used a variety of education law texts, and admittedly, each of these has been quite excellent. However,

I often felt that there was no one book that offered everything I was look-ing for in a text. As a result, this book arose as an effort to provide coverage of areas and issues of importance in education law. Although the chapters are organized sequentially, as much as this is possible in a book of this nature, each chapter can be read in isolation. It is important, too, to rec-ognize that coverage of certain topics might find a home in multiple chap-ters. For example, search and seizure is an issue for educators, but it also has an impact on student rights, and thus repetition is at times necessary.

David C. Young
St Francis Xavier University

Acknowledgements

Any prefatory note would be remiss without mentioning those who contributed to this book. Each of the authors has a demanding academic or legal career, and I acknowledge and appreciate their respective efforts in bringing to fruition their chapters.

I also extend a sincere debt of gratitude to Jeff Miller and the entire team at Irwin Law. From the first instance I pitched this idea, Jeff was unbelievably supportive and has been remarkably patient as the book has unfolded.

I also need to thank Wendy Kraglund-Gauthier for her outstanding proofreading and editing of the first draft of the manuscript. Her keen eye for detail is without equal!

As for my family, I would like to recognize the love of my parents, Clarke and Barbara Ann Young, and my late grandmother, Emma Dawson.

It goes almost without saying that the love and support of my wife Lori and daughter Emma have truly made this project possible. On more than one occasion they overlooked and tolerated my absence as I engaged in writing and research. For this and too many other things to name, I dedicate this book to them.

David C. Young
St Francis Xavier University

CHAPTER 1

From My Side of the Desk

A Case for School Law

Nora M Findlay

It was June 2000, and I had just been appointed vice-principal at a medium-sized high school in an urban centre in Saskatchewan. Prior to my appointment, I had been a teacher of English language arts at the secondary level for ten years. I recall going into the vice-principal's office for the first time in order to prepare for the upcoming school year and scouring the shelves, desk, and bookcase for a textbook — anything — that could assist me in my new role, which I somewhat naively assumed revolved around student discipline. At the time I held two undergraduate degrees, one in Arts and one in Education. Although a graduate degree or special certification was not a requirement for school-based administrative positions in the school division, I also had applied for, and been accepted into, part-time graduate studies at university. That fall, then, as I assumed my role as a high school vice-principal, I also embarked upon a Master's program in Educational Administration, and the first class I enrolled in was a course in education law.[1] The class engendered in me a keen interest in the law and its nexus with education and provided me, in part, with the knowledge I

---

1   See Anthony F Brown & Marvin A Zuker, *Education Law*, 4th ed (Toronto: Thomson Carswell, 2007) at 2–4 for a detailed description of education law that reflects the complexity of the field, in which they also distinguish the "sub-category of school law" that "includes areas that matter to principals, teachers, parents and students, including student safety and discipline, special education, parental harassment, school councils, student records, teachers' duties, and principals' duties" (*ibid* at 4). More succinctly, Thomas McMorrow, "Questioning the 'Law' in Education Law" (2014) 23 *Education and Law Journal* 209 defines education law at 209 as "the area of law, legal practice and scholarship which focuses on the intersection of the education system and the legal system."

had sought to inform my decision making in my work with students.[2] In the years that followed, I became increasingly more convinced, not only of the centrality of education law in the day-to-day practice of teachers and school-based administrators, but also of the need for educators to become legally literate.[3]

Education law is a part of a constellation of areas, such as curriculum and instruction, assessment and evaluation, and special education, that shape the role of contemporary educators; but as a foundational element in the daily practice of teachers and school-based administrators, its significance cannot be overstated.[4] Arguably, knowledge of education law serves the interests not only of educators but also of students, as Dr Gregory M Dickinson of Western University notes:

---

2   McMorrow, *ibid* at 221, mentions, as a point of interest, the lack of research indicating "the extent to which" educators at all levels "base their decisions on expressly legal considerations."

3   Charles J Russo & Douglas Stewart, in "The Place of Education Law in the International Community" (2001) *Education Law Journal* 18 at 19, argue that "educators need a broad-based understanding of the law that will not only enable them to recognise when legal problems are developing, but will also guide them in dealing effectively with situations after they have arisen." See also Mark Littleton, "Teachers' Knowledge of Education Law" (2008) 30 *Action in Teacher Education* 71 at 76, who suggests "inadequate legal knowledge may discourage risk taking and innovation" among teachers and that "uniformed teachers who grapple with difficult situations may elect the politically acceptable response in lieu of the legally correct response."

4   Eric M Roher & Simon A Wormwell, *An Educator's Guide to the Role of the Principal* (Aurora, ON: Aurora Professional Press, 2000) at 221, maintain "every action taken by a school board, school administrator, principal or teacher is founded upon a law which either permits those actions or limits them in some way," while Jay P Heubert, "The More We Get Together: Improving Collaboration Between Educators and Their Lawyers" (1997) 67:3 *Harvard Educational Review* 531 at 532, argues "the law affects such central educational matters as school governance, curriculum, pedagogy, staffing, the physical conditions under which educators and students work, and equality of educational opportunity." See also Sheila Stelck, "Walking the Tightrope: How Superintendents Respond to Challenging Rights Issues and the Role of Law" (2009) 18 *Education and Law Journal* 249 at 251, who observes that "law pervades the education system: it is the basis for the creation of schools, the formation of formal relationships within school, and it describes and prescribes the rights, duties and responsibilities of all those who work and study in the school system."

Like all professionals, educators — especially those with fiduciary[5] duties to vulnerable groups — should have an accurate understanding of their legal obligations and liability in their practice. Such knowledge benefits both educators and students: educators benefit from a sense of confidence in the legal propriety of their decisions and actions, and students benefit from educators' heightened awareness of legal boundaries including those determined by student rights, and the need to practise sound risk management. Educators also gain an appreciation of the extent to which their own rights and interests are protected under the law. (personal communication, 28 November 2014)

What might be described as an exponential growth of literature in the field of education law reflects the many perspectives from which it may be considered, such as a field of academic study or as an "applied rather than purely theoretical discipline"[6] that is a "valuable tool for practitioners."[7] A quick database search in November 2014, using the terms "education law" and "principal," for example, produced over 2,100 results for journal articles and dissertations alone. The literature is replete with studies[8] that have been conducted nationally and internationally[9] on teachers'

---

5   *Black's Law Dictionary*, 9th ed, defines a fiduciary as "a person who is required to act for the benefit of another person under matters within the scope of their relationship; one who owes to another the duties of good faith, trust, confidence and candor."

6   Charles J Russo, "School Law: An Essential Component in Your Toolbox" (2010) 75:9 *School Business Affairs* 36 at 36, maintains the decision in *Brown v. Board of Education of Topeka*, 347 US 483 (1954) "signaled the birth of the field known today as school law or education law" in the United States, while Brown & Zuker, above note 1 at 2, maintain "it is difficult to say exactly when education law evolved into a fully-developed field of law."

7   Russo, *ibid* at 36.

8   Perry A Zirkel, "Paralyzing Fear? Avoiding Distorted Assessments of the Effect of Law on Education" (2006) 35 *Journal of Law & Education* 461 at 486–87, and David Schimmel & Matthew Militello, "Legal Literacy for Teachers: A Neglected Responsibility" (2007) 77 *Harvard Educational Review* 257 at 260, specifically point to the large number of doctoral dissertations completed on the subject.

9   See, for example, Frank Peters & Craig Montgomerie, "Educators' Knowledge of Rights" (1998) 23 *Canadian Journal of Education* 29; Schimmel & Militello, *ibid*; Fatt Hee Tie, "A Study on the Legal Literacy of Urban Public School Administrators" (2014) 46 *Education & Urban Society* 192; Doug Stewart, "Legalisation of Education: Implications for Principals' Professional Knowledge" (1998) 36 *Journal of Educational Administration* 129; Bernard Moswela, "Knowledge of Educational Law: An Imperative to the Teacher's Practice" (2008) 27 *International Journal of*

and principals' legal literacy,[10] and, although there have been limitations noted,[11] the "cumulative consistency of their findings is significant."[12] An overwhelming number of these studies document findings that suggest teachers and school administrators lack a "fundamental understanding of school law,"[13] or that they "do not adequately comprehend the legal milieu in which they function on a daily basis."[14] Consequently, there also have been calls for increased legal knowledge among educators and administrators.[15] As well, the multifaceted nature of educators' roles[16] in the twenty-first century, in addition to what some have described as the

---

Lifelong Education 93; Nora M Findlay, "In-School Administrators' Knowledge of Education Law" (2007) 17 *Education and Law Journal* 177.

10   Jerome G Delaney, "The Value of Educational Law to Practising Educators" (2009) 19 *Education and Law Journal* 119 at 121, defines legal literacy as "the knowledge level that administrators have with respect to educational law and how it impacts on the governance of their schools."

11   See, for example, Michael Imber, "Pervasive Myths in Teacher Beliefs About Education Law" (2008) 30 *Action in Teacher Education* 88, or Peters & Montgomerie, above note 9 at 41.

12   Zirkel, above note 8 at 488.

13   Matthew Militello, David Schimmel, & H Jack Eberwein, "If They Knew, They Would Change: How Legal Knowledge Impacts Principals' Practice" (2009) 93 *NASSP Bulletin* 27 at 30.

14   Troy A Davies, "The Worrisome State of Legal Literacy Among Teachers and Administrators" (2009) 2 *Canadian Journal for New Scholars in Education* 1 at 6; Littleton, above note 3 at 72, points to teachers' "dismal comprehension of education law" and, at 75, to their "alarming lack of knowledge of education law and legal issues that pertain to their job."

15   See, for example, Schimmel & Militello, above note 8, Davies, *ibid* at 6–7, or Stewart, above note 9 at 140. Zirkel, above note 8 at 494, calls for greater effort at "fostering accurate, effective, and useful legal knowledge among educators at all levels, from preservice teachers to superintendents." See also Stelck, above note 4 at 269, who argues for school superintendents to have legal knowledge; knowing the "parameters of law" will allow them to act more "strategically" in their work. J Rene Gallant, "Advising Principals: Using the Law to Improve Schools and Support School Leaders" in Roderick C Flynn, ed, *Law in Education: Help or Hindrance?* (Proceedings of the fourteenth annual conference of the Canadian Association for the Practical Study of Law in Education, held in Jasper, AB, 27–30 April 2003) (Georgetown, ON: CAPSLE, 2004) at 424, believes that "educators should know the law so that lawyers are not the only profession that can speak with authority about legal problems in schools."

16   Russo & Stewart, above note 3 at 18, describe the growing "complexity surrounding schools" which results in "increasingly sophisticated management and teaching responsibilities" of educators. See also Stewart, above note 9 at 129.

"legalisation"[17] of education, would appear to require that teachers and administrators keep "informed and constantly upgrade their knowledge regarding policies, procedures, and the law."[18] Moreover, when models of school leadership are considered, an understanding of education law has been identified as one aspect of the professionalism[19] of educators since "the knowledge that teachers gain in the study of education law contributes to an efficient and orderly functioning of schools because they can accept responsibility for their practice as professionals and not simply as employees."[20] The importance of an understanding of education law has

17 Stewart, *ibid* at 131, describes the "processes of legalisation of education" which are "evident" in many countries, including Canada, "where there have been considerable increases in areas of legislative and common law influencing education policies and practices," and distinguishes them from "legalism" which "is the process of following rules and regulations, based on some formal aspect of law, as ends in themselves." See also Heubert, above note 4 at 537; Russo & Stewart, above note 3 at 18. Littleton, above note 3 at 76, refers to the effect of "the legalization of the educational environment." For a Canadian perspective, see also Findlay, above note 9 at 178; Brown & Zuker, above note 1 at 5–8; and Alan W Leschied, Gregory Dickinson, & Wendy Lewis, "Assessing Educators' Self-Reported Levels of Legal Knowledge, Law-Related Areas of Concern and Patterns of Accessing Legal Information: Implications for Training and Practice" (2000) 14 *Journal of Educational Administration and Foundations* 38.

18 Roher & Wormwell, above note 4 at 218.

19 See, for example, Delaney, above note 10 at 136; Tie, above note 9 at 204; Moswela, above note 9 at 102. Heubert, above note 4 at 543 and 567, makes an insightful comparison to individuals in other "human service fields [such] as health care" who would be expected to have had training and knowledge about legal principles affecting them. Leschied, Dickinson, & Lewis, above note 17, observe that legal knowledge, as an aspect of educators' professional knowledge, is linked to levels of accountability, as does Stewart, above note 9 at 132. See also Davies, above note 14 at 2.

20 Susan Sydor, "Teacher Education Needs More Education Law" (Paper delivered at the Canadian Association for the Practical Study of Law in Education Seventeenth Annual Conference, 29 April–2 May 2006, Montreal, QC) at 936. See also A Wayne MacKay & Lyle Sutherland, *Teachers and the Law*, 2d ed (Toronto: Emond Montgomery, 2006) at 196, who maintain that "some understanding of the legal framework within which schools operate is essential to being a good teacher"; Perry A Zirkel, "Guest Editor's Note" (2008) 30 *Action in Teacher Education* 2, suggests that models of "teacher leadership" extend also to "classroom teachers and specialists such as school psychologists and counselors" who are the "critical intersection . . . representing professional practice and legal requirements." See also Stewart, above note 9 at 141, who asserts principals are viewed not only as "instructional leaders but they are also seen as administra-

been linked to the role of in-school administrators,[21] especially in situations in which "knowledge of the legislative and common law issues and their interplay with constitutional and human rights principles is crucial to successful school administration."[22] Some studies show that many school administrators, in particular, desire more legal knowledge[23] and feel that an enhanced understanding may make them less vulnerable to potential litigation,[24] help them gain greater confidence in their decision

---

tive leaders responsible for a widening range of specialist concerns including legal risk management."

21   Sydor, above note 20 at 932, contends that "a more thorough and detailed knowledge of the acts and regulations appropriately belongs to the training of administrators because the majority of decisions and responsibilities for their application pertain to administrators"; the research of Schimmel & Militello, above note 8 at 265, suggests that the "school administration" was a "moderate or substantial source of legal information" for teachers second only to their primary source of "other teachers." See also Militello, Schimmel, & Eberwein, above note 13 at 39. See also Leschied, Dickinson, & Lewis, above note 17 at 63, who maintain "since school administrators are sources of legal information for their staffs, they are obvious targets for receiving considerably more legal education in their qualification programs."

22   See Robert G Keel, *Student Rights and Responsibilities: Attendance and Discipline* (Toronto: Emond Montgomery, 1998) at 172. While Roher & Wormwell, above note 4 at 221, specifically point to principals who "are both leaders and managers in their respective schools, it should be recognized that, among other things, an understanding of education law is essential to the effective management and operation of their schools." See also Stewart, above note 9 at 141, who argues principals are "viewed as instructional leaders but they are also seen as administrative leaders responsible for a widening range of specialist concerns including legal risk management."

23   See, for example, Delaney, above note 10; Findlay, above note 9; Tie, above note 9 at 198; Militello, Schimmel, & Eberwein, above note 13. Schimmel & Militello, above note 8 at 273, point to research that found both newly appointed and experienced principals identified "more legal knowledge" as a priority in their practices, especially since they were the source of legal knowledge for their staff.

24   *Zirkel*, above note 8 at 495, however, questions the perception of a "litigation crisis" in education cases in the United States, especially in light of "a steady and significant trend toward outcomes in favor of school defendants." Imber, above note 11 at 91, forthrightly dispels any such myth when he states "there is no litigation explosion in education, and there has not been one for at least 30 years"; Keel, above note 22 points to "reasonably consistent judicial support" for school officials in court cases. Louis LeBel, "Supreme Court of Canada Case Law Regarding Fundamental Rights in Education" (2006) 16 *Education and Law Journal* 137 at

making,[25] and help alleviate the stress of "managing legal matters" [26] in their schools. Other studies have revealed that some school principals have "terminated"[27] or "modified"[28] both curricular and extra-curricular programs because of "liability concerns."[29] Decisions I have made in my own administrative practice attest to this finding.

There are sound reasons for the inclusion of education law classes at the undergraduate and graduate levels. Dickinson provides a thoughtful rationale for teaching education law to teachers and school administrators:

> An education in law provides educators with a new lens through which to view and reflect on their practice; in particular, it affords a new mode of reasoning and a new set of values to bring to their decisions and actions, such as the legal meaning of procedural or administrative fairness, freedom of expression, equality of opportunity, and many other concepts that are embedded in educators' daily experiences at school. (personal communication, 28 November 2014)

Although the "centrality"[30] of courses in education law for American school leaders is reflected among the nearly 88 percent of the members of the University Council for Educational Administration (UCEA)[31] which offer courses in school law for their educational leadership programs, reasons for an apparent lack of undergraduate and graduate classes in

---

138, characterizes the Supreme Court of Canada "as deferential to the expertise of members of the educational community." See also MacKay & Sutherland, above note 20 at 196, who assert "the tradition of judicial deference to local school boards and political authorities is still alive and well in Canada." See also Davies, above note 14 at 2–3.

25 See Delaney, above note 10 at 127 and Findlay, above note 9. See also Leschied, Dickinson, & Lewis, above note 17, for a discussion of educators' self-assessed confidence levels.

26 Stewart, above note 9 at 140. See also Delaney, above note 10 at 132.

27 Sherman Joyce, "Keeping Schools from Being Sued" (2000) 65 *The Education Digest* 4 at 5.

28 *Ibid.*

29 *Ibid.* See also Davies, above note 14 at 5.

30 Russo, above note 6 at 36.

31 *Ibid.* Russo describes the UCEA as "an organization of doctoral degree-granting institutions in educational leadership" in the United States.

education law at many other universities[32] include "an already pressed curriculum, a lack of faculty expertise, a lack of budgetary resources, a discussion of legal topics included elsewhere, and an absence of need for legal education."[33] The need for "ongoing, and clearly focussed in-service courses on school law throughout principals' careers"[34] on a regularly scheduled basis has also been identified, in addition to recommendations for "periodic"[35] and "frequent"[36] in-service sessions on education law for practising teachers.[37] Knowledge of education law may be just one part of the "professional repertoire"[38] of teachers and administrators, but in my mind, it is a crucial part.

It does not necessarily follow, however, that with increased legal knowledge comes better decision making,[39] or the certainty that an educator

---

32 See for example, Littleton, above note 3 at 75, who points to a general lack of availability of education law courses in the United States and argues that the practice of "merely providing a unit of instruction within a course was found to be ineffective in improving one's knowledge level of education law." See also Leschied, Dickinson, & Lewis, above note 17, who observe that the levels and types of training for preservice teachers vary widely in Canada.

33 Davies, above note 14 at 6; Schimmel & Militello, above note 8 at 271. See also Darlene Y Bruner & Marilyn J Bartlett, "Effective Methods and Materials for Teaching Law to Preservice Teachers" (2008) 30 *Action in Teacher Education* 36 at 40, who outline various pedagogical approaches for teaching courses in education law to preservice teachers.

34 Stewart, above note 9 at 141.

35 Littleton, above note 3 at 75.

36 *Ibid.*

37 Militello, Schimmel, & Eberwein, above note 13 at 42, advocate for "regular professional development legal updates, [and] user-friendly resources" for principals. See also Leschied, Dickinson, & Lewis, above note 17 at 63, who recommend that school administrators should "receive frequent, regular and high-quality inservice updating education law issues."

38 Davies, above note 14 at 6.

39 See Davies, *ibid* at 6 for a practical example of this assertion involving duty of care and playground supervision; Suzanne R Painter, "Improving the Teaching of School Law: A Call for Dialogue" (2001) 2 *Brigham Young University Education and Law Journal* 213 at 215, cites the "disconnect between professional preparation and practice" in school leadership programs, for example, where "graduates steeped in instructional leadership may be unprepared to deal with workplace realities" and argues that the goal of administrators' preparation programs should be to develop "problem-solving" capability (*ibid* at 219).

or administrator will use this knowledge appropriately.[40] Arguably, what is needed is further exploration not only of the ways in which practising school administrators, for one example, make decisions in the workplace,[41] but also of how "educational law impacts the everyday practices of educators."[42] A lack of awareness of the relevant case law and legislation affecting their roles hinders teachers and administrators from exploring the "law's potential"[43] in their daily work; however, a knowledge of education law can "provide a framework for dealing with [the] problems and challenges"[44] they regularly encounter.[45]

---

40 Painter, *ibid* at 216, questions if students in administrative training programs with law courses, despite professing interest in the topic, are necessarily equipped to "employ their knowledge in the appropriate setting," since surveys of administrators' legal knowledge do not "measure the ways that administrators use or fail to use their legal knowledge in practice." See also McMorrow, above note 1 at 221, who questions whether "knowledge of the law will help educators both to act reasonably and to incorporate values of fairness and due process associated with the law into their decision-making." McMorrow, *ibid* at 215, is critical of "law-talk" which "displays a preoccupation with the articulation, identification, inculcation, and application of formal rules."

41 See, for example, Nora M Findlay, *The Problem of the Penumbra: Elementary School Principals' Exercise of Discretion in Student Disciplinary Issues* (PhD thesis, The University of Western Ontario, London, ON, 2012), online: ir.lib.uwo.ca/etd/689, which examines how school administrators negotiate within the legal parameters of discretion as it is delegated to them in legislation and school board policy in order to be faithful to their own value system in matters of student discipline. See also Gary L Anderson & Franklin Jones, "Knowledge Generation in Educational Administration from the Inside Out: The Promise and Perils of Site-Based, Administrator Research" (2000) 36:3 *Educational Administration Quarterly* 428. See also Carolyn Riehl et al, "Reconceptualizing Research and Scholarship in Educational Administration: Learning to Know, Knowing to Do, Doing to Learn" (2000) 36:3 *Educational Administration Quarterly* 391.

42 Delaney, above note 10 at 122. See also Leschied, Dickinson, & Lewis, above note 17.

43 McMorrow, above note 1 at 21.

44 Jerome G Delaney, *Legal Dimensions of Education: Implications for Teachers and School Administrators* (Calgary: Detselig, 2007) at 15.

45 Painter, above note 39 at 228, wonders if, by trying to provide school administrators with the "legal reasoning skills" to "inform decision-making," there may be a tendency to over-emphasize "the importance of the law to the exclusion of other frameworks for decision-making in education." See also, for example, Jacqueline A Stefkovich & Michael O'Brien, "Best Interests of the Student: An Ethical Model" (2004) 42:2 *Journal of Educational Administration* 197 at 198, who call for an integration of the "application of legal and ethical decision-making models" to allow school leaders to "make better-informed choices as they resolve

Notwithstanding the reasons I have cited advocating the need for increased legal knowledge for educators is the possibility such an understanding offers for enhanced decision making in two critical aspects of their practice. The first is in the area of student discipline.[46] The assertion that "some of the most prominent problems currently facing educators and school administrators are the result of legal mandates or legal concerns related to their abilities to act,"[47] especially in student behavioural issues, has considerable merit. One of the most challenging and time-consuming aspects of the in-school administrator's role is maintaining order and discipline — the twin legal imperatives that form the core of administrative practice, and without which the educational mission of the school could not be accomplished. Student behavioural concerns can be just as challenging and time-consuming for the classroom teacher. Some studies have suggested much of a principal's attention can be diverted from curriculum to disciplinary issues[48] or to spending a "disproportionate

---

problems in practice." Among these paradigms for analyzing ethical dilemmas are the ethics of justice, care, critique, the profession, and community (*ibid* at 199–200). Stefkovich & O'Brien also advocate for a decision-making model for school officials that determines the "best interests of the student" based on the correlates of "rights, responsibilities, and respect" (*ibid* at 202). Stelck, above note 4 at 270, maintains the law "complements ethical decision making" because it "combines norms with sanctions."

46 The research of Delaney, above note 10 at 124, reveals that an understanding of education law can provide educators with "various parameters" to aid in the decision-making process involving "student behaviour concerns" which are "often complicated" and complex. See also Tie, above note 9 at 194, who maintains that "a sound working knowledge of school law provides for order and discipline in school."

47 Painter, above note 39 at 215.

48 See, for example, Jennifer Birrell & J Paul Marshall, "Suspensions and Expulsions: Safer Schools for Whom?" in Roderick C Flynn, ed, *Students at the Centre* (Proceedings of the eighteenth annual conference of the Canadian Association for the Practical Study of Law in Education, held in Vancouver, BC, 22–24 April 2007) (Georgetown, ON: CAPSLE, 2008). See also the research of Findlay, above note 41 at 218, in which elementary principals estimated they spent from "10% to 80%" of their day on student disciplinary issues. See also Aaron Kupchik & Nicholas Ellis, "School Discipline and Security: Fair for All Students?" (2008) 39 *Youth & Society* 549 at 567, whose findings supported "reproduction theory which suggests that schools use discipline to reproduce existing social inequalities."

amount of time"[49] on social problems. My administrative experience supports these assertions; on any given day, much of my role as an in-school administrator may well have focussed on responding to the complex social issues in today's diverse and inclusive school settings. Without legal knowledge, school-based administrators may make capricious or arbitrary disciplinary decisions[50] and, within the broad discretion they are typically delegated, they may "unknowingly exceed their authority"[51] or "unknowingly fail to exercise their authority fully."[52] In short, they must know "where the law ends [and] discretion begins."[53] If teachers and principals acquire legal knowledge, they may be more inclined to "develop

---

49   Neil Dempster & Virginia Berry, "Blindfolded in a Minefield: Principals' Ethical Decision-Making" (2003) 33 *Cambridge Journal of Education* 457. See also John Michael Bundy, *Examination of Decision-Making Factors in Student Discipline by Idaho Secondary School Principals* (PhD thesis, The University of Idaho, 2006) at 101 [unpublished], who reasons principals' instructional leadership is also assumed in the "area of student behavioral management."

50   See Findlay, above note 41 at 281, for an in-depth analysis of certain influences and values that shape principals' discretionary decision making in student behavioural issues, such as the lack of importance some school officials may give to factors such as disciplinary history, academic performance, or age of students when determining disciplinary consequences. It is interesting to contrast this finding with Julian V Roberts & Nicholas Bala, "Understanding Sentencing Under the *Youth Criminal Justice Act*" (2003) 41 *Alberta Law Review* 395 at 412, who explain that age is "the most important mitigating factor relevant to young offenders" and that "correlation between age and severity of punishment is the one feature common to all Western juvenile justice systems." They also point out that "previous findings of guilt of the young person" are circumstances that must be taken into account in youth sentencing.

51   Heubert, above note 4 at 540.

52   *Ibid.* See also Matthew Militello & David Schimmel, "Toward Universal Legal Literacy in American Schools" (2008) 30 *Action in Teacher Education* 98 at 101, who cite "ignoring misbehaviour, permitting disruptions, and being intimidated by frivolous threats of legal action" as examples of teachers' failure "to act when they should."

53   Nora M Findlay, "At Law's End: In-School Administrators' Exercise of Discretion in Disciplinary Decision Making" in Michael Manley-Casimir & Alesha D Moffat, eds, *Administrative Discretion in Education* (Calgary: Brush Education, 2012) at 40.

school policies and practices,"[54] such as school codes of conduct,[55] that "abide with the law."[56] When educators' choice of disciplinary consequences can impact students' notions of fairness,[57] affect student outcomes,[58] or be

---

54 Tie, above note 9 at 195. See also Heubert, above note 4 at 566, who laments that those school board members who "set educational policy" in most school districts in America "are not obliged to acquire knowledge of the law." See also Findlay, above note 41 at 330–40, who found that some elementary principals did not appear rule bound or feel required to implement policy or follow legislation, and indicated they often did so only when it served their purpose. See also Linda LaRocque & Peter Coleman, "The Elusive Link: School-level Responses to School Board Policies" (1985) 31:2 *Alberta Journal of Educational Research* 149, who contend some school administrators do not seem to have "developed a keen sense of their responsibilities as policy implementers."

55 See Findlay, above note 41 at 384, about the need for "comprehensive codes of conduct" in schools. This study revealed not all schools had formalized codes of conduct, and that while some schools simply had a series of positive belief statements, in other schools the rules were just "understood." See also Brown & Zuker, above note 1 at 250, who point out that a school's code of conduct is a "critically important document, and that a student's right to "procedural fairness includes the right to know the school rules, i.e., what behavior is subject to punishment."

56 Tie, above note 9 at 195. See also Stelck, above note 4 at 268, who asserts "policy is created pursuant to law, and therefore must be authorized by and be consistent with the law in order to be valid." Sydor, above note 20 at 935, claims that teachers must move beyond a "policy and rules approach" and embark upon an "inquiry into the values, the spirit, and intention of what law seeks to accomplish in a pluralistic democracy."

57 See, for example, Martin D Ruck & Scot Wortley, "Racial and Ethnic Minority High School Students' Perceptions of School Disciplinary Practices: A Look at Some Canadian Findings" (2002) 31:3 *Journal of Youth and Adolescence* 185 at 192–93, whose research revealed that "minority status appears to be an extremely important predictor of student's [sic] perceptions of inequality regarding how they are treated by school authorities and police at school." See also Niki K Gall, *Alternative Education Students' Perceptions of the Overall Fairness of Safe School Rules, Punishments, and Rule Enforcement Practices in Ontario Schools* (Master's thesis, The University of Western Ontario, London, ON, 2010) [unpublished].

58 Bundy, above note 49 at 2, describes student discipline as an "age old concern" of school principals and at 113, suggests it is one of the "most contentious issues in the struggle for improving student achievement." Heubert, above note 4 at 568, argues that the law can be used, among other things, "to advance important policy objectives" and "to improve student performance." See also, for example, Linda M Mendez, & Howard M Knoff, "Who Gets Suspended from School and Why: A Demographic Analysis of Schools and Disciplinary Infractions in a Large School District" (2003) 26:1 *Education and Treatment of Children* 30.

the area of principals' practice that attracts the most frequent threats of lawsuits,[59] surely the plea for greater legal literacy to inform teachers' and principals' disciplinary decision making should not go unheeded.[60]

My second argument for increased legal knowledge for educators is grounded in the notion of student rights, embedded within a context of the "growing diversity of schools and the 'rights' awareness of students and their parents in the nearly thirty-five years since the entrenchment of the *Canadian Charter of Rights and Freedoms*[61] [which] have contributed to the challenges of administering a school district."[62] The tension between this conception of rights and traditional ideas of power and authority[63] may be difficult to reconcile, especially if teachers and principals have a misunderstanding about the rights of students.[64] Again, research suggests that teachers and school administrators are "not only uninformed about student rights,"[65] but

---

59   The research of Militello, Schimmel, & Eberwein, above note 13 at 37, reveals that student discipline is the area "about which school administrators are most likely to be threatened or sued," and although "very few of these threats resulted in litigation," one-third of the principals surveyed "reported that they have changed decisions regarding school discipline as a result of legal threats."

60   See Schimmel & Militello, above note 8 at 266.

61   *Canadian Charter of Rights and Freedoms*. Part 1 of the *Constitution Act, 1982*, being Schedule B to the *Canada Act 1982* (UK), 1982, c 11.

62   Stelck, above note 4 at 251.

63   See Greg Sitch & Sarah McCoubrey, "Stay in Your Seat: The Impact of Judicial Subordination of Students' Rights on Effective Rights Education" (2001) 11 *Education and Law Journal* 173 at 197, who contend "administrators are reluctant to discuss changes to their discretionary authority. This reluctance may be based on a fear that *Charter* scrutiny of administrative discretion would lead to the erosion or complete removal of that authority." As well, they believe "promoting and respecting students' rights might eliminate discipline issues through increased responsibility and respect for the rights of others" (*ibid* at 195).

64   Littleton, above note 3 at 71, argues that in America "teachers who are ignorant of the law are likely to deny students and parents the rights and privileges provided to them by the constitution and by federal and state laws." See also Sitch & McCoubrey, above note 63 at 174, who argue for greater awareness and understanding of the "extent and nature of students' rights."

65   See also Militello & Schimmel, above note 52 at 99. Peters & Montgomerie, above note 9 at 41, assert "it is apparent that few educators in the Western provinces have a firm grasp of the law as it pertains to various rights in education." Imber, above note 11 at 93, maintains that in the United States "many people, including many teachers, continue to believe that constitutional rights must be earned and that one of the ways to earn them is to grow up." This assertion is consistent with the research of Findlay, above note 41 at 344, who found elementary prin-

also are profoundly misinformed, and that principals, in particular, "*want* and *need* [emphasis in original] more information about the rights and responsibilities of their students and teachers."[66] Instead of protecting and respecting student rights in the school setting, educators and administrators "may tend to overreact and unknowingly violate students' constitutional rights;"[67] they may perceive students as having more extensive rights "than they actually do;"[68] or the rights of the "minority opinion"[69] may be "abridged at the expense of the majority or popular opinion."[70] Moreover, perhaps some teachers and principals are quite unaware[71] that the "doctrine of *in loco parentis*"[72] does not direct their actions[73] despite

---

cipals "appeared more inclined to interpret rights not as an entitlement, but in terms of a dominant notion of corresponding student responsibilities," while they also seemed to expect "students to be responsible and regulate their own behavior and to be aware of the rights of others" (*ibid* at 345).

66 Militello, Schimmel, & Eberwein, above note 13 at 41. Tie, above note 9 at 203, says "school administrators must also be able to accord the due process of the law to students and teachers, respect the constitutional rights and freedom of students and teachers, and act in a fair and reasonable manner."

67 Schimmel & Militello, above note 8 at 270, cite as examples "disciplining a student for wearing a T-shirt that criticizes the [American] president or for punishing a student who uses a personal website to criticize school policy."

68 Militello & Schimmel, above note 52 at 100.

69 Littleton, above note 3 at 76.

70 *Ibid.* See also Findlay, above note 41 at 260, whose research found that most of the elementary principals in the study exercised discretion in their disciplinary decision making based on what they thought was best for the group when seeking to find a balance between individual rights and those of the entire school.

71 Findlay, *ibid* at 360–62.

72 *Black's Law Dictionary*, 9th ed, defines *in loco parentis* as "relating to, or acting as a temporary guardian or caretaker of a child, taking on all or some of the responsibilities of a parent." Imber, above note 11 at 94.

73 Imber, *ibid*, also observes that in the US "for purposes of constitutional guarantees of freedom," teachers are "state actors, not parents." See also Russo & Stewart, above note 3 at 22. Mackay & Sutherland, above note 20 at xvii, maintain that in Canada, the doctrine "has been eroded almost to the point of extinction in the past several decades" and realistically speaking, has "little or no place in today's schools." Citing the Supreme Court of Canada's ruling in *R v Ogg-Moss* (1984), 11 DLR (4th) 549 (SCC), they write that the doctrine was seen to have "little, if any" relevance in institutions (Mackay & Sutherland, above note 20 at xix). They conclude teachers now "more commonly" act "in various capacities as agents of the state" (*ibid* at 195). See also Sitch & McCoubrey, above note 63 at 191, who contend *in loco parentis* is a "principle that is inappropriate when applied to a 21st century understanding of children's rights."

the expectations by stakeholders that they will "continue to perform all manner of parental functions on behalf of their students."[74] It follows that students may not be accorded their rights by teachers and administrators who, because of an incomplete understanding of the legal characterization of their role, exercise broad discretion[75] they wrongly believe they enjoy as "surrogate parents."[76] As a result, a greater awareness and an affirmation of students' rights are required on the part of educators in order to lessen the risk these rights would be abrogated by their discretionary decision making in disciplinary issues, for example. Despite the entrenchment of the *Charter*, if teachers and administrators are unaware of its guarantees, they may not be able to acknowledge the "child as a 'person' in his or her own right."[77] Educators must reconcile students' rights with notions of power and authority that are inherent in principal-student and teacher-student relationships and manifested through their decision making in disciplinary situations.[78] One way to accomplish this goal is to encourage teachers and administrators to learn about the rights of students so as to dispel and counter possible misconceptions. Another suggestion — to provide "guidance and training on strategies for disciplining children that respect them as people with rights and responsibilities to respect the rights of others"[79] — makes for sound educational decision making and good common sense.

A corresponding argument can be made for administrators and teachers to become versed in the best interests of the child as it is articulated in the United Nations *Convention on the Rights of the Child*,[80] a principle which is to "apply to *all* [emphasis in original] actions concerning children,

---

74 Imber, above note 11 at 94.

75 Findlay, above note 41 at 361.

76 Sitch & McCoubrey, above note 63 at 178.

77 Michael E Manley-Casimir, "The Rights of the Child at School" (1979) 19 *Education Canada* 9 at 10. Sitch & McCoubrey, above note 63 at 174–75, affirm the "recognition of children as persons" is a "twentieth century phenomenon" that is "set out in the *United Nations Convention on the Rights of the Child.*"

78 Ailsa M Watkinson, *Education, Student Rights, and the Charter* (Saskatoon, SK: Purich, 1999) at 195, believes some educators may feel their "professional autonomy" is challenged or may perceive the "erosion of their competence" as an inherent danger of considering student rights.

79 Canadian Coalition for the Rights of Children, *Best Interests of the Child: Meaning and Application in Canada* (Ottawa, ON; Canadian Coalition for the Rights of Children, 2009).

80 *United Nations Convention on the Rights of the Child*, 20 November 1989, United Nations General Assembly, Res. 44/25 [CRC].

including in the field of education."[81] Many educators justify their decision making by explaining that it is done in the students' best interests[82]; however, through ignorance, the principle may be applied too simplistically or superficially and may not always value or preserve student rights. It seems reasonable to assume that, without specific knowledge, all educators may not have the same understanding of the phrase, be unaware how best interests are determined, or be unable to determine when best interests have been met.[83] Accordingly, principals and school officials should gain an understanding of the *Convention on the Rights of the Child*, especially Article 28 that provides for ensuring that "school discipline is administered in a manner consistent with the child's human dignity and in conformity with the present Convention."[84] Without an awareness of the principle "as a primary consideration to guide decision-making"[85] on the part of educators, there is simply "no assurance"[86] that their decisions will be guided or informed by it.[87]

The argument for "a basic knowledge of the law"[88] is a valid one, although what knowledge should be gleaned and the best pedagogical approach for educators to take to acquire this information are open to de-

---

81 R Brian Howe & Katherine Covell, "Toward the Best Interests of the Child in Education" (2010) 20 *Education and Law Journal* 17 at 18, observe that Canada ratified the United Nations *CRC* in 1991, but point out that the principle "has not been applied in any serious way to elementary and secondary education in Canada" (*ibid* at 22).

82 See, for example, Findlay, above note 41 at 358–60. See also Paul T Begley "Leading with Moral Purpose: The Place of Ethics" in Tony Bush, Les Bell, & David Middlewood, eds, *The Principles of Educational Leadership and Management*, 2d ed (London, UK: Sage, 2010).

83 Howe & Covell, above note 81 at 29, worry that with the "wide discretionary power" delegated to school authorities, "there is little assurance that their decisions will be guided by the best interests of the child."

84 *CRC*, above note 80.

85 Howe & Covell, above note 82 at 22.

86 *Ibid* at 29.

87 *Ibid*. Howe & Covell worry that without an awareness of the principle, school officials may interpret best interests in "the traditional paternalistic manner."

88 Gallant, above note 15 at 423, suggests a basic knowledge of law "gives educators the ability to respond to the pressures of change in the legal regime and legislation and allows them to anticipate problems and challenges and respond confidently when they do arise."

bate.[89] An understanding of current, applicable case law; established legal principles such as the best interests of the child; relevant Supreme Court decisions; and education and human rights legislation would provide educators with an information base, thus enhancing the prospect that their decision making would reflect contemporary jurisprudence. Knowledge of school law, therefore, must be a priority in educators' and administrators' practice in order to benefit themselves, their students, and all other educational stakeholders.

> Perhaps the only constant in education law is that as it evolves to meet the demands of a constantly changing world, it is likely to remain of utmost importance for all those who are interested in the rights and opportunities of children. In fact, the seemingly endless supply of new statutes, regulations, and cases illustrates the need for educators to be ever vigilant as to how legal developments impact on their profession. The challenge for all educators, then, is to harness their knowledge of the ever-growing field of education law so that all schools can be made better places for children.[90]

In the years that have passed since I was that novice vice-principal searching for the elixir for my administrative practice, I have grown certain my knowledge of school law was instrumental in improving my practice, serving to inform my decision making — particularly in disciplinary issues — and giving me a solid foundation to reflect upon those decisions. By equipping themselves with knowledge of education law, educators and administrators will be in a better position to create educational settings where all learners will be afforded the opportunity to reach their greatest level of achievement. Our children and youth deserve no less.

---

89 See, for example, Painter, above note 39. See also Suzanne E Eckes, "Significant Legal Issues for Inclusion in Preservice Teacher Preparation" (2008) 30 *Action in Teacher Education* 25 at 27–33.
90 Russo & Stewart, above note 3 at 25.

CHAPTER 2

The Legal and Administrative Framework of Education in Canada

Frank Peters

A. INTRODUCTION

In attempting to describe or outline the basis for the legal and administrative structures that govern education in Canada today, one might be tempted to go back to section 93 of the *Constitution Act, 1867*[1] and possibly even stop there. There is a sense in which everything that we have today is based on the elements contained in that section, the wording of which is produced below:

> 93. In and for each Province the Legislature may exclusively make Laws in relation to Education, subject and according to the following Provisions:
> (1) Nothing in any such Law shall prejudicially affect any Right or Privilege with respect to Denominational Schools which any Class of Persons have by Law in the Province at the Union:
> (2) All the Powers, Privileges, and Duties at the Union by Law conferred and imposed in Upper Canada on the Separate Schools and School Trustees of the Queen's Roman Catholic Subjects shall be and the same are hereby extended to the Dissentient Schools of the Queen's Protestant and Roman Catholic Subjects in Québec.

The Preamble to this section sets the overall context for education in this country: the provinces are *god* and can exclusively make the laws that will govern education within their borders. While there may be limitations on the specifics of the laws they pass in relation to denominational

---

1   (UK), 30 & 31 Vict, c 3, reprinted in RSC 1985, App II, No 5. Sections 93(3) and (4) outline the procedures for appeals relating to conflicts regarding understandings of s 93(1) or (2).

education, no other jurisdiction can legislate in this domain — only the provinces can. And this jurisdiction is in relation to education in the full sense of the word, not limited to primary, secondary, or post-secondary; not confined only to educational institutions that receive public funding; not limited only to secular institutions, but applied to education in the broadest sense in which we can conceive of it, even to what we refer to as "home-schooling" or "home education."

However, to start from the legislative position accepted in 1867 would be to ignore the historical struggles, initiatives, and compromises, both social and political, that have emerged over the centuries as European settlers fought over and settled this part of North America. Cowan warns:

> We have been too prone to think that when emigrants arrived ... by some subtle process they became Canadian at the moment of arrival and that here Canadian history must begin .... To study the essential characteristics of Canadian life, one must follow the spreading colonial branches back to their root stock.[2]

While these comments are related specifically to emigration from Britain and other English-speaking countries, they are equally applicable to all immigrants.

Our educational structures are shaped by the laws that regulate them. The Preamble to the *Constitution Act, 1982*[3] states, "Whereas Canada is founded upon principles that recognize the supremacy of God and the rule of law . . . ." This forms the underpinning of how the Constitution as a whole must be understood and interpreted. We may not be clear just where God fits into our deliberations, but we are still committed to the idea that public life should be conducted in accordance with laws that have been passed in this country and the interpretations that the courts have provided.

The different actors in the educational enterprise behave in accordance with the powers and responsibilities given to them by the legislatures of their provinces. These laws may be normative as well as regulatory. They will, at times, attempt to ensure the values that the members of the public subscribe to are transmitted to the youth of today, whether these values be of a moral or a social nature or relate to specific knowledge and skills that

---

2   Helen I Cowan, "British Emigration to British North America" in William B Hamilton, *The British Heritage* (Toronto: University of Toronto Press, 1970) at 10; Donald J Wilson, Robert M Stamp, & Louis-Philippe Audet, *Canadian Education: A History* (Scarborough, ON: Prentice-Hall, 1970).

3   Being Schedule B to the *Canada Act 1982* (UK), 1982, c 11.

the government deems are essential for the development of the common good. The question of which values and which knowledge should be given a more privileged position in the curricula of the schools and post-secondary institutions is always a matter of contestation, but from a constitutional perspective, the provincial governments have the last word. It would be inappropriate to go much further without mentioning another limitation on provincial action in relation to education, namely, the *Canadian Charter of Rights and Freedoms*, adopted in 1982.[4] Arising out of widespread concern that both the international community and individual states needed to adopt safeguards to protect the rights of individual human beings in the face of specific legislation that might be approved in any particular jurisdiction, the United Nations adopted its *Universal Declaration of Human Rights* in 1948. The Government of Canada approved its *Bill of Rights* in 1960, but this granted individuals protection only in relation to federal legislation and action. The *Charter of Rights* was far-reaching in scope and broader in its reach than any previous legislation. Specifically,

32. (1) This *Charter* applies
(a) to the Parliament and government of Canada in respect of all matters within the authority of Parliament including all matters relating to the Yukon Territory and Northwest Territories; and
(b) to the legislature and government of each province in respect of all matters within the authority of the legislature of each province.

As it is part of the Constitution of Canada, the *Charter* clearly constrains the provincial governments in drawing up legislation. In a number of rulings, the courts have also stated that the *Charter* can apply to many, if not all, actions of school boards and of teachers, as education is clearly an area within the authority and control of each province. Although the *Constitution Act, 1867* is the most obvious foundation for the legal and administrative frameworks of education in Canada, it is still necessary to identify, insofar as we can, the basis on which the precise elements of that legislation were founded. While Canadian communities and those in the other colonies in what is today Canada were working out a satisfactory *modus vivendi* between different traditions, cultures, and religions, they were also grappling with the emerging understandings that society, in general, was placing on schooling and education, and the more liberal, democratic understandings of how society should function.

---

4   Part I of the *Constitution Act, 1982*, being Schedule B to the *Canada Act 1982* (UK), 1982, c 11 [*Charter*].

The fact that Canada, under the terms of the *Constitution Act, 1867,* grants exclusive rights to the provinces to make laws regarding education ensures that there will be considerable variety in the laws and practices that prevail from province to province. The nation itself developed in a piecemeal fashion as differing parts of the country were populated by European settlers, and as an awareness developed that some sort of political union between the disparate areas would be to the social and economic benefit of all.

The earliest use of the name "Canada" or its earlier version *Kanata* was at first applied only to the areas settled by the French colonists in the St Lawrence River region in the sixteenth century. Allegedly, the name emerged from a word used by two Aboriginal youngsters who directed Jacques Cartier, to Kanata, which apparently was a Huron-Iroquois word for a village or settlement,[5] one named Stadacona, which, in the sixteenth century, was located near modern-day Québec City.

In 1791, the British government applied the name "Canada" to two areas in what had been the colony of Québec. When the British government felt it necessary to acknowledge the different legal, linguistic, and religious regimes in the larger province of Québec, it divided it into two provinces. Lower Canada was predominantly Catholic and francophone; Upper Canada's traditions and religion were Protestant and British.

While the above paragraphs land us at the dawn of the nineteenth century, they point to two critical features of Canada's history and to the development of the educational structures throughout the country: heredity and environment.[6]

B. THE SETTLER INFLUENCE

In addition to the most obvious feature of their language, the earliest European settlers in this country brought their beliefs about religion and its place in their lives, and about family values and other social matters, such as child-rearing. The earliest visitors to Canada from Britain and continental Europe were generally not settlers. They came as explorers and as merchants, and were concerned that if the new territories were settled,

---

5   William B Hamilton, *The Macmillan Book of Canadian Place Names* (Toronto: Macmillan of Canada, 1978) at 21.

6   These two features are used as starting points for understanding the development of education in Canada by F Henry Johnson, *A Brief History of Canadian Education* (Toronto: McGraw-Hill, 1968).

they might lose their monopolies on whatever their trade was. The explorations and trading visits from both Britain and France throughout the 1500s were sporadic, though fairly continuous contact was kept up with the rich fishing grounds off the Newfoundland coast.

1) The Growth of Catholic Parochial Schools

In the early years of the seventeenth century, French settlers established themselves in LaHave, northwest of what is now Halifax and close to present-day Wolfville. Johnson mentioned that when Champlain returned to the Maritimes in 1615, he brought with him a number of Récollect friars who opened a school at that location.[7] A number of these friars continued west in 1615 with Champlain, landing first at Tadoussac and then going on to what became Québec City. Wherever they settled, the friars set up schools along the lines of the educational establishments they had operated in France prior to their crossing the Atlantic. Similarly, at Port-Royal, there was a boys' school and a girls' school operating by the 1640s. In the territory along the St Lawrence River settled by the French — New France — Récollect and Jesuit missionaries set up schools for boys, and missionary sisters, such as the Ursulines and the Sisters of the Hôtel Dieu, set up schools for girls. These basic primary schools were modelled on the *petits écoles* found throughout France: these schools were based on a parochial system of governance and control. In the mid-1630s, the Jesuits opened a secondary school in Québec in which classics, philosophy, and theology formed the major focus of the curriculum.

This was to be the pattern of schooling throughout French Canada until Britain took control of all the French lands, first as a result of the *Treaty of Utrecht* (1713)[8] and later as a consequence of the *Treaty of Paris*, which ended the Seven Years' War. The *Treaty of Paris* (1763) brought an end

---

7   *Ibid* at 11.

8   The *Treaty of Utrecht* (1713) brought to an end the War of the Spanish, a war waged entirely between European states — France, Britain, Spain, Holland, and parts of what is now Italy. The underlying concern in arriving at a peace was that a balance of power be maintained between these states. France had to cede some of its colonial territories and settlements to the other parties. Acadia changed hands and France also gave up any claim to Newfoundland; however, it maintained its possessions on Île-Saint-Jean and on Île Royale, known today as Prince Edward Island and Cape Breton respectively, and also control over the islands of Saint Pierre and Miquelon. The crown of Spain went to the grandson of Louis XIV, which was in keeping with the wishes of the dead king of Spain.

to the war, which was known in North America as the French and Indian War. Although war between France and Britain officially broke out in 1756, conflict between the two nations had actually erupted two years earlier.[9]

During the fifty years between the two treaties, an uneasy peace existed between France and England. The British settlers in New England became increasingly interested in expanding their colony north into Nova Scotia and pressured Britain to exercise her sovereignty more firmly. Hamilton[10] has pointed out that in addition to being concerned with protecting Britain's trade and territorial interests, this increased attention on Acadia/Nova Scotia was heavily influenced by an increase in anti-Catholicism. Catholicism was seen as being un-British and a possible threat to British control. There was also a fear that Catholics, through the dominant influence of the bishops, would support the anti-British sentiments being stirred up in New England.

2) The British Impact on Education

In North America, Britain was now faced with the urgency of having to govern an additional colony inhabited by about 60,000 French-speaking Catholics with their own culture and their own traditions. Realizing the tenuousness of their position in relation to the Aboriginal peoples, the British also wanted to ensure that those tribes friendly with the French continued to maintain that friendship and, thus, be less likely to ally themselves with other Aboriginal tribes who were siding with the increasingly restless settlers in New England.

Aware of the sensitive position from which they operated, the British continued to allow the French settlers, in what had previously been New France, to practise their religion, speak their own language, and operate

---

9 A major cause of the war was the fact that the British colonists were squeezed into a narrow strip of land on the east coast of the continent and were surrounded by the French settlers. In 1754 they tried to move into what is today Ohio and came into conflict with the French who already occupied that territory. The two countries, France and Britain, continued their battles along with their allies until 1763 when the *Treaty of Paris* brought the war to an end. France ceded all its remaining lands in French Canada to Britain in the terms of the treaty. Britain emerged as the clear victor in North America and in Europe. It also consolidated its imperial borders in Asia and the Caribbean and even gained a foothold in western Africa.

10 William B Hamilton, "Society and Schools in Nova Scotia" in Wilson, Stamp, & Audet, above note 2 at 87 [Hamilton, "Nova Scotia"].

socially with the same civil structures as they did before the Conquest. This was formalized when the British government passed the *Québec Act* in 1774 and these rights were enshrined for the French settlers. Whether or not the legislation helped persuade the French residents not to join the battle against the British crown in 1776 is questionable, but it did certainly inflame those advocating a break with Britain. It is equally clear that these rebellious forces did not receive any support either from the French settlers or their Aboriginal allies.

The British decision to prevent religious orders from taking in any new recruits had a strong detrimental effect on education and schooling in the former New France. Neither the Jesuits nor the Récollect friars were able to replace the clergy who returned to France or who died. A similar restriction was placed on the orders of nuns, and their numbers also dwindled. These restrictions resulted in a huge decline in the number of schools, as well as a drop in the overall level of general education and literacy in the lands recently acquired by Britain. At the same time, the vast majority of residents in this formerly French colony remained staunchly Catholic, though the demographic arrangements changed notably after the American Revolution.

The influx of English-speaking, Protestant settlers into these regions was insignificant in terms of the development of education and schooling. Like their counterparts in Nova Scotia, these immigrants to the Québec region and to southern Ontario demanded schools and action by the government. Education and schooling were put on the government agenda, and the government established a committee to look into the matter. This committee reported in 1789, recommending the establishment of a liberal arts college in Montréal in which no theology would be taught and thus religious bias would be avoided. This recommendation was opposed by the Catholics, who would not accept a non-sectarian university or non-sectarian, even if free, elementary and secondary schools. In the words of Sissons,[11] the "school would be sectarian or there would be no school."

The British settlers in Nova Scotia had also seen the beginnings of schooling in the early and middle decades of the eighteenth century. In 1711, the English residents at Annapolis Royal requested assistance from the Society for the Propagation of the Gospel (SPG) to open and operate

---

11   Charles Bruce Sissons, *Church and State in Canadian Education* (Toronto: Ryerson, 1959) at 132.

a school in that community.[12] This British-based organization provided both lay teachers and Church of England clergy to establish and operate schools, and in many cases, to replace expelled Catholic French priests and nuns. Like the Catholic Church, the Protestant Church also played a critical role in the development of education.

The SPG opened schools in Newfoundland at this time as well as in Acadia, and until the end of the century, it exercised a virtual monopoly on schools for English-speaking settlers in the Atlantic region. Central to the ethos of the Society was the belief that in order to ensure and maintain the Britishness of the colonies, it was essential to educate the children in the Anglican Church doctrines and to teach them to value "British Institutions."[13]

There were serious misgivings among the New England and Ulster-Scottish immigrants in regard to the close alignment between the governing structures in the colonies and the Anglican Church. Many of these new arrivals from New England were Congregationalists and had been influenced by the revivalist fervour of the 1740s known as the "Great Awakening." This movement stressed the importance of individual initiative in religion as well as in civil matters. The churches were governed in a democratic fashion by the congregations, whose members wanted the freedom to educate their children in the principles of their religion and in their beliefs regarding civic and social arrangements.

Similarly, the Ulster-Scottish Presbyterian immigrants were unhappy with the fact that Anglican Protestantism was virtually the "established church." Nonetheless, in the absence of support for any alternative system of schooling, they had to choose between not having their children educated, relying on the occasional visits of itinerant teachers, or sending their children to the SPG schools and risking what Hamilton called "doctrinal infection."[14]

In response to concerns expressed by SPG members that all the schools in the colony should support, sustain, and foster British culture, British traditions, and British religion, the civic government of Nova Scotia introduced legislation in 1766 to control and regulate teachers working in grammar schools. The legislation was not in the least concerned with academic qualifications, but rather with ensuring the *bona fides* of the

---

12   Hamilton, "Nova Scotia," above note 10 at 90 & 91.
13   *Ibid* at 91.
14   *Ibid* at 92.

teachers in relation to the Church of England.[15] It also made it clear that anybody involved with the "papist religion" could have nothing to do with these schools. Further, the law "gave official recognition that education was, at least in part, the responsibility of government."[16]

3) The Creation of Local School Boards

One additional aspect of their heritage that the emigrants from New England, the United Empire Loyalists, brought with them has continued to play a part in how we govern and operationalize schooling in Canada. One way in which the ideology of the Great Awakening had played itself out in the New England communities was that schools were controlled at the local level. A board of locally elected trustees hired the teacher, managed the day-to-day operation of the school and, through the local community, levied the taxes that supported the overall running of the enterprise. Insofar as they looked to higher levels of government, it was for financial, rather than regulatory, assistance. These local boards were the initial "school boards" which continue as features of our educational infrastructure in all provinces today; however, their role has evolved substantially in the two hundred years since they first emerged. Worth[17] explained that the original purposes for and understandings of school boards and school trusteeship represented a balancing between the three values of leadership, representation, and competence.

The presence of school boards is one feature of our foundations of education in Canada that can be identified in the early forms of schooling established prior to Confederation. Indeed, if we look at what I identify as the foundational pillars of our educational structures today, we can find that all of them, with one exception, were in place before 1800. "School boards" is one of those pillars, one of those lasting features.

Significant attention has been drawn to the fact that in the early years of Canada, religion, whether Catholic or Protestant, was integral to the development of schools and education systems at all levels.

---

15 *Ibid.*

16 *Ibid.*

17 W Worth, *Reflections on the Political Future of School Boards* (Paper delivered to the Trustees' Academy of the British Columbia Trustees' Association, Vancouver, BC, 1986.

... the history of the rise of public education in the provinces of Canada reveals, above all, the influence of the Protestant and Roman Catholic churches. The educational philosophy, aims, and broader objectives of the public education system reflected the moral and religious doctrines of the faith which had sponsored the founding of the institution.[18]

Canada, when its basic educational legislation was drawn up and enshrined as part of its Constitution in 1867, did not see fit to include articles similar to the first or the fourteenth amendments to the United States Constitution which effectively state that neither Congress nor state legislatures can make any laws regarding the "establishment of religion or prohibiting the free exercise thereof."[19] As schooling expanded and legislation governing the organization and conduct of schools became more sophisticated (and intrusive), the question of the appropriate place for religion(s) in a publicly supported school system was, and continues to be, a source of intense debate and contention.

4) The French Presence

A third element of the foundations of education can be identified in the *Québec Act of 1774*, namely, the acknowledgement of the French presence as a foundational culture and language, alongside that of England and English. Although this feature would not be fully enshrined in terms of education in most of Canada until after the adoption of the *Charter*[20] in 1982 and the court battles that followed in virtually every province, its origins can be found in the intent of the 1774 Act which guaranteed certain entitlements to the francophone population of Canada.

C. THE EMERGENCE OF EDUCATION LAW

When the report into the feasibility of establishing an education system in Québec was presented to government in 1789, it was abundantly clear that any effort to organize an education system in the region on non-sectarian grounds would meet intractable opposition from the vast majority of the population.[21] This forceful opposition made clear to the British government

---

18 William P Foster & Gayle Pinheiro, "Constitutional Protection of the Right to an Education" (1988) 11 *Dalhousie Law Journal* 759.

19 A Bartlett Giamatti, *A Free and Ordered Space* (New York: WW Norton, 1988).

20 Above note 4.

21 Sissons, above note 11.

the challenges they would face in trying to govern two distinct communities in the regions of what are now southern Ontario and southern Québec. The history, traditions, languages, and religions of the two groups of settlers were very different, and the groups would require different modes of government in order to flourish as distinct communities.

In 1791, the British Parliament approved a *Constitution Act*, dividing the British territory on the St Lawrence into Upper Canada and Lower Canada, each with an appointed Lieutenant Governor, an appointed Council, and an elected General Assembly. In Lower Canada the guarantees provided in the *Québec Act* of 1774 were renewed while in Upper Canada, British law was adopted. While Lower Canada was predominantly francophone and Catholic, there was also a significant number of Anglo-Protestants in the region. Similarly, though Upper Canada was made up largely of Anglo-Protestants, there was also a significant minority of Irish and French Catholics.

In Lower Canada, the United Empire Loyalists, while they continued to push government for support in establishing a colonial framework for education, carried on with their practice of setting up schools in towns and villages under the control and direction of their local elected officials. In response to the continuing pressures, the government, in 1801, approved the establishment of the Royal Institution for the Advancement of Learning to administer all schools set up in towns and villages at the request of a majority of the inhabitants. For a variety of reasons, "the French Canadians believed the whole Institution was an elaborate plot to Anglicize them."[22] This belief may not have been entirely without foundation as the first teachers appointed were all English Protestants. This choice and the government's initiative in allocating the monies from the Jesuit estates[23] to the Royal Institution were both seen as indications that neither the Institution nor the government was sincere in its support of French Catholics and the education system they desired. The Catholic bishop in Québec, Bishop Plessis, forcefully opposed the scheme. This opposition resulted in a boycott of the project, and it was not until 1818 that it got underway.

Around 1820, a grammar school was established in Québec and another in Montréal, both under the control of the Institution. These were

---

22 Johnson, above note 6 at 16.
23 When the Jesuit order was suppressed by Pope Clement XIV in 1773, their properties in Canada were confiscated by the British Crown; however, the Jesuits had virtually lost control over most of these properties in 1763.

elite schools to provide a classical education for sons of the British upper class. Enrolment in them was, at all times, small, and in the mid-1840s, the schools were merged with other high schools in these cities.

1) Early Education Acts

Although a small number of French Catholic students attended the schools run by the Royal Institution, the government was concerned that the arrangement continued to be viewed as a proselytizing agency and, thus, its efforts to expand educational opportunities in the colony were suffering. In order to address this concern, *The Fabrique Act* was adopted in 1824, setting up a system whereby the lay board of a parish (a *fabrique*) could allocate monies to the establishment and operation of a community school, independent of the Royal Institution. Johnson reported that by the mid-1830s, there were about 1,500 schools in Lower Canada and almost 1,400 of these were "trustee schools."[24]

The United Empire Loyalists in Canada West (southern Ontario) carried on their practice of local autonomy and opened a number of schools in the 1780s without any government assistance. After the establishment of Upper Canada in 1791, they continued to lobby the government forcefully to assist them in providing educational services for their children. However, "there were few persons in Europe and North America at the beginning of the 19th century who considered that government was responsible for education; such responsibility was held to lie in the hands of the church and the home."[25] Be that as it may, the United Empire Loyalists, probably

> because of their type . . . were important out of proportion to their numbers. Many ministers, doctors — the medical profession was pioneered by them — teachers, printers and other professional and technical men were comprised in the later American immigration. The major improvements in nearly all the arts from education to agriculture seem to have come into Canada by this route.[26]

---

24   Johnson, above note 6 at 18.
25   J Arthur Lower, *Canada: An Outline History* (Toronto: McGraw-Hill Ryerson, 1973) at 84.
26   Arthur RM Lower, *Colony to Nation: A History of Canada*, 3d ed (Toronto: Longmans, Green, 1957).

Upper Canada was a highly class-based society and the more established, wealthier classes exercised considerable power, both with the Lieutenant Governor and in the Executive Council. The first laws relating to education were in response to pressure from this elite sector. The *District Public Schools Act* (1807) identified eight communities in Upper Canada in which a grammar school could be operated with very generous public support. The sense in which these schools would be "public" was the same sense in which the famous historical schools of Rugby, Eton, and Harrow in Britain were called "public." In truth, they were elite, independent, fee-charging, and residential schools, totally inaccessible to most of the population — the "public."

Less than a decade later, the government passed *The Common School Act* (1816), which authorized the establishment of local schools. Their operation, however, would be expensive, and few children of poorer residents would be able to attend. Following its establishment in 1822, the General Board of Education took these schools under its authority. Bishop Strachan of Toronto was named as chairman of this board and for the next decade was, in practice if not in title, the superintendent of schools in Upper Canada.

A key element in Strachan's beliefs was that the Church of England should have been the established church in Canada as it was in England. He believed that if one were to be loyal to Britain, then one would have to belong to the Anglican Church. Consequently, he was very deliberate in appointing Anglican teachers to the schools under his control. Not only did he do nothing to accommodate Catholics, he openly attacked the loyalty of both Catholics and the large Methodist population in the colony. Not surprisingly, many parents refused to send their children to schools under the control of the Board of Education. Indeed, the board was abolished by the government in 1832, due, in large part, to the opposition to many of the partisan and bigoted positions advocated by Bishop Strachan.

Strachan's views on education appeared to match perfectly with those of the first Lieutenant Governor of Upper Canada, John Graves Simcoe. Lord Simcoe felt that education should be provided to "the select few . . . 'The Children of the Principal People of this Country' who would eventually become the country's leaders."[27] As far as education for the masses of other children, their needs ". . . may at present be provided for them by

---

27 J Donald Wilson, "Education in Upper Canada: Sixty Years of Change" in Wilson, Stamp, & Audet, above note 2 at 193.

their connections and relations."[28] It has been noted that Simcoe's elitist views on society and governance carried considerable influence long after his death in 1806. Bishop Strachan was clearly one who subscribed to the same views on matters relating to education, public schooling, and the proper ordering of society.

By the late 1830s, it was estimated, the population of the province of Upper Canada was about 400,000, but only a minute percentage of school-aged children attended school at any time. There was an awareness that a proper system of financing the education system would need to be devised if the large number of non-attenders were to be enabled to participate. The 1830s marked constant struggles between the reform-minded elements in the General Assembly and the more traditional supporters of the British elitist model of governance and of society. This tension was sometimes characterized as a clash between the British colonial view and what some saw as the unfortunate American influence: introducing ideas of democracy and advocating for an "irreligious" education system that would strike at the very bases of British traditions and beliefs. The disagreement over education was one of the many issues leading to the insurrections of 1837/38.

2) The *Act of Union* 1840: The "Dissentient" Clause

In his report following his investigation into the rebellions in both Upper and Lower Canada in 1837, Lord Durham recommended wide-ranging changes to how the British colonies in North America should be governed. He commented on the awful state of education and recommended that the two provinces be united. The British government quickly adopted this recommendation and passed an *Act of Union* in 1840. In the following year *The Common School Act* (1841) was passed.

The challenges associated with what Durham had described as "two races warring within the bosom of a single state"[29] presented particular difficulties in relation to schooling. In an effort to ensure that legislation would be acceptable to both the French Catholics and the English Protestants, the Act included what has come to be known as "the dissentient clause."[30] The Catholic clergy, though not initially forcefully opposed to

---

28 *Ibid.*

29 Johnson, above note 6 at 31.

30 This clause was introduced into the legislation at the committee stage of its readings, and traditional storytelling assumes that it was introduced in order to

the initiative, insisted that separate schools, in which Catholic children would be educated apart from their non-Catholic peers and taught in accordance with the teachings of the Catholic Church, had been part of educational arrangements in this country from the early seventeenth century, and any other system that did not permit this segregation would be unacceptable.[31] Anglicans, too, had concerns over the new system, with Bishop Strachan of Toronto arguing that the proposed system was just "imitating the irreligious scheme of our [American] neighbors."[32]

The interplay between Egerton Ryerson and the two major religious denominations was to continue right up to Confederation in 1867. However, on many other fronts, Ryerson established for the government solid positions in relation to the training and certification of teachers and the control over the curriculum and over texts; he also saw to the introduction of a supervisory and control system that monitored practices in schools in the province.

3) The *Constitution Act, 1867*: Provincial Rights

Given the differences in what had occurred over the previous two centuries in the disparate regions that came to the table in 1867, it should not be surprising that the provinces sought and obtained authority over edu-

---

placate the Catholic communities in Canada West. However, the preponderance of submissions advocating that the clause be included were from Anglican and Presbyterian clergymen who were concerned about the absence of religion from the schools and were requesting to use the King James Bible as a text in their schools. This clause permitted the religious minority to establish its own school in any district in which the teacher in the common school did not belong to the religion of the minority. The details of the clause were amended many times during the 1840s and 1850s with major arguments between Catholic clergy and Egerton Ryerson after the 1847 amendments that created a situation wherein separate schools would receive less public financial support than would the common schools. By then, Ryerson was chief superintendent of schools in Canada West (later Ontario), a position he would hold until his retirement in 1876. He was adamant that there was strong community support for the common schools and used as evidence the fact that only two separate Catholic schools had been established in the province since 1841.

31   This matter is dealt with thoroughly in Joseph Jean-Guy Lavoie, *A Study of the Ryerson-Charbonnel Controversy and Its Background* (Master's Thesis, University of Ottawa, 1971) [unpublished].

32   J Donald Wilson, "The Pre-Ryerson Years" in Neil McDonald & Alf Chaiton, eds, *Egerton Ryerson and His Times* (Toronto: Macmillan, 1978) at 39.

cational matters in the federal arrangement. Nor should it be a surprise that the different religious communities sought and obtained to have enshrined in the constitutional agreement whatever rights and privileges they had managed to have written into the laws in the provinces in the years before 1867.[33]

The *Constitution Act, 1867* was an Act of the British Parliament. The legal system that was adopted with the transfer of the last of the French lands to Britain in 1763 was that in place in Great Britain, with the exception of Québec, where civil matters were regulated by the traditions of French civil law. In other matters, all of Canada follows the principles of common law, where the laws are enacted by the provincial legislatures or by the federal parliament, and the laws are interpreted and adjudicated on by the courts. The decisions and interpretations of the courts then form the basis for future decisions in similar cases.

D. EDUCATION AND LAW IN POST-CONFEDERATION CANADA

If the constitutional bases for the governance of education were set in the pre-Confederation years, the more precise and practical meanings of some of these principles were anything but clear. What was unambiguous was the fact that the provinces were in charge of education within their own borders. In practice, the four original provinces (and subsequently the six additional ones also) adopted the system of establishing school boards as statutory bodies to govern the school systems. This choice was not as a result of any constitutional requirement, but rather a pragmatic decision to continue with practices that appeared to meet the needs of both the provincial governments and the emerging local communities. In the years since Confederation, each province has dealt with how best to develop a legal framework within its borders and how best to adapt that framework to deal well with emerging and changing issues.

In attempting to narrow the possible perspectives relating to the legal matters, I will approach the development and implementation of the provincial laws — and on occasion, the Constitution — from a number of angles. First, in Section E, I discuss the always-with-us matter of church and state in Canadian education. I then discuss, in Section F, some matters

---

33 Sir Charles Tupper, Premier of Nova Scotia in 1867 and later to become prime
    minister, indicated that without the provisions relating to separate schools,
    Confederation would never have been agreed to.

dealing with centralization and decentralization. In Section G, I discuss a number of issues pertaining to politics and education: these may persist or recur but they take on a particular significance at a particular time and then move (or not) towards the wings.

E. CHURCH AND STATE IN EDUCATION

1) New Brunswick

What quickly emerged as contentious following Confederation was the interpretation of section 93(1) dealing with the rights and privileges in relation to denominational schools. When the province of New Brunswick approved a *Common School Act* in 1871, the Roman Catholic community was outraged and claimed that the practices that had been in place since the adoption of the *Parish School Act* in 1858, and which the Catholics assumed would continue after Confederation, had been totally discarded. Section 8 of the 1858 Act stated:

> The Board of Education shall, by regulation, secure to all children whose parents do not object to it, the reading of the Bible in Parish schools and the Bible when read in Parish schools by Catholic children, shall, if required by their parents or guardians, be the Douay[34] version, without note or comment.[35]

Under the Act, the Acadians had been permitted to build their own schools in wholly French areas of the colony as well as in mixed communities. They were permitted to teach religion in their schools, and they received government grants.[36] Needless to say, the Catholic community believed that the requirements of the new law to exclude religious instruction and make the schools explicitly non-sectarian violated the guarantees that they had in law prior to Confederation. The matter was

---

34   The Douay Bible was an English translation of The Vulgate, which was the approved Latin translation and compendium of the Bible, largely done by St Jerome in the late fourth and early fifth centuries. The Bible translation was completed in the English Catholic College in Douay, northern France, between 1582 and 1610 and endorsed by the Catholic Church for use in English-speaking Catholic communities and institutions.

35   William B Hamilton, "Society and Schools in New Brunswick and Prince Edward Island" in Wilson, Stamp, & Audet, above note 2 at 117.

36   Louis-Philippe Audet, "Educational Developments in French-Canada after 1875," in Wilson, Stamp, & Audet, *ibid* at 352.

discussed in Parliament and was also ruled on in the Supreme Court of New Brunswick, which upheld the validity of the legislation. So, too, did the Judicial Committee of the Privy Council.[37]

While an accommodation was worked out between the provincial government and the Catholic clergy on most of the religious issues pertaining to schools, there was still forceful opposition among the general Acadian population to the idea of the schools being supported by general property taxes on the public. This opposition led to riots in the Miramichi region, and when attempts were made to arrest some of the rioters, two men were killed.[38]

2) Manitoba

This confrontation was to be only the first of a number during the coming decades in which the constitutionally protected rights in regard to denominational schools would be challenged. One of the most noted challenges relates to what is referred to as the "Manitoba School Question." The province of Manitoba was formed in 1870 out of what had until 1868 been part of Rupert's Land. In that year, the British government purchased all of Rupert's Land from The Hudson's Bay Company and granted it as a gift to the federal government of Canada, which renamed it the Northwest Territories. In recognition of the fact that the region did not have any traditional governing structures before this time and acknowledging that more than 80 percent of the population was Métis and Catholic,[39] the federal government, in drawing up the *Manitoba Act*, saw fit to incorporate the term "or practice" alongside the phrase "by Law" in section 22(1) of the Act, as modifications and expansions on the 1867 legislation.

The federal government arrived at this agreement after discussions and negotiations with the predominantly Métis population of the region led by Louis Riel. Bishop Taché of St Boniface had prevailed on Riel to have denominational schools acknowledged in the legislation as well as the

---

37 Manoly R Lupul, "Education Crisis in the New Dominion to 1917" in Wilson, Stamp, & Audet, *ibid*. In this chapter the author deals extensively with this and other challenges that arose in relation to authority of provincial governments during the fifty years following Confederation.

38 *Ibid* at 272.

39 It should be noted that Lupul, above note 37 at 274, provided numbers that indicate the Protestant population was almost equal to the Catholic population when the *School Act* was approved in 1871.

other significant demands he had already made. The negotiations were anything but amicable. They were complicated by a number of underlying fears, including the fear among the Métis that they would lose the land that they had settled and farmed to the influx of settlers from Ontario. Those moving west from Ontario were afraid that the settlers in the Northwest Territories were essentially "savages," with little or no appreciation for or understanding of the Anglican Church or the British way of life. There were some grounds for the fears of both groups. Nonetheless, the legislation establishing Canada's fifth province incorporated almost all of Riel's requests. Treaties were concluded with the First Nations; the legislation acknowledged parity between the French and English languages; denomination rights were protected in education; and provision was made for the protection of local customs and traditions.

However, the demographic realities changed quickly, and so, too, did the province's social demographics. Within twenty years of providing the security demanded and obtained in the *Manitoba Act*, the constitutional applecart was upended dramatically. As the Protestant population took control of the province, and as the percentage of the overall population who were Catholic dropped drastically, and the number of non-francophone residents rose far beyond that of the francophone population, demands to abolish the linguistic/cultural and denominational constitutional privileges increased.[40] By far, the greatest number of new residents in Manitoba came from Ontario. It was estimated that by 1890, approximately 45 percent of the residents of Manitoba had been born in Ontario.[41]

In 1890, the legislature did away with denominational schools and abandoned the privileged status of the French language in the province of Manitoba. After protracted legal battles in Manitoba, Ottawa, and London, the Judicial Committee of the House of Lords ruled in 1895 that

> [t]he 1890 law, although *intra vires* did in fact affect the minority's rights and privileges unfavourably; through double taxation the minority suffered hardships after 1890, which the federal government was constitutionally bound to remedy.[42]

---

40   Throughout the 1880s, Ontario had experienced an increase in bigotry against the francophone population and against the use of French in schools. There had also been a number of public elections in which "no Popery" was a significant political issue.

41   Wilson, above note 32 at 274.

42   *Ibid* at 276.

After the 1896 election, an agreement of sorts was worked out between Prime Minister Laurier and Manitoba Premier Greenway. In the public schools, religious instruction would be permitted at the end of the school day and a Catholic teacher had to be employed by the board of trustees for every twenty-five Catholic students in a school. Furthermore, where ten or more students spoke any language other than English, the teacher was required by the agreement to use a method of bilingual instruction — a directive that Lupul says was guaranteed to create chaos.[43]

The agreement was seen as being as much about placating the electorate in Ontario and Québec as about sorting out matters in Manitoba.[44] The entire series of events highlights the political power and the force of public persuasion in matters of public policy. It also highlights the reality that short of the employment of military force, there may be no way to force an unwilling province or a legislature to comply with a legal or constitutional obligation.

Nonetheless, the patriotic fervour generated by the First World War provided an opportunity for governments across the country to require, with little danger of serious opposition, that English would be the language of instruction in all public schools. As a result, the Manitoba accommodations for Catholic and French students were done away with.

3) Ontario

Trying to understand the implications of section 93 was a matter that was to return and remain with Canadian courts throughout the years. Early in the 1900s, Ontario had to deal with the issue of the inextricable links between many of the rural Catholic boards in the northern part of the province and the French language. Years of evidence of poor teaching and little learning had prompted the government to insist on basic levels of training for all teachers, a move supported by many English-speaking Catholics. However, some members of the Catholic hierarchy, clergy, and boards of trustees claimed that the new regulation interfered with their right to hire members of religious orders for the Catholic schools even without any provincial permit.

43 *Ibid* at 277.
44 WL Morton, "Manitoba Schools and Canadian Nationality, 1890–1923" (1951) 30 *Report of the Annual Meeting of the Canadian Historical Society* 51.

By 1910 the issue had been taken up by those interested in obtaining equal rights for the French language in Ontario. Bishop Fallon of London spoke out publicly in favour of the government's efforts to improve the quality of instruction in the schools. In somewhat intemperate language, he criticized the "alleged bilingual school system which teaches neither English nor French, encourages incompetency, gives a prize to hypocrisy, and breeds ignorance."[45]

Matters came to a head in 1912 with the introduction of a regulation which severely limited the extent to which French could be used in schools either as a language of instruction or as a subject to be taught. The French members of the Ottawa Catholic School Board insisted on their right to employ more than twenty Christian Brothers without teaching authority. As the conflict played out, the schools were closed.

A case was brought by an English-speaking trustee, R Mackell, who argued that the term "class of persons" in section 93 referred to either Protestants or Catholics in a religious sense and had no linguistic connotations. This interpretation was upheld through the courts and ultimately decided by the Ontario Supreme Court in 1916. "Roman Catholics together form the meaning of the section a class of persons, and that class cannot be subdivided into other classes by consideration of the language by whom that faith is held . . . ."[46]

4) Alberta and Saskatchewan

When Alberta and Saskatchewan came into Confederation in 1905, they brought with them a legislative framework very similar to that in existence in Ontario — the religious minority within a public school district, whether Protestant or Catholic, could, if it so wished, establish a separate school system in that district. By the 1920s, considerable attempts had been made to develop a funding structure that would ensure fairness between the two systems while respecting the right of the taxpayer to decide which system the money should go to; however, this right was severely curtailed in Alberta and Saskatchewan. Two cases, *McCarthy v City of Regina and Regina Board of Public School Trustees* (1918) and *McCarthy v City of Regina and Regina Board of Public School Trustees* (1917), established for both

45   Charles Bruce Sissons, *Bi-lingual Schools in Canada* (Toronto: JM Dent & Sons, 1917) at 80.

46   Wilson, above note 32 at 285.

provinces that once a separate school district was established in a region, then all those professing the same faith as those establishing the district were automatically residents and supporters of that district and liable to taxation for the support of the district. In essence, the minority of the minority establishing the district were bound by the will of the majority of that minority.[47] The Appeal Court of Alberta came to a similar conclusion in 1976.[48]

In two later cases from Alberta, the courts further refined understandings relating to the establishment of separate schools. In *Starland School Division No 30 v Alberta*,[49] the judge indicated that he would not "explore the mind and conscience of electors to determine their faith for public and separate education purposes." The electors would be considered to be of the faith they declared. In the *Jacobi v Newell No 4 (County)* case some years later,[50] the judge ruled that a separate school district must have a denominational purpose. There must be, in other words, an intent to provide a religious experience for those students of the Catholic faith for whom the school district is primarily, though not exclusively, established. According to this ruling, if there is no denominational purpose, the system cannot be established, and if it were, it would not enjoy any constitutional protection.

However, there have been additional skirmishes in relation to denominational rights in both provinces. In Alberta, the constitutionality of certain boundary expansions has been a cause of contention.[51] In Saskatchewan, questions in proceedings that are underway centre on whether the government may constitutionally provide grants to Catholic schools on behalf of non-Catholic students.[52] The rights of the religious minorities safeguarded in section 93 of the *Constitution Act, 1867* are constitutional requirements, but a provincial government is not precluded from permitting the establishment of and even funding schools operated by other religious

---

47 *McCarthy v City of Regina and Regina Board of Public School Trustees*, [1918] 3 WWR 302 (PC); *McCarthy v City of Regina and Regina Board of Public School Trustees* (1917), 32 DLR 755 (Sask SC).

48 *Schmidt v Calgary (Board of Education)*, 1975 CanLII 254 (ABQB).

49 1988 CanLII 3528 (ABQB).

50 [1994] AJ No 1063 (QB).

51 *Aspen View Regional School Division v The Attorney General of Alberta and Lakeland Roman Catholic Separate School District*. The case was brought to a close before going to court.

52 Proceedings between *Christ the Teacher Roman Catholic Separate School Division No 212 and Good Spirit School Division No 204, and the Government of Saskatchewan.*

denominations. All provinces permit religiously operated schools, and many provide some financial support on certain conditions. This is constitutionally permitted.

In no case do provincial governments fund private schools as generously as they do public schools, so the private schools are all fee charging. A rough estimate would indicate that about 5 percent of Canadian students are in private schools and that most of these schools are denominational. Generally, these schools are subjected to the same scrutiny as are public schools in terms of their academic standards, adherence to provincial education regulations, and financial operations.

Several school jurisdictions in Alberta permit the operation of an interdenominational *Logos* Christian-based program in some of their schools at parental request and where numbers can sustain the program. Similarly, a number of what were formerly private schools have worked out agreements with the public jurisdictions that permit them to maintain their denominational integrity and work within the public school system with the addition of an intermediate board with clearly defined responsibilities. This arrangement allows the erstwhile private school to receive full funding and provides access to supplementary resources and professional development opportunities that would otherwise not have been available.

5) Québec

For a number of years, the Parti Québécois has sought to implement a policy of secularism in all public operations in Québec. This commitment emerged partly as a result of the requirements that reasonable accommodation be made in areas where the provincial government felt that *Charter* interpretations clash with traditional provincial practices. The Québec *Charter of Values* was first discussed in the provincial Assembly in May 2013 and formally introduced in October of that year.[53] In essence, it was similar in its message to *Laïcité*, which has been central to French social policy since the early years of the century, and which distinguishes clearly between the private and the public citizen. Religion, its practice, and its symbols are all seen as being associated with the private person and

---

53   Bill 60, *Charter affirming the values of State secularism and religious neutrality and of equality between women and men, and providing a framework for accommodation requests*, 1st Sess, 40th Leg, Québec, 2013.

having no place in the public sphere. Consequently, all displays of overt religious symbols or emblems would be banned in Québec under the *Charter of Values* and, clearly, religious dress such as the hijab, the niqab, the burqa would be illegal. Considerable opposition to the Québec *Charter* emerged, and in addition to the reactions from established churches, there was extensive criticism from human rights groups and the Canadian and Québec bar associations. When the Liberal Party took power following the election in 2014, the implementation of the *Charter* was put on hold.

In the years leading up to the introduction of the Québec *Charter of Values*, the government faced challenges in the Supreme Court of Canada on a number of issues. First, there was a case of refusing to allow a young Khalsa Sikh to wear a kirpan to school although satisfactory agreements addressing safety concerns had been reached with the school board.[54] It should be noted that there had been two earlier cases dealing with the concerns around kirpans and both decisions, as well as this one, were decided in favour of the students.[55]

The Québec government has also had to deal with two matters relating to its required secondary school course in Ethics, introduced in September 2008. The first of these[56] dealt with a claim by two parents that the mandatory course, in the Ethics and Religious Culture (ERC) program, would cause serious harm to their children because of the conflicting ideas to which they would be exposed. The parents also claimed that what the program was designed to do would infringe on their children's rights to freedom of conscience and religion. The Supreme Court denied the appeal and pointed out that "[i]t is not enough for a person to say that his or her rights have been infringed. The person must prove the infringement on a balance of probabilities."

In the second case,[57] the court dealt with an appeal by Loyola High School against the minister of Education's refusal to grant the school an exemption from having to teach the ERC course. The minister was permitted to grant

---

54 *Multani v Commission scolaire Marguerite-Bourgeoys*, 2006 SCC 6.

55 The earlier case was *Tuli v St Albert Protestant Board of Education* (1985), 8 CHRR D/3906 (Alta QB). The second case was *Pandori v Peel Board of Education* (1990), 12 CHRR D/364, aff'd (1991), 3 OR (3d) 531 (Div Ct). See also Mary S Martin, *The 1990 Kirpan Case: Cultural Conflict and the Development of Equity Policy in the Peel District School Board* (PhD thesis, Ontario Institute for Studies in Education, University of Toronto, 2011) [unpublished].

56 *SL v Commission scolaire des Chênes*, 2012 SCC 7 at para 23.

57 *Loyola High School v Quebec (Attorney General)*, 2015 SCC 12.

an exemption if the proposed alternative was deemed to be equivalent. He indicated that since the alternative course would be taught from a Catholic perspective, it could not be equivalent. The Supreme Court allowed the appeal and indicated that the minister's requirement that all aspects of the Loyola program be taught from a neutral perspective, "including the teaching of Catholicism, limited freedom of religion more than was necessary given the statutory objectives. As a result, it did not reflect a proportionate balancing and should be set aside."[58] While the appeal was allowed, the matter was sent back to the minister for reconsideration.

6) Human Rights

Before leaving the topic of religion and schooling, it is appropriate to mention the complex matter of the changes to school law aimed at ensuring that bullying of youngsters because of sexual orientation is eradicated from all schools. Initiatives that require school boards to allow for the adoption of Gay–Straight Alliances in all schools where students request them[59] have encountered much push back from a variety of religious groups, though the media appear to have focused disproportionately on comments from some members of the Catholic community. While there appears to be unanimity in all efforts to ensure a safe, welcoming school environment for all students, complications seem to have arisen in relation to what these initiatives should or might be called.

On a different, but related, topic, the government of Alberta has been involved in rewriting its education legislation for some years. A new *Education Act* was given royal assent in 2012 but has not yet been proclaimed as all necessary regulations are not yet in place. There is a point of interest relating to the matter of sexual orientation that emphasizes the political nature of law-making. Section 16 of the new law has the heading "Diversity and respect." The paragraph in the original version of the Bill read:

> All courses or programs of study offered and instructional materials used must reflect the diverse nature and heritage of society in Alberta, promote understanding and respect for others and honour and respect the *Canadian Charter of Rights and Freedoms* and the *Alberta Human Rights Act*.

---

58 *Ibid*, headnote
59 A Gay–Straight Alliance is a student-driven initiative primarily in middle and high schools, whereby students can meet in a safe place to support one another, talk about issues related to sexual orientation and gender identity and expression, and work to end homophobia and transphobia.

Serious and forceful (and effective) opposition to this wording emerged from Christian home-schoolers. They argued that both the *Charter* and the Alberta human rights legislation had been used as "hammers" in the past to require Christians to remain silent on matters that they considered wrong and sinful. They objected to the prominent and even dominant positions these documents were given in directing how education and educating should be carried out in Alberta. The government modified the section of the new *Education Act*. It now reads:

> Diversity and respect
> 16(1) All courses or programs of study and instructional materials used in a school must reflect the diverse nature and heritage of society in Alberta, promote understanding and respect for others and honour and respect the common values and beliefs of Albertans.
> (2) For greater certainty, the courses or programs of study and instructional materials referred to in subsection (1) must not promote or foster doctrines of racial or ethnic superiority or persecution, social change through violent action or disobedience of laws.

The references to the *Charter* and to the *Alberta Human Rights Act* have been removed. The stated opposition appears to be solely to the protections that both of these statutes provide in relation to sexual orientation. The extent to which the government's acquiescence to the demands of this small group will affect the application of the overall legislation is unknown.[60]

Some of the points that I have raised are clearly linked to denominational/religious issues while others may also be tied to other issues such as human rights or freedom of expression. The areas frequently overlap, providing courts and people of good will with the challenge of unravelling the intertwined strands.

---

60   In relation to the issues raised by the Alberta government's acquiescence in this situation, it would be informative to refer to the two readings identified below. In relation to the place of secularism in society, it is worth reading Charles Taylor, *The Meaning of Secularism* (Charlottesville, VA: Institute for Advanced Studies in Culture, University of Virginia, 2010) [reprinted with permission from (2010) 12 *The Hedgehog Review* 23]. In Peter D Lauwers, "Religion and the Ambiguities of Liberalism Pluralism: A Canadian Perspective" (2007) 37 *Supreme Court Law Review* 1, he analyzed, compared, and considered the implications for society of both convergence pluralism and accommodation pluralism.

F. CENTRALIZED CONTROL VERSUS LOCAL AUTONOMY

Under the original administrative frameworks established in the 1800s, the number of school systems in every province was bound to increase massively as immigrants settled each region, and so they did. In Saskatchewan, there were over 4,000 school districts by 1918. By the early 1930s, the number of school districts had reached more than 3,800 in Alberta. In Ontario, there were almost 3,500 different districts in 1950. There were over 270 school districts in Prince Edward Island in 1970, over 430 in New Brunswick in 1967, and over 300 in Newfoundland in 1964.[61] In the mid-1940s, British Columbia had more than 800 districts in operation.[62]

By 1970, the population of Canada had grown to more than twenty-one million from about six million in 1900. That of itself would have accounted for a sizable increase in the number of children in schools. Other factors were also in play, however. First of these was the considerable emphasis placed on universal, free, and compulsory schooling for all children between certain ages. A second factor was that the compulsory element was diligently enforced, not just in law but in practice.[63] A third factor that played a notable part in the expansion of schooling and increase in number of school districts was the large number of immigrants to Canada; many immigrants settled in rural areas and — particularly in western Canada — established homogeneous communities and set up their own educational structures within the legal and administrative contexts set out by their province. As early as 1901, a little over 12 percent of the population of about six million indicated that they were not born in Canada. In every decade up to 2000, the percentage indicating that they were born outside Canada was above 14 percent, and at any given time, any of the census figures would have a substantial number of children who — though born in Canada and attending Canadian schools — had parents who had been born abroad.[64]

---

61   These figures are to be found in a number of different places. See R Carney & Frank Peters, "Governing Education: The Myth of Local Control" in James Lightbody, ed, *Canadian Metropolitics: Governing Our Cities* (Toronto: Copp Clark, 1995) at 240–68.

62   Johnson, above note 6 at 113.

63   See, for example, *Perepolkin v British Columbia (Superintendent of Child Welfare)* (1957), 11 DLR (2d) 245 (BCCA).

64   The extent to which immigration had been a significant contributor to population growth in Canada, and consequently, to the expansion of the number of school

Provinces tried to come to grips with the huge numbers of school jurisdictions even early in the twentieth century but had little success. From a political perspective, the areas that would be most affected were the rural areas, and these constituencies were generally unwavering in their commitment to maintaining local control of their educational affairs. Even today, when more than 80 percent of the Canadian population lives in urban areas, every province has a disproportionately large number of rural schools.

Although the underlying tensions between local autonomy and centralized control have been present in Canadian education since the end of the eighteenth century, in the last forty years, they have featured prominently in educational politics and governance across the country. It is not surprising that any attempt to reduce the number of districts by means of amalgamations is seen as a move towards centralization and a loss of local control. Centralization has been made somewhat more difficult because governments have been unable to demonstrate that the substantial financial savings they have used as justifications for the changes have, in fact, materialized. Many educators, however, point to the programmatic improvements and enrichment that can emerge when the sizes of schools are closer to optimal.

Only comparatively recently, and following a number of rulings from the Supreme Court of Canada,[65] have provinces such as Alberta, Ontario, and Saskatchewan adopted funding frameworks for public schools that allow for an equal allocation to each school board for comparable students. This has necessitated a pooling of what had been the traditional source of funding for education: the property tax base. This system was unavoidably inequitable in that the amount of money available from this source of revenue varied wildly from one location to another. However, as a system on which funding of schools was based, it had the apparent virtues of age and tradition; it was also a system over which the local school board exercised some control.

It is worth commenting that although the pooled system of funding undeniably establishes a "more equal" system of allocating financial resources, the system may not be fair in terms of whether students of different

---

districts is dealt with thoroughly in Monica Boyd & Michael Vickers, "100 Years of Immigration" (2000) 58 *Canadian Social Trends* (Statistics Canada Cat no 11-00).

65 See, for example, *Public School Boards' Assn of Alberta v Alberta (Attorney General)*, [2000] 2 SCR 409; and *Ontario English Catholic Teachers' Assn v Ontario (Attorney General)*, [2001] 1 SCR 470.

abilities are receiving the resources needed so that they can obtain "equal benefit of the law," as required by the *Charter*.[66] Nor does the equal funding do anything to ensure adequacy of funding in terms of overall systems' needs. It may well be that in some provinces what prevails at certain times is "an equality of inadequacy" in funding and the school boards have no means to provide more funding to overcome these shortfalls.

The Alberta ruling mentioned above is also interesting in that the Court reiterated the fact that public school boards enjoy no constitutional protections. They are governed by each province and derive whatever powers they have from the provincial statutes. This had been hinted at in a ruling in Salmon Arm, British Columbia, in the 1950s when school trustees were told that if they were unable to fulfill their statutory duty their only recourse was to resign. Nonetheless, there has never been a case where the Supreme Court of Canada stated clearly that school authorities are arms of the government to assist the government in carrying out responsibilities under section 93 of the *Constitution Act, 1867*.

G. POLITICS AND EDUCATION

In 1976, following a review of policies relating to education in Canada, members of an OECD[67] panel concluded that ". . . Canadian education policy may be one of the least 'politicized' in the world." Legal, educational, and social historians would likely quibble with the accuracy of such a

---

66 Above note 4, s 15.

67 Organization for Economic Co-operation and Development, *Reviews of National Policies for Education: Canada* (Paris: OECD, 1976) at 3. The paragraph continued:

> . . . Indeed it is as if the attempt has been made in this field since the beginning to avoid party-political controversy at all cost. Study of the rather meager Provincial Parliamentary debates on education reveals little evidence of political controversy in the realm of educational policy, except for some occasional recent debates on financing separate and private schools. The political parties make few if any statements on specific educational matters and, in the vase of Quebec, the second largest of the Provinces, there is no clearly formulated concept of educational policy set in the context of a comprehensive framework of general social policies. Reforms in education are almost totally pragmatic, or so generally conceived and relying so heavily on United States, British, and French models, more or less adapted to Canadian conditions, that the opportunity for any party political conflict is, for all practical purposes, excluded.

sweeping claim, but it is difficult to imagine that anybody would make a similar claim in relation to the past forty years.

1) Pre-*Charter* Deference to School Authorities

Many decisions are contested, even when discussed and supported on all sides by "experts." In the case of many educational decisions, the only agreed-on matter is that improvement is needed, but the precise nature of the problem to be addressed, as well as the improvement needed, is frequently contested. In these situations, there is rarely agreement on the means that should be adopted and implemented. This is where the decision makers find themselves having to pick through competing proposals, demands, facts, and fantasies. There is no need for politics when everybody is in agreement on both the ends to be attained and the best, most appropriate means to be used. However, these felicitous occasions rarely, if ever, arise in the educational domain.

Decision makers are also caught up in the conundrum that Habermas[68] presented us with. The law is a statement of how things are. They direct our actions but frequently leave where we have discretion, and this permits us to interpret and apply the law in the manner most closely aligned with the norms and values we would most want to promote. In this sense, the interpretation of the law, of the policy, of the rule is absolutely critical. Many decisions we are wont to think of as objective are, in reality, political and subjective, laced with traces of the values we think are important.

Historically, considerable deference was given to educational authorities under the broad mandate that they enjoyed to ensure proper order in the running of the school. Students were to follow rules regarding dress and length of hair and even colour of hair. Boys were suspended for wearing jeans and for having long hair. Boys and girls were suspended because the school authorities did not like the colour of dye they had used in their hair or for wearing inappropriate clothing: the logo might be offensive or the clothing might not cover enough skin. Similarly, school authorities were granted extensive freedoms in placing students in whatever class they deemed appropriate, frequently without involving the parents in the decision. This was an era of considerable deference to the authority of

---

68   Jürgen Habermas, *Between Facts and Norms* (Cambridge, MA: MIT Press, 1996).

educators. One might have expected this to change with the *Charter* and, in some respects, it has.

2) The Challenge of Meeting Special Needs

One area in which some notable, if slow, change has occurred relates to children with special needs. Even before the adoption of the *Charter* in 1982, interest had developed in providing appropriate education for children with severe disabilities, children who had previously been excluded from school.[69] The struggle to ensure that these children would be permitted to attend school has been referred to as the struggle for "platform rights."[70] The years since the adoption of the *Charter* have seen a notable increase in changes to legislation and funding and in the amount of litigation relating to the provision of educational services for students with severe educational, physical, and/or mental challenges.[71] This area is clearly one in which parental wishes and educational expertise from time to time clash.

MacKay and Burt-Gerrans[72] claimed that even though *Elwood v The Halifax County Bedford District School Board* was settled out of court, the fact that the judge granted an injunction permitting Luke to remain in the classroom until the case was resolved in court was in itself a breakthrough. It suggested that the law could be used to challenge a school system's experts. Furthermore, in considering the best interests of the child, the deference that had been traditionally granted to educational experts would be balanced against the knowledge and wishes of the parents. It

---

69   An example of this change is the case of *Carrière (Next friend of) v Lamont (County No 30)*, [1978] AJ No 131 (SCTD). The significance of this case is highlighted by Dick Sobsey with Kent Cameron, "A Brief History of the J.P. Das Developmental Disabilities Centre" (2008) 36 *Developmental Disabilities Bulletin* 251 at 265. The Supreme Court of Alberta, Trial Division, upheld this decision in 1984 but though it upheld Shelly Carrière's right to attend school, it found that it had no authority to make any ruling as to the quality or appropriateness of the schooling she should receive.

70   See, among others, A Wayne MacKay & Janet Burt-Gerrans, "Inclusion and Diversity in Education: Legal Accomplishments and Prospects for the Future" (Paper delivered at the Canadian Association for Community Living National Conference, Mississauga, Ontario, 3–5 November 2002).

71   This entire area is covered in considerable detail by Joyce D Clayton, *Implications of Charter Litigation for Special Education Policy in Canada* (PhD Thesis, University of Alberta, 2011) [unpublished].

72   See above note 69.

has been pointed out that in the years before the *Charter* and for a decade after its introduction, courts paid considerable deference to educational administrators and "experts" in cases where the best interests of students with special needs were being considered.[73] Two notable decisions — one handed down in 1997 and the other, fifteen years later — have contributed much to the foundation upon which our understanding of educating children with special needs is built.

The first of these cases was *Eaton v Brant County Board of Education*.[74] The school board appealed a decision of the Ontario Court of Appeal that the *Charter* required a legal presumption in favour of integration in a regular classroom if children with special needs were to benefit from their *Charter* right to equality. The Supreme Court of Canada overturned this decision and, in doing so, indicated that what was required was a reasonable accommodation of the student based on a thorough identification and analysis of the student's special characteristics and needs. While the Court appeared to indicate a continued deference to educational experts, it was clear that a school system would have to establish that the proposed placement was not merely one of convenience or least expense or the only one available in the school, but rather based on the specific characteristics and needs of the particular student.

The case of Jeffrey Moore, decided in the Supreme Court of Canada in 2012,[75] represents an incredible progress in understanding from the *Carrière* decisions. Jeffrey was diagnosed as being severely dyslexic and received remedial support in his school in North Vancouver, British Columbia. The school district specialists indicated that he needed additional, more intense support; however, the school district closed down the facility that provided this service prior to his being able to avail of it. The school system reading experts advised Jeffrey's parents that the program he needed was only available in a private school. They enrolled him in that school at great personal expense.

After Jeffrey's successful completion of school, his father, Frederick, filed a complaint with the BC Human Rights Tribunal claiming that his son was denied a "service customarily available to the public" to which he

---

73   Monica A Williams & Robert B MacMillan, "Litigation in Special Education (1978–1995) Part I: From Access to Inclusion" (2000) 10 *Education & Law Journal* 349 at 350.

74   [1997] 1 SCR 241.

75   *Moore v British Columbia (Education)*, 2012 SCC 61 [*Moore*].

was entitled under section 8 of the BC *Human Rights Code*.[76] The Tribunal agreed with Moore; however, the government and the school board appealed to the province's Supreme Court, and the Tribunal decision was set aside. Moore then appealed this loss to the Court of Appeal, but a majority of the Court of Appeal dismissed his claim. Eventually, in its decision, the Supreme Court of Canada agreed with most of the findings of the BC Human Rights Tribunal.

The Court found that Jeffrey had, indeed, been deprived of access to a "service customarily available to the public." It stated that Jeffrey was entitled to "education generally" but because of his dyslexia, he needed assistance to enable him to gain access to and benefit from that education. The Court stated forcefully that

> [a]dequate special education . . . is not a dispensable luxury. For those with severe learning disabilities, it is the ramp that provides access to the statutory commitment to education made to all children in British Columbia.[77]

The service to which Jeffrey was entitled was that to which all students were entitled. Special education would be the means by which he gained meaningful access to general education. The Court pointed out (in agreement with the Human Rights Tribunal) that when considering whether or not Jeffrey had been subjected to discrimination, the correct comparator group should be the general body of students and not other students with dyslexia. It would be easy to conclude that he was not discriminated against if the latter group was the comparator sector. The school board could show that nobody with severe dyslexia received the treatment they needed, so all were treated the same; no individual was discriminated against.

MacKay and Burt-Gerrans referred to the 1987 case[78] of *Hickling v Lanark, Leeds & Grenville Roman Catholic Separate School Board*, which was ultimately decided in court, on appeal from a decision of the Human Rights Board of Inquiry. The school had placed all the students with special needs in a segregated setting as it did not have proper accommodations to meet their individual needs. The Catholic school board applied to have the decision judicially reviewed and the court held that since the school did not have the appropriate amenities to accommodate any of the students

---

76 RSBC 1996, c 210.
77 *Moore*, above note 75 at para 5.
78 MacKay & Burt-Gerrans, above note 70 at 4.

with special needs, there was no discrimination. The court also pointed out that it was better to leave decisions of this sort to educational experts.

The decision in the *Moore* case twenty-five years later clearly demonstrates that the criteria used in deciding on discrimination in relation to special needs placements should change. Assuming that all other provinces have made a similar statutory commitment to the education of all children, the ruling appears to be far-reaching. This is just one area in which educational structures and the laws governing those structures have been adapted and rewritten to better incorporate a greater sensitivity to the rights of parents and of students.

3) Student Searches in the Context of Rights

We have developed deeper insights into the purposes of schooling and become more attentive to issues of fairness and equity. There are a number of additional areas where our understandings of rights appear to have evolved and where the understandings appear to be based in a changed political understanding. I next refer to three cases involving searching students or their property in schools.

The first two cases, *R v JMG*[79] and *R v M(MR)*,[80] deal with boys who were found guilty of possession of marijuana and school administrators who were found to be blameless in terms of how the cases were handled in the schools. In the *JMG* case, the principal was informed that James was seen putting drugs into his sock just prior to classes starting. The principal brought the youth to the office and told him of the allegations. The young man then swallowed a hand-rolled cigarette that was assumed to contain drugs. The principal became engaged in a struggle with the young man and, in the process, found a small foil package in the sock which the principal identified as marijuana. The principal called the police and handed over the drugs. The young man was charged under the *Young Offenders' Act*, found guilty, and fined $25. The decision was appealed to the Divisional Court, which overturned the conviction. It decided that the evidence was inadmissible because the principal, acting as a police agent, had violated JMG's *Charter* right protected under section 8. The court found that the marijuana had been seized in violation of the *Charter* and was inadmissible in evidence.

---

79 (1986), 33 DLR (4th) 277 (Ont CA) [*JMG*].
80 (1998), 166 DLR (4th) 261 (SCC).

The Attorney General appealed this decision, and the Ontario Court of Appeal found that the principal had acted appropriately, in accordance with his responsibilities to maintain order and safety in the school and on the basis of credible information. He was not acting as a police agent and for him to call the police without verifying whether JMG did have drugs would have been irresponsible. Being in school, JMG could expect less privacy than had he been elsewhere, and so his section 8 rights were not violated. Nor were his section 10 rights violated because students who are "detained" by school officials for questioning on school matters are not understood to be detained in the sense in which the word is understood in criminal law.

The second case deals with a junior high school student from Nova Scotia. The vice-principal was informed that MRM would be selling drugs at the school dance that evening. When MRM arrived at the dance with a friend, the vice-principal, Mr Cadue, asked both students to go to his office. Prior to the search, Cadue called the police and waited until a plainclothes police officer arrived before beginning the questioning. The vice-principal searched the students and found a small cellophane bag containing marijuana in MRM's sock, which he then gave to the police officer. The officer determined that the bag contained marijuana and arrested MRM, informing him that he had the right to have an adult present when any further questions were asked. MRM attempted to contact his mother but was unsuccessful and indicated that there was nobody else he wished to get in touch with. The constable, MRM, and Cadue then searched MRM's locker but found no more drugs.

In the Divisional Court trial, Dyer J found that the vice-principal was acting as a police agent as a result of his having had a prior conversation with the police officer. He excluded the evidence obtained in the search and dismissed the case. The Nova Scotia Court of Appeal overturned that decision, found that the vice-principal was acting as an educator, and that there had been no violations of MRM's *Charter* rights. This decision was appealed to the Supreme Court of Canada, which upheld the decision of the Nova Scotia Appeal Court and found MRM guilty.

The reasoning of the majority (Major J dissented) was very similar to that of the Court of Appeal in the *JMG* case. Justice Major's dissent was based, in part, on his appearing to accept the interpretations of Dyer J that there had been an agreement between Cadue and the police officer and that, to some extent, Cadue had been "coached" in how to proceed. In his view, Cadue was acting as a police agent, and the evidence should not have been admitted.

Both cases point clearly to the deference paid to school authorities and the acknowledgement by the courts that school administrators have an arduous task in ensuring that schools are safe and orderly places, free from drugs. The rights of the students are clearly considered to be of lesser significance. Students should understand that their right to be protected from unreasonable search and seizure is lessened because they are in school and their right not to be detained is also reduced because by the nature of their being in school, they are already detained, though not in the legal sense.

The third case, R v AM, may, in some ways, be surprising.[81] The police in Sarnia, Ontario, had an open invitation from the principal of one of the high schools to bring sniffer dogs into the school at any time. One day in 2002, they did this without any specific request from the school authorities. They searched the building and found a knapsack belonging to AM to which a sniffer dog reacted. Without a warrant, the police officer opened the backpack and found illegal drugs. AM was charged with possession of cannabis marijuana and psilocybin for the purpose of trafficking.

The defence argued that AM's right to a reasonable degree of privacy under section 8 of the *Charter* had been violated and the evidence should be excluded. Justice Hornblower agreed on the basis that there were two illegal searches, one by the sniffer dog and the second by the police officer. The Crown appealed to the Ontario Court of Appeal, but the appeal was denied. At the Supreme Court of Canada, the result was the same. A majority of the Supreme Court dismissed the appeal.

The Court this time emphasized the rights of the student and pointed out that the search by the police was without a warrant and had not been requested by the school. It pointed out that a teenager should have an expectancy of privacy from "the random and speculative scrutiny of the police." Furthermore, students who move from place to place during their school day may use their backpacks as repositories for many personal and "private" objects. "This expectation is a reasonable one that society should support."[82] In what appears to be a notable departure from the form of language used in earlier cases, the Court stated:

---

81 2008 SCC 19.

82 *Ibid* at para 63.

> [While the sniffer-dog search] may have been seen by the police as an efficient use of their resources, and by the principal of the school as an efficient way to advance a zero-tolerance policy, these objectives were achieved at the expense of the privacy interest (and constitutional rights) of every student in the school . . . . The *Charter* weighs other values, including privacy, against an appetite for police efficiency.[83]

This ruling appears to have the potential to alter the way in which school officials take on board the *Charter* rights of students and, in particular, their privacy rights.

The area in which the rapid change in technologies continues to affect how schooling must be done is challenging and intimidating. The unprecedented access to information has altered the nature of teacher–student relationships. In addition to its being a hugely beneficial resource, it has been found that technologies can be great distractions in the classroom unless their use is monitored appropriately. This is an area that educators are constantly working with in order to ensure that technologies are providing optimal benefits to schools in terms of student learning and financial expenditures.

New technologies have also altered the ways in which students relate to one another and this has emerged as a crucial area in the administration and general operation of schools. Social media allow student-to-student interaction on a constant basis, and the various modes of communication are constantly being adapted.[84] Technologies allow students to group together in cliques, form flexible groups for a variety of purposes, and make and discard "friends" in an impersonal and nonchalant fashion. Social media have facilitated the creation of situations in which individuals or groups of students are harassed and bullied by others, often under an apparent cloak of anonymity. This belief that they cannot be identified has apparently emboldened some members of these groups of bullies and created situations far more violent and serious than might have emerged had the individuals been operating face-to-face. Furthermore, personal information and details, including photographs, at times sexually explicit, are shared, leaving the sender vulnerable to being harassed and even

---

83   *Ibid* at para 15.

84   A small listing of readily available apps for social interactions include Fling, Snapchat, Chat for Omegle, WhatsAPP, KIK, and Instagram, not to mention the ubiquitous Facebook. Most of these apps are constantly being refined and updated, and the dangers associated with their use need to be constantly reassessed.

blackmailed, either by the direct recipient of the information/photograph or a third party with whom it has been shared.

It has become a truism that teenagers are consumed by their addictions to the Internet and to the devices that link them to cyberspace, and it is here that they often develop their sense of self-worth and confidence — or lack of it. Many young people discover that they are happier with their online friends than with those around them. For many, their online interactions are more influential in the development of their values than are family, school, or personal friends.

The issue of online bullying is one that schools must deal with.[85] The problem is a social one, but by virtue of the amount of time students spend in school, schools are often in the position to deal most effectively with both the perpetrators and the victims. Provincial legislators are amending their education acts to provide school authorities with sweeping authority to deal with bullying that may originate outside school hours and off school property. It is unlikely that the challenges relating to advancing technology and the hazards of cyberspace will disappear in the near future. In the meantime, educators will be faced with the need to educate all students to the benefits and risks associated with social media, in particular. They will also have to reconcile the rights of all students to safety and privacy.

As a final point, it is worth noting that the courts have been consistent in emphasizing the significant role that teachers play in the education of the young. They have consistently emphasized the significance of the teacher as mentor and role model. Never have the courts more forcefully recognized the understanding of the role of the teacher in assisting in the formation of appropriate values in the young. Whenever a teacher's

---

85   This very broad topic is addressed in the following documents, but this list is by no means comprehensive:

Shaheen Shariff, *Confronting Cyber-bullying: What Schools Need to Know to Control Misconduct and Avoid Legal Consequences* (New York: Cambridge University Press, 2009); Jonas Kiedrowski, William Smale, & Tatiana Gounko, "Cellular Phones in Canadian Schools: A Legal Framework" (2009) 19 *Education and Law Journal* 41; Ruth Broster & Ken Brien, "Cyber-Bullying of Educators by Students: Evolving Legal and Policy Developments" (2010) 20 *Education and Law Journal* 35; Eric M Roher, "Dealing with Off-School Conduct: Cyberbullying, Drug Dealing and Other Activities outside of School Premises" (2012) 21 *Education and Law Journal* 91; Katherine Ng, "Digital Dilemmas: Responding to Cyberbullying in Nova Scotia" (2012) 22 *Education and Law Journal* 63.

behaviour has been construed as likely to poison the atmosphere in the school, the courts have disciplined that teacher and at times removed him or her from teaching.

H. SUMMARY

The frameworks that underpin and guide the administrative and legal structures in education in Canada have emerged out of our unique histories and traditions. At their roots, they are statements that we do things in this manner because we believe that this is the correct way to do things. And we arrive at this point as a result of the interactions that have taken place over centuries between peoples from differing backgrounds and cultures and with differing languages and religions and with disparate social values. Changing histories and changing times cause us to adapt our perspectives and consider the importance of specific values and, if necessary, alter our laws to meet the needs of an emerging society. We have maintained some practices and laws from the past, and we have rejected others. Some we have modified to meet changed circumstances and demands.

By any standards we choose to use, Canada has a very successful education system. Highly qualified teachers assist students in acquiring appropriate learning that is relevant for today's world. They provide a safe, caring, challenging, and supportive environment in which children are able to develop and prosper. There is significant broad-based parental and community involvement in our schools and in policy formulation, and the programs in the schools are adapted to meet the wants and needs of parents, students, and society.

As we continue to challenge our educators and our law-makers to ensure that both the administrative and legal frameworks remain relevant and up-to-date, we need to remember the adage that "there are two kinds of fools: those who say this is old and therefore good and those who say this is new and therefore better." Our society will not be well served unless there is a mindful approach to both law-making and to the operation of our school systems: an approach that places appropriate emphasis on the values inherent in what we do and how we do things just as much as on the form and content of the law or of the program. Our changed societies demand an open, generous, principle-based approach that acknowledges the rights of all people from all backgrounds, creeds, and cultures. Our legislative and policy frameworks need to encapsulate those values, and our schools need to be assiduous in modelling and implementing them.

Section 27 of the *Charter* tells us, "This *Charter* shall be interpreted in a manner consistent with the preservation and enhancement of the multicultural heritage of Canadians."[86] Successful implementation of this directive in our schools, as well as a serious operationalization of other *Charter* sections that deal with student rights, will contribute significantly to ensuring that our society continues to be well served by our schools as it develops and sustains the generous, pluralistic, multicultural society of which we are rightly so proud.

---

86 See above note 4.

CHAPTER 3

The Role of Courts in Education

Shirley Van Nuland

A. INTRODUCTION

The *Constitution Act, 1867* affords education in Canada special status through section 93, which outlines that the provinces are assigned legislative authority in all education matters. Specifically,

> In and for each Province the Legislature may exclusively make Laws in relation to Education, subject and according to the following Provisions:
> (1)   Nothing in any such Law shall prejudicially affect any Right or Privilege with respect to Denominational Schools which any Class of Persons have by Law in the Province at the Union . . . .[1]

Provinces have authority to make laws that relate to education subject to certain safeguards for denominational schools. The one exception to the federal government not interfering in educational matters is the power that it has over education of Aboriginal peoples, that is, "persons governed by the *Indian Act* and Federal agreements with Bands or Band Councils."[2]

In 1982, the *Canadian Charter of Rights and Freedoms* was entrenched in the *Constitution Act, 1982*.[3] As a key element of the *Constitution Act, 1982*, the *Charter* is supreme as the law in Canada. All law or legislation is to be consistent with the provisions of the *Constitution Act, 1982*; if not, the law

---

1   *Constitution Act, 1867* (UK), 30 & 31 Vict, c 3, s 93 (distribution of legislative powers), reprinted in RSC 1985, App II, No 5.
2   Anthony Brown & Marvin Zuker, *Education Law*, 4th ed (Toronto: Thomson Carswell, 2007) at 3.
3   Part I of the *Constitution Act, 1982*, being Schedule B to the *Canada Act 1982* (UK), 1982, c 11 [*Charter*].

or legislation has no force or effect.[4] The *Charter* has established the rights and freedoms for all Canadians regardless of residence. As the courts hear cases that involve the impact of the *Charter*, the provinces are forced to adjust their legislation to comply with the standards of the *Charter* as interpreted by the courts. *Charter*-based issues that come before the courts in Newfoundland and Labrador now have an impact on schools in Manitoba or British Columbia. To avoid challenges in their own courts, all provinces need to be attentive to other jurisdictions.

Education in Canada is directed also by a plethora of rules found in statutes and regulations that grant and impose a formidable collection of powers and duties to those involved with it. Most often, these statutes and regulations are located in provincial education acts and their attendant regulations that govern the obligations of schools and school boards, the duties of teachers and principals, the responsibilities of the minister of education, the funding of schools, and so on. Further statutes and regulations directing responsibilities of educators and applying to others outside the realm of education include, but are not limited to, the *Criminal Code*, collective bargaining legislation, human rights codes, the *Youth Criminal Justice Act*, the *Child and Family Services Act*, the *Copyright Act*, and the *Municipal Freedom of Information and Protection of Privacy Act*.

B. THE COURTS

As with education, each province is responsible for organizing and administering aspects of its own judicial system[5] subject to sections 91 and 92 of the *Constitution Act, 1867*. All Canadian jurisdictions, with the exception of Nunavut, have three levels of court. Nunavut has Canada's first, and only, single-level court in which judges may hear any type of case. The remainder of the country's judicial levels are explained as follows:

---

4   *Constitution Act, 1982*, s 52(1), being Schedule B to the *Canada Act 1982* (UK), 1982, c 11.

5   Information on the provincial/territorial courts for each jurisdiction may be found at the following sites: Alberta (https://albertacourts.ca), British Columbia (www.courts.gov.bc.ca), Manitoba (www.manitobacourts.mb.ca), New Brunswick (www.gnb.ca/Cour/index-e.asp), Newfoundland and Labrador (www.court.nl.ca), Northwest Territories (www.nwtcourts.ca), Nova Scotia (www.courts.ns.ca), Nunavut (www.nunavutcourts.ca), Ontario (www.ontariocourts.ca), Prince Edward Island (www.gov.pe.ca/courts), Québec (www.tribunaux.qc.ca/mjq_en), Saskatchewan (www.sasklawcourts.ca), and Yukon (www.yukoncourts.ca). Websites are current as of 27 May 2016.

1) The first level consisting of provincial or territorial courts is created by provincial or territorial laws that define the scope of the courts' authority; these courts hear the majority of cases that come into the Canadian courts.

2) The next level consists of superior or supreme courts which are created by the *Constitution Act, 1867* and have "inherent jurisdiction." In other words, the courts are able to hear any matter that comes before them.

3) The third level of courts, that is, courts of appeal, hear appeals from the lower courts' decisions; these cases are heard generally by three judges, or more if the province's chief justice opines that the case requires more for deliberation.

These courts, based on their level, are responsible for civil, criminal, and family cases and appeals from arbitrations; they also hear reviews and appeals from some administrative boards and tribunals in their respective areas of law, subject to statutory limitations. The decisions that these courts determine are applicable to the individuals involved in the specific case but also are useful for future cases.

At the national level, the Canadian courts include two specialized courts (the Tax Court and the Military Courts); the Federal Courts; and the Supreme Court of Canada.[6] The Federal Courts — that is, the Federal Court (trial-level court) and the Federal Court of Appeal — judge on issues as specified in federal statutes such as "interprovincial and federal–provincial disputes, intellectual property proceedings (e.g. copyright), citizenship appeals, *Competition Act* cases, and cases involving Crown corporations or departments of the Government of Canada."[7]

The Supreme Court of Canada is the highest court in the land and "the final authority on the interpretation of the entire body of Canadian law, whatever its source."[8] As Canada's final court of appeal, the Court, within its mandate, deals "with issues of law which are of public importance . . . or of such a nature or significance as to warrant decision by the Court"[9] from an extremely wide jurisdiction since potentially it may hear an appeal from any court or tribunal in the country. McCormick describes the Court as "a Canadian court developing a Canadian jurisprudence in a way

---

6   Department of Justice Canada, *Canada's Court System*, online: www.justice.gc.ca/eng/csj-sjc/ccs-ajc/pdf/courten.pdf.

7   *Ibid* at 8.

8   Peter Hogg, *Constitutional Law of Canada*, 4th ed (Toronto: Carswell, 1997) at 217.

9   Supreme Court of Canada, online: www.scc-csc.ca/court-cour/sys-eng.aspx.

that is both visible and relevant to an increasingly large segment of the Canadian public."[10]

Iacobucci, a former Supreme Court justice, summarized the distinctive nature[11] of the Court as a bilingual court that deals with matters emerging from civil law and common law jurisdictions in the country. The Court's membership is composed of judges from both civil law and common law backgrounds acting as a constitutional court and as the supreme court of the country. Court judges lead a unified judicial system that may hear appeals from provincial and federal courts. These cases may involve issues of private law (e.g., torts, contracts, and property) and public law (e.g., labour, administrative, taxation, and patents).

The Court also hears appeals from the Federal Court of Appeal and the provincial/territorial courts of appeal. It rules on the legality of bills submitted by the government and questions referred to it by the federal Cabinet. The decisions that this Court determines are applicable to the individuals involved in the specific case and also contribute to caselaw. As such, these judgments contribute to all areas of law within and throughout Canada. Since the advent of the *Charter*, the Court is "at centre stage in some of the country's most dramatic policy debates."[12] The adoption of the *Charter* changed the nature of questions coming to the Court, thus increasing the Court's role in politically and socially important issues, especially in rights, constitutional, and statutory interpretation.[13]

C. ADMINISTRATIVE TRIBUNALS

Various tribunals and boards handle disputes over administrative rules or regulations such as human rights complaints (e.g., Human Rights Tribunal), labour issues (e.g., Labour Relations Board), and refugee claims (e.g., Immigration and Refugee Board). These differences and disputes are addressed outside of the court system. Although the tribunals may resemble courts, they are not part of the court system. Administrative tribunals derive their authority from the statutes that created them and concentrate

---

10   Peter McCormick, *Supreme at Last: The Evolution of the Supreme Court of Canada* (Toronto: James Lorimer, 2000) at 166.

11   Frank Iacobucci, "The Supreme Court of Canada: Its History, Powers and Responsibilities" (2002) 4 *Journal of Appellate Practice and Process* 27 at 33–34.

12   Donald R Songer, *The Transformation of the Supreme Court of Canada* (Toronto: University of Toronto Press, 2008) at 6.

13   *Ibid* at 6–7.

on distinct areas of law. Certain restraints are placed on tribunals; they are "bound by the law, to render decisions to be in an equal and predictive manner and to act in accordance with law and social values."[14] The procedure before these administrative bodies is usually less formal than courts demand. When individuals or groups perceive that they have been treated unfairly in educational situations by government or school board actions, they appeal to the judicial system, whether the courts or tribunals, for their involvement. If required, the issue in dispute may be referred to the courts. The courts are involved with tribunals through a supervisory role to ensure that they act within their legal responsibilities and that their procedures are fair.

D. APPLYING DECISIONS

While provincial and local school systems have far-reaching authority to regulate publicly funded schools, the Canadian courts and tribunals, to a degree, influence and shape education and policy through their verdicts. Many decisions, especially those provided by the Supreme Court of Canada and more so since the implementation of the *Charter*, have been rendered in areas such as human rights, equality, freedom of expression, freedom of religion, school excursions, and discrimination. Courts and tribunals have overturned the decisions of democratically elected bodies, such as school boards, which, in turn, has furthered social change.

Generally, courts are reluctant to interfere with decisions made by school boards, but will invalidate any board action considered to be arbitrary, capricious, or beyond the board's legal authority.[15] In *Lutes (Litigation Guardian of) v Prairie View School Division No 74*, Barclay J specifically states, "The court should, except when dealing with a *Charter* argument, refrain from ruling on the rightness or wrongness of a decision of a school as long as the school was acting within its jurisdiction in carrying out discipline."[16]

In section 32(1) the *Charter* outlines that it is applicable "(a) to the Parliament and government of Canada in respect of all matters within the authority of Parliament including all matters relating to the Yukon Territory

---

14   Beverley McLachlin, "Rules and Discretion in the Governance of Canada" (1992) 56 *Saskatchewan Law Review* 167 at 168.

15   Martha M McCarthy, Nelda H Cambron-McCabe, & Stephen B Thomas, *Legal Rights of Teachers and Students* (Boston, MA: Allyn and Bacon, 2004) at 5.

16   [1992] SJ No 198 (QB) [*Lutes*].

and Northwest Territories; and (b) to the legislature and government of each province in respect of all matters within the authority of the legislature of each province."[17] Since school boards are under the legislative authority of each province, the courts early on determined that the *Charter* applied to school board activities and proceeded on this assumption when issues relative to school boards were brought forward. The Supreme Court proceeded on the assumption that school boards are part of government and, therefore, the *Charter* applied in *R v M(MR)*: "The actions of school officials as an extension of government are subject to the *Charter*."[18] The lower courts and tribunals in considering the question had arrived at a similar conclusion. The *Charter* was applied in the following two cases, but was not limited to these:

1) *Metropolitan Separate School Board v Taylor*: "the actions of the board must be regarded as the actions of the 'legislature' or 'government' of the province within the meaning of s. 32 of the *Charter*, and thus subject to its requirements in accordance with its terms."[19]
2) *Lutes*: ". . . except when dealing with a *Charter* argument."[20]

The *Charter* applies to those bodies[21] over which either the federal or provincial government exerts "routine or regular control."

E. JUDICIAL DECISION MAKING

When examining issues to inform their decision making, the judiciary studies statutes, constitutions, caselaw, and so on; this is often referred to as the "legal model." Statutes and attendant regulations, including policy/program memoranda and bylaws, are promulgated by a body, for example, a provincial legislature or school board authorized to proclaim these. In education, statutes and regulations for elementary and secondary schools

---

17 Above note 3.
18 *R v MRM*, [1998] 3 SCR 393 (headnote).
19 [1994] OJ No 1870 at para 8 (Gen Div).
20 *Lutes*, above note 16.
21 Other instances where the courts indicate that the *Charter* applies to provincial legislation and includes the actions of delegated decision makers are noted in *R v H*, [1985] AJ No 567 at para 13 (Prov Ct Youth Div); *McKinney v University of Guelph*, [1990] 3 SCR 229 at 271–73; *Douglas/Kwantlen Faculty Assn v Douglas College*, [1990] 3 SCR 570 at 584–85; and *Eldridge v British Columbia (Attorney General)* (1997), 151 DLR (4th) 577 at 608 (SCC).

are determined by the provincial/territorial governments with the requirement that school boards implement these. Decision making is also informed by caselaw — a body of judgments or established legal doctrine from previous cases developed by judges over time in deciding cases before them. The same type of case coming before judges in one jurisdiction may assist the judiciary in determining decisions elsewhere. Since individuals continue to pursue issues through the courts, caselaw is in constant development.

The purpose of the courts and tribunals is to resolve disputes as expeditiously and impartially as possible while upholding the law in question. Where a straightforward application of the legal model is difficult, where the law is unclear, or where precedent cannot be easily and objectively applied, "judges must apply their own interpretations of how existing law fits the present case."[22] Some laws and constitutions "are at high levels of abstraction, and therefore are unavoidably vague."[23] Where clarification of the law is required, the court accepts a law-making or policy-making role since the wording of the law may be open to legitimate interpretations. While this kind of clarification occurs in the lower courts, it is seen most often in cases heard by the Supreme Court.

The principle of judicial independence must be present for judges to adjudicate; judges function independently from the bodies that appoint them, and their decisions impartially must reflect their legal interpretation of the law and not government policy. Those judging must be competent, deciding as impartially as possible without undue influence, and, where necessary, "use their discretion to choose the interpretation that to them appears to be the most just. Thus, one secondary purpose of courts is to create rules to fill in the gaps left by legislation."[24]

Social conditions and past practices or experiences influence the development of statutes. "Law is often used as a method of social change, a way of bringing about planned social change by the government."[25] For example, since 2012 anti-bullying legislation has received assent in many

22   Songer, above note 12 at 175.
23   Ian Greene, *The Courts* (Vancouver: University of British Columbia Press, 2006) at 17.
24   *Ibid* at 5–6.
25   Steven Vago & Adie Nelson, *Law and Society* (Toronto: Pearson Prentice Hall, 2004) at 17.

provinces, including Nova Scotia,[26] Manitoba,[27] and Québec;[28] the intent is to reduce bullying and cyberbullying, which has become a social problem. These matters are specifically addressed in education acts with clarification of the roles and responsibilities for principals, teachers, students, and others. If required, the courts may be called upon to enforce this legislation. In 1986, Sussel and Manley-Casimir wrote: "The field of education is so intricately related to other important walks of life, it often becomes the battleground for important debates on issues of social policy."[29] The following cases provide illustrations of this belief.

1) *Moore v British Columbia (Education)*

Educators have found themselves before the courts and tribunals on many occasions, resulting in decisions that have had a significant impact on provincial legislation or school board policy. One such case, *Moore v British Columbia (Education)*,[30] took fifteen years to resolve. The *Moore* case moved through the legal system from the British Columbia Human Rights Tribunal through to the Supreme Court of Canada. It is an example of the various levels of court system in process.

Jeffrey Moore was diagnosed with dyslexia, a severe learning disability (SLD), and required intensive remedial instruction. In his early school days, he received assistance within the public school system. In Grade 2, he was designated as having an SLD, which allowed for additional funding from the ministry to support his learning. He required further intensive remedial instruction and was due to receive it outside his public school at the local diagnostic centre. Due to government cutbacks, however, the centre was set to be closed by the school board and was not to be replaced with equivalent educational services. Now Jeffrey's required assistance was available only in the private school system. He completed his schooling

---

26　Bill 30, *Promotion of Respectful and Responsible Relationships Act*, 4th Sess, 61st Leg, Nova Scotia, 2012 (assented to 17 May 2012).

27　Bill 18, *The Public Schools Amendment Act (Safe and Inclusive Schools)*, 2nd Sess, 40th Leg, Manitoba, 2012.

28　Bill 56, *An Act to Prevent and Stop Bullying and Violence in Schools*, 2nd Sess, 39th Leg, Québec, 2012 (assented to 15 June 2012).

29　Terri A Sussel & Michael E Manley-Casimir, "The Supreme Court of Canada as a 'National School Board': The *Charter* and Educational Change" (1986) 11 *Canadian Journal of Education* 313 at 322.

30　At the Supreme Court level: 2012 SCC 61 [*Moore* SCC].

in private schools that specialized in teaching children with learning disabilities.

In May 1997, Jeffrey's father, Frederick Moore, filed a human rights complaint against the district school board, and in August 1999, included the British Columbia Ministry of Education. A violation of section 8 of the British Columbia *Human Rights Code* was cited.[31] The complaint was that Jeffrey had suffered discrimination and had been denied a "service . . . customarily available to the public": an education.

From October 2001 to December 2002, the British Columbia Human Rights Tribunal held over forty-three days of hearings, giving its decision on 21 December 2005. The case continued to be debated until the Supreme Court of Canada ruled in 2012. The question that faced the Court was whether the special education program provided by a British Columbia district school board to Jeffrey infringed the *British Columbia Human Rights Code* and, if it did, what was the appropriate remedy under the *Code*. Was Jeffrey Moore denied meaningful access to education programs that he needed to address his disability? Should "service . . . customarily available to the public" mean education generally, or special education?

The Human Rights Tribunal[32] concluded that the district school board had failed to provide Jeffrey with the level of support he needed and that the ministry of Education provided inadequate funding for SLD students and failed to appropriately monitor the delivery of special education services provided by the school district. The Tribunal ordered damages and systemic remedies against the district school board and the ministry of Education. It ordered reimbursement for the costs of Jeffrey's private school tuition and $10,000 in damages for pain and suffering. It also ordered a wide range of sweeping systemic remedies against both the school district and province, including rewriting the funding methodology for special education and centralizing oversight of individual special education programs within the ministry of Education.[33]

Both the school board and the government applied for judicial review of the Tribunal decision. After fourteen days of hearing in 2007, Dillon J of

---

31 RSBC 1996, c 210, s 8, says that there is discrimination if a "person . . . without a bona fide and reasonable justification . . . den[ies] to a person or class of persons any accommodation, service or facility customarily available to the public" on the basis of a prohibited ground.
32 *Moore v British Columbia (Ministry of Education)*, 2005 BCHRT 580.
33 *Ibid* at paras 1019–25.

the British Columbia Supreme Court[34] determined that the Tribunal had erred. The Tribunal had compared Jeffrey's situation to that of the general student population, rather than to what the British Columbia Supreme Court considered to be the appropriate comparator group: other students with special needs. Thus, the Tribunal decision was set aside.

The Moores appealed the BC Supreme Court's decision to the Court of Appeal. With five days of hearings in 2009, the majority of members of the British Columbia Court of Appeal[35] agreed with the British Columbia Supreme Court and upheld the judicial review decision to set aside the Tribunal decision. The court noted: "Jeffrey Moore received more special education services than any other student in his school."[36] In dissent, however, Rowles JA held that the appeal should be allowed since special education within the school system is the means by which students with learning disabilities are able to achieve, to have "meaningful access" to educational services. Further, Rowles JA stated that the use of the comparator analysis by the court was unnecessary and inappropriate.

In 2012, in a unanimous decision,[37] the Supreme Court of Canada[38] held that Jeffrey Moore had been denied meaningful access to the educational programs he needed to address his disability and accordingly was discriminated against in a manner that could not be reasonably justified. The Court determined that "this appeal is therefore substantially allowed,"[39] thus reinstating the Tribunal's damages award against the district school board, but overturning the damages award and denying the systemic remedies ordered against the ministry of Education.

The *Moore* decision has distinct implications for school boards. The Supreme Court clarified procedural steps for school boards prior to making changes to educational programs for students with learning disabilities. To ensure that the rights of students with disabilities to accommodation are taken into account, school districts must take a proactive approach to budgeting and programming. In this case, the school board's

> failure to consider financial alternatives completely undermines what is, in essence, the District's argument, namely that it was justified in providing no meaningful access to an education for Jeffrey because it had no

34   *British Columbia (Ministry of Education) v Moore*, 2008 BCSC 264 at para 149.
35   *British Columbia (Ministry of Education) v Moore*, 2010 BCCA 478.
36   *Ibid* at para 175.
37   It is no small matter when the Supreme Court decides a case unanimously.
38   *Moore* (SCC), above note 30.
39   *Ibid* at para 71.

economic choice. In order to decide that it had *no* other choice, it had at least to consider what those other choices were.[40]

Although the Court believes that school boards are owed deference in implementing their policies and goals, when deciding which programs must be changed or removed, financial considerations without a full needs-based analysis cannot be the sole reason. This decision places an impetus on school boards to establish an integrated decision-making structure. Budgetary decisions cannot be made when isolated from student and program needs. All board officials must share relevant information to ensure that budget decisions and program cuts are decided after genuine consideration of the impact on students with special needs.

In addition, the Tribunal, one dissenting judge from the Court of Appeal, and the Supreme Court of Canada selected a comparator group (students with special education needs) while the BC Supreme Court and two of the three judges selected the general student population as the comparator group to determine if Jeffrey had been discriminated against. Selecting the comparator group of general students deviates from previous human rights cases where the comparator group was those students with special education needs with different diagnoses than those of the complaint. "The court has charted a new course with respect to comparator groups when assessing whether a child has received differential treatment."[41] This direction will garner attention and discussion in future decisions.

This decision reaffirms that human rights law requires service providers to make their services accessible to persons with disabilities. Once a barrier is identified, the service provider must provide accommodation to overcome that barrier, unless to do so would cause an undue hardship. The basis for measuring the adequacy of a program will not be a comparison with other students and their education, but an assessment of whether the program provides meaningful access to education. This requires a program appropriate for the student in question.

Students with learning disabilities require specific accommodation in order to benefit from educational services. The accommodation is not an extra or special service, but "rather the measures needed for students to benefit equally from the education system. And the measures must be

---

40   *Ibid* at para 52.
41   A Wayne MacKay, Lyle Sutherland, & Kimberley D Pochini, *Teachers and the Law: Diverse Roles and New Challenges*, 3d ed (Toronto: Emond Montgomery, 2013) at 122.

adequate to ensure meaningful access,"[42] states the Council of Canadians with Disabilities, one of many interveners in the case.

While provincial governments control the funding mechanism, appropriate financing of school boards is crucial. School districts make program choices within the grants determined by provincial governments. In this case, the Court stated that the school board's budgetary crisis was due, in part, to the lack of funding; the Court's decision stated that the "Province was liable for the District's discriminatory conduct towards Jeffrey cannot be sustained."[43] This perceived contradiction — that is, a lack of funding from the province versus the school board's claim that the province did not provide sufficient funds — was not explained further.

The *Moore* decision affirms that for students with learning disabilities, special education is not the service; it is the means by which those students obtain meaningful access to the general education services available to all students: "Adequate special education . . . is not a dispensable luxury for those with severe learning disabilities"[44] and "it is the ramp that provides access to the statutory commitment to education made to *all* children . . . ."[45] The "service" is education. Access to education and to the service must be meaningful, a way to balance the diverse needs of individuals. A legal duty exists to accommodate a student with special needs.

2) *Bain (Guardian ad litem of) v Calgary Board of Education*[46]

It is a well-established fact that teachers assume a duty of care to their students, imposed on them because of the distinctive character of their work. This special student–teacher relationship finds its basis in common law, which clearly establishes the duty of care. Teachers are to be attentive and careful in situations where students are involved to ensure that students are not exposed to any unnecessary risk of harm.

Kevin Bain, a nineteen-year-old student in Grade 11 enrolled in a vocational school, went on a forestry products tour with four other students and one teacher-supervisor for a three-day, two-night trip to British Columbia.

---

42 Council of Canadians with Disabilities, "The Moore Case: Summary of Key Points," online: www.ccdonline.ca/en/humanrights/litigation/Moore-Case-Key-Findings-9Nov2012.

43 *Ibid.*

44 *Moore* (SCC), above note 30 at para 5.

45 *Ibid.*

46 (1993), [1994] 2 WWR 468 (Alta QB) [*Bain*].

A detailed itinerary was provided, and permission forms were signed and returned by parents. One evening when the planned activity was a movie night, the students insisted on mountain climbing. "To save the trip from going sour,"[47] the teacher acquiesced and drove the students to the base of the mountain where he left them alone. The students "were dressed only in shorts, T-shirts and runners, . . . had not eaten supper; and . . . took with them no map, no water, no provisions, no extra clothing, and no flashlight or other signalling device."[48] There was no marked trail; the teacher and the students were not familiar with the terrain. Kevin fell from a rock face and suffered a severe permanent brain injury as well as other injuries.

This case represents a watershed of sorts since the justice making the decision did not rely upon the "prudent parent" test.[49] The case was heard in the Alberta Court of Queen's Bench by Virtue J. Justice Virtue believed that school excursions are valuable and do not need to be dangerous: "Properly planned outdoor recreation programs are, in my view, one of the best ways to develop these essential attributes [a healthy sense of self-worth and self-reliance] in people of all ages, and they should be encouraged."[50] Justice Virtue found that the teacher owed a duty of care to Kevin in this student–teacher relationship, even though Kevin was over eighteen. The teacher did not meet the standard of care and was found negligent, since there was a reasonably foreseeable risk of harm. Even though the student had not voluntarily assumed the risk of injury, he had failed to "take proper steps for his own safety."[51] In the decision, the student was found 25 percent liable while the teacher and school board were apportioned 75 percent liable. Damages awarded totalled more than $3 million.

This case dealing with an excursion, or field trip, confirms that a standard of care existed, that the teacher failed to meet the standard of care, that the teacher "who had considerable experience in hiking in the wilderness, failed to take the steps which a leader would be expected to take before allowing inexperienced students, of any age, to undertake such an

---

47 Ibid at para 23.
48 Ibid at para 47.
49 Jon Heshka, "Canada's Legal Standard of Care for Outdoor Education" in Roderick C Flynn, ed, *Proceedings of the Sixteenth Annual Conference of the Canadian Association of the Practical Study of Law in Education* (Toronto: CAPSLE, 2006) 221 at 232.
50 *Bain*, above note 46 at para 53.
51 *Ibid* at para 59.

unsupervised hiking expedition in an area without marked hiking trails."[52] In its decision, the court listed specialized skills required for excursions through its criticism of the teacher's actions or omissions. In effect, the court said that educators must be attentive to

> the duty of a leader to familiarize himself with the terrain, to warn the students of dangers of which he was or ought to have been aware, to plan a route that would avoid the dangers, and to make certain that all the students were aware of the route and agreed to follow it, and were aware of the need to stay together . . . remained to see that his instructions were being followed . . . to properly prepare the students to meet the risks they would face.[53]

Throughout the decision, the court outlined the additional skills required beyond those listed above. Heshka determined that "this is the first instance of a court prescribing skills of any sort to a teacher leading groups in the outdoors."[54] The court held that the excursion was an "extension of the classroom" because it was approved by the school board and subject to the same duty and standard of care as in the classroom. The court found three failures in the teacher's supervision: (1) permitting an unplanned hike, (2) failing to supervise the hike, and (3) failing to take precautions and avoid risks. This case is instructive in terms of supervision. Teachers should not deviate from school board–approved field trip itineraries. A spontaneous outing can attract liability if accidents and injuries occur. Teachers and administrators need to anticipate and arrange for adequate supervision for all activities, including school board–approved excursions.

Bain has influenced current standards of practice and school board policies. School boards have established protocols for excursions and use the suggested "risk management" practices[55] to minimize risk exposure to those participating. Risk management, "a process of planning, organizing and controlling activities that contain an element of risk to the participant,"[56] includes risk identification, risk management strategies (avoiding, reducing, and transferring risk), selection and implementation of appro-

---

52 *Ibid* at para 48.
53 *Ibid.*
54 Heshka, above note 49 at 232.
55 Melanie Warner & Teresa Drijber, "School Excursions: Avoiding a Trip to Court" (Fall 2005) *Education Law News* 9, online: Borden Ladner Gervais http://blg.com/ en/News-And-Publications/Documents/publication603_EN.pdf.
56 *Ibid* at 14.

priate strategies, and monitoring/reviewing results. Implementation of risk management should ensure that standards of care are met.

3) *Ross v New Brunswick District No 15*

While employees' off-duty activities and comments/postings are usually of no interest to employers, employers would and should be concerned that these activities and comments could have a negative impact on a work environment. Such is the situation that was determined in *Ross v New Brunswick School District No 15*.[57]

On 21 April 1988, David Attis, a Jewish parent of two children, sent a letter of complaint to the New Brunswick Human Rights Commission against School District 15 in Moncton, New Brunswick. Attis claimed that Malcolm Ross, a teacher employed by the school board, had violated section 5(1) of the *New Brunswick Human Rights Act* through statements and publications that were "anti-racist, bigoted and discriminatory." Even though his children were not taught by Ross, the parent objected that the school board, by allowing Ross to teach, ignored his writings and permitted him to model racist and anti-Jewish views for the students. While Ross did not present his views in class, his views and writings "were well-publicized in the community."[58]

The board of inquiry[59] found that the school board contributed to the "poisoned environment," especially for Jewish students, by failing to respond to Ross's actions. This failure hindered student learning and other educational services that the school board was required to provide. The board issued an order that provided four criteria: (1) that Ross be placed in a leave of absence, without pay, for eighteen months; (2) that he be appointed to a non-teaching job if a non-teaching job became available and he was qualified; (3) that his employment cease at the end of eighteen months if he had not been offered and accepted a non-teaching position; and (4) that, if at any time, he published, wrote, or sold anti-Jewish material, his employment with the school board would be terminated.[60]

---

57 [1996] 1 SCR 825 [*Ross*].
58 Maurice Green & Margaret Correia, "Freedom of Speech and Teachers' Duties: *Ross* Revisited" (1993) 5 *Education and Law Journal* 361 at 362.
59 *Attis v New Brunswick (School District 15)*, [1991] NBHRBID No 1.
60 *Ross*, above note 57 at 828.

The case moved to the New Brunswick Court of Queen's Bench,[61] which quashed part of the order since it was beyond the jurisdiction of the board of inquiry. It further determined that the board had no jurisdiction to make the order that restricted Ross's activities outside the classroom when he was no longer a classroom teacher. The remaining parts of the order were upheld.

This decision was appealed to the New Brunswick Court of Appeal.[62] This court found against the board of inquiry because the activities that attracted the complaint were outside of school. Ross's constitutional right to freedom of expression had priority; the board of inquiry order did not meet "a specific purpose so pressing and substantial"[63] to override his *Charter* rights.

The case was given leave to appeal to the Supreme Court of Canada, which decided that Malcolm Ross was to be removed from his teaching duties because of his anti-Semitic views. In its finding to dismiss him from his position as a teacher, the Court outlined the relationship between the school and society and defined the role of the school:

> A school is a communication centre for a whole range of values and aspirations of society. In large part, it defines the values that transcend society through the educational medium. The school is an arena for the exchange of ideas and must, therefore, be premised upon principles of tolerance and impartiality so that all persons within the school environment feel equally free to participate.[64]

The Court criticized the school board for failing to provide for a positive environment and cited from the board of inquiry what role a board must undertake:

> In such situations it is not sufficient for a school board to take a passive role. A school board has a duty to maintain a positive school environment for all persons served by it and it must be ever vigilant of anything that might interfere with this duty.[65]

By failing to act, the school board appeared to condone and support Ross. The school board had failed to take a proactive response.

---

61 *Ross v New Brunswick School District No. 15* (1991), 121 NBR (2d) 361 (QB).
62 *Ross v New Brunswick School District No. 15* (1993), 142 NBR (2d) 1 (CA).
63 *R v Zundel*, [1992] 2 SCR 731 at 733.
64 *Ross*, above note 57 at para 42.
65 *Ibid* at para 50.

The Court outlined how teachers must act in a manner that respects the rights of their students. It emphasized this as a driving factor of its decision: that education of the young is extremely important and that importance is to be valued:

> Young children are especially vulnerable to the messages conveyed by their teachers. They are less likely to make an intellectual distinction between comments a teacher makes in the school and those the teacher makes outside the school. They are, therefore, more likely to feel threatened and isolated by a teacher who makes comments that denigrate people's characteristics of a group to which they belong. Furthermore, they are unlikely to distinguish between falsehoods and truth and more likely to accept derogatory views espoused by a teacher. The importance of ensuring an equal and discrimination-free education environment, and the perception of fairness and tolerance in the classroom are paramount in the education of young children. This helps foster self-respect and acceptance by others.[66]

The Court recognized the important role that teachers undertake:

> Teachers are inextricably linked to the integrity of the school system. Teachers occupy positions of trust and confidence, and exert considerable influence over their students as a result of their positions. The conduct of a teacher bears directly upon the community's perception of the ability of the teacher to fulfil such a position of trust and influence, and upon the community's confidence in the public school system as a whole.[67]

The Court accepted the premise that teachers have a fiduciary duty towards students. Clearly, teachers have a responsibility to be attentive to the well-being of their students. Acceptance of this understanding helps ensure public confidence in the education system.

The Court held that the board of inquiry was correct in finding that continuing Ross's employment constituted discrimination:

> Public school teachers assume a position of influence and trust over their students, and must be seen to be impartial and tolerant. By their conduct, teachers, as "medium" of the educational message (the values, beliefs and knowledge sought to be transmitted by the school system), must be perceived as upholding that message. A teacher's conduct is evaluated

---

66 *Ibid* at para 82.
67 *Ibid* at para 43.

on the basis of his or her position, rather than whether the conduct occurs within or outside the classroom.[68]

In applying the test that evolved out of *R v Oakes*,[69] the Court found that limiting the teacher's freedom of religion and freedom of thought, belief, opinion, and expression, as the teacher claimed had occurred, was justified. The
objective is sufficiently important since eliminating discrimination supports one of Canada's goals to prohibit disseminating ideas "based on racial
or religious superiority."[70]

Dismissing the teacher was reasonable and demonstrably justified
since allowing him to carry on teaching would permit him to continue influencing children. His dismissal as a teacher ensured that he would have
no more influence upon his students and that "educational services are discrimination free."[71] The Court determined that limiting Ross's freedoms was
necessary to achieve an environment free of discrimination, thus showing
that "proportionality between the effects of the order and the objective"[72]
existed. It avowed that through their conduct, "teachers must be perceived
to uphold the values, beliefs and knowledge sought to be transmitted by the
school system."[73]

4) *RT v Durham Catholic District School Board*

A thirteen-year-old Grade 8 student (VK) used Facebook to send email
messages, impersonate some students, and make death threats. The target student described how she was affected by threatening emails, such
as "U DON'T WANT ME TO GET MAD BECAUSE ILL KILL YOU RIGHT IN UR
SLEEP OR SCHOOL ON MONDAY" and "I am gonna come to school on Monday and kick ur ass. im gonna kill u. ok? ok!" She said she felt isolated, had
troubled sleep, and was afraid for herself and her family. She was closing
the blinds at home and always watching over her shoulder. Further, there
was evidence that her sister, also a student at the school, felt the negative

---

68 *Ibid* at headnote.
69 [1986] 1 SCR 103.
70 Alisa M Watkinson, *Education, Student Rights and the Charter* (Saskatoon, SK:
Purich, 1999) at 50.
71 *Ibid* at 51.
72 *Ibid* at 52.
73 Stuart Piddocke, Romulo F Magsino, & Michael E Manley-Casimir, *Teachers in
Trouble: An Exploration of the Normative Character of Teaching* (Toronto: University
of Toronto Press, 1997) at 179.

impact of the threats. The target student's father informed the school's administration of his concern for his daughter's safety and noted that he had got in touch with the police and Facebook. Facebook closed VK's account three times, but she reopened it. The principal recommended expulsion of VK from all of the board's schools, and the School Board Expulsion Hearing Committee agreed.

The school board considered the impact that these actions had on school climate. It examined the mitigating factors and the additional factors listed in Ontario Regulation 472/07,[74] section 2 (student's inability to control behaviour, inability to understand the foreseeable consequences of behaviour, or presence in the school does not create an unacceptable risk to the safety of any person) and section 3 (student's history, use of progressive discipline, harassment of the said student due to race, ethnic origin, religion, disability, gender or sexual orientation, or to any other harassment, effect of expulsion on student's ongoing education, student's age, or development of student's individual education plan, with three conditions). By considering each factor individually, the board determined if and to what degree the factor had been addressed. This approach ensured that the student's well-being was addressed appropriately. The board determined that it would expel VK from her school only.

Although the infraction did not occur at the school or during any school-related activity, VK's return to her school was seen to have a negative impact on school climate. This situation made the board decision distinct. In reviewing the mitigating and other factors, the board determined that there was no evidence to suggest that the student was unable to control her behaviour or understand the foreseeable consequences of her behaviour. The fear of serious harm that the Facebook communication had generated and knowing that one of its students was enrolled at the same school as the target attended led the board to determine that a negative school climate would exist and would continue to exist. The school board determined that expulsion was appropriate.

As required by Regulation 472/07, the Child and Family Services Review Board examined the expulsion decision to establish if the school board acted within its authority.[75] The review board unanimously found that the student's threats against another student through Facebook, although not occurring at school or during a school-related activity, were

---

74   *Behaviour, Discipline and Safety of Pupils*, O Reg 472/07.
75   *RT v Durham Catholic District School Board*, 2008 CFSRB 94.

"very detrimental" to the school climate under section 310(1) of Ontario's *Education Act*.[76] The review board further determined that the school board could not have taken any other steps to fulfill its duty to ensure the emotional and physical safety of other students attending the school. The review board stated, "The fear of significant harm generated by the Facebook communications and the subsequent knowledge that this was committed by one of the pupils of the school leads the Board to find the school climate was negatively impacted." It thus upheld the school board's decision since it would not be possible for VK to return to her home school.

This case highlights the urgent need for policy makers to engage teachers, students, and parents to help create a school environment that reduces the incidence of bullying. "The unlikely perpetrators such as victims of school bullying occurrences can be[come] perpetrators within the cyberbullying context."[77] This idea expands the issue of bullying further than the "school yard bully." This decision is important[78] because it represents the first case in which "cyberbullying" has been specifically recognized as falling within the context of the recent amendments to section 310(1) of the *Education Act*. The expanded authority to expel students for conduct not directly related to school activities includes the ability to address cyberbullying. At time of writing, the issue of expelling a student from school for cyberbullying had not been tested in the courts.

F.   THE IMPORTANCE AND IMPACT OF THE COURTS

Since 1982, when the *Charter* was introduced as part of the *Constitution Act, 1982*, the impact of the *Charter* has been noted in many education-based cases. One dramatic outcome of the *Charter* and the courts' decisions with a *Charter* basis is its importance in shaping national standards in education.[79]

---

76   RSO 1990, c E.2.

77   Kwesi Johnson, *Building Better Schools Not Prisons: A Review of the Literature surrounding School Suspension and Expulsion Programs and the Implication of Such Programs on the Lives of Racial and Ethnic Minority Students* (MA Thesis, Ontario Institute for Studies in Education, University of Toronto, 2012).

78   Jason Green, "Student Expulsion for Cyberbullying Upheld on Appeal" *Hicks Morley News* (15 May 2009), online: https://hicksmorley.com/2009/09/17/school-board-update-3/#a3.

79   A Wayne MacKay & Lyle Sutherland, *Teachers and the Law*, 2d ed (Toronto: Emond Montgomery, 2006) at xiii.

Decisions of the courts, arbitration boards, labour boards, teacher registration bodies, and so forth have significant impact on educational policy, rules, and regulations, which, in turn, affect teachers, students, and school boards. The decisions of the cases cited above illustrate this impact. The results of addressing a school board's decision to close a program, a field trip that deviated from its original agenda, a teacher's out-of-school activities, and a student's posting of messages on Facebook have contributed to an improved environment for those most vulnerable: children. These cases and others have obligated governments, school boards, and schools to develop or modify policy.

The impact of court decisions, especially those of the Supreme Court of Canada, is seen through ripple effects. Other courts review the decisions and use these to inform their own decision making. Other bodies — for example, government agencies and school boards — also review these decisions and alter their actions and policies (e.g., acts, regulations, policies, and bylaws) accordingly and where required to reflect the courts' judgments. This multiplier effect from courts' decisions means that many more people than those presenting before the courts are affected by what happens there.[80]

The courts have stated that maintaining a safe and positive learning climate is essential; there is a clear link between such a school climate and the academic and social progress of students.[81] If students are fearful, they cannot learn; if students feel safe, an environment exists to help them learn. This idea sets a standard of what is required in schools. In *Ross*, it was determined that the school is to be a place safe to seek, receive, form, and exchange ideas and opinions and must be free from discrimination and violence, free from a "poisoned environment." Society wants its values to be transmitted to its members; the school is one vehicle expected to incorporate these values in its program and goals.

The onus of maintaining a safe and positive climate is also set on school boards. The Supreme Court in *Ross* stated, "A school board has a duty to maintain a positive school environment for all persons served by it and it must be ever vigilant of anything that might interfere with this duty." School boards are answerable for the actions of their staff and, therefore,

---

80 Songer, above note 12 at 169–70.
81 A Wayne MacKay, *Respectful and Responsible Relationships: There's No App for That: The Report of the Nova Scotia Task Force on Bullying and Cyberbullying* (Halifax, NS: Nova Scotia Task Force on Bullying and Cyberbullying, 2012) at 52, online: http://ssrn.com/abstract=2123494.

must provide clear direction on their responsibilities. They must take pro-active and effective actions to ensure "a positive school environment."

The focus on the fiduciary duties of teachers and other educators to act as trustees of vulnerable students accords with the need to be proactive with respect to maintaining safety, a positive environment, and protection from bullying and cyberbullying. Cases such as *Ross* and *Bain* emphasize the fiduciary, or trust, relationship between a teacher and a student, and recognize that the teacher is a role model for students, both in and outside the classroom. Teachers have significant influence over their students. While being positive role models can be a heavy load for them, it is essential "in maintaining a credible and accessible education system."[82]

In addition, courts help shape legislative behaviour. Since they do not operate in a vacuum, legislatures should be aware of the political and judicial environment. It is expected that as they work to produce public policy, formally or informally, they "collect information that ultimately influences how they will react in the creation, or in the enactment, of a policy."[83] In drafting and enforcing educational legislation, governments have the power, authority, and obligation to uphold democratic values and ensure that their legislation is in concert with the *Charter*.[84]

In their commentary on the Supreme Court, Sussel and Manley-Casimir state that there was a "gradual movement of the Canadian Supreme Court into the arena of educational policy making in Canada."[85] Their observations on judicial decisions regarding education-related matters are being realized, namely, that these decisions extend into Canadian provinces and school districts. Their second observation, that these decisions "may well contribute to a greater trend toward centralizing educational governance,"[86] cannot be confirmed definitively.

The cases decided by the Court have served to bring about some changes in certain areas of education. Some decisions have had weighty implications[87] for educational policy — for example, special education, school at-

---

82 Watkinson, above note 70 at 198.

83 Teena Wilhelm, "The Policymaking Role of State Supreme Courts in Education Policy" (2007) 32 *Legislative Studies Quarterly* 309 at 311.

84 Watkinson, above note 70 at 201.

85 Sussel & Manley-Casimir, above note 29 at 325.

86 *Ibid* at 326.

87 Jonathan L Black-Branch, *Rights and Realities: The Judicial Impact of the* Canadian Charter of Rights and Freedoms *on Education, Case Law and Political Jurisprudence* (Aldershot, UK: Ashgate, 1997) at 180.

tendance, and school prayer. Other rulings have served to maintain the status quo or have strengthened the control of school boards in matters of program and school discipline, as examples. The courts, through case decisions, influence standards of practice and school board policies and thus, have an impact on the process of education.

CHAPTER 4

Educator Rights and Duties

David C Young

A. INTRODUCTION

Effective educators possess an understanding of the system in which they work. They are well aware that schooling is an enterprise charged with a serious responsibility: providing an avenue as well as a means for teaching and learning. As a result, each year from September until late June children of appropriate age from across the country congregate in schools where teachers try to provide for each student in their classes an *appropriate* education. From the school buses that shuttle children to and from their homes, to the local community school, to the teachers and support staff employed by school boards, to the policy makers enacting directives that drive the system, public education is governed by many competing forces. To the lay person, most of these forces often appear hidden, and, in fact, many teachers are also oblivious to them. Yet, good teachers recognize that public education does not exist in a vacuum and is, indeed, context dependent on several factors: these include but are not limited to legal and policy dimensions.

It is neither assumed nor expected that teachers or administrators be lawyers. However, it is incumbent upon educators to have a healthy respect and appreciation for the manner in which the law has an impact on what they can and cannot do in schools. This chapter will discuss the dynamics of education in Canada with particular reference to the legal and policy dimensions.

B. A LEGAL OVERVIEW OF THE PUBLIC SCHOOL SYSTEM

Most Canadian educators are employed by the public school system. The genesis for this system, in which enrolment is open, is based on the principles of public funding and of provincial control, and dates back to Confederation. In fact, the legitimacy of this system is found in section 93 of the 1867 *British North America Act*.[1] Section 93 reads as follows: "In and for each Province the Legislature may exclusively makes Laws in relation to Education." As Bezeau points out, section 93 resulted in education becoming an unequivocal and exclusive provincial responsibility.[2] It should also be noted that although constitutional power in the territories was initially vested in the federal government by virtue of the *Constitution Act, 1871*,[3] much, if not all, of this power has since been delegated to the governments of the Yukon and Northwest Territories, as well as Nunavut.[4] Therefore, since Confederation, education is and continues to remain a responsibility of the provincial and territorial governments.

Because Canada is a vast country, characterized by common elements among the provinces and territories, each province or territory also lays claim to its own unique history and culture. The provinces and territories each have a department or ministry of education, which develops policies that give structure to, and at the same time regulate, the public school system. The primary vehicle through which the provincial and territorial governments give structure to the public school system within their respective jurisdictions is by means of a statute with a name such as the *Education Act* or *Public Schools Act*. This Act, which varies based on the province or territory, can outline issues such as the rights and duties of students, parents, teachers, and administrators. As an example, section 17 of the British Columbia *School Act* specifies the responsibilities of a teacher as including among other things "designing, supervising and assessing educational programs and instructing, assessing and evaluating individual students and groups of students."[5] Other issues that are often addressed include duration of the school year and the establishment of school boards. In addition to such an Act, provincial governments routinely pass regula-

1   Later named the *Constitution Act, 1867* (UK), 30 & 31 Vict, c 3, reprinted in RSC 1985, App II, No 5.
2   Lawrence M Bezeau, *Educational Administration for Canadian Teachers*, 2d ed (Toronto: Copp Clark, 1995) at 18.
3   (UK), 34–35 Vict, c 28, s 4.
4   Forrest W Parkay et al, *Becoming a Teacher*, 3d Canadian ed (Toronto: Pearson, 2009) at 116.
5   RSBC 1996, c 412.

tions under the Act. Unlike statutes, which are debated in the legislature, regulations can be enacted by the minister of Education or the provincial cabinet. Generally, regulations are detailed and technical, and provide further clarity in terms of the implementation of the Act itself. For example, one Ontario regulation provides details in regard to the identification and placement of exceptional students.[6]

1) The Public System within a Broad Context

Given that most educators are employed in the public school system, educators should also be aware that once they sign their first contract with a school board, they will also normally become a member of a teacher union or federation. Membership in a union is compulsory in each province and territory, although the form these unions take will vary depending on the geographic locale. In most provinces, one union represents all teachers, but there are some notable exceptions. In Québec and New Brunswick, for example, union membership is divided along linguistic lines; in Ontario, teachers belong to one of four federations based on factors such as religion, language of instruction, and grade level taught.[7] The union provides a host of supports, including but not limited to the provision of counselling services and legal advice; it will also negotiate, on behalf of teachers, collective bargaining agreements with the employer.[8]

Besides the public school system, there are other types of educational arrangements in Canada. First, section 91(24) of the *Constitution Act, 1867* is relevant in that the federal government is charged with the responsibility of "Indians and Lands reserved for Indians." Thus, the government of Canada funds, either partially or fully, elementary, secondary, and post-secondary education for registered First Nations and Inuit people. This arrangement has resulted in the Department of Indigenous and Northern Affairs Canada either directly operating schools or transferring control over schooling to band councils for individual reserves. As well, under another configuration, Aboriginal children will attend provincial public schools, with the cost of their education funded by the federal government.[9]

---

6   *Identification and Placement of Exceptional Pupils*, O Reg 181/98.
7   William Rodney Dolmage, *So You Want to Be a Teacher: The Guide to Teaching as a Career Choice in Canada* (Toronto: Harcourt Brace, 1996) at 44.
8   Jonathan C Young, Benjamin Levin, & Dawn Wallin, *Understanding Canadian Schools: An Introduction to Educational Administration*, 4th ed (Toronto: Nelson, 2007) at 290–91.
9   Bezeau, above note 2 at 83.

Another alternative to the public school system are independent or private schools, which are educational institutions not directly governed by the province. These schools, sometimes organized around religion, operate in every Canadian province, although their total enrolment is not significant. In fact, the highest percentage of students enrolled in private schools is in Québec, which accounts for only 9 percent of the total student population in the province.[10] Unlike public schools, which are open to all children, private schools essentially admit whom they want based on predefined criteria. Furthermore, public schools, which receive full government funding and charge no tuition, stand in stark contrast to private schools, which receive little government funding, and thus charge fees.

Interestingly enough, there have been ongoing efforts to extend public funding to these independent or private schools. In the 1996 case of *Adler v Ontario*,[11] two groups of parents, Jewish and Christian Reformed, who for religious reasons sent their children to private schools, launched a legal challenge focused on the Ontario government not providing funding for these institutions. Although the Supreme Court of Canada rejected the argument advanced by the parents, the Court indicated that a government could, if it so desired, extend funding to private schools.[12] A related 1999 case, *Waldman v Canada*,[13] centred on the issue of extending funding to a parent who opted to send his children to a private Jewish day school. In hearing the case, the United Nations Human Rights Committee found that the failure of the government of Ontario to not fund this private school was discriminatory, given that the province already provided full funding for Roman Catholic schools. The *Waldman* case can be seen as a victory for those who support the private school movement; however, because the United Nations Human Rights Committee has no real enforcement mechanism, the practical impact of this litigation is limited.

A final arrangement that may have an impact on educators is that of home-schooling. The most recent estimates from 2011/2012 indicate more than 20,000 students in Canada are home-schooled.[14] Among the reasons

---

10   Young, Levin, & Wallin, above note 8 at 160.

11   [1996] 3 SCR 609.

12   David C Young, "Education Law and Multiculturalism: Beyond the Quintet" in JM Mangan, ed, *Social Foundations of Education Coursebook, 2008–2009* (London, ON: The Althouse Press, 2008) 197.

13   *Waldman v Canada*, Communication No 694/1996: Canada. 05/11/99. CCPR/C/67/D/694/1996.

14   Deani A Neven Van Pelt, *Home Schooling in Canada: The Current Picture* (Vancouver: Barbara Mitchell Centre for Improvement in Education, Fraser Institute, 2015).

most often voiced by parents for opting to home-school their children is dissatisfaction with the public school system or religious or philosophical objection to their child attending a public school.[15] Today, most provinces permit children to be educated at home. However, the legislation normally stipulates that the instruction must be the equivalent of that provided by the public school system. As the Ontario *Education Act* states in section 21(2): "A person is excused from attendance at school if, (a) the person is receiving satisfactory instruction at home or elsewhere."[16]

C. WHY TEACHERS NEED TO UNDERSTAND THE LAW

Many teachers assume, oftentimes incorrectly, that they know and understand the law. Teachers believe that simple common sense is all that is required in guiding their public and private behaviour.

> Yet, the prevalence of litigation involving teachers reveals a disconnection between theory (as a preservice teacher) and practice (as an inservice teacher). The law is complex and multi-faceted; it can be bewildering to even those with formal legal training. Teachers need not be lawyers, but they do need some understanding of the law and its implications for professional practice and off-duty conduct.[17]

If you are an educator, keep in mind that your field of employment is arguably heavily regulated and the potential for lawsuits is a fact of life. Common sense is a valuable ally in avoiding litigation, but an understanding and appreciation of the law as it relates to teaching would serve you well.

When it comes to education law, you may believe that the topic has little value for you. When studying litigation involving educators, a common retort from teachers is "that would never happen to me." Certainly, most school employees will spend their entire careers free of legal entanglements. However, lawsuits exact a tremendous toll on all parties, and it is important to recognize that even if a teacher is exonerated by a court of law, the stigma associated with litigation never truly disappears. In a study involving preservice and graduate education students at Memorial University of Newfoundland, Delaney found that exposure to education

---

15   Young, Levin, & Wallin, above note 8 at 129.
16   RSO 1990, c E.2.
17   David C Young, Wendy L Kraglund-Gauthier, & Andrew Foran, "Legal Literacy in Teacher Education Programs: Conceptualizing Relevance and Constructing Pedagogy" (2014) 24 *Journal of Educational Administration and Foundations* 7.

law (1) raised awareness levels and understanding in terms of the impact of the legal system on education; (2) led to sound decision making involving legal issues; (3) fostered a degree of professionalism; and (4) raised the self-confidence of teachers.[18] Without question, each of these benefits underscores the sheer value that exposure to legal principles and procedures can have for educators. Although we oftentimes claim ignorance is bliss, this is not a legal defence and ultimately, ". . . knowledge of education law is more effective as a protector than as a healer and it is better to have a solid understanding of education law than it is to study the relevant statutes after the fact."[19] As Sydor points out:

> When teacher education includes instruction about the legal context of schooling, teachers are better prepared to do their work. They have a better understanding of what is required of them from a legal perspective and are consequently less likely to misstep in their professional duties. Teachers who understand the boundaries of their roles with pupils, parents, colleagues and administrators are less likely to be intimidated by the actions of others and more likely to exercise their authority with reason and perspective. From a practical standpoint, the knowledge that teachers gain in the study of education law contributes to an efficient and orderly functioning of schools because they accept responsibility for their practice as professionals and not simply as employees.[20]

The preceding discussion has emphasized the point that educators should be well informed in terms of the law. "As caregivers to the most vulnerable sector of the populace, children, teachers are inextricably woven into the fabric of the educational, social and legal lives of their charges. That they need to be well-informed in all these contexts seems . . . almost a foregone conclusion."[21]

---

18   Jerome G Delaney, "The Value of Educational Law to Practising Educators" (2009) 19 *Education and Law Journal* 119 at 123.

19   Gary L Reglin, "Public School Educators' Knowledge of Selected Supreme Court Decisions Affecting Daily Public School Operations" (1990) 7 *Research in Rural Education* 17 at 17.

20   Susan Sydor, "Teacher Education Needs More Education Law" (Paper delivered at the seventeenth annual conference of the Canadian Association for the Practical Study of Law in Education, Montréal, Québec, 2006) at 936.

21   Alan W Leschied, Wendy J Lewis, & Greg M Dickinson, "Assessing Educators' Self-Reported Levels of Legal Knowledge, Law-Related Areas of Concern and Patterns of Accessing Legal Information: Implications for Training and Practice" (2000) 14 *Journal of Educational Administration and Foundations* 38 at 66.

D. SOURCES OF SCHOOL LAW

Historically, the legal status of a teacher was defined by the doctrine of *in loco parentis* (in place of the parent). Although a teacher may still act in place of the parent during the school day, in the current context the legal status of a teacher is defined largely by the state through statutes.[22] Building on this, if you were asked to provide a list of laws that would affect what you can and cannot do as a teacher, it is safe to assume that without much effort and in very short order you could compile a number of sources. Figure 4.1 below provides some of the major sources of school law.[23] When looking at this, keep in mind this is a hierarchy; more specifically, as federal pieces of legislation, both the Constitution and the *Charter* are paramount, and apply uniformly to all provinces and territories. The *Education Act* and regulations, which are provincial in scope and will thus vary based on jurisdiction, fall below federal law in terms of supremacy. School board policies fall below the *Education Act*, and at the bottom of the hierarchy are school policies.

Figure 4.1   Major sources of school law for each province or territory

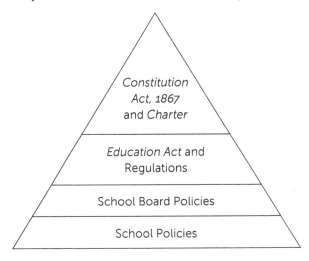

---

22   A Wayne MacKay, Lyle I Sutherland, & Kimberley D Pochini, *Teachers and the Law*, 3d ed (Toronto: Emond Montgomery, 2013).

23   *Ibid.*

First, the *Constitution Act, 1867* is relevant since, as was discussed previously, section 93 gives control of public education to the provinces. Section 93 also acts as a protection mechanism for denominational (religious) rights and privileges that existed at the time a province joined Confederation. Thus, the Constitution is important when we consider Roman Catholic separate school boards, which exist in Alberta, Saskatchewan, and Ontario, as this document provides for their legal legitimacy.

Another federal piece of constitutional legislation that fundamentally impacts public education is the *Charter of Rights and Freedoms*, enacted in 1982.[24] The *Charter*, as outlined in section 32(1)(b), applies only to government action and government actors, but not to the private sector. Thus, the *Charter* applies generally to publicly funded school boards as well as to the employees of such boards.[25] If you teach in a private school, however, the *Charter* has less significance. Private school teachers are more affected by provincial human rights codes than by the *Charter*. Public school educators should be aware that the students they teach have *Charter* rights. As was pointed out in a 1969 United States Supreme Court case, *Tinker v Des Moines Independent Community School District*, which involved wearing black armbands to protest the Vietnam War, students do not "shed their constitutional rights ... at the schoolhouse gate."[26] Although an American case, the decision in *Tinker* has been cited with favour by several Canadian courts. As a result, it is important to remember that the whole school community possesses rights enshrined in the *Charter*.

Although not exhaustive, among the most common school-related issues addressed by the *Charter* are the following: freedom of conscience and religion; expression; peaceful assembly and association; life, liberty, and the security of person; search and seizure; and detention. In section 15(1), the *Charter* prohibits discrimination on the basis of race, national or ethnic origin, colour, religion, sex, age, or mental or physical disability. It should be clear that rights and freedoms outlined in the *Charter* are extensive. However, they are not unfettered or absolute, as section 1 states that these rights and freedoms remain subject to reasonable limits as prescribed by law.

This discussion of sources of school law would be incomplete if school board and school policies were not mentioned. Certainly, every board and

---

24   Part I of the *Constitution Act, 1982*, being Schedule B to the *Canada Act 1982* (UK), 1982, c 11 [*Charter*].

25   MacKay, Sutherland, & Pochini, above note 22 at 69.

26   393 US 503 at 506 (1969).

school in Canada has developed policies unique to their own particular context. For example, the Ottawa-Carleton District School Board policy on bus cancellations due to inclement weather is typical of protocols boards may enact. An example of a school policy would be the code of student conduct implemented at Fredericton High School, Canada's oldest English high school.

E. THE ROLE OF THE COURTS

In Canada, each province and territory has its own system of courts, and provincial courts are routinely involved in hearing cases concerning public education.[27] However, for our purposes attention will be limited and directed to the Supreme Court of Canada. As the highest court of law in the country, the Supreme Court plays a very significant role. "First, its rulings are binding on all other courts in Canada. Second, controversial cases in all areas of law may be taken to the Supreme Court for a ruling that will provide clear direction to the lower courts, and thus a common interpretation of the law across Canada. Third, the Supreme Court is responsible for determining how the various clauses in the Constitution will be interpreted."[28]

Through an examination of the role played by the courts in relation to education, three salient points emerge. First, it would appear that oftentimes courts have become the ultimate arbiters of issues pertaining to law and policy. The Canadian Senate was likened by Sir John A Macdonald to a "place of sober second thought." In a similar fashion, courts are now routinely called upon to provide some semblance of clarity to vexatious issues. However, it is interesting to note that some commentators, including former Alberta premier Peter Lougheed, former Saskatchewan premier Allan Blakeney, and former federal justice minister John Crosbie, have lamented the rise in judicial power. According to these three politicians, judicial supremacy has surpassed parliamentary supremacy.[29] Certainly, it is interesting to consider whether an unelected judiciary exercises more influence than the elected federal parliament or provincial and territorial legislatures.

---

27 See Lori Hausegger, Matthew Hennigar, & Troy Riddell, *Canadian Courts: Law, Politics and Process* (Don Mills, ON: Oxford University Press, 2009).

28 Young, Levin, & Wallin, above note 8 at 111.

29 Kent Roach, *The Supreme Court on Trial: Judicial Activism or Democratic Dialogue* (Toronto: Irwin Law, 2001) at 3–4.

Second, an oft-voiced and somewhat related criticism levied against courts is the charge of judicial activism. Judicial activism is often wrapped up in claims that in their deliberations, judges allow their political leanings and predilections to influence their legal reasoning. Hausegger, Hennigar, and Riddell comment, "While it is clear that judges have increased their policy-making in the *Charter* era, there is little consensus as to whether the rate of activism is proper and, more generally, whether the increased judicial policy-making under the *Charter* has been beneficial."[30] Ultimately, as Roach correctly points out, judicial activism is a complex topic and one that will continue to prompt debate.[31]

A third and final point to note in regard to the courts is the whole notion of constitutional interpretation. In a very real sense, it would appear that courts have embraced the notion of the Constitution as akin to a "living tree." "Thus," write Hausegger, Hennigar, and Riddell, "the justices have rejected the notion that the meaning of the Constitution is 'frozen' — set at the meaning the framers would have intended. Instead, the Court has taken a 'progressive' approach to constitutional interpretation, which involves adjusting the meaning of the documents' provisions to keep up with changes in society and its values."[32] As Antonio Lamer, a former Supreme Court of Canada chief justice, stated in *Reference re Motor Vehicle Act (British Columbia) S 94(2)*, "If the newly planted 'living tree' which is the *Charter* is to have the possibility of growth and adjustment over time, care must be taken to ensure that historical materials . . . do not stunt its growth."[33]

Suffice it to say that decisions rendered by courts across the country have the capacity to wind their way into teachers' classrooms and affect what educators do.

F. TEACHER DUTIES, RIGHTS, AND RESPONSIBILITIES

1) Legal Parameters

It is important to recognize that the public school system in Canada is largely defined as secular. For example, section 76 of the British Columbia *School Act* stipulates that schools are to be secular, and furthermore, "no

---

30   Above note 27 at 370.
31   See above note 29.
32   Above note 27 at 121.
33   [1985] 2 SCR 486 at para 52.

religious dogma or creed is to be taught."[34] The 1988 Ontario case of *Zylberberg v Sudbury Board of Education* is a prime example of the intersection between religion and education.[35] At stake was a regulation dictating that opening and closing exercises in schools would consist of reading scriptures or other suitable readings, or the recitation of the Lord's Prayer or a similar prayer.[36] Ultimately, the Ontario Court of Appeal struck down the regulation, indicating that one religion cannot be given primacy.[37] Besides *Zylberberg*, the *Canadian Civil Liberties Assn v Ontario (Minister of Education)* illustrates the tensions between religion and public schools.[38] This 1990 case revolved around an Ontario regulation which mandated two periods of religious instruction per week, as well as a claim that the religious instruction curriculum developed by the Elgin County Board of Education displayed a Christian point of view, thereby resulting in a form of religious indoctrination. In hearing the case, the Ontario Court of Appeal reversed a lower court decision, finding that the regulation as well as the curriculum did result in a form of indoctrination. The conclusion to be drawn from both of these cases is that "in short, public schools were [and are] to be secular."[39]

The *Education Act* and regulations in each province and territory provide educators with parameters as to legal rights and responsibilities. For example, the New Brunswick *Education Act* specifies the duties of a teacher in section 27.[40] Accordingly, teachers are expected to fulfill the following responsibilities:

(a) implement the prescribed curriculum;

(b) identify and implement learning and evaluation strategies that foster a positive learning environment aimed at helping each pupil achieve prescribed learning outcomes;

(c) maintain a deportment consistent with his or her position of trust and influence over young people;

(d) exemplify and encourage in each pupil the values of truth, justice, compassion and respect for all persons;

34 Above note 5.

35 (1988), 65 OR (2d) 641 (CA) [*Zylberberg*].

36 Young, above note 12.

37 Anthony F Brown & Marvin A Zuker, *Education Law*, 2d ed (Scarborough, ON: Carswell, 1998) at 127.

38 (1990), 71 OR (2d) 341 (CA).

39 Greg M Dickinson & W Rod Dolmage, "Education, Religion, and the Courts in Ontario" (1996) 21 *Canadian Journal of Education* 363 at 370.

40 SNB 1997, c E-1.12.

(e) attend to the health and well-being of each pupil;

(f) maintain his or her professional competence; and

(g) assist in the development and implementation of the school improvement plan and cooperate in the preparation of the school performance report.

The list provides a legal framework within which teachers are expected to
perform their role. Similar provisions can be found in the respective act of
each province and territory.

When considering the many duties of an educator, it is reasonable to
posit that the most important duty is that of teaching. In public education,
"teachers are largely constrained as to what curriculum is taught, and the
school boards through approved resources largely dictate the techniques
used."[41] However, this comment is not intended to suggest that school
boards have unfettered power or that educators are completely muzzled.
In regard to the former, the 2002 case of *Chamberlain v Surrey School District
No 36* is telling.[42] In its decision, the Supreme Court found the decision by
the school board to ban three books that dealt with same-sex parenting was
unreasonable. The Court noted the decision to ban the books was driven
by religious considerations, which ultimately led to a lack of respect being afforded same sex–parented families. As such, the board was ordered
to reconsider the decision to ban the books in light of its own internal
policies as well as the principles of tolerance and non-sectarianism upon
which the British Columbia *School Act* was built. In reference to educators specifically, *Morin v Prince Edward Island Regional Administrative Unit
No 3 School Board* involved a Grade 9 teacher showing a video titled *Thy
Kingdom Come, Thy Will Be Done* to a language arts class in advance of an
assignment dealing with what religion means to people. The video, which
was highly critical of religious fundamentalism, upset several students
and parents. In response, the principal instructed the teacher not to show
the video again and cancelled the assignment. At the heart of this case is
the question of whether the teacher's academic freedom and freedom of
speech had been infringed through the actions of the principal. Ultimately, the Prince Edward Island Court of Appeal found that the actions of the
principal did infringe the teacher's freedom of expression.[43] As the Court
noted:

---

41 Kenneth Crook & Derek Truscott, *Ethics and Law for Teachers* (Toronto: Nelson,
2007) at 131.

42 2002 SCC 86.

43 2002 PESCAD 9 [*Morin* (CA)].

What is being dealt with in this case is the freedom of teachers to carry out their mandate in a free and democratic society without fear that a whiff of controversy could spell the end of their careers — or result in suspension or other punishment. Is education not well served by a stimulating debate, discussion of different points of view, exposure to different perspectives? Should not teachers be encouraged to challenge students, to raise topical issues, rather than be intimidated from raising anything that might be controversial?[44]

Yet, as Waddington correctly points out,[45] despite the decision in the *Morin* case, which points to the fact teachers enjoy some right to freedom of expression in the classroom, this right should be exercised responsibly and guided by careful planning and consultation. In the absence of this, teachers may run afoul of the law when they engage in unorthodox teaching methods or teach material deemed socially unacceptable. As the trial court stated in *Morin*, "... freedom of expression does not grant teachers ... the right to teach whatever they like to their students as a captive audience."[46]

2) Codes of Ethics

In addition to the *Education Act*, most provincial teacher associations have their own codes of ethics, which outline conduct expected of members of the teaching profession. As Delaney points out,[47] most codes of ethics offer guidelines in terms of the responsibilities of teachers to each of the following: students, employer, colleagues, parents, personal professional development, and professional association.

Of particular importance for educators in regard to codes of ethics is conduct with teaching colleagues. Codes of ethics frown upon educators publicly criticizing other members of the profession. As the Nova Scotia Teachers Union (NSTU) Code of Ethics states in article II(a), "The member should not make defamatory, disparaging, condescending, embarrassing, or offensive comments concerning another member."[48] In this regard, the 1987 *Cromer* case from British Columbia is telling. The appellant, who was

---

44   *Ibid* at para 96.
45   David I Waddington, "A Right to Speak Out: The *Morin* Case and Its Implications for Teachers' Free Expression" (2011) 42 *Interchange* 59 at 74.
46   1999 CanLII 4418 (PEISCTD).
47   Jerome G Delaney, *Legal Dimensions of Education: Implications for Teachers and School Administrators* (Calgary: Detselig Enterprises, 2007) at 87.
48   Online: www.nstu.ca/the-nstu/about-us/about-nstu/code-of-ethics/.

a teacher, had children enrolled in the same district in which she taught. At a heated public meeting held at her son's school, Cromer openly criticized a school counsellor. The counsellor complained to the British Columbia Teachers' Federation, which found that Cromer had violated the Code of Ethics when she criticized a colleague. Cromer appealed this decision, stating that when she criticized the counsellor she was speaking as a parent, not as a teacher. In its ruling, the British Columbia Court of Appeal expressed this view: "I do not think people are free to choose which hat they will wear on what occasions."[49] As such, a teacher is always a teacher, and openly criticizing other members of the profession is always inappropriate.

Teachers must also keep in mind that codes of ethics routinely specify that one's off-duty conduct needs to conform to acceptable standards of behaviour. According to the NSTU Code of Ethics, "the member should so conduct themselves in their private life that no dishonour may befall them or through them to the profession."[50] The case involving British Columbia teacher Christopher Kempling is illustrative of this point. Between 1997 and 2000, Kempling wrote a series of letters to the editor of a local newspaper, the *Quesnel Cariboo Observer*, in which he made discriminatory statements about homosexuality. In response, the British Columbia College of Teachers cited Kempling for professional misconduct, namely, "conduct unbecoming" a member of the College and subsequently recommended a one-month suspension of his teaching certificate. Although no direct evidence was entered to support the position that Kempling's writings resulted in a "poisoned school environment," the College of Teachers believed that such an inference could be drawn.[51]

G. ISSUES OF MISCONDUCT

Educators need to recognize that they serve as role models for those under their charge. Consequently, as the preceding discussion has shown, actions both in and outside the classroom will be subject to scrutiny. There is no shortage of cases involving teachers who have committed misconduct, but the most heinous are those involving teachers engaged in inappropriate relationships with their students. Teachers stand in a position of trust towards their students; any abuse of this position of trust is reprehensible.

---

49   As cited in Bezeau, above note 2 at 399.
50   Above note 48, art VII.
51   Greg M Dickinson, "The Problem of Heretic Teachers: *Kempling v. British Columbia College of Teachers*" (2005) 40 *McGill Journal of Education* 383 at 389.

1) Inappropriate Relationships with Students

Consider the 1996 case of Yves Audet, a twenty-two-year-old teacher in northern New Brunswick. While on summer break, Audet and a friend visited a local nightclub where they encountered one of Audet's former fourteen-year-old students, who was at the establishment accompanied by two cousins. Although the safest course of action would have been for Audet to simply leave the nightclub, he spent the evening with his former student. To further complicate matters, the group eventually wound up at a cottage, and at a certain point during the evening, Audet engaged in oral sex with his student. At trial, the Supreme Court of Canada established a reverse onus provision for teachers in regard to the position of trust they hold; that is, it is assumed that at *all* times a teacher is in a position of trust.[52] Thus, this position of trust extends to off-duty as well as to on-duty conduct. Section 151 of Canada's *Criminal Code*[53] makes it an offence to touch, either directly or indirectly, any part of the body of a young person for sexual purposes. Furthermore, section 153 of the *Code* states that "consent" is not a defence to this charge.

Parents entrust their children with teachers and expect that educators will act responsibly in the discharge of their duties. As Delaney correctly points out:

> Teachers and school administrators are very vulnerable to the accusations of students. It is imperative that they be very cautious in their behaviours towards children. Avoiding any unnecessary contact is wise advice especially at the higher levels of schooling (i.e., upper elementary, junior and senior high). At the primary and lower elementary levels students very commonly hug their teachers; it is not suggested that teachers reject overt signs of affection. However, teachers should act professionally and with moderation in these situations. Teachers need to be conservative in the degree of affection they show their students, depending of course on the particular situation they find themselves in.[54]

In an age where real or alleged sexual misconduct by teachers is a fact of life, teachers need to be prudent in their actions with students. Remember that false allegations have been brought forward by students, and these allegations have exacted tremendous tolls. Besides obvious precautions, such as not closing the classroom door, particularly when with

---

52 *R v Audet*, [1996] 2 SCR 171.
53 RSC 1985, c C-46 [*Code*].
54 Above note 47 at 72–73.

a single student, teachers should remember that their role *in loco parentis* does not equate to the role of a parent: teachers are not entitled to the same degree of physical intimacy as parents.[55] In fact, even touching a student's shoulder might not be prudent in the current context. This situation is troubling and somewhat alarming. Educators are faced with walking a tightrope between caring for students and keeping an appropriate degree of professional distance. This is a tenuous line, and one to be cognizant of in professional practice.

2) Improper Role Modelling

While cases involving inappropriate sexual relationships may grab media headlines, the issue of teacher misconduct extends beyond this dimension. Consider, for example, the case of Jim Keegstra, a teacher from Eckville, Alberta, who espoused anti-Semitic sentiments and insisted that his students accept his views, to the point where, if they failed to do so, their grades would be reduced. Keegstra was charged under the *Criminal Code* with unlawfully and willingly promoting hatred against an identifiable group. Keegstra claimed that his freedom of expression rights as guaranteed by section 2(b) of the *Charter* had been violated, and although the Supreme Court of Canada agreed with this argument, it found that the violation was justified under section 1.[56]

For an educator, the Keegstra case is relevant in that teachers must be seen to be impartial in and outside of the classroom. Thus, a teacher is always a teacher. As the Supreme Court of Canada pointed out in the 1996 case *Ross v New Brunswick School District No 15*, which involved an educator who published anti-Semitic propaganda, "teachers do not necessarily check their teaching hats at the school yard gate and may be perceived to be wearing their teaching hats even off duty."[57]

Consequently, teachers need to recognize that even in their off-duty time, their conduct is subject to limitations. They arguably have restrictions placed on their freedoms that other members of society do not. This perception is certainly not new, as the following female teacher's contract from 1915 illustrates.

---

55 Eleanor Doctor, "Someone Else's Nightmare: Sexual Misconduct in Schools" (Paper presented at the annual conference of the Canadian Association for the Practical Study of Law in Education, Toronto, 25–27 April, 1999).

56 *R v Keegstra*, [1990] 3 SCR 697.

57 [1996] 1 SCR 825 at para 44.

. . . not to keep company with men; to be home between the hours of 8:00 p.m. and 6:00 a.m. unless in attendance at a school function; not to loiter downtown in ice cream stores; not to leave town at any time without the permission of the chairman of the board; and not to get in a carriage or automobile with any man except her father or brother.[58]

While an educator may feel that having limitations placed upon personal freedoms is patently unfair, it is part of what to expect in the role.

3) Denominational Cause

Teachers who accept a position with a Roman Catholic separate school board are arguably held to an even higher standard of accountability. In a Roman Catholic school board, a teacher may be terminated for "denominational cause." Denominational rights and privileges are enshrined in section 93 of the *Constitution Act, 1867*, as listed below:

(1) Nothing in any such Law shall prejudicially affect any Right or Privilege with respect to Denominational Schools which any Class of Persons have by Law in the Province at the Union;

(2) All the Powers, Privileges, and Duties at the Union by Law conferred and imposed in Upper Canada on the Separate Schools and School Trustees of the Queen's Roman Catholic Subjects shall be and the same are hereby extended to the Dissentient Schools of the Queen's Protestant and Roman Catholic Subjects in Quebec;

(3) Where in any Province a System of Separate or Dissentient Schools exists by Law at the Union or is thereafter established by the Legislature of the Province, an Appeal shall lie to the Governor General in Council from any Act or Decision of any Provincial Authority affecting any Right or Privilege of the Protestant or Roman Catholic Minority of the Queen's Subjects in relation to Education;

(4) In case any such Provincial Law as from Time to Time seems to the Governor General in Council requisite for the due Execution of the Provisions of this Section is not made, or in case any Decision of the Governor General in Council on any Appeal under this Section is not duly executed by the proper Provincial Authority in that Behalf, then and in every such Case, and as far only as the Circumstances of each Case require, the Parliament of Canada may make remedial Laws for the due Execution of the Provisions of this Section and of any Decision of the Governor General in Council under this Section.[59]

---

58   Brown & Zuker, above note 37 at 239.
59   *Constitution Act, 1867*, above note 1, s 93.

So, if a province joined Confederation with denominational rights and privileges intact, then these rights and privileges were essentially "frozen in time." Further, section 29 of the *Charter* permits for these denominational rights and privileges to take precedence over the *Charter* itself. As section 29 states:

> Nothing in this Charter abrogates or derogates from any rights or privileges guaranteed by or under the Constitution of Canada in respect of denominational, separate or dissentient schools.[60]

In commenting on the importance of section 29, Bezeau makes the following observation:

> This clause gives denominational rights and privileges established when the provinces entered Canada precedence over any provisions of the *Charter*. It prevents *Charter* challenges to denominational rights and privileges and also prevents the use of those in establishing a case of discrimination under the *Charter* by those who are denied such right and privileges.[61]

As a consequence, privacy rights as well as lifestyle choices are restricted for a teacher employed by a separate school board. Simply put, any teacher working for a Roman Catholic board must respect church doctrine, as a failure to do so could result in termination. In fact, adherence to Catholic doctrine is a bona fide occupational requirement (an essential in order to properly fulfill the role). For example, in the 1987 *Casagrande v Hinton Roman Catholic Separate District No 155* case from Alberta, a female teacher employed by the Hinton Roman Catholic Separate School Board was dismissed after her second pregnancy while unmarried. Ultimately, a board of reference as well as the Court of Queen's Bench in Alberta agreed that premarital sex was a direct violation of Catholic doctrine, and as such, termination based on denominational cause was justified.[62] In another denominational cause case from British Columbia, Margaret Caldwell was dismissed from her teaching position at a private Catholic institution, St Thomas Aquinas High School, because she married a divorced man in a civil ceremony, thus violating two tenets of the Catholic Church. Caldwell's case was heard by the Supreme Court of Canada, which, in 1984, ruled that adherence to Catholic doctrine was a bona fide job requirement,

---

60 *Charter*, above note 24, s 29.
61 Above note 2 at 23.
62 1987 CanLII 3358 (Alta QB).

and consequently her termination was justified in that she lacked the qualifications required to teach in a Catholic school.[63]

4) Social Media Indiscretions

In discussing teacher misconduct, it would be remiss if the issue of social media was not raised. Online postings, even if seemingly innocent, can result in serious consequences. Consider that, in 2006, Millersville University in Pennsylvania refused to grant an education degree to a student who had posted a photo to her *MySpace* page in which she was seen wearing a pirate hat and drinking from a cup, with a caption attached that read "Drunken Pirate." Although the university cited additional factors in refusing to grant the degree, the online photo almost certainly factored heavily into the equation. As the Ontario College of Teachers has pointed out, "maintaining professional boundaries in all forms of communication, technology related or not, is vital to maintaining the public trust."[64] Teachers are wise to act professionally when using sites such as Facebook and to ensure that their privacy settings are intact.

H. CORPORAL PUNISHMENT AND THE USE OF FORCE

Another area of law with which teachers need to be familiar is corporal punishment and the use of force. As Delaney points out, "the term, corporal punishment, conjures up images in days gone by of teachers strapping students for the most trivial of reasons such as not knowing how to spell a word or for not knowing the answer to a question from their Social Studies textbook."[65] In the current context, corporal punishment has been, to a large measure, abandoned, and in many circumstances, its very use is prohibited. Still, section 43 of the *Criminal Code* does permit the use of force. As it states: "Every schoolteacher, parent or person standing in the place of a parent is justified in using force by way of correction toward a pupil or child, as the case may be, who is under his care, if the force does not exceed what is reasonable under the circumstances."[66] There has been continued debate on whether section 43 violates the equality rights of

---

63 *Caldwell v St Thomas Aquinas High School*, [1984] 2 SCR 603.
64 Ontario College of Teachers, *Professional Advisory: Use of Electronic Communication and Social Media* (Toronto: Ontario College of Teachers, 2011) at 3.
65 Above note 47 at 67.
66 Above note 53.

children as specified in the *Charter*. The 2004 case of *Canadian Foundation for Children, Youth and the Law v Canada (Attorney General)* provided some clarity in this regard when the Supreme Court of Canada upheld the constitutionality of section 43. The Court further asserted that parents and teachers should use only "minor corrective force of a transitory and trifling nature."[67] The Court went on to state that the following would be seen as unreasonable:

1) hitting a child under two years of age
2) corporal punishment of teenagers
3) the use of objects in disciplining a child
4) slaps or blows to the head
5) degrading and inhumane treatment
6) corporal punishment that causes injury

Although the use of force to defend oneself is perhaps necessary in extreme circumstances, the use of force to correct a student should be avoided. Even though section 43 has been affirmed by the Supreme Court of Canada, a teacher who uses physical force may still face civil or criminal charges, as well as discipline from his or her employer. Thus, as MacKay, Sutherland, and Pochini quite rightly point out, "regardless of the state of the law, teachers should always seek other options to avoid physical confrontations with students."[68]

I. NEGLIGENCE

While on a school-sponsored field trip to a local conservation authority, a group of female students you are supervising asks if it might be possible to go for a swim at the nearby beach. As a teacher with both training and experience, you are apprehensive about such an outing. Because you are a non-swimmer, your level of unease is even more heightened. In spite of this, you eventually agree, and you and your students head to the beach for a swim. As you pace back and forth on the beach, you notice that a breeze has picked up, and some waves are now visible. Still, you feel it is unnecessary to interrupt the girls as they play in the water. In an instant, however, all changes as you quickly realize that because of the strong breeze, two of your students are now experiencing difficulty. In the turmoil that ensues,

---

67   [2004] 1 SCR 76 at para 40.
68   Above note 22 at 43.

efforts are made by other students to rescue the two students. In the end, despite concerted efforts, two of your students drown.

This scenario is drawn from a 1972 case, *Moddejonge v Huron County Board of Education*, in which two fourteen-year-old students lost their lives.[69] It will, it is hoped, serve as a reminder of how quickly accidents can happen and how educators must always exercise good judgment and common sense. Ultimately, teachers cannot be too careful in safeguarding the students under their charge.

Generally, schools are safe places, but despite educators' best efforts, accidents can and do happen. When an accident occurs, people seek to uncover the cause, and in so doing, normally attach blame to an individual or party. Negligence on the part of teachers generally occurs through one's actions or inactions. Oftentimes, in determining negligence, courts will attempt to ascertain if the level of supervision provided by the teacher was appropriate. Courts may also seek to determine if the accident was reasonably foreseeable. As MacKay points out:

> Everyone has a duty to conduct himself in such a way so as not to harm others. In order for liability to arise it is necessary that the harm caused and the person injured should have been "reasonably foreseeable." The test often used by the courts is whether a "reasonable person" would have foreseen the accident . . . . If it is foreseeable that someone might be harmed, it is necessary for a person to take whatever steps a reasonable or prudent person would take to avoid injury.[70]

Certainly, in supervising students, it is impossible for teachers to eliminate all threats of injury; it is, however, incumbent upon teachers to reduce threats that are "reasonably foreseeable."

In terms of the standard of care teachers owe to their students, courts have and continue to generally rely upon the "careful parent" standard set down by Lord Esher in the 1893 case of *Williams v Eady*. The case, which involved a student being injured when a jar of phosphorous exploded, resulted in the headmaster being held liable for improperly storing the phosphorous. In his decision Lord Esher stated the following:

> [T]he schoolmaster was bound to take such care of his boys as a careful father would take of his boys, and there could be no better definition of the duty of a schoolmaster. Then he was bound to take notice of the

---

69   (1972), 25 DLR (3d) 661 (Ont HCJ).

70   A Wayne MacKay, *Education Law in Canada* (Toronto: Emond Montgomery, 1984) at 109–10.

ordinary nature of young boys, their tendency to do mischievous acts, their propensity to meddle with anything that came in their way.[71]

According to the careful parent standard, teachers are expected to use the same degree of care in supervising their students as reasonable parents would in looking after their own children. Courts of law in Canada routinely reaffirm this standard in determining negligence on the part of teachers. Keep in mind that the standard of care for teachers is a bit of an enigma in that education is perhaps the only profession where this standard is based on parental behaviour.[72] As such, several courts have modified the "careful parent" standard in cases involving physical education teachers, thus holding them to the higher standard of a "skilled and competent practitioner." Still, "it is unclear when the parentally based (careful parent) as opposed to the professionally based (competent instructor) test will be invoked by the courts in any given case."[73]

The potential for negligence is very real for educators. Student injury exacts tremendous tolls on the victim. Although vicarious liability dictates that employer school boards assume liability for the actions of their employees, this picture is incomplete. Negligence claims can be quite impactful for the teacher in whose class the injury was sustained. Emotional and psychological turmoil can follow a teacher, even if she or he is exonerated by a court. In thinking about negligence, teachers are well advised to give serious thought to the following as outlined in MacKay, Sutherland, and Pochini:

1. the age of the student or students;
2. the nature of the activity (is it inherently dangerous, or did the student do something unforeseeable to make it dangerous?);
3. the amount of instruction received by the student;
4. the student's general awareness of the risks involved;
5. the approved general practice and, in particular, any school policies regarding this practice;
6. the foreseeable risk of danger; and
7. previous accidents in similar circumstances.[74]

---

71 (1893), 10 TLR 41 at 42, discussed in A Wayne MacKay & Greg M Dickinson, *Beyond the "Careful Parent": Tort Liability in Education* (Toronto: Emond Montgomery, 1998) at 10.
72 See Bezeau, above note 2 at 343.
73 Mackay & Dickinson, above note 71 at 41.
74 Above note 22 at 18.

Each of the above is important in terms of curricular planning. As well, teachers should note the value of implementing risk-management policies in the classroom. According to MacKay and Dickinson, the following questions should be addressed:

1. What are the risks?
2. What can be done to eliminate or reduce the risks?
3. Are the benefits worth the risks?[75]

Athough teachers want to safeguard all students under their charge, a fear of litigation should not deter them from doing activities that could be educationally valuable to their students. Further, in reflecting on negligence and risk management, teachers are wise to keep in mind what happened to Humpty Dumpty: foreseeing potential sources of danger and reducing them will do much to protect students from being injured.

1) Educational Malpractice

As MacKay and Dickinson point out, teachers are rarely sued for failing at arguably the most important aspect of their job: teaching.[76] However, some parents have attempted to pursue litigation against school boards, schools, and educators on the grounds that the system failed to adequately educate their son or daughter. These lawsuits, grounded in the tort of negligence, are commonly referred to as "educational malpractice." Brown and Zuker define educational malpractice as "the alleged failure to impart knowledge or to teach practical skills."[77] Foster argues that the following scenarios could give rise to an educational malpractice lawsuit: (1) failing to provide adequate instructional programs; (2) failing to provide adequate instruction and evaluation of student progress; (3) failing to identify exceptionalities, or provide accommodations when a student is identified as exceptional; (4) failing to provide competent staff; (5) misleading or failing to advise students regarding their academic progress; (6) failing to maintain proper discipline; (7) failing to assign adequate and appropriate materials; and (8) failing to adopt adequate and appropriate methods of instruction.[78] Certainly, this list encapsulates many of the tasks educators routinely perform in the scope of their duties.

---

75 Above note 71 at 100.
76 *Ibid* at 103.
77 Above note 37 at 103.
78 William F Foster, "Educational Malpractice: A Tort for the Untaught" (1985) 19 *University of British Columbia Law Review* 161 at 171–72.

An examination of the litigation surrounding educational malpractice would suggest that courts have thus far been unwilling or reluctant to recognize this as a valid claim. The leading case in this area, from 1976, is *Peter W v San Francisco Unified School District*, in which a student alleged that the school system failed to provide an adequate education, as well as failed to address his reading disability, thus resulting in the plaintiff graduating from high school with only a Grade 8 reading ability. It was further alleged that because of an inability to read, the plaintiff suffered loss of income. The California Court of Appeal found that the plaintiff had no case, as a duty of care had not been established. Further, from a policy perspective, there was an obvious concern that if this case was successful, it would lead to others initiating similar lawsuits. As the Court stated: "To hold them [school boards] to an actionable 'duty of care' in the discharge of their academic functions, would expose them to the tort claims — real or imagined — of disaffected students and parents in countless numbers."[79] In the 1978 case of *Donohue v Copiague Union Free School District*, the New York Supreme Court found, like the Court in *Peter W*, that it was not the role of the judiciary to interfere in matters of public education.[80]

In the Canadian context, the 1996 case of *Gould v Regina (East) School Division No 77* is noteworthy. In rejecting the claim of educational malpractice, the court noted it had no role to play in measuring educational quality. Further, "only if the conduct is sufficiently egregious and offensive to community standards of acceptable fair play should the courts even consider entertaining any type of claim in the nature of educational malpractice."[81]

Although courts have been slamming the proverbial door shut on educational malpractice lawsuits, the rationale provided by the court in *Gould* is worth reiterating. Actions or inactions that are deemed offensive or egregious might warrant a tort of educational malpractice proceeding with success. It seems logical, too, that there exists more opportunity for success if these suits are advanced early in one's education, rather than after the fact.[82]

---

79   60 Cal App 3d 815 at 825 (1976) [Peter W].
80   64 AD 2d 29 (NY App Div 1978).
81   [1997] 3 WWR 117 at para 47 (Sask QB) [*Gould*].
82   Above note 22 at 57.

J. SEARCH AND SEIZURE

Search and seizure is yet another issue that educators need to be aware of in the school context. Section 8 of the *Charter* stipulates that Canadians have the right to be free from unreasonable search or seizure. In the 1998 Nova Scotia case of *R v M(MR)*, the Supreme Court of Canada provided some clarity in this regard.[83] As a means of background, a vice-principal of a junior-high school had been informed by students that another student was planning on selling drugs at an upcoming dance. On the evening of the dance, the vice-principal had the student come to the office, where a search of the student was conducted by the vice-principal. As the search was undertaken, an RCMP officer, who had been called pursuant to board policy, stood by and observed. During the search, marijuana was uncovered, at which point the police officer advised the student he was being placed under arrest. At trial, the Supreme Court of Canada ruled that in maintaining proper order and discipline, school officials, without a warrant, can search students and seize prohibited items.

Generally speaking, in conducting searches of students and lockers, the following, derived from the 1985 United States Supreme Court case of *New Jersey v TLO*, is relevant.[84]

1) The search must be justified at its inception; in other words, there must be reasonable grounds to conduct the search.
2) The search must be reasonable in light of the age and sex of the student, as well as the nature of the infraction.

The criteria that school administration must adhere to in regard to searches is much lower than the "probable cause" requirement placed on law enforcement. Thus, schools should avoid conducting searches on behalf of the police and limit searches to those that deal with order and discipline.

The 2008 Supreme Court of Canada decision in *R v AM* is also relevant to this discussion.[85] This case centred on a standing invitation from the principal of St Patrick's High School in Sarnia, Ontario, to the police to conduct random sniffer dog searches for drugs. Ultimately, the Court ruled that random, or dragnet, searches should be avoided; there must be reasonable grounds for conducting such a search.

---

83 [1998] 3 SCR 393.
84 469 US 325 (1985).
85 2008 SCC 19.

Here are a few last points pertaining to school locker searches:

1) If the school owns the property, such as a locker, the school does not need permission to search it.
2) If students rent lockers, they should be advised that the property is still owned by the school and subject to searches by school staff at any time.
3) It is recommended that students , as well as another staff member, be present during a locker search. This protocol prevents claims that the evidence was planted.

In conducting searches, educators must always act in accordance with the law and never forget that a search must be justified at its inception. There must be reasonable grounds for conducting the search. In *R v M(MR)*, Cory J provided some insight into the nature of reasonableness:

> The following may constitute reasonable grounds in this context: information received from one student considered to be credible, information received from more than one student, a teacher's or principal's own observations, or any combination of these pieces of information which the relevant authority considers to be credible. The compelling nature of the information and the credibility of these or other sources must be assessed by the school authority in the context of the circumstances existing at the particular school.[86]

K. REPORTING OF CHILD ABUSE

Child abuse is yet another issue that teachers must grapple with. Because teachers have daily contact with children, they are in a unique position to observe potential cases of physical, sexual, and emotional abuse and maltreatment. Section 22(2) of the Nova Scotia *Children and Family Services Act* contains a detailed list of circumstances under which a child would require protective services:

> A child is in need of protective services where
> (a) the child has suffered physical harm, inflicted by a parent or guardian of the child or caused by the failure of a parent or guardian to supervise and protect the child adequately;
> (b) there is a substantial risk that the child will suffer physical harm inflicted or caused as described in clause (a);

---

86   Above note 83 at para 50.

(c)   the child has been sexually abused by a parent or guardian of the child, or by another person where a parent or guardian of the child knows or should know of the possibility of sexual abuse and fails to protect the child;

(d)   there is a substantial risk that the child will be sexually abused as described in clause (c);

(e)   a child requires medical treatment to cure, prevent or alleviate physical harm or suffering, and the child's parent or guardian does not provide, or refuses or is unavailable or is unable to consent to, the treatment;

(f)   the child has suffered emotional harm, demonstrated by severe anxiety, depression, withdrawal, or self-destructive or aggressive behaviour and the child's parent or guardian does not provide, or refuses or is unavailable or unable to consent to, services or treatment to remedy or alleviate the harm;

(g)   there is a substantial risk that the child will suffer emotional harm of the kind described in clause (f), and the parent or guardian does not provide, or refuses or is unavailable or unable to consent to, services or treatment to remedy or alleviate the harm;

(h)   the child suffers from a mental, emotional or developmental condition that, if not remedied, could seriously impair the child's development and the child's parent or guardian does not provide, or refuses or is unavailable or unable to consent to, services or treatment to remedy or alleviate the condition;

(i)   the child has suffered physical or emotional harm caused by being exposed to repeated domestic violence by or towards a parent or guardian of the child, and the child's parent or guardian fails or refuses to obtain services or treatment to remedy or alleviate the violence;

(j)   the child has suffered physical harm caused by chronic and serious neglect by a parent or guardian of the child, and the parent or guardian does not provide, or refuses or is unavailable or unable to consent to, services or treatment to remedy or alleviate the harm;

(ja) there is a substantial risk that the child will suffer physical harm inflicted or caused as described in clause (j);

(k)   the child has been abandoned, the child's only parent or guardian has died or is unavailable to exercise custodial rights over the child and has not made adequate provisions for the child's care and custody, or the child is in the care of an agency or another person and the parent or guardian of the child refuses or is unable or unwilling to resume the child's care and custody;

(l)   the child is under twelve years of age and has killed or seriously injured another person or caused serious damage to another person's
property, and services or treatment are necessary to prevent a recurrence and a parent or guardian of the child does not provide, or
refuses or is unavailable or unable to consent to, the necessary services or treatment;

(m) the child is under twelve years of age and has on more than one occasion injured another person or caused loss or damage to another
person's property, with the encouragement of a parent or guardian
of the child or because of the parent or guardian's failure or inability
to supervise the child adequately.[87]

If teachers observe any of the above factors, they are expected to act
in accordance with established guidelines and file a report. A report can
also be made based on third-party reports, hearsay, or overheard conversations. Teachers are not to conduct an investigation into possible child
abuse but rather to leave the investigating to the authorities. Becoming
involved in an ongoing case could hamper efforts to prosecute alleged offenders. The safest course of action is to simply report a suspicion. Teachers should report suspected cases of abuse to the appropriate authorities;
in most instances, doing so requires that a report be made to police or to
the Children's Aid Society or equivalent organization. It is also extremely
important for teachers to remember that reporting should not be delegated to someone else, such as the school principal.

In short, if an educator suspects that abuse is occurring, the educator must file the report. In some jurisdictions such as Ontario, the duty
to report is ongoing; if, for example, the Children's Aid Society does not
respond to an initial report, it is incumbent upon the educator to follow up
and report suspicions again.[88] And rest assured that unless the reporting
is done falsely or maliciously, no legal action will be taken against you.
Any failure to report can have serious consequences. The Nova Scotia *Children and Family Services Act* states that upon conviction, a failure to report
can result in a fine of not more than $5,000 or to imprisonment not ex-
ceeding one year, or to both.[89]

As MacKay, Sutherland, and Pochini note, "teachers are normally reti-
cent to involve outside authorities and initiate the trauma of a child abuse

---

87   SNS 1990, c 5.
88   See Anthony F Brown, *Legal Handbook for Educators*, 6th ed (Toronto: Carswell,
2009) at 38–39.
89   See above note 87.

investigation. They are also concerned about the reaction of parents who are the object of suspicion. However, it is incumbent upon teachers and other professionals to err on the side of caution when deciding to report."[90] Certainly, reporting suspected cases of child abuse is not easy, but teachers must always act in the best interests of their students, since a failure to act can result in tragedy. Further, in protecting youth from abuse, inter-agency cooperation is imperative. Everyone entrusted with looking after the most vulnerable in society — children — must make a concerted effort to protect them.

L. FINAL THOUGHTS

At the beginning of this chapter it was pointed out that effective teachers understand the system in which they work. Again, it is worth reiterating that a knowledge and understanding of the public education system is important. In fact, a knowledge of how and why the system is organized as it is will make any teacher better.

Certainly, from the preceding discussion it is clear that public education is a complex enterprise. A web of policies and laws regulate the teaching profession. Classroom teachers need to bear in mind that their conduct will be governed to a large degree by regulations that stipulate what they can and cannot do. In the 1980s television police drama *Hill Street Blues*, Sgt Phil Esterhaus (played by Michael Conrad) always ended roll call by advising, "let's be careful out there." Teachers are wise to remember those words, as they will serve them well in their professional practice.

---

90 MacKay, Sutherland, & Pochini, above note 22 at 194.

CHAPTER 5

Student Rights

Nadya Tymochenko

This chapter will identify and discuss the rights of students attending elementary and secondary school in Canada. The topics addressed in this chapter include student rights as they relate to attendance, denominational rights to education, student rights pursuant to the *Canadian Charter of Rights and Freedoms*[1] (the *Charter*) such as the right to freedom of expression, and the right to freedom of religion. While it is not possible to cover the legislation and caselaw of each province in detail, selected cases and legislation from across Canada will be reviewed.

It is important to note that student rights and obligations in education are seldom discrete. For example, the right to privacy in the educational setting is an issue that is addressed in student discipline with respect to the right of educators to conduct searches of student belongings and their person. Student discipline will be reviewed in detail in another chapter, and will only tangentially be addressed as it relates to the student rights addressed in this chapter.

A. THE RIGHT TO EDUCATION AND THE DUTY TO ATTEND

It is a common misconception that the *Constitution Act, 1867*[2] and/or the *Charter* provide a right to publicly funded education for elementary and secondary aged children and youth.[3] While section 93 of the *Constitution Act,*

---

1   *Canadian Charter of Rights and Freedoms*, Part I of the *Constitution Act, 1982*, being Schedule B to the *Canada Act 1982* (UK), 1982, c 11 [*Charter*].
2   *Constitution Act, 1867* (UK), 30 & 31 Vict, c 3, reprinted in RSC 1985, App II, No 5.
3   *Adler v Ontario*, [1996] 3 SCR 609 at para 47.

1867[4] identifies that education is a matter under the exclusive jurisdiction of the provinces of Canada, it does not provide a guarantee that education will be provided without fees or even provided at all.[5]

Each province has established a publicly funded education system that is outlined in provincial legislation. Legislation across Canada provides for compulsory, publicly funded education with attendance requirements from the age of five or six to either the age of sixteen or eighteen. In New Brunswick,[6] the *Education Act* at subsection 8(1) provides that, "Subject to subsection (2) the Minister shall provide free school privileges under this Act for every person who is of school age and who (a) has not graduated from high school, and (b) is a resident of the Province." Compulsory attendance is provided for in subsection 15(1):

> Except as provided in section 16 and subject to subsection (2), a child is required to attend school in the school in which the child is placed by the superintendent concerned under section 11 (a) beginning on the first school day of a given school year if, on or before the thirty-first day of December of that school year, the child will have attained the age of five years, and (b) until the child graduates from high school or attains the age of eighteen years.[7]

Failure by a parent to require the attendance of their child, where he or she is not excused, may lead to a provincial offence.[8]

In Ontario, a student is excused from compulsory attendance where he or she is provided with an alternative educational program.[9] Compulsory attendance in Ontario extends to the age of eighteen, and begins at the age of six,[10] unless the student is registered and attending full day kindergarten, in which case the duty begins at the age of four.[11] However, parents do not have to register children for kindergarten.[12] Therefore, the duty of attendance once they are registered seems hollow since the parent

---

4   *Constitution Act, 1867*, above note 2.
5   *Ibid*, s 93, which states that "in and for each Province the Legislature may exclusively make Laws in relation to Education . . . ."
6   *Education Act*, SNB 1997, c E-1.12, s 8(1).
7   *Ibid*, s 15(1).
8   *Ibid*, s 15(7).
9   *Ibid*, s 21(2).
10 *Education Act*, RSO 1990, c E.2, s 21(2) [Ontario *Education Act*].
11 *Ibid*, s 21(4).
12 *Ibid*.

can withdraw the child from school and wait until the age of six to register their child again.[13]

These rights and duties with respect to the provision of education for children and youth are consistent with the United Nations *Convention on the Rights of the Child*, which provides at Article 28 that:

> 1. States Parties recognize the right of the child to education, and with a view to achieving this right progressively and on the basis of equal opportunity, they shall, in particular:
> (a) Make primary education compulsory and available free to all;
> (b) Encourage the development of different forms of secondary education, including general and vocational education, make them available and accessible to every child, and take appropriate measures such as the introduction of free education and offering financial assistance in the case of need.[14]

The compulsory attendance provisions as set out in the legislation in Alberta were the subject of a *Charter* challenge in 1986 in *R v Jones*.[15] Mr Jones was charged with three counts of truancy subject to subsection 180(1) of the *Alberta School Act*[16] with respect to each of his three children. He eventually appealed his charges to the Supreme Court of Canada on the grounds that the compulsory attendance provisions in the Act were contrary to his right to freedom of religion and the principles of fundamental justice, as guaranteed by the *Charter*.[17]

The compulsory attendance provisions in the Act provided exception for those children attending a private school approved by the Department of Education. Mr Jones operated a private school, educating approximately twenty students, including his own children. However, he argued that it was contrary to his religious beliefs to apply for approval of his private school "because . . . requesting the state for permission to do what he is authorized by God to do would, he asserts, violate his religious convictions."[18] The constitutional question stated for the Court was whether the compulsory attendance provisions and the private school approval process was contrary to subsection 2(a) (freedom of religion) or section 7 (security of the person) of the *Charter*.

---

13 *Ibid*, s 1(1).
14 *Convention on the Rights of the Child*, 20 November 1989, 1577 UNTS 3, art 28.
15 [1986] 2 SCR 284 [*Jones*].
16 *Alberta School Act*, RSA 1980, c S-3 [now RSA 2000, c S-3].
17 *Charter*, above note 1.
18 *Jones*, above note 15 at 291.

The appellant argued that the registration and certification process outlined in the legislation would require him to acknowledge that the government, and not God, had the "final authority over the education of his children,"[19] and, as such, compliance would be contrary to his religious beliefs. The Court held that the compulsory attendance requirements could not be administered by provincial authorities "in a manner that unreasonably infringes on the right of parents to teach their children in accordance with their religious convictions. The interference must be demonstrably justified."[20] The Court found that the requirements for certification required by the legislation provided a minimal intrusion on religion, stating:

> No proof is required to show the importance of education in our society or its significance to government. The legitimate, indeed compelling, interest of the state in education of the young is known and understood by all informed citizens. Nor is evidence necessary to establish the difficulty of administering a general provincial educational scheme if the onus lies on the educational authorities to enforce compliance. The obvious way to administer it is by requiring those who seek exemptions from the general scheme to make application for the purpose. Such a requirement constitutes a reasonable limit on a parent's religious convictions concerning the upbringing of his or her children.[21]

The Supreme Court also rejected the appellant's argument that the compliance provisions deprived him of his liberty. The Court found that the provisions did not violate the principles of fundamental justice, despite the fact that the sanction was not adjudicated by a court.[22]

Thus, while students do not have a constitutionally protected right to education, the Supreme Court has upheld the notion of the compulsory provision of education as being "a compelling interest" of the state.[23] As such, there is significant protection provided to the provision of publicly funded elementary and secondary education.

---

19   *Ibid* at 295.
20   *Ibid* at 298.
21   *Ibid* at 299–300.
22   *Ibid* at 308.
23   *Ibid* at 299.

B. THE RIGHT TO FRENCH LANGUAGE EDUCATION

The right and obligation to attend school in Canada includes the right to attend a school taught in either English or French, depending upon the background of the rights holder and the number of students exercising the same right. In Ontario, French language minority rights holders can attend either public French language schools or Catholic French language schools, both operated by their respective school boards.[24] The *Charter*, at section 23, identifies the rights of minority language students as follows:

23(1) Citizen of Canada
(a) whose first language learned and still understood is that of the English or French linguistic minority population of the province in which they reside, or
(b) who have received their primary school instruction in Canada in English or French and reside in a province where the language in which they received that instruction is the language of the English or French linguistic minority population of the province, have the right to have their children receive primary and secondary school instruction in that language in that province.

(2) Citizens of Canada of whom any child has received or is receiving primary or secondary school instruction in English or French in Canada have the right to have all their children receive primary and secondary school instruction in the same language.

(3) The right of citizens of Canada under subsections (1) and (2) to have their children receive primary and secondary school instruction in the language of the English or French linguistic minority population of a province
(a) applies wherever in the province the number of children of citizens who have such a right is sufficient to warrant the provision to them out of public funds of minority language instruction; and
(b) includes, where the number of those children so warrants, the right to have them receive that instruction in minority language educational facilities provided out of public funds.

The responsibility to establish a school because numbers warrant has been the subject of many appeals to the Supreme Court of Canada.

---

24   Ontario *Education Act*, above note 10, s 33 [elementary school students] and s 36 [secondary school students].

In *Arsenault-Cameron v Prince Edward Island*,[25] the Minister of Education denied the request of French language rights holders to have an elementary school program provided in their community of Summerside. The minister accepted that the number of students who were rights holders as per section 23 warranted instruction in French; however, the minister did not agree that instruction should be provided in Summerside. Instead, the minister thought that the students should be transported to another community that was within the average travel time for students across the province. The Supreme Court indicated that in order to receive an equivalent education, section 23 rights holders had to be treated differently than the majority.[26] The Court identified the primary issue as whether or not the French language school board had the power to determine the location of French language minority schools for rights holders.[27]

The Supreme Court indicated that a purposive reading of section 23 of the *Charter*[28] means that provinces are required to redress past injustices to official minority language rights holders by providing them with access to education in their own language "in circumstances where community development will be enhanced."[29]

The Minister of Education in the *Arsenault-Cameron* case did not place value on the location of the facility where student rights holders would attend school, testifying that students were transported all over the province to access educational services. The key issue for the minister was the quality of the programming that might be provided. In the minister's opinion, the fact that there were a number of French language cultural institutions in Summerside confirmed that a school was not necessary for the French language and culture to flourish there. The Supreme Court disagreed with the minister's approach and stated:

---

25 [2000] 1 SCR 3 [*Arsenault-Cameron*].

26 With respect to the duration of bus rides, s 23 *Charter* rights-holders would be comparing the duration between attendance at an English language school and a French language school, whereas English language students would have no other choice. Thus, s 23 rights-holders might be discouraged from attending a French language school if the bus ride was longer than the ride to an English language school, even if the bus ride to the French language school was consistent with provincial averages. The ability of students to participate in activities in their community would also be impacted by the length of the bus ride for s 23 rights-holders.

27 *Ibid* at 11.

28 Above note 1.

29 *Arsenault-Cameron*, above note 25 at 25.

In fact, the existence of French cultural institutions in Summerside highlights the incongruity of the absence of a school and cannot be used to support the argument proposed by the minister. The expert evidence of Ms Angeline Martel, supported by all other witnesses for the appellants, indicates that the school is the single most important institution for the survival of the official language minority, which is itself a true beneficiary under section 23.[30]

The Supreme Court of Canada in *Mahe v Alberta*[31] identified that there should be two considerations for the provision of education in a community for section 23 rights holders: the number of students who would be attending and the costs associated with the provision of education. The way in which the Court should determine the number of students who will potentially take advantage of their section 23 rights was outlined in *Mahe* as an estimate between the total number of rights holders in the community and the number who are known to be demanding the provision of services.[32]

In the *Arsenault-Cameron* case, the Ministry of Education had not calculated an estimate of the potential number of students who might take advantage of French language education; thus, the Court did not permit the government to dispute the numbers that were determined by the appellant's expert. The minimum threshold required by the provincial regulations was met according to the appellant's expert.[33]

The Court did not accept the minister's testimony that pedagogically the existing number of students was not sufficient. The Court held that if the number of students were not pedagogically sufficient, the regulation should not have included that number as its threshold for the provision of instruction.[34] Thus, the appellants satisfied the first factor of the analysis. The Ministry of Education had consistently indicated that cost was not at issue; as such, the Court found that the second step in the analysis outlined in *Mahe* was not necessary.[35]

The management and control of instruction and facilities for section 23 rights holders was considered to be critically important by the Supreme Court in *Mahe*.

---

30   *Ibid* at 29.

31   [1990] 1 SCR 342 [*Mahe*].

32   As reviewed in *Arsenault-Cameron*, above note 25 at 28.

33   *Ibid* at 29.

34   *Ibid* at 26–28.

35   *Ibid*.

First, they are essential to the preservation and enhancement of minority language education and culture . . . management and control are necessary "because a variety of management issues in education, e.g., curricula, hiring and expenditures, can affect linguistic and cultural concerns". Second, the right to management and control furthers the remedial goals of s. 23. Empowerment is essential to correct past injustices and to guarantee that the specific needs of the minority language community are the first consideration in any given decision affecting language and cultural concerns.[36]

Prince Edward Island had a provincial school board representing French language rights holders (the "Board"). Thus, in accordance with the principles articulated by the Supreme Court in *Mahe*, the Supreme Court found that the minister's decision not to offer French language education in Summerside was unconstitutional because the minister did not have the discretion to substitute his decision for the Board, which had met the necessary provincial requirements, and thus should have the right to management and control of the instruction and the facilities to meet the needs of section 23 rights holders.[37]

C. DENOMINATIONAL SCHOOLS

Funding for linguistic minorities is not the only constitutional student right that exists with respect to educational funding. As identified above, section 93 of the *Constitution Act*, 1867 provided the provinces with jurisdiction over education. Section 93 also ensures minority rights in education, stating:

> In and for each Province the Legislature may exclusively make Laws in relation to Education, subject and according to the following Provisions:
> (1) Nothing in any such Law shall prejudicially affect any Right or Privilege with respect to Denominational Schools which any Class of Persons have by Law in the Province at the Union:
> (2) All the Powers, Privileges, and Duties at the Union by Law conferred and imposed in Upper Canada on the Separate Schools and School Trustees of the Queen's Roman Catholic Subjects shall be and the same are hereby extended to the Dissentient Schools of the Queen's Protestant and Roman Catholic Subjects in Quebec:

---

36 *Ibid at* 34–35.

37 *Ibid at* 42.

(3) Where in any Province a System of Separate or Dissentient Schools exists by Law at the Union or is thereafter established by the Legislature of the Province, an Appeal shall lie to the Governor General in Council from any Act or Decision of any Provincial Authority affecting any Right or Privilege of the Protestant or Roman Catholic Minority of the Queen's Subjects in relation to Education:

(4) In case any such Provincial Law as from Time to Time seems to the Governor General in Council requisite for the due Execution of the Provisions of this Section is not made, or in case any Decision of the Governor General in Council on any Appeal under this Section is not duly executed by the proper Provincial Authority in that Behalf, then and in every such Case, and as far only as the Circumstances of each Case require, the Parliament of Canada may make remedial Laws for the due Execution of the Provisions of this Section and of any Decision of the Governor General in Council under this Section.[38]

The *Constitution Act* provisions were a compromise at Confederation to ensure that minority religious education rights would be respected.

The protection afforded to minority denominational rights holders continues in Ontario, but not in Québec. The constitutional protection for Protestant rights holders in Québec was eliminated with the creation of linguistic school boards in 1993.[39] In Ontario, however, legislation in 1986 expanded the provision of public funding for Catholic schools to include grades 11, 12, and 13 (grade 13 has since been eliminated from the Ontario curriculum). This extension of public funding to Catholic secondary schools was challenged in the *Bill 30 Reference*[40] on the basis that it was contrary to the equality rights guaranteed by subsection 15(1) of the *Charter* and also violated the right to freedom of religion in subsection 2(a) of the *Charter*. It was argued that these rights were not saved by section 29 of the *Charter* because only rights under the *Constitution* itself were subject to section 29.[41]

During the *Bill 30 Reference*, the Court reviewed the background to the *Constitution Act* provisions and stated:

The protection of minority religious rights was a major preoccupation during the negotiations leading to Confederation because of the perceived

---

38 *Constitution Act, 1867*, above note 2, s 93.
39 *Reference re Education Act (Quebec)*, [1993] 2 SCR 511.
40 *Reference re Bill 30, An Act to Amend the Education Act (Ontario)*, [1987] 1 SCR 1148 [*Bill 30 Reference*].
41 *Ibid.*

danger of leaving the religious minorities in both Canada East and Canada West at the mercy of overwhelming majorities. Given the importance of denominational educational rights at the time of Confederation, it seems unbelievable that the draftsmen of the section would not have made provision for future legislation conferring rights and privileges on religious minorities in response to new conditions.[42]

Those who opposed the legislative extension of funding argued that it was contrary to subsection 15(1)[43] and subsection 2(a)[44] of the *Charter* "in that it provided full funding for Roman Catholic secondary schools but not for other secondary schools, denominational or non-denominational, in the province."[45] The Supreme Court held that section 29 of the *Charter*, which provides that "Nothing in this *Charter* abrogates or derogates from any rights or privileges guaranteed by or under the Constitution of Canada in respect of denominational, separate or dissentient schools"[46] meant that the rights and privileges protected by subsection 93(1) were not subject to *Charter* review.[47]

The Supreme Court of Canada held that subsection 93(3) of the *Constitution Act* did not limit the right of provinces to augment the rights of denominational school supporters,[48] and that Bill 30 was "a valid exercise of the provincial power to add to the rights and privileges of Roman Catholic separate school supporters under the combined effect of the opening words of s. 93 and s. 93(3) of the *Constitution Act, 1867*."[49]

However, the Court also stated that section 29 of the *Charter* was not necessary to provide protection to rights holders. The Court stated:

> What is less clear is whether s.29 of the *Charter* was required in order to achieve that result. In my view, it was not. I believe it was put there simply to emphasize that the special treatment guaranteed by the consti-

---

42 *Ibid* at para 27.

43 The *Charter*, above note 1, provides: "Every individual is equal before and under the law and has the right to the equal protection and equal benefit of the law without discrimination and, in particular, without discrimination based on race, national or ethnic origin, colour, religion, sex, *age* or mental or physical disability" [emphasis added].

44 Section 2(a) of the *Charter*, *ibid*, states: "Everyone has the following fundamental freedoms: (a) freedom of conscience and religion."

45 *Bill 30 Reference*, above note 40 at para 78.

46 *Charter*, above note 1, s 29.

47 *Bill 30*, above note 40 at para 81.

48 *Ibid* at para 21.

49 *Ibid* at para 29.

tution to denominational, separate or dissentient schools, even if it sits uncomfortably with the concept of equality embodied in the *Charter* because it is not available to other schools, is nevertheless not impaired by the *Charter*. It was never intended, in my opinion, that the *Charter* could be used to invalidate other provisions of the Constitution, particularly a provision such as s.93 which represented a fundamental part of the Confederation compromise. Section 29, in my view, is present in the *Charter* only for greater certainty, at least in so far as the Province of Ontario is concerned.[50]

The extension of public funding for grades 11, 12, and 13 came with the caveat that Catholic secondary schools would have open access. Thus, while Catholic elementary schools are restricted to Catholic rights holders, any resident may attend a Catholic secondary school within the appropriate jurisdiction.[51]

D. THE RIGHT TO RELIGIOUS FREEDOM

Legal challenges to educational funding based on religion and equality have also been brought by other groups in Ontario. In 1996, the Supreme Court of Canada heard an appeal arguing that "the current education funding scheme in the province of Ontario violates the appellants' religious and equality rights as guaranteed by ss. 2(a) and 15 of the *Canadian Charter of Rights and Freedoms*."[52]

In *Adler v Ontario*, one of the appellants sought funding for Jewish day schools and the other appellant, the Elgersma family, sought funding for independent Christian day schools. The Supreme Court of Canada summarized their arguments as follows:

> The appellants advance, in essence, two *Charter* arguments. The first is that s. 2(a)'s guarantee of freedom of religion requires the province of Ontario to provide public funding for independent religious schools. The second is that, by funding Roman Catholic separate schools and secular public schools at the same time as it denies funding to independent religious schools, the province is discriminating against the appellants on the basis of religion contrary to s. 15(1).[53]

---

50 *Ibid* at para 63.
51 Ontario *Education Act*, above note 10 at s 42(13).
52 *Adler*, above note 3 at para 1.
53 *Ibid* at para 26.

The Court found that Ontario could choose to extend funding to both Jewish and Christian day schools, but that section 2(a) did not create a positive obligation on the Province to do so. The Court stated:

> However, an *ability* to pass such legislation does not amount to an obligation to do so. To emphasize, s. 93 defines the extent of the obligations of the province to set up and fund denominational schools when public schools are established. In this respect it is a comprehensive code thereby excluding a different or broader obligation regarding denominational schools, while not restricting the plenary power of the province to establish and fund such other schools as it may decide.[54]

The Supreme Court held that the funding of public schools and the decision not to fund private religious schools was "immune from *Charter* attack and therefore does not violate s. 15(1) of the *Charter*."[55] Thus, the funding of Catholic schools is guaranteed by the Constitution, but the funding of other denominational schools in Ontario is a political decision. Ontario has chosen not to fund other private religious schools.

The review by the courts of the religious rights of students has not been limited to funding for denominational schools. The expression of one's religion while attending school is also a right that students in Canada have sought. In both Ontario and Québec, students of the Orthodox Sikh creed sought the right to wear metal-bladed kirpans (ceremonial daggers) while attending school, despite a ban for safety reasons.[56]

In Ontario, a student of the Peel District School Board through his father, Harbhajan Singh Pandori, appealed the board decision prohibiting the wearing of kirpans by anyone in a school building.[57] The policy of the board was found to be contrary to the *Human Rights Code*[58] of Ontario by a board of inquiry. The Peel Board appealed the decision to the Divisional Court, and in 1991, the Divisional Court upheld the decision of the Board of Inquiry and leave to appeal to the Court of Appeal was denied. The Board of Inquiry found that there was a lack of kirpan-related incidents of violence to support a ban, and that accommodation of the kirpan was

---

54   *Ibid* at para 48 [emphasis in original].
55   *Ibid* at para 50.
56   *Peel Board of Education v Ontario Human Rights Commission*, 1991 CanLII 7356 (Ont Div Ct) [*Peel Board*]; *Multani v Commission scolaire Marguerite-Bourgeoys*, [2006] 1 SCR 256 [*Multani*].
57   *Peel Board*, above note 56.
58   RSO 1990, c H.19.

possible by ensuring that it was worn under the individual's clothing and safely secured so as not be easily removed.[59]

The Supreme Court of Canada in 2006 heard a similar case pursuant to section 2(a) of the *Charter*.[60] The school board's council of commissioners prohibited a student from wearing a kirpan to school as required by his religion. The Court was asked to determine whether or not the refusal was a breach of the student's freedom of religion.[61]

The issue came to the attention of the council of commissioners when Gurbaj Singh accidentally dropped his kirpan. As a result, the governing body of the school decided to prohibit all students from carrying kirpans on the basis that to do so was contrary to the Code of Conduct which prohibited students from carrying weapons and dangerous objects while at school.[62] The Supreme Court of Canada found that the student's refusal to wear a symbolic kirpan made of a material other than metal, thus rendering the kirpan harmless, was based on the student's sincerely-held religious convictions. In fact, as a result of the school board's refusal to allow the student to carry his kirpan, the student registered and began attending a private school. Thus, the school board's refusal deprived the student of his right to attend a publicly funded school.[63]

The Supreme Court of Canada found that the student's right to religious freedom was breached by the school board. On an analysis pursuant to section 1 of the *Charter*,[64] the respondent school board tried to demonstrate that the objective being pursued by the school board was "sufficiently important to warrant limiting a constitutional right,"[65] and that the school board's method of pursuing its objective was "proportional to the objective in question."[66]

The objective of student and staff safety in schools was determined by the Court to be a sufficient, pressing, and substantial objective to "warrant overriding a constitutionally protected right or freedom."[67] The Court

59 *Peel Board*, above note 56.
60 *Charter*, above note 1.
61 *Multani*, above note 56 at 265.
62 *Ibid* at 266.
63 *Ibid* at 282.
64 Section 1 of the *Charter*, above note 1, states: "The *Canadian Charter of Rights and Freedoms* guarantees the rights and freedoms set out in it subject only to such reasonable limits prescribed by law as can be demonstrably justified in a free and democratic society."
65 *Multani*, above note 56 at 282.
66 *Ibid*.
67 *Ibid* at 283.

commented that the minimal impairment test at section 1 of the *Charter* did not require the impairment to be the least intrusive option,[68] but the Court questioned whether or not the absolute prohibition of wearing kirpans was within a "range of reasonable alternatives"[69] open to the school board to address their concerns.

The school board argued that "to allow the kirpan to be worn to school entails the risks that it could be used for violent purposes by the person wearing it or by another student who takes it away from him, that it could lead to a proliferation of weapons at the school, and that its presence could have a negative impact on the school environment."[70] The school board also argued "the presence of kirpans in schools will contribute to a poisoning of the school environment." They maintained that the kirpan is a symbol of violence and that it sends the message that using force is the way to assert rights and resolve conflict, compromises the perception of safety in schools, and establishes a double standard.[71]

The Supreme Court did not consider the evidence supportive of the school board's arguments that the kirpan was a symbol of violence and that it would poison the school environment. The Supreme Court found that these arguments failed to respect the Sikh religion and the tradition of multiculturalism in Canada.[72] Moreover, the Court stated:

> Religious tolerance is a very important value of Canadian society. If some students consider it unfair that Gurbaj Singh may wear his kirpan to school while they are not allowed to have knives in their possession, it is incumbent on the schools to discharge their obligation to instill in their students this value that is . . . at the very foundation of our democracy.[73]

The Court found that there had not been a single violent incident reported involving a kirpan in a school in the 100 years that Sikh students had been attending Canadian schools. It followed that the risk that such an incident would occur was very low.[74] Thus, the Court held that the absolute prohibition of all kirpans was not proportional to the objective of safety. "An absolute prohibition would stifle the promotion of values such as

---

68   *Ibid* at 285.
69   *Ibid.*
70   *Ibid* at 287.
71   *Ibid.*
72   *Ibid* at 297.
73   *Ibid* at 296.
74   *Ibid* at 288.

multiculturalism, diversity, and the development of an educational culture respectful of the rights of others."[75] The decision prohibiting the student from wearing his kirpan was declared null, and the Supreme Court of Canada imposed the conditions of wearing the kirpan in school that were outlined by the court at first instance.[76]

E. *LOYOLA HIGH SCHOOL v QUEBEC (ATTORNEY GENERAL)*

In a recent decision, *Loyola High School v Quebec (Attorney General)*,[77] the Supreme Court of Canada considered the religious freedom of a private Catholic boys' school in Québec, Loyola, to teach a course prescribed by the Ministry of Education in a manner consistent with its Catholic identity and purpose.

The Ministry of Education in Québec required all schools, publicly and privately funded, to teach a course called Ethics, Religion, and Culture (ERC course). This course was intended to be taught from a neutral, cultural perspective, which Loyola considered contrary to its identity and purpose as a Catholic school. While the ministry permitted private schools to seek an exemption from teaching the course if they taught an equivalent course, it denied the exemption to the course proposed by Loyola on the ground that it was faith-based and therefore, not an equivalent course.

The first issue that was addressed by the Supreme Court of Canada was whether Loyola, as a school, could have a right to religious freedom. The Court found that the members of its community, which would arguably

---

75 *Ibid* at 296–97.
76 *Ibid* at 298. The court of first instance set the following conditions for wearing a kirpan at school: the kirpan must be worn under the student's clothes; the kirpan must be carried in a sheath made of wood, not metal, to prevent it from causing injury; the kirpan must be placed in its sheath and wrapped and sewn securely in a sturdy cloth envelope, and that this envelope be sewn to the *guthra*; school personnel must be authorized to verify, in a reasonable fashion, that these conditions were being complied with; the student must be required to keep the kirpan in his possession at all times, and its disappearance must be reported to school authorities immediately; and in the event that there is a failure to comply with the conditions set, the student would lose the right to wear the kirpan at school.
77 2015 SCC 12 [*Loyola*].

include its student community, had a right to freedom of religion, which would be expressed through their decision to attend Loyola.[78]

Loyola argued that it should be permitted to teach the portions of the course regarding the ethics of Catholicism and other religious traditions and Catholic doctrine from a Catholic perspective, not a neutral, cultural perspective. The minister maintained that this would not satisfy the purpose of the course, and that teaching from any religious perspective, including a religious institution teaching its religion from its perspective, could not be equivalent to the ministry's course. The Supreme Court held that:

> . . . prescribing to Loyola how it is to explain Catholicism to its students seriously interferes with freedom of religion, while representing no significant benefit to the ERC Program's objectives. In a context like Quebec's, where private denominational schools are legal, this represents a disproportionate, and therefore unreasonable interference with the values underlying freedom of religion of those individuals who seek to offer and who wish to receive a Catholic education at Loyola. On the other hand, I see no significant impairment of freedom of religion in requiring Loyola to offer a course that explains the beliefs, ethics and practices of other religions in as objective and neutral a way as possible rather than from the Catholic perspective.[79]

The minority of the Court would have permitted Loyola to teach the course as proposed. The majority of the Court remitted the matter back to the minister for reconsideration.

F. THE RIGHT TO FREEDOM OF EXPRESSION

A student's right to freedom of expression, while inherent and essential in the educational process, has seldom been tested in Canada. Its parameters

---

78 *Ibid.* The Supreme Court of Canada, in a prior decision *SL v Commission Scolaire des Chênes*, 2012 SCC 7, denied the appeal of Catholic parents of children attending a publicly funded school that was required to teach the ERC course who argued that their children should be exempt from the course, as it was contrary to their religious beliefs. They argued that it was their responsibility to pass on the tenets of the Catholic religion and that the ERC course was contrary to their observance of the Catholic faith. The Court found that the parents were not able to demonstrate that their religious rights were infringed by having their children taught the ERC course.

79 *Loyola*, above note 77 at para 6.

have been reviewed by courts in the United States with respect to discipline, and it is from these decisions that some Canadian school boards responsible for elementary and secondary schools inform their policies and procedures regarding acceptable communication.[80] The leading case in the US is *Tinker v Des Moines Independent Community School District*,[81] decided by the United States Supreme Court in 1969. The students in this case were suspended from school for wearing black armbands as a way to protest the Vietnam War. The Supreme Court found that the decision of the school to ban the wearing of armbands was contrary to the students' right to freedom of speech. The Court held that, "First Amendment rights, applied in light of the special characteristics of the school environment, are available to teachers and students. It can hardly be argued that either students or teachers shed their constitutional rights to freedom of speech or expression at the schoolhouse gate."[82]

The United States Supreme Court found that the action of wearing armbands to protest the war was a "silent, passive expression of opinion, unaccompanied by any disorder or disturbance."[83] There was no evidence that the students' actions interfered with the educational programming at their school; as such, the Court found that there were insufficient grounds to prohibit students from wearing the armbands. The Court held that:

> A student's rights therefore, do not embrace merely the classroom hours. When he is in the cafeteria, or on the playing field, or on the campus during the authorized hours, he may express his opinions, even on controversial subjects like the conflict in Vietnam, if he does so without 'materially and substantially colliding with the rights of others [*Burnside v Byars*, at 749]. But conduct by the student in class or out of it, which for any reason — whether it stems from time, place or type of behavior — materially disrupts classwork or involves substantial disorder or invasion of

---

80 Hurtful, harmful, and sometimes illegal communication off-school grounds utilizing technology has become a significant issue for Canadian elementary and secondary schools. Whether students are communicating about teachers, administrators, or students, this form of communication, called cyberbullying and cyberaggression, can have devastating effects on the target or victim of the communication. This form of expression shall not be addressed explicitly in this chapter, but is reviewed in the chapter regarding student discipline.

81 393 US 503 (1969) [*Tinker*].

82 *Ibid* at 506.

83 *Ibid* at 509.

the rights of others is, of course, not immunized by the constitutional guarantee of freedom of speech."[84]

The United States Supreme Court's creation of the standard of "material disruption and/or substantial disorder" before a student's right to free speech may be suspended has been used in several cases, including some involving cyberbullying.[85] However, the United States Supreme Court has distinguished the treatment of student speech in protest from that which is related to school-sanctioned events or programming.

G. BETHEL SCHOOL DISTRICT NO 403 v FRASER (NO 84-1667)

In *Bethel School District No 403 v Fraser (No 84-1667)*,[86] Fraser, a secondary school student, gave a sexually explicit and graphic speech to an assembly of six hundred grade nine students. The purpose of the speech was for nominating a fellow student for student government, which was a school-sponsored educational activity. The students in attendance were required to attend the assembly or another school activity. Fraser's speech had been reviewed by two teachers, both of whom warned him that it was inappropriate and would likely lead to disciplinary consequences if spoken. Students, hearing the speech by Fraser, responded in a variety of ways, including being shocked and confused. As a result of the speech, Fraser was suspended for three days and prohibited from competing for Valedictorian. He appealed his suspension up to the US Supreme Court, alleging that his First Amendment right to free speech had been violated as a result of the discipline imposed.[87]

The United States Supreme Court distinguished between the free speech accorded to adults and that which is permissible to students performing educational activities. The Court noted that educators, acting *in loco parentis*, needed to be able to protect students, who are a captive audience, while attending school.[88] The Court held that:

> ... the School District acted entirely within its permissible authority in imposing sanctions upon Fraser in response to his offensively led and indecent speech. Unlike the sanctions imposed on the students wearing

---

84   *Ibid* at 512–13.

85   See Chapter 8 for a fulsome review of cyberbullying issues.

86   478 US 675 (1986).

87   *Ibid*.

88   *Ibid* at 684.

armbands in *Tinker*, the penalties imposed in this case were unrelated to any political viewpoint. The First Amendment does not prevent the school officials from determining that to permit a vulgar and lewd speech such as [the] respondent's would undermine the school's basic educational mission. A high school assembly or classroom is no place for a sexually explicit monologue directed towards an unsuspecting audience of teenage students. Accordingly, it was perfectly appropriate for the school to disassociate itself to make the point to the pupils that vulgar speech and lewd conduct is wholly inconsistent with the "fundamental values" of public school education.[89]

While there may have been grounds to argue that the speech caused disruption to the educational purpose of the assembly and offended the rights of others, the United States Supreme Court chose to review the actions from the perspective of school-sanctioned programming and to distinguish the approach from the decision in *Tinker*.

H. *HAZELWOOD SCHOOL DISTRICT v KUHLMEIER*

Another important case, *Hazelwood School District v Kuhlmeier*,[90] reviewed the First Amendment rights of students as they applied to a school newspaper that formed part of a journalism course. The process for publishing the school newspaper involved the requirement that a draft version of the paper be reviewed and approved by the school principal. In the instant case, there were two articles that the principal identified as inappropriate. The first article was unacceptable with respect to the risk that it would identify students who had provided information on a confidential basis and because the content might not be suitable for the school's youngest students and the younger siblings of students attending the school. The second article was determined by the principal to be inappropriate because it was critical of a student's father, who did not have an opportunity to defend his actions. Because there were two articles that were not acceptable, the principal required two pages from the newspaper to be removed in order to have the paper printed and distributed within the deadline.[91]

The United States Supreme Court held that the issue in *Tinker*, which was related to non-sanctioned student speech, needed to be distinguished

---

89   *Ibid* at 685–86.
90   484 US 260 (1988) [*Hazelwood*].
91   *Ibid*.

from circumstances in which the speech was related to school curriculum activities. The Court held that:

> Educators are entitled to exercise greater control over this second form of student expression to assure that participants learn whatever lessons the activity is designed to teach, that readers or listeners are not exposed to material that may be inappropriate for their level of maturity, and that the views of the individual speaker are not erroneously attributed to the school.[92]
>
> . . . Accordingly, we conclude that the standard articulated in *Tinker* for determining when a school may punish student expression need not also be the standard for determining when a school may refuse to lend its name and resources to the dissemination of student expression. Instead we hold that educators do not offend the First Amendment by exercising editorial control over the style and content of student speech in school-sponsored expressive activities, so long as their actions are reasonably related to legitimate pedagogical concerns. . . . It is only when the decision to censor a school-sponsored publication, theatrical production, or other vehicle of student expression has no valid educational purpose that the First Amendment is so "directly and sharply implicate[d]" as to require judicial intervention to protect students' constitutional rights.[93]

The Court found the principal's decision to have the two pages containing the offending stories removed to be appropriate given the timeframes for publication. Alternatively, had there been sufficient time, the principal could have required amendments to be made to the articles to make them more suitable to their audience as well as to address the privacy concerns and the failure to have a subject of one of the articles given an opportunity to respond to the allegations about him included in the article.

I.   *LUTES (LITIGATION GUARDIAN OF) v PRAIRIE VIEW SCHOOL DIVISION NO 74*

In Canada, elementary and secondary educators have had few cases to guide their decisions regarding the right of students to freedom of expression. A case heard by the Saskatchewan Court of Queen's Bench, *Lutes (Litigation Guardian of) v Prairie View School Division No 74*,[94] unfortunately

---

92   *Ibid* at 271.
93   *Ibid* at 272–73.
94   1992 CanLII 7997 (Sask QB).

provides no guidance to educators with respect to the factors that might be considered by a court when school discipline has violated a student's right to freedom of expression and the court is conducting a section 1 *Charter* analysis. Chris Lutes, a student of Milestone High School in the Prairie View School District, sang the song "Let's Talk About Sex" while he passed the assistant director of education on the sidewalk during the school's lunch break. Chris was disciplined for singing a "banned song" and being rude and disrespectful to the assistant director. The discipline imposed was a month of lunchtime detentions and the reason given for the detention was, in part, for singing an "inappropriate song." But the lyrics of the song were in fact about safe sex.[95]

The Saskatchewan Court, on a motion for an interim injunction, held that Chris's section 2(b) *Charter* right to freedom of expression was breached when he was disciplined and that the discipline could not be upheld by section 1 of the *Charter* because the decision to discipline Chris was based on an "overreaction to an inoffensive song that carried a powerful message."[96] The court did not identify when or under what circumstances imposing discipline contrary to a student's section 2(b) *Charter* right to freedom of expression might be saved by section 1 of the *Charter*.

J. *PRIDGEN v UNIVERSITY OF CALGARY*

In Canada, there has been a decision at the post-secondary level with respect to off-campus communication leading to discipline,[97] which also assists in identifying protected expression at the elementary and secondary level. The Alberta Court of Appeal decision in *Pridgen v University of Calgary*,[98] regarding two university students, provides educators with some insight as to how a Canadian court might apply a student's *Charter* right to freedom of expression in an elementary or secondary school context.

Keith and Steven Pridgen were students at the University of Calgary, and were enrolled in a course called Law and Society (LWSO). Their professor, Aruna Mitra, was teaching the course for the first time, and in their opinion, as well as that of other students, she did not do a particularly good job. One of the students in the course created a Facebook page called

---

95   *Ibid.*
96   *Ibid* at para 30.
97   *Pridgen v University of Calgary*, 2012 ABCA 139 [*Pridgen*].
98   *Ibid.*

"I no longer fear hell, I took a course with Aruna Mitra."[99] The Pridgens and others joined the Facebook group and made postings.[100]

Steven Pridgen posted the comment: "Some how I think she just got lazy and gave everybody a 65 . . . that's what I got. does anybody know how to apply to have it remarked?"[101] Much later in the year, Keith Pridgen posted the following:

> Hey fellow LWSO homees.
>
> So I am quite sure Mitra is NO LONGER TEACHING ANY COURSES WITH THE U OF C!!!!! Remember when she told us she was a long-term professor? Well actually she was only sessional and picked up our class at the last moment because another prof wasn't able to do it . . . lucky us. Well anyways I think we should all congratulate ourselves for leaving a Mitra-free legacy for future LWSO students![102]

Concerns about the content of the Facebook page were communicated to the university by Professor Mitra. The university proceeded on the basis that a complaint about non-academic misconduct had been made. As a result, both Keith and Steven were disciplined.

Keith Pridgen received twenty-four months of probation, a requirement that he write a letter of apology to Professor Mitra, and that he refrain from posting or circulating material about Professor Mitra or the university's faculty "that may be defamatory" or "unjustifiably bring the University of Calgary's and/or the Faculty of Communication and Culture into disrepute."[103] Steven was found guilty of non-academic misconduct on the basis that he was a member of the site, not as a result of the comment that he posted regarding his grade of 65 per cent. The discipline letter from the Dean stated in part: "You lent credence to this misconduct by your association with the site and the tacit concurrence with the tenor of its name."[104]

Steven, Keith, and other students who were disciplined as a result of their involvement with the site appealed the Dean's decision to the university's Review Committee. The committee upheld Keith's discipline but reduced the period of academic probation from twenty-four months to six months, and upheld Steven's discipline and imposed a further academic

---

99   *Ibid* at para 6.
100 *Ibid*.
101 *Ibid* at para 7.
102 *Ibid* at para 11.
103 *Ibid* at para 19.
104 *Ibid* at para 21.

probationary period of four months. Both Keith and Steven were denied an appeal to the university's Board of Governors and, therefore, sought judicial review of the university's decisions.[105]

The Court on Judicial Review found that the university had violated Keith and Steven's right of freedom of expression guaranteed by section 2(b) of the *Charter* when it imposed discipline. The court held that the violation of their right to freedom of expression was not saved by section 1 of the *Charter*. The university further appealed the decision to the Court of Appeal, which held:

> The chambers judge in this case considered whether the infringement of the Pridgens' freedom of expression was justifiable under section 1. She rightly noted that freedom of expression, while vitally important in a democratic society, is not an unqualified right. The University must be able to place reasonable limits on speech on campus in order, for example, to maintain a learning environment where there is respect and dignity for all. Criticism and debate are essential to ensuring the place of universities as centres for discussion.
>
> In this case, however, the chambers judge concluded that the critical opinions made by the students, although some were not particularly gracious, had utility in encouraging discussion and providing feedback to current and future students. The imposition of discipline in this case went beyond what was necessary to achieve the objective of the *Student Misconduct Policy* to maintain an appropriate learning environment.[106]

The decision in *Pridgen* supports a conclusion that elementary and secondary schools may impose disciplinary consequences for a student's expression to ensure a proper learning environment. This objective is broader than the limit on speech that "is inconsistent with the school's 'basic educational mission'"[107] as in *Hazelwood*, or "materially disrupts classwork or involves substantial disorder or invasion of the rights of others,"[108] as in *Tinker*. However, the limit imposed on the student's freedom of expression as identified in *Pridgen* must be proportional to the school's goals as set out in their discipline policy or Code of Conduct.

A determination of whether or not a limit to expression is proportional to the objective of the learning institution will depend on the circumstances, which would arguably include not only the specific expression and the limit

105 *Ibid*.
106 *Ibid* at paras 124–25.
107 *Hazelwood*, above note 90 at 266.
108 *Tinker*, above note 81.

to that expression, but also the impact that the expression might have on students and/or the learning environment. The Court of Appeal acknowledged a variety of considerations in determining whether a student's right to freedom of expression might be limited, specifically, "fostering an environment of open exchange of ideas, the prevention of incivility, intimidation, disrespect and fear, and the fostering of a safe environment to discuss and debate contemporary issues within and among a diverse student body."[109]

In elementary and secondary schools, arguably the objectives of the school can include teaching students to understand that the ways in which they express themselves have consequences, such that they learn the value of respectful communication and expression of ideas. Student codes of conduct can also aim to create a balance between the need for safe spaces for learning, teaching students about the value of freedom of expression and respecting that students have a right to express themselves.

K. THE RIGHT TO PRIVACY AT SCHOOL (SEARCH AND SEIZURE)

The *Charter* protects students from unreasonable search and seizure by school administrators. Section 8 of the *Charter* provides that: "Every person has the right to be secure against unreasonable search or seizure."[110] The issue of what constitutes a reasonable search was considered by the Supreme Court of Canada in *R v MRM*.[111]

MRM was a senior elementary student on his way to a school dance. Earlier in the day, the vice-principal of the school, who was also supervising the school dance, had been told by several students that MRM was planning to sell drugs during the dance. The students who had reported

---

109 *Pridgen*, above note 97 at para 127.
110 *Charter*, above note 1.
111 [1998] 3 SCR 393 [*MRM*]. In cases when a breach of s 8 of the *Charter*, above note 1, is found, s 24(2) of the *Charter* may be applied. It states: "Where, in proceedings under subjection (1), a court concludes that evidence was obtained in a manner that infringed or denied any rights or freedoms guaranteed by this *Charter*, the evidence shall be excluded if it is established that, having regard to all the circumstances, the admission of it in the proceedings would bring the administration of justice into disrepute."

this information to the vice-principal were, in his opinion, reliable sources of information.[112]

When the vice-principal saw MRM enter the school and proceed to the dance, he asked him to come to the office. The vice-principal also called the police. While a plain clothes officer was in the vice-principal's office with MRM, the vice-principal told MRM that he was suspected of being in possession of drugs and that the vice-principal was going to conduct a search. The vice-principal asked MRM to empty his pockets and unroll his socks while they were in the presence of the plain clothes police officer. The vice-principal saw that there was a bulge in MRM's sock and asked him to remove and turn over what was later confirmed by the police officer to be a cellophane bag containing marijuana. The marijuana was given over to the police. A search of the student's locker was also conducted, but there were no inappropriate items found.[113] The Supreme Court of Canada found that, despite the presence of a police officer, the officer was not involved in the search and the vice-principal was not acting as an agent of the police. Thus, the Supreme Court did analyze the student's rights on the basis that the search was conducted by the police.[114]

The application of the *Charter* to the vice-principal's search of MRM was not disputed by either party; however, it was argued by the Crown that the *Charter* analysis by the Supreme Court of Canada should consider the special circumstances in elementary and secondary schools. The Supreme Court identified that there was a difficult balance that had to be made between student rights and safety:

> The question presents potentially conflicting values and principles. On one hand, it is essential that school authorities be able to react swiftly and effectively when faced with a situation that could effectively disrupt the school environment or jeopardize the safety of the students . . . . Yet schools also have a duty to foster the respect of their students for the constitutional rights of all members of society. Learning respect for those rights is essential to our democratic society and should be part of the education of all students. These values are best taught by example and may be undermined if the students' rights are ignored by those in authority.[115]

---

112 *MRM, ibid.*
113 *Ibid* at 402–3.
114 *Ibid* at 411–12.
115 *Ibid* at 401–2.

The Supreme Court of Canada found that students, while attending school, did have a subjective expectation of privacy of their person and that such an expectation was objectively reasonable,[116] but that the expectation of privacy in a school setting would be less than in other settings or circumstances. The Supreme Court noted that students understand that teachers and administrators have a responsibility to create safe environments in which certain substances and articles might be prohibited. Moreover, students appreciate that measures, such as searches and seizures, might need to be taken to ensure that the school was free of dangerous or inappropriate substances and articles.[117]

The Supreme Court of Canada identified the following test for searches of students in elementary and secondary school settings:

1. A warrant is not essential in order to conduct a search of a student by a school authority.

2. The school authority must have reasonable grounds to believe that there has been a breach of school regulations or discipline and that a search of a student would reveal evidence of that breach.

3. School authorities will be in the best position to assess information given to them and relate it to the situation existing in their school. Courts should recognize the preferred position of school authorities to determine if reasonable grounds existed for the search.

4. The following may constitute reasonable grounds in this context: information received from one student considered to be credible, information received from more than one student, a teacher's or principal's own observations, or any combination of these pieces of information which the relevant authority considers to be credible. The compelling nature of the information and the credibility of these or other sources must be assessed by the school authority in the context of the circumstances existing at the particular school.[118]

---

116 *Ibid.* The Supreme Court of Canada also identified that searches of student lockers have been reviewed by the US courts with respect to the impact that the school's degree of control over the locker has on the student's subjective expectation of privacy and its objective reasonableness. See also *Zamora v Pomeroy*, 639 F2d 662 (1981); *People v Overton*, 301 NYS2d 479 (1969); *State in Interest of TLO v Engerud*, 94 NJ 331 (1983), aff'd 469 US 325 (1985).

117 *MRM*, above note 111.

118 *Ibid* at headnote.

The search itself, the Supreme Court of Canada cautioned, must also be reasonable.[119] A reasonable search would comply with the following factors:

1. The first step is to determine whether it can be inferred from the provisions of the relevant *Education Act* that teachers and principals are authorized to conduct searches of their students in appropriate circumstances. In the school environment such a statutory authorization would be reasonable.

2. The search itself must be carried out in a reasonable manner. It should be conducted in a sensitive manner and be minimally intrusive.

3. In order to determine whether a search was reasonable, all the surrounding circumstances will have to be considered.[120]

The Supreme Court of Canada held that the search conducted by the vice-principal in the present case was consistent with the Supreme Court's expectations. It was authorized by the legislation, there was reasonable information to believe that the student was in possession of a prohibited substance, the search was minimally intrusive, and it was conducted in the privacy of the vice-principal's office.[121]

Thus, students have a right to privacy of their person that must be respected while they are in attendance at school. While students at school do not have the same expectation of privacy as when they are in public spaces, school administrators need to have a reasonable basis to believe that the student might be in possession of contraband. Moreover, the search of the student that is conducted must itself be reasonable.[122]

---

119 In 2015 a female student in a Québec secondary school was asked to remove her clothing to her underwear behind a screen in the presence of two female staff members as part of a search for drugs. The student had allegedly sent a text message to another student offering to sell that student drugs. See Allan Woods, "Quebec Reviewing Policies after Strip Search of Girl, 15, at School" *Toronto Star* (18 February 2015).

120 *MRM*, above note 111 at para 54.

121 *Ibid.*

122 See also *Gillies (Litigation guardian of) v Toronto District School Board*, 2015 ONSC 1038, in which a mandatory breathalyzer test prior to entering a graduation dance was held to breach the students' *Charter* rights against unreasonable searches.

L. *R v AM*: THE "SNIFFER DOG CASE"

The expectation of privacy not only applies to a student's body, but also to the student's personal carry-alls, such as backpacks, purses, and gym-bags. In *R v AM*,[123] the issue before the Supreme Court of Canada was a school administrator's right to conduct random searches at a secondary school using the assistance of a police dog. Often referred to as the "sniffer dog case," the issue was the standard required to conduct searches using police dogs. The principal of a secondary school in Sarnia had communicated an open invitation to the police to conduct searches at the school using police dogs trained to identify, by smell, drugs and other illegal substances. Given the nature of the standing invitation, these searches were to be random and involve the entire school body.[124]

On the day at issue, the police attended the school with a sniffer dog based on the principal's open invitation. There was no particular suspicion that a student might be in possession of drugs. The principal told students to remain in their classrooms while the dog and two police officers conducted the search, which lasted approximately ninety minutes.[125] The dog did successfully identify a backpack that was left in the school gymnasium along with other student backpacks. The police conducted a search of the backpack and uncovered illegal drugs.[126]

The Supreme Court of Canada distinguished this search from the search conducted in *MRM* because it was conducted by police officers and a dog, rather than administrators at the school. According to the principal, he did not believe that under the same circumstances he would have authority to conduct such a search.[127] The youth court judge agreed with him. According to the youth court judge, "there was no credible information to suggest that a search was justified and no reasonable grounds to detain the students. The detention aggravated the unreasonableness of the search."[128]

The Supreme Court of Canada noted that the latitude that is given to school administrators when they are conducting searches should not also be given to the police, just because the police are conducting searches on

---

123 *R v AM*, [2008] 1 SCR 569.
124 *Ibid* at 587–88.
125 *Ibid* at 589 and 592.
126 *Ibid* at 589–90.
127 *Ibid* at 592.
128 *Ibid*.

school premises.[129] The Supreme Court in *MRM* did not hold that school buildings attracted a specific standard for searches, but rather that school administrators had a different standard from police to which they would need to comply before conducting the search of a student. In other words, the standard applied to school administrators would not automatically apply to police dog searches just because they were being conducted in a school.[130]

The Supreme Court of Canada also found the fact that students left their backpacks and other bags in the gym during the search did not mean that those students lost their privacy rights to their bags. There was no reason to believe that the students were consenting to a search of their bags because the bags were left in the gym. The Supreme Court found that backpacks would objectively attract privacy,[131] they are an important repository for personal items given the "itinerant lifestyle" that students lead.[132] Moreover, the Supreme Court held that, subjectively, backpacks would attract privacy because students had a reasonable expectation that the police would not randomly search their backpacks just by virtue of them being at school.[133]

The Crown argued that the students did not have privacy rights to illegal drugs in their backpacks uncovered by a sniffer dog, and that the search is minimally intrusive because the dog only communicates the fact that there is an illegal drug in the bag. There are no other contents revealed by a dog when it is sniffing. However, the Crown's distinction between legal and illegal contents in a student's bag was not accepted. The Supreme Court of Canada held that it is not the object of the search that determines the privacy right, but rather the circumstances of the search, such as where it takes place and the impact of the search on the individual whose privacy interests were impacted by the search.[134]

The Supreme Court of Canada also ruled that the appropriate test for sniffer dog searches of personal property was that of *reasonable suspicion*, a diminished standard from that which applies to searches by the police of a person, which requires prior judicial approval. The standard is also diminished from that which applies to school administrators conducting

---

129 *Ibid* at 599–600.
130 *Ibid* at 600.
131 *Ibid*.
132 *Ibid* at 606.
133 *Ibid*.
134 *Ibid* at 585–86.

a search of a student, which is *reasonable belief.* The Court found that a sniffer dog search by the police did not require a warrant because the dog search was very narrow; the dog would only smell contraband and would identify nothing else in the backpack. On a more practical level, if the police had sufficient reason to get a warrant, the dog would not be necessary, as the police would have enough information to conduct the search without the dog.[135]

The standard of evidence required for sniffer dog searches is one of reasonable suspicion. Principals cannot ask the police to attend a school to conduct such a search without a reasonable suspicion of contraband in the school. A general belief that one or more students will be in possession of drugs in the school building at any given time, as was the belief in the present case, was not sufficient to meet the standard of *reasonable suspicion.*[136] The Supreme Court of Canada concluded there was insufficient evidence to conduct a sniffer dog search at the school, and the section 8 *Charter* rights of the student whose backpack was identified by the dog and searched by police were violated.[137]

The Supreme Court of Canada also considered the issue of whether the principal had breached the students' right against detention pursuant to section 9 of the *Charter* when they were ordered to remain in their classrooms for the duration of the police search, which lasted approximately ninety minutes. The principal made the announcement over the school's public address system for students to remain in their classrooms "for the mutual benefit of the police and the school population."[138] The Supreme Court further found that the principal's "announcement should be seen as action by the school principal pursuant to the *Education Act* to maintain order and discipline in the school. It was not itself a *Charter* breach."[139]

The *Education Act*[140] in Ontario requires that principals maintain discipline and order in the school as well as pay assiduous attention to health and comfort of students.[141] Under either provision the principal could have argued that it was not in the best interests of students to be walking hallways and using their lockers and the washrooms while a sniffer dog was

---

135 *Ibid* at 620–21.
136 *Ibid* at 621.
137 *Ibid.*
138 *Ibid* at 622.
139 *Ibid.*
140 Ontario *Education Act*, above note 10.
141 *Ibid*, ss 265(1)(a) and (j).

trying to do its duty. Therefore, despite the search being the responsibility of the police and a police act, the control of students during the search was still an act by the principal and the principal's responsibility.

In summary, students have rights pursuant to section 8 of the *Charter* to be protected from wrongful searches. The principal searching a student's person must have a *reasonable belief* that the student is in possession of a prohibited article or substance, such as a weapon or illegal drug. A principal must also conduct the search in a reasonable manner. The search must be minimally invasive; it must be done in private and respect the student's dignity. In the case of a search by police with a dog in a school, there must be a *reasonable suspicion* that a student has contraband. Similarly, the search must respect the students by ensuring that they come to no harm during the search process. This might require them to remain in their classrooms for a period of time, which is not unlawful detention pursuant to section 9 of the *Charter*.

M. SECTION 43 OF THE *CRIMINAL CODE*

Thus far in this chapter, it has been demonstrated that students have the protection of the *Canadian Constitution* and *Canadian Charter of Rights and Freedoms*, not only with respect to denominational education, French language education, freedom from discrimination on the basis of religion, but also freedom from unlawful searches. Yet, section 43 of the *Criminal Code* of Canada,[142] states: "Every school teacher, parent or person standing in the place of a parent is justified in using force by way of correction toward a pupil or child, as the case may be, who is under his care, if the force does not exceed what is reasonable under the circumstances."[143]

The constitutionality of this section was challenged by the Canadian Foundation for Children, Youth and the Law, also known as Justice for Children and Youth (JCY);[144] however, the section survived. Neither the Superior Court of Ontario nor the Ontario Court of Appeal issued the declaration requested. The Supreme Court of Canada heard the case, but ultimately did not issue the declaration either.

---

142 *Criminal Code*, RSC 1985, c C-46.

143 *Ibid*, s 43.

144 *Canadian Foundation for Children, Youth and the Law v Canada (Attorney General)*, [2004] 1 SCR 76 [*Canadian Foundation for Children*].

JCY sought a declaration from the Supreme Court of Canada that section 43 of the *Criminal Code*[145] violated section 7 of the *Charter*[146] for its failure to provide procedural protection to children and because it was not in the best interests of children, as it was over broad and too vague; that it violated section 12 of the *Charter*[147] because it constituted cruel and unusual treatment; and that it violated section 15(1) of the *Charter*[148] because it denied children protection from assault, which is given to adults.

The first argument made by JCY was that laws affecting children must be in their best interests, and section 43 did not meet this test. However, the Supreme Court of Canada held that "best interests of the child" was a legal principle, but not a principle of fundamental justice,[149] and could be subordinated to other legal considerations.[150]

It was also argued by JCY that the phrase "reasonable under the circumstances" was too vague for constitutional purposes, but the Supreme Court of Canada clarified by outlining the circumstances in which the application of force would be considered reasonable. The Supreme Court held that the application of force must be for education or correction, and the child must be of an age that they can be educated or corrected; for example, a baby cannot be the subject of the section 43 exemption.[151] Further, if the child is being corrected or educated, the activity cannot involve harm to the child.[152] Nor can the act include "cruel, inhuman or degrading treatment."[153]

---

145 *Criminal Code*, above note 142, s 43.

146 *Charter*, above note 1, s 7 states: "Everyone has the right to life, liberty and security of the person and the right not to be deprived thereof except in accordance with the principles of fundamental justice."

147 *Ibid*, s 12 provides: "Everyone has the right not to be subjected to any cruel and unusual treatment or punishment."

148 *Ibid*, s 15(1) of the *Charter* provides: "Every individual is equal before and under the law and has the right to the equal protection and equal benefit of the law without discrimination and, in particular, without discrimination based on race, national or ethnic origin, colour, religion, sex, *age* or mental or physical disability" [emphasis added].

149 *Canadian Foundation for Children*, above note 144 at 92. As a legal principle, it is commonly applied in family law, education law, and other areas of law that involve children and youth.

150 *Ibid* at 95.

151 *Ibid* at 98.

152 *Ibid* at 100.

153 *Ibid* at 101.

With respect to the context of the use of section 43 in the education realm, the Supreme Court noted the following:

> Contemporary social consensus is that, while teachers may sometimes use corrective force to remove children from classrooms or secure compliance with instructions, the use of corporal punishment by teachers is not acceptable. Many school boards forbid the use of corporal punishment, and some provinces and territories have legislatively prohibited its use by teachers: see, e.g. *Schools Act, 1997*, S.N.L. 1997, c. S.12.2, s.42; *School Act*, R.S.B.C. 1996, c.412, s.76(3); *Education Act*, S.N.B. 1997, c.E.1.12, s.23; *School Act*, R.S.P.E.I. 1998, c. S.2.1 s.73; *Education Act*, S.N.W.T. 1995, c.28, s.34(3); *Education Act*, S.Y. 1989-90 c.25. This consensus is consistent with Canada's international obligations, given the findings of the Human Rights Committee of the United Nations noted above. Section 43 will protect a teacher who uses reasonable, corrective force to restrain or remove a child in appropriate circumstances. Substantial societal consensus, supported by expert evidence and Canada's treaty obligations, indicates that corporal punishment by teachers is unreasonable.[154]

Lastly, the Supreme Court of Canada considered the argument by JCY that section 43 was contrary to section 15 of the *Charter*[155] because it discriminated against children and youth on the basis of age by protecting adults from the use of force, but not a child or a youth.

The Supreme Court of Canada applied the test in *Law v Canada (Minister of Employment and Immigration)*,[156] to decide whether or not section 43 discriminated against children and youth. The test in *Law*[157] requires that there be a "(1) pre-existing disadvantage; (2) correspondence between the distinction and the claimant's characteristics or circumstances; (3) the existence of ameliorative purposes or effects; and (4) the nature of the interest affected."[158] With the application of the test in *Law*, the Supreme Court held, "Section 43 is not arbitrarily demeaning. It does not discriminate. Rather, it is firmly grounded in the actual needs and circumstances of children. I conclude that s. 43 does not offend s. 15(1) of the *Charter*."[159]

---

154 *Ibid* at 103–4.
155 *Charter*, above note 1.
156 [1999] 1 SCR 497 [*Law*].
157 *Ibid*.
158 *Law*, as cited in *Canadian Foundation for Children*, above note 144 at 110.
159 *Ibid* at 117.

N. PHYSICAL RESTRAINTS

Physical restraints continue to be used by teachers to protect students from harming themselves and others. In some cases, students who pose a risk of harm to themselves and others cannot be de-escalated, and it is necessary to carry out physical interventions. The best practice when school boards approve the use of restraints by teachers or teaching aides is for school boards to have trained staff and developed procedures that identify the reasonable response to students who are at risk of harming themselves or others. Section 43 of the *Criminal Code*, therefore, protects teachers from being subject to criminal sanctions in instances where the use of force is warranted.

The use of restraints to protect students from the risk of being harmed by other students and to protect students from harming themselves is related to the concept of exclusion from a classroom or from a school, which is provided for in the Ontario *Education Act*.[160] Exclusion is intended to be used as a method to protect the physical or mental well-being of students, and is authorized under the Ontario *Education Act*, at section 265(1)(m), which states: "subject to an appeal to the board, to refuse to admit to the school or classroom a person whose presence in the school or classroom would in the principal's judgment be detrimental to the physical or mental well-being of the pupils."[161]

O. EXCLUSION FROM SCHOOL

Prior to 2003, principals in Ontario, usually with the support of their superintendent of education, excluded parents, strangers, and other adults from school buildings when their behaviour was detrimental to the physical or mental well-being of students in the school. The provision was also used to prevent students from accessing classrooms or a school that was not the student's own. Whether or not students with behavioural needs could similarly be excluded, however, was an issue of contention. School boards did from time to time exclude students and some children's advocates and advocates for children with disabilities argued that they did so without authority because "person" in section 265(1)(m) of the *Education Act* did not include students.

---

160 Above note 10.
161 *Ibid.*

Following the Ontario Court of Appeal's decision in *Bonnah (Litigation Guardian of) v Ottawa-Carlton District School Board*,[162] it was clear that a student could also be a "person" for the purposes of exclusion pursuant to subsection 265(1)(m) of the *Education Act*,[163] and that a principal could exclude a student from his/her school if that student was, in the opinion of the principal, detrimental to the physical or mental well-being of students in that school.

Pursuant to subsection 265(1)(m) of the *Education Act*, students may, therefore, be excluded from their classroom and be required to receive instruction in a different room, one that might be solitary or have only a few students. The student may also be excluded from the school building. The excluded student's parent can appeal the exclusion to the school board's board of trustees, seeking to have the exclusion quashed and their child returned to school. During the period of exclusion, the student remains a student of the school board and continues to have the right to receive educational services. However, the reasons for and circumstances of the exclusion may make the provision of educational services very difficult to provide.

An exclusion does not have any legislated duration; thus, a student could be excluded until they are no longer age and/or grade appropriate for the school from which they are excluded. Subsection 265(1)(m) of the *Education Act* does not prohibit a student's parent from trying to have their child register at a different school. The principal of the receiving school has the authority to decide whether or not there is sufficient evidence to make a judgment about the student being detrimental to the physical or mental well-being of the students in the receiving school. However, if the exclusion was appealed and denied by the board of trustees, arguably a principal of a different school within the same jurisdiction would have sufficient reason to believe that the student would also be a risk if admitted.

The recent decision of the Human Rights Tribunal of Ontario, *RB (Next friend of) v Keewatin-Patricia District School Board*,[164] reviewed the application of subsection 265(1)(m) by a principal who determined that it was necessary to exclude RB from the school until specific conditions were met.

Prior to the exclusion, RB's parent brought a human rights application against the school board alleging that her son had suffered discrimination on the basis of disability in grades 2 and 3 because the school board was

162 (2003), 64 OR (3d) 454 (CA).
163 Above note 10.
164 2013 HRTO 1436.

not meeting his educational needs. RB was diagnosed with "Pervasive Developmental Disorder: Not Otherwise Specified," as well as an intellectual disability in the mild range and Attention Deficit Hyperactivity Disorder. He was also seeing a therapist to assist with anxiety. RB posed challenges for the school with respect to his behaviour, and the relationship between his mother and the school administration and teachers was not positive.

RB's mother advocated for a full-time, one-on-one educational assistant to support RB with his behaviour and learning needs. However, the school did not provide him with the support that she requested. In RB's grade 2 year, the vice-principal informed RB's mother that RB's access to an educational assistant would be reduced to half of the school day. When issues arose with RB's behaviour at school and were reported to his mother, she would critically respond that the behaviour was the fault of the school and the result of his lack of educational assistant support. Over time, there was less and less constructive dialogue between home and school, although RB's mother was prolific with her emails to the school.

In grade 3, RB received access to an educational assistant based on a shared support model for the whole school day. He also received other supports such as time with a special education resource teacher, and speech and language pathology services, all of which were set out in his Individualized Education Plan (IEP). However, the relationship between the school and home did not improve, nor did RB's behaviour.

On 15 October 2012, a behaviour plan was developed by the school to assist with RB's self-regulation. A copy of the plan was forwarded to his mother on Friday, 19 October 2012. But, RB was excluded from the school on Monday, 22 October 2012. His exclusion was for behaviour including "swearing, using profanity, spitting, yelling, cutting a child's sweater, stomping on a child's leg, throwing material and being non-compliant with his teacher, educational assistant, Vice-Principal and Principal."[165] RB's return to school was conditional upon the completion of a psychological assessment by the school board's psychologist and the principal's judgment that his return would not compromise the physical and mental well-being of the students in his class. During the period of exclusion, RB was provided with instruction from a teacher for three hours per week at the local library, and he demonstrated improvement in reading during the period of his exclusion.

---

165 *Ibid* at para 98.

The psychological assessment was completed and contained several recommendations for RB's educational program. It also found that RB was no longer a risk to other student's physical or mental well-being. In addition to specific programming, the psychologist also recommended that RB not return to school until there was a "resolution of the 'human rights issue' because the relationship between SF and the school was fraught with discord and lack of trust."[166] Relying on this statement, the school board made it a condition that the human rights application filed by RB's mother be completed before RB could return to school. RB did return to school, but it was by order of the Human Rights Tribunal in an interim decision dated 25 January 2013.[167]

The Human Rights Tribunal of Ontario held that RB had suffered discrimination on the basis of disability. In particular, the Tribunal found that the period of his exclusion was without appropriate educational instruction. The Tribunal stated: "When a student is excluded from school, he is denied an education. No one would suggest that providing a student with three hours of instruction per week in a public library, regardless of the effectiveness of that instruction, is an appropriate education."[168] Moreover, the Tribunal held that the reasons for the exclusion were insufficient and the failure to return RB to school following the psychological assessment was inappropriate. The Tribunal found that the behaviours exhibited by RB consisted largely of swearing and uttering profanities, which did not constitute behaviour supporting an exclusion from school. Further, the return to school should not have been predicated on his mother withdrawing her human rights application, which is a legal right.

While the decision does not define when it would be appropriate to exclude a student, it does identify that swearing and profanity are insufficient reasons to support an exclusion from school. Moreover, while excluded, a student must receive more than three hours of instruction per week. The right to education is not forfeited because a student is excluded from his or her school.

The right to attend school might not yet be enshrined in the *Charter*,[169] but once it is provided to children and youth by legislative means without cost, it is very difficult to eliminate that student's right to receive publicly funded education. In all of the provinces, publicly funded education

---

166 *Ibid* at para 102.
167 2013 HRTO 130.
168 Above note 164 at para 256.
169 Above note 1.

includes the right to French language education where numbers warrant, and in some provinces, the right to denominational education remains protected.

Further, students have rights while attending school that are protected by the *Charter*. They have the right to religious freedom, and they have the right to privacy, whereby they cannot be unreasonably searched. Moreover, a student's right to freedom of expression has been applied to post-secondary education and will certainly apply to protect the rights of students to communicate, provided that their expression does not violate the Codes of Conduct and expectations for civil discourse in their schools.

The rights of students to attend school and their rights while in school must be protected, and students are best placed to identify and advise when their rights have been breached. Teaching students about their rights and the recourse they have to protect their rights not only assists them to ensure that they are afforded appropriate protections, but also provides an opportunity to develop a culture that is respectful of rights.

CHAPTER 6

Educators' Negligence and Liability

Theresa Shanahan[1]

A. INTRODUCTION

Accidents in schools can result in negligence lawsuits against educators. Educators are responsible for taking all reasonable steps to provide a safe and positive learning environment for students. School safety and the duty to supervise students underpin educators' liability for negligence. The legal concept of risk management and the law of tort shape educators' duties in this area.

School accidents fall under tort law. A "tort" is a wrong that is compensable in damages. Tort law allows a court to hold liable someone who is found legally responsible for another's loss or injury. The objective of tort law is to restore the injured party to the position they would have enjoyed had the wrong not occurred. There are two kinds of torts. An *intentional* tort is deliberate harm to another person, such as assault or defamation. Intentional torts result in criminal proceedings. An *unintentional* tort is the unintentional harm to another person caused by a person's actions or failure to act. Unintentional torts result in civil proceedings. Negligence is an unintentional tort. This chapter is concerned with unintentional torts; specifically, this chapter will address educators' liability for negligence in

---

1   This chapter draws upon my unpublished teaching materials — in particular, my curriculum and course materials on negligence and liability of educators for various courses I have created and taught — including the "Ethics and Legal Studies in Education" online tutorial which I created at the Faculty of Education, York University, for the bachelor of education students studying to become teachers, and also curriculum material I created for the Principal's Qualifications course.

their care and supervision of their students. The focus of this chapter is on educators' liability for accidents leading to student injury.

B. WHAT IS NEGLIGENCE? THE LEGAL ELEMENTS OF NEGLIGENCE

Negligence is unintentional harm caused by the failure to eliminate un-reasonable risks of injury. A risk is "unreasonable" if it could have been reduced or eliminated by common sense. Negligent actions in education can involve civil lawsuits against teachers, principals, and school boards. The legal elements of negligence include the following:

1) a *duty of care* owed, as in educators having a duty of care to their students
2) a *standard of care*, in this case, the "educator's standard of care," to prevent reasonably foreseeable risks of harm
3) a *breach* of the standard of care, namely, conduct that falls below the standard of care
4) *damage*, or quantifiable harm, to the plaintiff as a result of the breach
5) *causation* — that is, the harm or damages done must flow from the breach of the duty[2]

C. THE EDUCATOR'S DUTY OF CARE

Teachers and principals have a duty of care towards their students. Educators' duties towards their students are set out and governed by legal statutes as well as in the common law. Supervising and keeping students safe is one of an educator's most important duties. This duty includes maintaining order and discipline in the school environment. Educators are thus responsible for the health, comfort, and welfare of students. Supervision requires that educators watch and direct student activities.

In Canada, an educator's duty to supervise underpins the law of negligence and liability of educators. It is established and defined in both statute (legislation) and common law (caselaw). Every province in Canada has an array of education statutes that organize the education system and set out the duties and responsibilities of teachers, principals, and school boards, and the minister responsible for education. For example, the On-

---

2   See *Hussack v Chilliwack School District No 33*, 2011 BCCA 258 at para 33 [*Hussack*], citing *Mustapha v Culligan of Canada Ltd*, 2008 SCC 27 at para 3.

tario *Education Act*,[3] and its regulations, organizes the education system and sets out numerous duties of teachers under section 264(1) and numerous duties of principals under section 265(1). Similar statutory provisions can be found in each provincial education statute. In Ontario, the educator's duty to supervise is articulated under the *Education Act* in this way:

Duties of teacher
264. (1) It is the duty of a teacher and a temporary teacher,

discipline
(e) to maintain, under the direction of the principal, proper order and discipline in the teacher's classroom and while on duty in the school and on the school ground;[4]

Further, under Regulation 298 of the Ontario *Education Act*:

20. In addition to the duties assigned to the teacher under the Act and by the board, a teacher shall,
(a) be responsible for effective instruction, training and evaluation of the progress of pupils in the subjects assigned to the teacher and for the management of the class or classes, and report to the principal on the progress of pupils on request;
(b) carry out the supervisory duties and instructional program assigned to the teacher by the principal and supply such information related thereto as the principal may require;
(c) where the board has appointed teachers under section 14 or 17, co-operate fully with such teachers and with the principal in all matters related to the instruction of pupils;
(d) unless otherwise assigned by the principal, be present in the classroom or teaching area and ensure that the classroom or teaching area is ready for the reception of pupils at least fifteen minutes before the commencement of classes in the school in the morning and, where applicable, five minutes before the commencement of classes in the school in the afternoon;
(e) assist the principal in maintaining close co-operation with the community;
(f) prepare for use in the teacher's class or classes such teaching plans and outlines as are required by the principal and the appropriate supervisory officer and submit the plans and outlines to the principal or the appropriate supervisory officer, as the case may be, on request;

3   RSO 1990, c E.2.
4   *Ibid*, s 264(1)(e).

(g) ensure that all reasonable safety procedures are carried out in courses and activities for which the teacher is responsible;

(h) co-operate with the principal and other teachers to establish and maintain consistent disciplinary practices in the school.[5]

Similar statutory provisions apply to principals under Ontario's *Education Act*:

Duties of principal

265. (1) It is the duty of a principal of a school, in addition to the principal's duties as a teacher,

discipline

(a) to maintain proper order and discipline in the school; . . .

care of pupils and property

(j) to give assiduous attention to the health and comfort of the pupils, to the cleanliness, temperature and ventilation of the school, to the care of all teaching materials and other school property, and to the condition and appearance of the school buildings and grounds;

report to M.O.H.

(k) to report promptly to the board and to the medical officer of health when the principal has reason to suspect the existence of any communicable disease in the school, and of the unsanitary condition of any part of the school building or the school grounds;

persons with communicable diseases

(l) to refuse admission to the school of any person who the principal believes is infected with or exposed to communicable diseases requiring an order under section 22 of the *Health Protection and Promotion Act* until furnished with a certificate of a medical officer of health or of a legally qualified medical practitioner approved by the medical officer of health that all danger from exposure to contact with such person has passed;

access to school or class

(m) subject to an appeal to the board, to refuse to admit to the school or classroom a person whose presence in the school or classroom would in the principal's judgment be detrimental to the physical or mental well-being of the pupils; and

visitor's book

(n) to maintain a visitor's book in the school when so determined by the board. R.S.O. 1990, c. E.2, s. 265; 1991, c. 10, s. 6; 2010, c. 10, s. 17.[6]

---

5   See *Operation of Schools — General*, RRO 1990, Reg 298, ss 20(a)–(h).
6   Sections 265(1)(a), (j), (k), (l), (m), & (n) of the *Education Act*, above note 3.

D. PROFESSIONAL GOVERNING BODIES FOR EDUCATORS

In addition to provincial education statutes and regulations, at least one province, Ontario, has created a professional governing body for educators, the Ontario College of Teachers (OCT), which is responsible for governing the education profession, ensuring competence and discipline, and licensing teachers for practice. In Ontario, the OCT statutes and regulations constituting and governing the College of Teachers further articulate educators' legal duties, including the duty of care in terms of professional standards of practice.[7] For example, a regulation of the *Ontario College of Teachers Act* sets out the definition of "professional misconduct" and includes under section 11, "Failing to supervise adequately a person who is under the professional supervision of the member."[8]

Most Canadian provinces have professional associations and organizations that advocate for teachers or principals. Members of these organizations are subject to duties set out in the statutes and regulations constituting the organization, and they include educators' duties owed to their students that involve keeping them safe. For example, the Ontario *Teaching Profession Act*, section 14(f), states teachers have a duty to "concern [themselves] with the welfare of [their] pupils" while they are under their care.[9] Finally, educators' duties are set out in the common law, or judge-made law established through court cases. Caselaw fleshes out the black-letter law and illustrates and distinguishes what the duty of care looks like in specific circumstances.[10] If teachers fail in their duties to protect students from reasonable risks of harm or fail to maintain order and discipline, they may be found liable for any injuries that result. Negligence cases in education most often involve a teacher's failure to supervise students, as this lack often leads to injuries.

---

7   For example, in Ontario, see the *Ontario College of Teachers Act, 1996*, SO 1996, c 12 and its regulations. See also Ontario College of Teachers, "Standards of Practice," online: www.oct.ca/public/professional-standards/standards-of-practice; Ontario College of Teachers, "The Ethical Standards for the Teaching Profession." online: www.oct.ca/-/media/PDF/Standards%20Poster/standards_flyer_e.pdf.

8   *Professional Misconduct*, O Reg 437/97, sets out the definition of professional misconduct.

9   For example, in Ontario, see the *Teaching Profession Act*, RSO 1990, c T.2.

10   It is important to note that other sources of education law such as policy statements, bylaws, and guidelines may be looked to in a court case to establish the standard of practice expected, but they would not in and of themselves initially ground an action of negligence.

E. THE EDUCATOR'S STANDARD OF CARE: THE CAREFUL AND PRUDENT PARENT RULE

The scope of an educator's duty of care is defined by legislation and caselaw. This definition is referred to as the "educator's standard of care." The standard of care that educators are responsible for meeting is known as the "careful and prudent parent rule." Educators are to act as a reasonably careful and prudent parent when carrying out their professional duties, teaching and supervising their students. The standard is not inflexible or uniform; it varies from case to case. Every situation gives rise to different factors that determine whether the educator in the circumstances has met the standard of care.

Williams v Eady[11] established the educator's standard of care. The case has been upheld in more recent cases such as *Myers (Next friend of) v Peel County Board of Education*,[12] the leading Canadian case on negligence in education. This case is significant and very helpful for educators because it established factors to be considered in determining whether supervision is appropriate and meets the educator's standard of care in a given situation. The 1981 Ontario case went to the Supreme Court of Canada. It involved a fifteen-year-old boy who attempted to dismount from gymnastic rings in the exercise room of the school. His spotter, another student, had wandered off, and no teacher supervision was present. Upon dismount, the plaintiff student injured himself on the substandard matting of the exercise room floor. The Court found the plaintiff contributorily negligent for 20 percent of his injuries. The teacher who failed to provide adequate supervision was found negligent and held liable for 80 percent of the student's injuries. The Court stated the teacher should have realized that children will wander off, so delegating another student to be spotter was not sufficient supervision and fell below the educator's standard of care. The Court held that the teacher in this case did not act as a "careful and prudent parent." A "careful and prudent parent" would not provide substandard matting when more protective mats were available and, further, would not allow a student to engage in potentially dangerous maneuvers without adult supervision. According to this and other caselaw, appropriate supervision is determined by

---

11   (1893), 10 TLR 41 at 42.
12   [1981] 2 SCR 21 [*Myers*].

1) the number of students being supervised (More students require more supervision.)
2) the nature of activity Is it inherently dangerous? Are there foreseeable risks to the activity? (More sophisticated activities require more supervision.)
3) the age and maturity of the students participating (Younger students require more supervision.)
4) the degree of skill and training received by the students in connection with the activity
5) the condition of equipment (Poor equipment poses potentially greater risk of injuries and requires greater supervision.)
6) the competency, capacity, special needs, and intelligence of students participating (Younger and less capable students require more supervision; students need an awareness of the risks involved.)
7) the location of the activity
8) the history of accidents involving the same or similar activity or circumstances

Appropriate and reasonable supervision is central to the determination of an educator's negligence and liability. The absence of supervision does not itself constitute negligence, nor does the presence of supervision prevent liability of negligence. It is the reasonable *quality* of the supervision that matters in negligence and liability. Supervision does not need to be perfect. The case of *Hentze (Guardian ad litem of) v Campbell River School District No 72*, reiterated this duty of care in relation to supervision of students:

> The law does not, of course, require that school authorities keep students under constant supervision at all times. The standard is that of the reasonably careful and prudent parent. How the standard is to be applied in any given case will depend upon many factors, including the nature and size of the area to be supervised, the number and ages of the students involved, and the nature of the activity or activities that are in progress.[13]

1) Legal Doctrines That Inform the Educator's Standard of Care

An educator's responsibility and authority as reflected in the educator's standard of care is informed by various historical legal principles. At common law, educators are seen to act as parental delegates; they stand

---

13   [1994] BCJ No 1876 at para 14 (CA).

in the place of the parent or *in loco parentis* in their responsibility and authority over children under their supervision. Scholars suggest, however, that this principle has been diminished over time and has largely been replaced in the Canadian context by teachers' statutory duties. The principle of *in loco parentis* is no longer considered the primary basis for educators' authority over students.[14] Its application has also been limited in an institutional setting by recent Supreme Court caselaw such as *R v Ogg-Moss*[15] where, citing Wells J, in *North Carolina v Pittard*, Dickson J observed:

> The relationship of *in loco parentis* does not arise from the mere placing of a child in the temporary care of other persons by a parent or guardian of such child. The relationship is established only when the person with whom the child is placed intends to assume the status of a parent by taking on obligations incidental to the parental relationships particularly that of support and maintenance.[16]

Although the principle of *in loco parentis* is limited in its application in the modern-day school setting, it does find its way into the law of negligence for educators because it is the starting point for any discussion of the educator's standard of care as the careful and prudent parent.[17]

A second legal principle that informs a teacher's authority is the notion that educators are state or government agents in the delivery of compulsory schooling. This is known as the legal doctrine of *parens patriae*, which has its historical roots in English common law. The doctrine, its name is Latin for "parent of the country," typically refers to the state's duty to care for its citizens. It grants the power and authority of the state to protect persons who are legally unable to act on their own behalf. It emerges prominently in child welfare caselaw where the need arises to act for the protection of those who cannot care for themselves. It encompasses the state and its agents acting as guardians.[18] Compulsory schooling laws in Canada are emanations of the *parens patriae* authority of the state requir-

---

14   See A Wayne MacKay, Lyle Sutherland, & Kimberley D Pochini, *Teachers and the Law*, 3d ed (Toronto: Emond Montgomery, 2013) at 8–13 for a discussion of the legal role and status of teachers.
15   [1984] 2 SCR 171.
16   263 SE2d 809 at 811 (NC App 1980).
17   See above note 14 at 15.
18   For a compelling and thorough discussion of the doctrine of *parens patriae* as it relates to public schooling in both Canadian and American contexts, see Jason Blokhuis, *Parens Patriae: A Comparative Legal Study of Sovereign Authority and Public Education Policy in the Province of Ontario and the State of New York* (PhD Dis-

ing parents to share (temporarily during the school day) custodial authority over their children with state agents (educators) and allow educators to exercise care and control over children for the purposes of education.[19]

The relationship between parents, children (as students), and the state (in the form of educators as state agents) has also been characterized by legal analysts as a stewardship, or a fiduciary, relationship.[20] A *fiduciary relationship* is a legal and ethical relationship of trust and confidence between two people, the fiduciary and the principal. Fiduciary duty is not grounded in tort law per se.[21] Courts have found a fiduciary duty, however, in the relationship between a parent and child.[22] In the education setting, the *in loco parentis* principle suggests that the teacher–student relationship may give rise to a fiduciary duty in certain situations whereby the educator is the fiduciary and the student is the principal. The fiduciary relationship imposes a very high duty of care on the educator who must act in the interest of the student.[23]

2) Critique of Rule and Legal Doctrines

The legal doctrines of *in loco parentis, parens patriae,* and fiduciary duty inform the educator's standard of care. However, these doctrines have been variously critiqued by scholars. The *parens patriae* doctrine and the fiduciary characterization of the educator–student relationship have been disparaged as treating children as chattel or property and as insinuating that child-rearing is a state function.[24]

---

sertation, University of Rochester, NY, Graduate School of Education and Human Development, 2009) [unpublished].

19 *See E (Mrs) v Eve*, [1986] 2 SCR 388 for a discussion of the *parens patriae* doctrine by the Supreme Court of Canada.

20 See Blokhuis, above note 18 at 17 for a discussion and critique. See also Barbara Bennett Woodhouse, "Hatching the Egg: A Child-Centered Perspective on Parent's Rights" (1993) 14 *Cardozo Law Review* 1747; ES Scott & RE Scott, "Parents as Fiduciaries" (1995) 81 *Virginia Law Review* 2401.

21 Anthony F Brown & Marvin Zuker, *Education Law*, 4th ed (Toronto: Thomson Carswell, 2007) at 164.

22 *M(K) v M(H)* (1992), 96 DLR (4th) 289 at 323 (SCC).

23 For an extensive discussion of the caselaw on fiduciary duty as it may apply to the education setting, see Brown & Zuker, above note 21 at 164–72.

24 See Stephen L Carter, "Parents, Religion, and Schools: Reflection on Pierce, 70 Years Later" (1997) 27 *Seton Hall Law Review* 1194; see also Carl E Schneider, "On

The educator's standard of care, the "careful and prudent parent rule," has also been found inadequate when compared to the standard of the skilled, expert practitioner that other professionals are held to. In fact, some caselaw on teachers' negligence refers to a modified, alternative, or higher standard of care for certain educational situations involving inherently risky activities, such as in coaching or teaching specialized and potentially dangerous subjects such as shop class or science labs. This alternative standard is that of the skilled and competent practitioner teacher as measured by specialized skill, knowledge, and training necessary to properly teach and supervise these activities.[25] The British Columbia Supreme Court clearly annunciated this in *Madsen v Mission School District No 75*:

> The standard of a careful or prudent parent as modified by the various factors listed in decisions such as those discussed above, will many times lead to an adjusted test or a test of less than direct application. A teacher may often be dealing with a classroom activity that an ordinary parent would not competently be able to conduct or control. The course objectives and the design of the curriculum are factors which an ordinary person might not understand well. The most common differentiating factor referred to in the decisions is the number of students in the teacher's charge. In a context where a teacher would be expected, through experience and training, to deal more appropriately with a matter than a parent would ordinarily be capable of, the test likely approaches the standard of a competent teacher acting reasonably in the circumstances. Such a standard would be more directly amenable to evidence of professional standards and would more closely resemble the tests applied to others in occupations requiring experience and knowledge.[26]

Conversely, the careful and prudent parent rule has been criticized for imposing a higher standard for educators than for non-educators or even parents because it includes not just reasonableness but also carefulness and prudence.[27] Nevertheless, these notions have contributed to our understanding of the educator's standard of care. Educators must anticipate un-

---

the Duties and Rights of Parents" (1995) 81 *Virginia Law Review* 2477, cited in Blokhuis, above note 18 at 17.

25 See, for example, *Thomas (Next Friend of) v Hamilton (City) Board of Education* (1994), 20 OR (3d) 598 (CA); *Myers*, above note 12; *Thornton v Board of School Trustees of School District No 57 (Prince George)* (1976), 73 DLR (3d) 35 (BCCA) [*Thornton*].

26 [1999] BCJ No 1716 at para 28 (SC).

27 A Wayne MacKay & Gregory M Dickinson, *Beyond the "Careful Parent": Tort Liability in Education* (Toronto: Emond Montgomery, 1998) at 11.

reasonable, unexpected, reckless behaviour of students and others that could harm their students and they must protect against it. Today, the standard requires something more than parental supervision; it requires a greater level of control and oversight by teachers who must not rely on students to follow their instructions.

F. BREACH OF CARE, CAUSATION, AND DAMAGES

A teacher must take reasonable steps to minimize risks of foreseeable injury to students. If teachers' conduct falls below the educator's standard of care — that is, if they do not act like reasonably careful and prudent parents — but no injuries result from the conduct, they may be reprimanded by their board, criticized by their students' parents, and/or disciplined by a professional governing body or professional association. However, if nothing untoward happened as a result of their breach, they cannot be successfully sued for negligence. If, however, the teachers' conduct breaches the educator's standard of care and does result in injuries, they may be sued for negligence by the injured student(s) and their parents or guardians, and held liable for compensatory damages. Damages are meant to compensate the victim and are usually monetary. The purpose of damages or compensation is to put the injured party, as far as money can do so, in a pre-breach position.

For a teacher to be guilty of negligence, the plaintiff (student) must prove that his or her injuries were caused by the teacher's breach of the educator's standard of care. There must be a connection between the teacher's actions or omissions and the student's injury. In investigating causation, courts look at proximity and remoteness between the teacher's actions and the student's injury. Courts also use the "but for" test to determine causation, meaning they ask: "*but for* the teacher's actions or inaction, would the student have been injured?" In order to establish causation, an injury must also have been "reasonably foreseeable." A freakish accident or an unpredictable turn of events does not qualify as reasonably foreseeable.

G. WHEN AND WHERE IS AN EDUCATOR LIABLE FOR NEGLIGENCE?

Anybody can sue for harm done to them but not everyone will be found responsible for the harm by a court of law; in other words, not every action or failure to act will be deemed by a court to be negligent. For a civil negligence lawsuit to succeed and for the defendant to be found negligent, the plaintiff must prove each of the legal elements of negligence outlined above (duty of care, standard of care, breach of the standard, damages, and causation) to a "balance of probabilities." Therefore, if a plaintiff can prove to a balance of probabilities that an educator had a duty of care towards a student under the specific circumstances of the case to prevent reasonably foreseeable harm, that the educator's actions or inaction fell below the educator's standard of care (that of the careful and prudent parent), and that the educator's actions or inaction caused quantifiable damages to the student, then the educator could be found negligent.

An educator's duty of care towards students to properly supervise and keep them safe arises in the following areas or circumstances: (1) in the classroom, (2) in the schoolyard, (3) outside of school hours, (4) at school board–sanctioned excursions and field trips, (5) while students are being transported to and from school-sponsored activities, (6) during physical education, sports, and recreation, and (7) during shop, home economic, or science classes.

Negligent supervision can also happen around school safety issues. For example, educators can be found negligent in their supervision of students in circumstances of discrimination and harassment, bullying, and violent conduct towards students. Moreover, the scope of an educator's duty of care is expanding with technology, social media, and the Internet. The educator's duty to keep students safe now also extends to activities online and in cyberspace under certain circumstances where the culture and safety of students in the school are affected.

H. VICARIOUS LIABILITY

Vicarious liability is the legal principle that holds a person responsible for the acts of another. Through this principle, school boards are liable for their employees' actions and for the means of carrying out authorized activities, such as transportation on field trips. In most negligence cases involving public schools, the school board provides legal defence for their employee (teacher or principal). Vicarious liability is an important protection for teachers, but it is not absolute.

For school boards to be liable for the improper supervision by educators, educators must have acted within the scope of their employment or authority. Acting within the scope of employment means the activity that resulted in the negligence claim must be connected to the teacher carrying out his or her job. Generally, courts have found when school board employees carry out activities related to school board education programs, they are acting within the course of their employment. If the educators were acting within the scope of their employment and are found guilty of negligence and liable for damages, these damages would be paid by the school board's insurance company.

All public school boards across Canada are insured for negligence liability; however, if the educator was acting outside the scope of employment — for example, conducting an unapproved field trip during which a student is injured — the teacher may be held personally liable for damages if found guilty of negligence. Even if negligent teachers acted within the scope of their employment, their school board may sue the teachers to recover the cost of damages.

The limitations of the scope of the legal principle of vicarious liability emphasize the importance for teachers to secure approvals for all field trips and activities. This is emphasized in the case of *Beauparlant v Board of Trustees of Separate School Section No 1 of Appleby*,[28] where a teacher took seventy students, by truck, to a concert outside of town. The truck, which had not been safety-inspected, broke down on the highway en route to the concert, and several children sustained severe injuries. The teacher had not obtained school board permission for the concert, and the court decided that the concert was not connected to students' school curriculum. The teacher was found personally liable for damages because the court determined the teacher had acted outside the scope of employment on the unsanctioned field trip.

I. STUDENT LIABILITY AND THE VOLUNTARY ASSUMPTION OF RISK

1) Students' Contributory Negligence

In determining a teacher's negligence, a court will consider whether the student contributed to her or his injury. Students can be found negligent as well and can be held responsible for part or all of their injuries. This legal principle is known as "contributory negligence." Courts will divide, or apportion, the amount of liability between each party in the case. Apportionment of liability means, for example, that a court can find a teacher

---

28 *Beauparlant (Next friend of) v Appleby Separate School Section No 1*, [1955] 4 DLR 558 (Ont HCJ).

75 percent liable for a student's injuries and the student 25 percent liable for the injuries. Students also can be held completely liable for their injuries. Consequently, if a school implements reasonable supervision practices and policies, educators may not be held negligent at all for accidents causing injuries.

This was the outcome in the British Columbia case of *Gu (Litigation guardian of) v Friesen*,[29] where the court considered whether the student involved in an accident at recess was contributorily negligent. The eleven-year-old student was giving her friend a "piggy-back" ride during recess at which time another classmate ran over and pushed her, causing both students to fall. The student giving the ride fractured an elbow and sued for negligence against the school, alleging that the school was negligent in its supervision of the students at recess. She also sued the classmate who pushed her and the classmate's parents. The defendants (the school board and educators, the classmate who pushed her, and the classmate's parents) claimed that the plaintiff student was contributorily negligent in engaging in piggy-backing.

At trial, it was established that the school had extensive playground safety policies, including a "no pushing rule," known to the students and staff. The school had one teacher on recess duty supervising approximately seventy students. The court found that the supervision provided over recess was reasonable given the students were eleven and twelve years old and did not warrant constant supervision. Moreover, the court determined that the size of the playground was not large, and the activities in question were not extremely dangerous or risky; nor were they unsanctioned. Finally, the court found that school supervision policies and practices were in place and being acted upon when the accident happened. Consequently, the court dismissed the claim against the school board and educators, stating that they were not negligent. The court also found that "piggy-backing" was an innocuous activity and dismissed the contributory negligence claim against the plaintiff. However, it found that the boy who did the pushing was liable for the injury and should have known the risk involved in pushing, which caused the accident.

---

29 *Gu (Litigation guardian of) v Friesen*, 2013 BCSC 607.

2) Standard of Care for Students

Students have a duty to act with reasonable care for their own safety, in other words, to act reasonably for their age. To be held negligent, students must be able to appreciate the consequences of their actions. The standard of care for students is that of a reasonably prudent student of same age, intelligence, and experience. If students act within this standard of care, they are not liable for their injuries. Courts have interpreted this standard for students generously: a student has to do something quite careless to be held liable for his or her injuries. For example, in *Mainville v Ottawa Board of Education*, the court ruled that students under six years of age ("tender age") are too young to be found negligent or contributorily negligent.[30] However, in the case of *Bartosek v Turret Realties Inc*, the Ontario Court of Appeal found a six-year-old boy 50 percent responsible when he rode his bicycle down a ramp and into the path of an oncoming vehicle.[31]

3) Voluntary Assumption of Risk

When students and/or parents fully comprehend and consent to the legal risks of an activity that results in injury, educators may be protected from liability by the legal principle of voluntary assumption of risk. This principle is difficult to prove, and courts are reluctant to impose it in educational settings. It does arise, however, in students' participation in sports and games. Where students voluntarily participate in sports or games knowing the risks involved, and where injury results, educators may be protected from liability if they have removed unreasonable, foreseeable risks associated with the activity and if the student and/or parents or guardian have consented to the known risks. However, educators must be able to show that the student knew the risks of injury involved in the activity, accepted the risks, and accepted the legal liability for any loss or damage suffered.[32] Establishing this is difficult, so written acknowledgement of the risks involved in the activity and written consent to those risks by the student or a parent or guardian is extremely helpful in establishing that a student or parent understood the risks and consented to them. It is also important to establish that the students and parents were capable

---

30 (1990), 75 OR (2d) 315 (Ct J).
31 2004 CanLII 10051 (Ont CA).
32 Eric Roher & Simon A Wormwell, *An Educator's Guide to the Role of the Principal*, 2d ed (Aurora, ON: Canada Law Book, 2008) at 61.

of understanding the risks and consenting to them. For example, signed consent forms are meaningless if the signing student is too young to understand them or if the forms are in a language that the students and/or parent do not understand.

Thomas (Next Friend of) v Hamilton (City) Board of Education[33] is an example of a case where a court exonerated a teacher because of a "voluntary assumption of risk" on the part of a student and his parents. It is a leading case establishing grounds for negligence and liability in the gymnasium or during physical education or sports activities. In this 1994 Ontario case, a sixteen-year-old high-school student and experienced football player suffered a neck injury while playing football on the school team, resulting in his quadriplegia. The student's parents argued that their son should not have been allowed by the school to play football on the school team because of his fatigue and poor physical condition. They also argued the teacher-coach should have known that their son had a long, slender neck, making him vulnerable to injury. The parents further alleged that the teacher-coach was negligent for failing to instruct students on proper tackling which, they argued, had led to the injury to their son. They sued the teacher-coach and school board for negligence. The lower court dismissed the action against the teacher and school board. The injured student's parents appealed, but the appeal court upheld the decision after examining the teacher's coaching methods and instruction. The court held that football is inherently dangerous and that the student and his mother had consented to the normal risks of the game, that is, they had voluntarily assumed the normal risk inherent in the game. The student's mother had signed a consent form indicating she knew of, and consented to, these risks.

4) Permission Forms

A permission form is evidence that a teacher has informed parents or guardians about students' activities, and that both the adults and students have given informed consent. *Informed consent* is permission given with knowledge of the possible consequences, risks, and benefits of an activity. People giving the informed consent must be capable of understanding the possible risks and consequences, which must be spelled out in a clear and comprehensible way in a language they understand.

---

33   Above note 25.

As an acknowledgement that an activity is "acceptable," a permission form may discourage a parent or guardian of a student from suing. However, a permission form does not waive liability of educators who improperly supervise or who fail to remove foreseeable risks of harm to students under their supervision. Consequently, permission forms are of limited value as educators cannot contract out of the duty of care owed to students under their supervision, and a student and/or parents or guardian cannot waive the rights of a minor. A permission form is simply evidence that a parent or guardian views the activity as suitable. The teacher still owes a duty to the students to protect them from foreseeable harm. If teachers are negligent, they can be sued even if the parent or guardian of the injured child consented to the activity and signed a permission form. This applies especially to activities that the court determines unreasonably risky or dangerous.

Caselaw and legal scholarship in this area suggests that permission forms are not standardized, but it is good practice to include at minimum the following information:

1) the nature and purpose of the activity
2) any special risks, possible consequences, or unusual factors
3) the date, time, and location of the activity
4) supervision to be in place during the activity
5) transportation arrangements
6) a reminder that student injury insurance coverage may be purchased
7) the cost of the activity
8) information about meals or special clothing
9) identification of relevant medical conditions and a consent for medical assistance, if appropriate[34]

J. OCCUPIER'S LIABILITY

Occupier's liability holds an owner or occupier of a building or premises liable for injuries suffered on those premises. The legal notion of occupier's liability emerged from the English common law. At first in the common law, occupiers of premises or land had no liability to other persons who were injured while passing in, through, or over their land. Gradually, however, this began to change in the common law. English courts began

---

34   For a detailed discussion on permission forms see Roher & Wormwell, above
     note 32 at 78–81, and also MacKay & Dickinson, above note 27 at 69–71.

to recognize and compensate injury as a result of negligent upkeep of land and premises but also began to distinguish the duty owed to three types of entrants to land: trespassers, licensees, and invitees. Every Canadian province has an *Occupiers Liability Act*. These statutes have codified the common law principles and, in some cases, extended or reduced the duty of care owed to people entering lands depending on whether they are invited on to the lands, are licensed to be on the lands, or if they are trespassing on the lands.

"Occupiers" include people in physical possession of premises and people responsible for the condition of premises or the activities carried on there. In educational settings, occupiers include educators, that is, school boards and principals who are responsible for the upkeep and safety of the school premises. Students are considered invitees at the school they attend. As invitees (as opposed to licensees or trespassers) on school premises, students are owed the highest standard of care.

The general duty requires occupiers to take reasonable steps in making their premises safe. Occupiers owe a duty to take reasonable care in all circumstances that people enter the premises and to make reasonably safe while there the personal property brought on the premises by those people. This duty of care does not require occupiers to remove every possibility of danger. The test is one of reasonableness, not perfection.

Under the various provincial occupier liability statutes, Canadian school boards have an obligation to take reasonable steps to ensure the safety of persons on school premises, including during after-school hours and for a non-school activity or a non-school group. In fact, the law requires that the school premises must be safe even for trespassers in the school. The premises include the school building and the school grounds, parking lot, fences, trees surrounding the schoolyard, and playgrounds. Justice Martinson described the scope of the duty under the BC statute in the 2008 British Columbia Supreme Court case *Wilde v The Cambie Malone Corporation*:

> The goals of the *Act* are to promote, and indeed, require where circumstances warrant, positive action on the part of occupiers to make their premises reasonably safe: *Waldick v. Malcolm*, 1991 CanLII 71 (SCC), [1991] 2 S.C.R. 456 at 477.
>
> Section 3 of the *Act* states:
>
> 3(1) An occupier of premises owes a duty to take that care that in all the circumstances of the case is reasonable to see that a person, and the person's property, on the premises, and property on the

premises of a person, whether or not that person personally enters on the premises, will be reasonably safe in using the premises.

(2) The duty of care referred to in subsection (1) applies in relation to the
    (a) condition of the premises,
    (b) activities on the premises, or
    (c) conduct of third parties on the premises.

The duty of care imposed by the Act is to take reasonable care in the circumstances to make the premises safe. That duty does not change, but the factors which are relevant to an assessment of what constitutes reasonable care will necessarily be very specific to each fact situation — thus the proviso "such care as in all circumstances of the case is reasonable": *Waldick* at 472.

The *Act* does not impose a duty on Malones to take reasonable care to insure that persons using the premises will be absolutely safe. The standard is reasonableness: *Milina v. Bartsch* (1985), 1985 CanLII 179 (BC SC), (1985), 49 B.C.L.R. (2d) 33 (S.C.); and *Dyke v. British Columbia Amateur Softball Assn.*, 2008 BCCA 3, 2008 (CanLII) at 19. Occupiers are not insurers.

The care that must be taken by an occupier differs according to the nature and use of the premises.[35]

Therefore, the normal duty owed by the educator is one of reasonable care to ensure that people are reasonably safe in using the land and premises regarding all aspects of the conditions of the premises, the activities undertaken on the premises, and the conduct of third parties on the premises. This is illustrated in the case of *Cox (Litigation Guardian of) v Marchen*,[36] where a principal and school board were found negligent when a high-school student nearly severed her Achilles tendon while walking through a door. The door had an exposed, sharp, jagged metal edge at the bottom which caught her foot on closing. The school principal and maintenance staff conducted monthly health and safety inspections of the school building, but were not aware of the condition of the door. The court found the principal should have been conducting weekly inspection as per his responsibilities under the provincial *Education Act* and regulations and, hence, he had failed to take reasonable precautions to prevent harm to the students. The court held that his system of inspection for the door was inadequate and that he had failed to act as a careful parent.

---

35   2008 BCSC 704 at paras 34–37.
36   2002 CanLII 36967 (Ont SCJ).

A trespasser on a property may assume risks of injury entering a property, but a trespasser is still owed a duty of care. Educators must not create any danger to a person entering the property even as a trespasser or recklessly disregard the safety of a person entering their property if they are aware of that person's presence on the property. If they are aware that people are using their property, they must not fail to do anything that would cause damage or injury, or act with disregard to the fact that damage or injury might occur to the trespasser. If the principal fails to ensure reasonable safety and injury results to someone using the land or premises, then the educators (principal and school board as their employer) may be sued for negligence and damages awarded against them.

K. NEGLIGENCE CASELAW

1) Negligence in the Classroom

Normally, educators have to ensure that there is a system of supervision in place in the classroom appropriate to the age, maturity, and number of children in the class. Adequate supervision does not mean perfect or constant supervision. It does involve reasonable supervision to prevent foreseeable injuries and to eliminate foreseeable dangers.

Misir v Children's Rehabilitation Centre of Essex County[37] is a leading Canadian case establishing grounds for negligence and liability when in the classroom. In this 1989 Ontario case, a teacher left her special education class momentarily to help a student in the hall. While the teacher was out in the hallway, a boy in class who had no history of such behaviour grabbed, twisted, and fractured another student's arm. The teacher and school board were sued for negligence by the injured student's parents for improper supervision of the class. The court found that the teacher's absence was only for a short period and for a legitimate reason because the student in the hallway was also owed a duty of supervision and required assistance. Further, the court decided the sudden attack was not foreseeable. For these reasons, the court ruled that the teacher was not negligent and that it would be "absurd" to hold her liable under these circumstances.

McCue v Etobicoke (Borough) Board of Education[38] is another case establishing grounds for negligence and liability in the classroom. While seated in a classroom before the teacher arrived, a high-school student was struck in the eye by a paper clip shot from an elastic band by another stu-

37 [1989] OJ No 1653 (Dist Ct).
38 [1982] OJ No 1934 (HCJ).

dent. As a result, the injured student lost sight in one eye. The injured student sued his classmate, the teacher, the school principal, and the school board, alleging improper supervision. In response, the defendant student alleged that the plaintiff had voluntarily assumed the risk of injury by participating in the horseplay, and that he was negligent himself and had contributed to or caused his own injury. The court found that, although the defendant had a history of errant behaviour, this pattern of behaviour had not been observed by or reported to the teacher, or to any other member of the school board; therefore, the court found the educators were not aware of it.

The court ruled that liability was limited to the two students responsible for firing the paper clip. Because previous incidents had gone unreported, the court found that the injury was not foreseeable by the teacher, principal, or school board; therefore, the court found that the educators were not negligent and not liable for the injury. However, it did find that both boys contributed to the situation and it apportioned liability between them with the defendant being 80 percent responsible for the injury and the plaintiff being 20 percent responsible for the injury because "both [boys] knew that to propel a paper clip at another person by means of an elastic band, or otherwise, was dangerous and involved the risk of striking other person or persons in such a manner as could cause injury."[39]

The caselaw outlines the following factors to consider when determining liability for classroom incidents during a teacher's absence:

1) the reason for the absence (Was being absent a legitimate part of the teacher's duties?)
2) the duration of the absence (How long was the teacher absent? Was it momentary?)
3) the time of the accident (Was it before, during, or after class time?)
4) the age, competency, and involvement of the students (Did they participate in the horseplay?)
5) the known history of previous incidents (Is there a pattern that points to a foreseeable risk?)

2) Negligence in the Schoolyard

Central to the determination of negligence in the schoolyard is whether a school has an appropriate system of supervision in place and whether the

---

39   *Ibid* at para 34.

teachers were implementing the system of supervision. Courts will also consider whether the system of supervision was the cause of the accident. *Plumb (Guardian ad Litem of) v Cowichan School District No 65*[40] is a leading case establishing the grounds for negligence and liability in the schoolyard. In this 1993 British Columbia case, a student was sitting in a schoolyard a short distance away from a game of catch. An errant throw hit the student, resulting in an eye injury. The student believed he was sitting a safe distance away from the game, and his parents sued, alleging that teachers on yard duty were negligent in their supervision.

The court ruled against the parents, stating that a game of catch is not inherently dangerous. The players were not doing anything that would have put other students at risk of injury. The court held that a "careful and prudent parent" would have found the distance between the players and the injured student sufficiently safe. It stated, however, that schools should have a system of yard supervision in place to protect students from injuries. Teachers are liable for any injuries resulting from failure to observe this system.

Analyses of this and other cases suggest that educators have duties such as the following when developing a system of schoolyard supervision: (1) a duty to warn students about dangers, (2) a duty to oversee activities, (3) a duty to furnish secure and adequate resources, and (4) a duty to obtain prior parental consent for participation in an activity not part of a regular school program. For example, in the case of the latter, if a school-wide baseball game is organized but is not part of the regular curriculum, parents must consent to their child's participation.[41]

Brost v Board of Trustees of Eastern Irrigation School District Division No 44[42] is another early leading case establishing the grounds for negligence and liability in the schoolyard. In this 1955 Alberta case, a six-year-old girl was injured during recess when she fell off a swing. A teacher was in charge of the playground during recess, but there was no direct supervision of swings. The court found that the teacher did not act as a "careful and prudent parent" would and that the girl's injury resulted from this failure. It found that swinging too high was a foreseeable risk. The court exonerated the teacher but found the principal and school board liable for negligence because of their failure to provide a systematic plan for playground supervision during recess. This case suggests that a teacher's

---

40   (1993), 83 BCLR (2d) 161 (CA).
41   Roher & Wormwell, above at note 32 at 70.
42   [1955] 3 DLR 159 (Alta SCAD).

duty to provide supervision is not without limits: lack of supervision must cause the injury and improper supervision must have caused the injury, or liability cannot be established.

Caselaw in this area demonstrates that to meet the standard of the careful and prudent parent, schools must have a supervision policy in place as well as appropriate rules of conduct for the schoolyard for students. These rules must be clear, known, and enforced by staff and communicated to the students. This precaution, in addition to the presence of a supervisor on the playground, will militate against negligence findings.[43] In determining whether proper supervision was in place, courts will also consider the ratio of supervisors to the number of students in the playground; the kinds of activities in which the students are engaged in the playground; the age, maturity, and (dis)ability of students being supervised; the weather conditions at the time of the accident; and the nature of the location or physical setting being supervised.[44]

3) Before and after the School Day

Generally, educators are not responsible for accidents occurring outside of "normal" school hours. For example, in the case of *Sked (Litigation guardian of) v Henry*,[45] a student fell off a car hood in the school's parking lot after hours. There had been no history of students engaging in this kind of behaviour. The court ruled that there was no breach of a duty to supervise because no such duty was established. Yet, there are exceptions to this rule. When a student habitually arrives early or stays late, for example, a parental expectation of supervision is created. In this situation, educators need to establish clear and reasonable policies on supervision before and after school, communicate the policies to parents, and follow the policies. Other exceptions to the rule that educators are not responsible for accidents outside of "normal" school hours include these:

1) when on school-sponsored activities
2) accidents on school property occurring a "reasonable time" after school hours, usually 15 minutes before and after school

---

43 *Little (Litigation Guardian of) v Chignecto Central Regional School Board*, 2004 NSSC 265 [*Little*]; *Dyer v Halifax School Commissioners* (1956), 2 DLR (2d) 394 (NSSC); *Walsh v Buchanan*, [1995] OJ No 64 (Gen Div).
44 *Little*, above note 43.
45 (1991), 28 MVR (2d) 234 (Ont Ct Gen Div).

3) supervision time provided before or after school to meet parents' needs, such as late pick-up arrangements
4) after-school teacher activities which are within the scope of teachers' employment, such as sports or study classes
5) emergencies, such as storms, which extend normal school hours
6) under the principle of "occupier's liability," when an after-hours accident related to the poor condition of the school occurs[46]

Teachers are responsible for some after-school supervision and can be the subject of a disciplinary hearing as well as negligence. In the case of *Ontario College of Teachers Discipline Committee v Kowal*,[47] an occasional teacher was trying to "beat the school buses" off the elementary school grounds at the end of the day. The teacher left the school at 3:05 right after the end of the school day without accounting for all the students in his class. Two students in his class were left alone and unattended in the schoolyard. They missed their buses. The teacher expressed his regret and apologized, stating that he had checked the schoolyard before he left but he did not recognize the students. He also indicated he had little experience with primary age schoolchildren and admitted he should have taken more time with school dismissal procedures.

The school board disciplined the teacher, and the matter was referred to the Ontario College of Teachers for discipline to determine if the teacher's actions amounted to professional misconduct. The College found that leaving the students unattended after school in the schoolyard, failing to follow the procedures was professional misconduct. It referred to the testimony of the children about the emotional impact of being left unattended. Indeed, one student expressed anxiety about returning to school in case the teacher lost him again. The College said the teacher's actions amounted to psychological or emotional abuse of the students, violating the professional misconduct regulations. The teacher was reprimanded by the College, had his certificate suspended for three months, and was required to take at his own expense a course on instruction emphasizing classroom management and teacher accountability. Although this was a disciplinary case, not a negligence case, the analysis of the teacher's duty is applicable to determining the educator's standard of care in negligence. The case shows that teachers are responsible for supervision of their stu-

---

46 Roher & Wormwell, above note 32 at 70–71. See also MacKay, Sutherland, & Pochini, above at note 14 at 29–31.
47 2014 LNONCTD 3.

dents and must manage the end-of-the-day dismissal beyond the school bell in a professional manner.

As a general rule, educators are not responsible for injuries students suffer away from school property or travelling to and from school on their own. However, this rule does not apply when known hazards are close to the school. Educators in this situation must eliminate risks associated with these hazards. Doing so might include employing a crossing guard at busy intersections or fencing off a steep ravine. Educators must also warn parents and students of these hazards and develop school policy accordingly.

4) Field Trips

Educators are responsible for the safety of students when they take students on school-related and school board–approved field trips. In these circumstances, the educator's standard of care applies to activities and excursions off school property. *Bain (Guardian ad litem of) v Calgary Board of Education*[48] is a leading case in establishing grounds for negligence and liability on field trips. In this 1993 Alberta case, a teacher conducting an overnight forestry excursion deviated from the school board–approved itinerary by permitting students to hike alone and unsupervised. No precautions were taken. A nineteen-year-old student fell while hiking and suffered severe and permanent brain injury. The teacher and school board were sued for negligence because of inadequate supervision. The court found the school board liable for the teacher's actions. The student was found contributorily negligent and apportioned 25 percent liability for the injury. The teacher was apportioned 75 percent liability. The court held the excursion was an "extension of the classroom" because it was approved by the school board and subject to the same duty and standard of care as the classroom. It found three failures in the educator's supervision: (1) permitting an unplanned hike, (2) failing to supervise, and (3) failing to take precautions and avoid risks.

This case demonstrates that teachers must not deviate from board-approved field trip itineraries. Spontaneous outings attract liability if accidents and injuries occur. Teachers need to anticipate and arrange adequate supervision for every activity on school board–approved excursions.

A field trip is any school-organized educational activity involving students that takes place away from school. The school board must approve

---

48   [1994] 2 WWR 468 (Alta QB).

field trips, and teachers must submit a form to their principals request-ing approval. If teachers conduct a field trip without approval from their board, they may be held personally liable for any injuries. The custodial parents or guardians of each student under eighteen participating in the field trip must give written consent to a field trip. If a student is in a joint custody family situation, written consent from both parents is required.

Field trips should also have an educational purpose communicated to students and their parents or guardians. They should be prepared for as if they are classroom activities: doing so means having a lesson plan out-lining how the educational objectives of the trip will be met. The teacher in charge of the field trip should leave an itinerary with the principal in case of an emergency. Trip arrangements and emergency plans should be prepared and communicated to all students, parents, volunteers, and staff involved in the trip. Expectations for conduct and consequences should be clearly communicated to students and parents. Information on how to contact parents, as well as student medical information, should be col-lected and on hand throughout the trip.

Certain activities that are deemed high risk, unsafe, or irrelevant to the curriculum are generally not approved by school boards. These may include trips to amusement parks, as well as water sport activities such as scuba diving, white water rafting, and swimming parties at private or non-regulated pools, rivers, or lakes. Teachers are wise to consider the fol-lowing when planning and implementing a field trip:

1) student safety
2) the age, maturity, experience, health, emotional capabilities, excep-tionalities, and cultural backgrounds of all students
3) funding
4) transportation arrangements
5) risks associated with the planned activities, including weather, geog-raphy, and condition of equipment
6) adequate supervision in accordance with the school board's teacher-student supervision ratios, which includes ensuring that supervisors are all over eighteen years of age and do not have a criminal record.[49]

---

49 For detailed discussions of risk management strategies pre- and post-excursion, see Brown & Zuker, above note 21 at 178–81, and see also Roher & Wormwell, above note 32 at 76–78.

a) Medical Emergencies

Medical emergencies on field trips pose potentially challenging situations for teachers. Because teachers stand in *loco parentis* to their students, they have a duty to render assistance to students if they are in peril. Teachers are obligated to exercise positive conduct towards a student in a medical emergency. They must act like a reasonably careful or prudent parent and render assistance competently. The standard of care required of a teacher in a medical emergency varies depending on circumstances and risks. Teachers must be aware of students' medical conditions and their required medications in case of an emergency. If students under eighteen years of age have life-threatening medical conditions, their teacher must get directions for treatment from the students' parents or guardians; students over eighteen years of age can give their own consent.

In a medical emergency, however, when obtaining the consent of a parent or guardian is not possible, students under eighteen are presumed to have the mental capacity to provide consent for their medical treatment, unless there is evidence to the contrary. If a student is unable to give consent — for instance, if unconscious — consent is not necessary. In this situation, a teacher must do what is best for the student. Furthermore, the teacher in charge needs to make sure that all adult supervisors are aware of any existing medical conditions.

On a field trip it is important to have sufficient staff who are properly trained to administer appropriate medication and also trained to cope with emergencies. Field trips far from medical centres (such as a camping ground) may be inappropriate for a student requiring medical treatment. Teachers should try to arrange for a parent or guardian of the student to attend, so that the parent may look after the child. Teachers planning field trips should determine how they might deal with medical emergencies as part of their preparation. For example, they should know where the nearest hospital is and how to get to it, and ensure that staff members who are trained in basic emergency procedures are present.

In the case of *Moddejonge v Huron County Board of Education*,[50] two young girls drowned on a camping field trip. The supervising teacher was a non-swimmer; nevertheless, he took some of the students down to the lake for a swim. Two of the girls, one of whom was a non-swimmer, were carried out by the current towards a dangerous drop-off and began to struggle. A third girl came to their rescue and managed to save one of

---

50 (1972), 25 DLR (3d) 661 (Ont HCJ).

the girls, but in the process, she herself drowned. The supervising teacher who could not swim could not rescue the girls and had to return to camp to get help. The court found that the supervising teacher was negligent and his conduct fell below the standard of care of the careful and prudent parent. The court also held the school board vicariously liable for the teacher's conduct, finding he was acting within the course of his employment. This case illustrates that teachers must be aware of and prepared for any potential hazards or emergencies that may be encountered during a field trip.

b) Transportation Related to School Events

Travel arrangements are important to consider when planning field trips or school events. School boards in Canada are generally held responsible for student safety on field trips or to school-sponsored events. School boards are vicariously liable for negligence related to school board–owned transportation, namely, school buses. If a means of transportation is not owned by the school board, courts will consider the degree of control the school board has over the means of transportation: for instance, whether a bus company is an independent contractor or is an agent of the school board. Transportation may include school buses, public transportation, private vehicles, or any other form of school board–approved transportation.

Teachers must arrange and supervise all aspects of transportation, including accommodations for students with special needs. If students are under eighteen years of age, teachers must notify parents of the mode of transportation and obtain their consent. Volunteer drivers on field trips must be approved by the principal and have school board–approved motor vehicle liability insurance. A teacher must act as a "reasonably careful and prudent parent" towards students travelling in the teacher's car. The school board is vicariously liable for the teacher's actions as long as the teacher is transporting students to school activities.

If students volunteer to drive, they must have signed consent from the vehicle's owner. The principal may refuse to allow a student to drive on a field trip if it is deemed unsafe or inappropriate. All volunteer drivers, including school board employees, should inform their insurance company of the field trip. The insurance company will add this information to the employee's file to ensure coverage in the case of an accident. Volunteer drivers should make sure that their vehicle is safe.

If students have arrangements to be picked up at school by their parents after an event, the principal or teacher must supervise them until the parents arrive. If students are to make their own way home after an event, parents must be informed, especially if it is very late, if the students are young, or if known hazards are close to school. If a student has to be sent home early from a field trip, the parents should be contacted and the student's safe return arranged. Doing this may mean that the student is picked up by their parents or guardian or is driven home by a teacher.

5) Emergence of a Higher Standard of Care

a) Sports and Physical Education

The general standard of care imposed by the courts for sports and physical education has been the careful and prudent parent;[51] however, scholars suggest that courts are also inclined to impose a higher standard of care than what a regular classroom teacher is to meet: that of a "reasonably skilled physical education teacher," who would have the expert knowledge, skills, and level of competency required to carefully and prudently supervise students participating in these kinds of activities.[52] The educator's role is to supervise students to ensure that they are not exposed to unreasonable risk in the performance of any inherently dangerous activity that they have not been properly trained to do.[53] Other considerations in determining negligence include the nature of the activity, the student's age, ability, and training in the activity, and the condition of the equipment involved. Courts will generally consider school board policies and practices around implementing sport activities as evidence as to what educators consider reasonable precaution in sports. They may also view established practices as set out in provincial government or physical education association safety guidelines to determine customary practices and reasonable expectations in athletic fields.

Catherwood (Guardian ad litem of) v Heinrichs[54] established the grounds for negligence and liability in the gymnasium or during physical education or sports activities. In this 1996 British Columbia case, a sixteen-year-old student suffered a broken wrist after falling from a tree. He had climbed the tree while waiting to go to bat during a school baseball game.

---

51   See *McKay (Next friend of) v Saskatchewan Govan School Unit No 29*, [1968] SCR 589 at 593–94; *Myers*, above note 12.

52   MacKay, Sutherland, & Pochini, above note 14 at 36–38.

53   *MacCabe v Westlock Roman Catholic Separate School District No 110*, 2001 ABCA 257 at para 35.

54   [1996] BCJ No 1373 (SC) [*Catherwood*].

Supervising teachers participated in the game. Other students did not report to the teachers that the student was climbing the tree, and the tree was too dense for teachers to see the student. The student sued the teachers and the school board, alleging negligent supervision during the baseball game. The court found the student was owed a standard of care of "a careful and prudent parent of a large family," taking into account the student's age and capacity and any inherently dangerous conditions. The court held the teachers did not breach this standard of care. They had participated in the baseball game as role models to ensure the safety of students under their care. Moreover, the student's injury was not foreseeable, since he was mature and there were no other incidents of students injuring themselves while climbing trees.

This case illustrates that "reasonable" teacher supervision depends on the circumstances. According to the *Catherwood* case, appropriate supervision during physical exercise is determined, in part, by

1) the circumstances of the injury
2) the relevant school board policies
3) the supervisors' instructions regarding student conduct
4) the ratio of students to supervisors
5) the inherent dangers associated with the activity in question
6) the age and maturity of the students
7) the weather conditions for outdoor activities
8) the hazards in or around the area of supervision
9) any special circumstances concerning student(s) involved

Thornton illustrates a modified standard of care for physical education teachers, namely, that of a

> reasonable and careful parent, taking into account the judicial modification of the reasonable-and-careful parent test to allow for the larger-than-family size of the physical education class and the supraparental expertise commanded of [the teacher].[55]

In this British Columbia case, after performing a somersault from a springboard during gymnastics class, a fifteen-year-old student was tragically injured and became quadriplegic. The physical education teacher had added a jumping box to the activity, making it more dangerous. The court found the teacher negligent for creating a dangerous situation.

---

55 *Thornton*, above note 25 at 57.

The teacher appealed this decision. The appeal court found there was an inherent and foreseeable danger in gymnastics but the teacher's actions increased, instead of minimized, the risk of injury. In this case, the court identified the following factors to consider in determining negligence in physical exercises:

1) suitability of attempted exercise to students' age and mental/physical condition
2) adequate and progressive training and coaching of students in the activity to avoid dangers
3) adequate and suitably-arranged equipment
4) appropriate supervision considering the inherent dangers of the activity[56]

The caselaw on negligence in sports and physical education classes points to the need for educators to be proactive and preventive in their coaching. The cases demonstrate the importance for teachers to provide adequate instruction and training in a particular sport or activity. Doing this may include proper training for coaches and adhering to physical education and sport guidelines. For example, when educators are supervising sports, following the provincial physical education association guidelines has an impact on the appropriate supervision. These guidelines establish appropriate levels of supervision for students in sports, athletic, and physical education activities. Teachers and coaches should develop lesson plans for physical education classes as well as for practices that demonstrate their knowledge and skill — especially around proper techniques for complicated sports. They must also show that each student has been trained properly and progressively in the sport in question. They need to ensure that their own training is up-to-date and to have evidence of their training as coach/instructor for the particular activity.

These concerns were evident in *Hussack v Chilliwack School District No 33* when, in 2009, the Supreme Court of British Columbia held that the Chilliwack School District was liable for injuries sustained by a Grade 7 student playing field hockey in physical education class. The court found that the student did not have the appropriate experience and the proper instruction to play the sport. The decision was appealed to the BC Court of Appeal and the original decision was upheld.[57] The teacher's conduct in this case fell below the educator's standard of care because he allowed

---

56 *Ibid* at 58.
57 *Hussack*, above note 2.

the student to participate in the sport knowing he had no exposure to field hockey. The court found that the student, who had a history of chronic absenteeism, also lacked the basic requisite skills to play field hockey. In the middle of the game, the plaintiff student had chased down another student who was on a breakaway and attempted to check her from behind. She swung her stick and struck him in the nose. He was taken to hospital. The injury did not result in brain injury, but the student complained of worsening symptoms during the weeks after the injury.

This case shows that a teacher must be able to prove that the students were trained and coached in a progressive way that ensures they have the skills to do the sport/activity and if a student does not have the skills, the teacher should not allow the student to participate. Safety is the paramount concern. Taken together, the caselaw suggests that, in certain situations involving dangerous or risky activity that requires special skill and expertise, courts are more likely to hold teachers to a professional standard of expertise rather than a parental standard of care. This standard applies to sports and physical education classes and also to shop, home economics, and science classes.

b) Shop, Home Economics, and Science Lab Classes

The caselaw suggests that teachers of classes that involve inherently dangerous activities need to establish proper safety procedures and provide students with proper instructions about possible risks and safety precautions. They should maintain proper supervision throughout the class and warn students of particular dangers during the class.[58] Safety policies must be implemented and routinely reviewed, and students must be provided with written safety manuals that provide instruction on how to use specialized equipment. To meet the educator's standard of care, teachers must consider and address

1) the condition of the machines
2) the history and knowledge of machine malfunctions[59]
3) the characteristics of the students participating in the class, including their age and (dis)ability
4) the foreseeable risks of injury in the activity[60]

---

58 *Brown v Essex (County) Roman Catholic Separate School Board*, [1990] OJ No 1455 (HCJ).
59 *Jahangiri-Bojani (Guardian ad litem of) v Brudderer*, 2001 BCSC 1371.
60 *Dziwenka (Next friend of) v Alberta* (1971), [1972] SCR 419.

5) the use of appropriate safety equipment such as safety glasses

6) the need to instruct students about potential hazards, such as splat-tering of chemicals

7) the need to instruct students about the proper procedure around chem-icals[61]

In this area of negligence cases, courts are imposing an alternative stan-dard of care which goes beyond that of the reasonably careful and prudent teacher practitioner: meeting this standard involves a greater degree of supervision and demands the skill and competence of a professional edu-cation practitioner.[62]

L. ACCOUNTABILITY FOR BULLYING, SCHOOL VIOLENCE, AND DISCRIMINATION

Courts are increasingly finding that part of the educator's standard of care includes preventing bullying, violence, and discrimination in the schools. In the case of *North Vancouver School District No 44 v Jubran*,[63] Azmi Jubran was being bullied and harassed by other students for a number of years on the basis of his perceived sexual orientation. The other students made anti-gay slurs, and among other things, Azmi was spit on, kicked, and slammed into lockers. The student and his parents notified his school and school board about the bullying. After an investigation, the school at-tempted to address the problem by, for example, educating the offending students and imposing discipline and sanctions (including suspensions and detentions) for the conduct. The harassment, however, continued.

Azmi Jubran eventually filed a human rights complaint against the school board for their lack of success in eliminating the harassment and bullying. The school maintained they did respond, but the bullying just continued. The British Columbia Court of Appeal found the school board in breach of their duties under the BC *Human Rights Code* for not provid-ing proactive, preventive, and ongoing measures to combat homophobic bullying.[64] The court found the school board's response was inadequate. Although the educators had implemented progressive discipline strat-egies, they had failed to adopt new strategies when the initial responses

---

61 *James v River East School Division No 9*, [1976] 2 WWR 577 (Man CA).

62 MacKay, Sutherland, & Pochini, above note 14 at 33–36.

63 2005 BCCA 201.

64 RSBC 1996, c 210.

did not curb the misconduct. The court also noted that while the school addressed incidents of bullying, it did not address the underlying and pervasive homophobia throughout the school organization that was needed to ensure a safe school environment.

Although this was a human rights case, it could have proceeded as a negligence case as the court found that the educators had failed in their duty to supervise and keep the student safe, ultimately holding the school liable for the bullying happening within it. In effect, the court in the *Jubran* case found that the educators' actions and responses to the bullying fell below the standard of care, and it held the educators and school board liable for damages.

The existing common law and statutory laws pertaining to the educator's standard of care provide the framework for the tort of bullying. This case serves as a caution for educators whose inaction or inadequate reaction to stop known bullying, harassment, and discrimination within the school can lead to negligence lawsuits and findings of liability and damages. Educators' duty of care towards their students includes the duty to intervene and stop bullying occurring in the school or on the school grounds. Moreover, schools and school boards must establish and implement effective policies to assist educators in stopping bullying and harassment.[65]

The standard of care of the careful parent also applies to technology and social media websites. Educators may be liable for students' online or out-of-school bullying and harassment that affects the safety, health, and well-being of students at their school if they knew or should have reasonably known about it. This duty, as it pertains to discrimination, has been described by the Supreme Court of Canada as follows: "A school board has a duty to maintain a positive school environment for all persons served by it and it must be ever vigilant of anything that might interfere with this duty."[66]

---

65   There is a new trend in Canada towards negligence lawsuits for bullying; yet, as of the date of writing, there are no reported judgments. However, the US Supreme Court has held that school boards can be held liable where the harassment is severe, pervasive, and objectively offensive and deprives the victim of the educational benefit of the school. See *Davis v Monroe County Board of Education*, 526 US 629, headnote at 1, which defined the standard of educator's liability as "deliberate indifference." See also *Patterson v Hudson Area Schools*, 551 F3d 438 (6th Cir 2009).

66   *Ross v New Brunswick School District No 15*, [1996] 1 SCR 825 at para 50.

M. CONCLUSION

Negligence in the educational setting revolves around the significant parental, supervisory role of teachers. The important role of educators has been summed up by the Supreme Court of Canada in this way:

> Teachers and principals are placed in a position of trust that carries with it onerous responsibilities. When children attend school or school functions, it is they who must care for the children's safety and well-being. It is they who must carry out the fundamentally important task of teaching children so that they can function in our society and fulfil their potential. In order to teach, school officials must provide an atmosphere that encourages learning. During the school day they must protect and teach our children. In no small way, teachers and principals are responsible for the future of the country.[67]

While the *in loco parentis* legal principle may not define the full educational authority and status of teachers, it still influences the educator's standard of care in the careful and prudent parent rule, which is central to any discussion of negligence and liability of teachers. The historical common law duty of care imposed on teachers has been expanded and clarified by courts, statutes, and numerous government regulations and policies. Taken together, the law indicates that teachers must protect their students from unreasonable risk of harm.

Indeed, the complex, multifaceted, and expanding role of the contemporary teacher comes with increased exposure to risk and suggests that educators cannot simply act as a regular parent in exercise of their duties towards their students, but instead must supervise their students with the attention of a *careful and prudent* parent. This standard has been criticized as unduly onerous and as requiring something beyond parental vigilance, impossible to meet in a modern-day schooling context given the variety of students' social and educational needs. But Canadian courts have repeatedly upheld the careful and prudent rule as the educator's standard of care.

As outlined in this chapter, in some circumstances involving specialized activities that require a higher skill level such as physical education, shop classes, or science labs, courts have held educators to a higher standard of care requiring professional competence and specialized expertise rather than simply parental competence and expertise. Educators do not

---

67   R v MRM, [1998] 3 SCR 393 at para 35.

have to be perfect in their supervision of students, but the standard of care for today's educators requires a greater degree of oversight by teachers: teachers must anticipate dangers and the potential for students' reckless behaviour and protect against it.[68]

Preventing negligence involves "risk management."[69] This includes identifying, reducing, or eliminating foreseeable risk in schools in a manner that meets the educator's standard of care. Each year, educators should review, evaluate, and revise school safety policies and systems of supervision in their schools. Up-to-date policies should be communicated to the school community and implemented effectively. A system of routine follow-up and ongoing monitoring of the success or limitations of safety procedures and strategies across school activities and the school premises should be put in place. Achieving this may involve a post-event survey of participants evaluating the education experience and what was learned. For educators that means identifying what safety strategies worked, what strategies did not work, what safety issues arose, and how the activity can be reorganized to ensure a better and safer educational experience.

---

68 *Myers*, above note 12.
69 For a full discussion of risk management for educators, see Brown & Zuker, above note 21 at 87–88.

CHAPTER 7

Issues of Misconduct

Justice Marvin A Zuker (retired)

A. INTRODUCTION

As the world continues to change at a rapid pace, educators in the twenty-first century face a wide variety of challenges. As teachers enter the field of education, it is necessary that they come equipped with a body of knowledge that can help them to navigate through different elements of their career. One of the most important areas that teachers must be informed about is their legal position within society, as well as the obligations and duties that go along with that position.

Unfortunately, preservice education programs for teachers do not always, if at all, cover the legal context and implications of our education system in Canada in enough depth to prepare educators for the legal elements of their role in society. In Canada, more specifically according to the *Criminal Code* of Canada, members of certain professions are deemed to be in a "position of trust." Due to their role in society, teachers are most often considered to be in a position of trust. Working so closely with children, as well as being responsible for the safety and well-being of those children, heightens teachers' moral, ethical, and legal obligations.

It is the unique relationship between teacher and student that legally obligates teachers to maintain a duty of care towards those they teach. Parents entrust teachers to the care of their children while the parents are not present, and this responsibility is not taken lightly within our legal system. The *Education Act* of Ontario,[1] for example, defines and explains the parameters of what is referred to as *"in loco parentis."* In simple terms,

---

1   RSO 1990, c E.2, as amended.

188 / Marvin A Zucker

teachers take on the role of the parent while students are under their care, subject, of course, to statutory considerations.

One of many Ontario regulations pertaining to teachers is "a teacher shall be responsible for effective instruction, training and evaluation of progress of pupils in the subjects assigned to the teacher."[2] Apart from a teacher's basic duties within the classroom, there are also "supervisory duties." These duties are more closely linked to the safety of students and remain within the spectrum of responsibility.

It is important to note that due to the natural connection between teachers and school boards, standards of ethical behaviour extend outside the school setting. Teachers are seen to be representatives of the school board for which they work and, therefore, have a responsibility to uphold certain values held by the board when they are out in the community. The various duties and responsibilities of teachers are extensive and often stretch beyond the settings of the classroom and school. For this reason, teachers need to be aware of what they may be held accountable for.

B. DETERMINATION OF A POSITION OF TRUST

The "position of trust" has been referenced and assessed in the context of our criminal courts where teachers have been charged with actions not acceptable for appropriate and responsible student–teacher relationships. In 1984, the Committee on Sexual Assault against Children and Youth developed the report *Sexual Offences against Children*, otherwise known as the Badgley Report, in an effort to further protect children against crimes of a sexual nature.[3] The committee felt it important to deem teachers as well as those in other professions to be in a position of trust or authority.

Although teachers are seen today to hold a position of trust within society, Parliament did not fully accept the recommendations put forth in the Badgley Report. Instead, Parliament wanted the evaluation of each individual case to be recognized as an important part of the process when determining whether or not a person was in a position of trust or authority. Despite the fact that a position of trust is present in most cases involving teacher and student relationships, Parliament was careful not to construct a legal situation that automatically held teachers in a position of

---

2   *Operation of Schools — General*, RRO 1990, Reg 298, as amended.
3   Committee on Sexual Offences against Children and Youths, *Sexual Offences Against Children* (Ottawa: Supply and Services Canada, 1985) [Badgley Report].

trust or authority without looking further into the unique circumstances of each case. Of the utmost importance was the protection of children against possible sexual predators. With the safety of children remaining an obvious priority, Parliament also set out to protect teachers from any legal unfairness based solely upon their occupation.

The submission of the Badgley Report resulted in amendments to the *Criminal Code* of Canada.[4] In various sexual assault and sexual exploitation cases involving teachers, the nature of the relationship between the teacher and student is evaluated within the context of a position of trust or authority; for example, section 153(1) of the *Code* outlines the offence of sexual exploitation as follows:

> 153.(1) Every person commits an offence who is in a position of trust or authority towards a young person, who is a person with whom the young person is in a relationship of dependency or who is in a relationship with a young person that is exploitative of the young person, and who
> a) for a sexual purpose, touches, directly or indirectly, with a part of the body or with an object, any part of the body of the young person;
> or
> b) for a sexual purpose, invites, counsels or incites a young person to touch, directly or indirectly, with a part of the body or with an object, the body of any person, including the body of the person who so invites, counsels or incites and the body of the young person.

The implications of being found in a position of trust can greatly affect the outcome of a criminal case. The definition and interpretation of being in a position of trust has been the central issue of several cases.

In *R v Audet*,[5] the position of trust was a central factor. At a night club in Campbellton, New Brunswick, the accused, Yves Audet, a twenty-two-year-old physical education teacher, encountered a student he had previously taught. The complainant had just celebrated her fourteenth birthday and was accompanied by two of her female cousins. Both of the complainant's cousins were in their twenties and had purchased a few beers for the fourteen-year-old while at the night club. Audet indicated surprise upon seeing his underage student at the venue.

After spending the evening together at the night club, Audet's male friend, who had accompanied him, suggested that they all go to a cottage,

---

4   *Ibid. Criminal Code*, RSC 1985, c C-46 [*Code*].
5   [1996] 2 SCR 171 [*Audet*]. See, more recently, *R v Zhou*, 2016 ONCJ 547, where the accused was sixteen and the complainant fourteen years of age.

the three young women included. The three cousins agreed, and once they were at the cottage, Audet complained he was not feeling well and went to lie down in another room. Not long after this, the complainant went into the same room, and although there were two beds in the room she lay down beside Audet. At some point during the night, both Audet and the complainant woke up and proceeded to engage in oral sex. Audet admitted that he had started the touching initially.

The trial judge found that Audet was not in a position of trust or authority towards the complainant at the time of the incident, a decision upheld by the Court of Appeal. The trial judge found that there was sufficient circumstantial evidence to conclude that Audet was not in a position of trust the evening that the events occurred. Some critical aspects of the case that most affected his decision were the role of the complainant's cousins, the setup of the bedroom, the young age of the accused, and the fact that Audet had neither made a sexual pass at the complainant at the cottage nor invited her to the cottage.

It was decided by the Supreme Court of Canada, however, that the trial judge had erred in law. The trial decision was overturned and replaced with a guilty verdict. Although Parliament did not make it possible to automatically assume teachers to be in a position of trust or authority in every circumstance, it is not enough for a trial judge to determine the nature of a relationship without a thorough application of section 153 of the *Code*. Consent of a minor is not relevant in determining whether or not a position of trust was breached. A person charged under s. 153.1(1) cannot raise the young person's consent as a defence according to section 153.1(3) of the *Criminal Code*, as amended.

In another important case concerning the position of trust, *R v Aird*,[6] a twenty-eight-year-old tutor was charged with having a sexual relationship with an underage student he was tutoring. Again, a critical issue in this case was determining whether or not Aird was in a position of trust towards the complainant. Aird was a second-year student in teachers college with an undergraduate degree in mathematics. The complainant was a female student in Grade 12. She was sixteen years of age when the two met in the fall of 2008. Aird's practicum teaching placement was at an elementary school in Waterloo where he was assigned to a Grade 8 class. The complainant's sister, a student in the class where Aird had been placed, brought home a flyer about the appellant showing that he had his univer-

---

6   2013 ONCA 447.

sity degree in mathematics. The complainant's mother requested that she pay Aird to tutor her high school–aged daughter in mathematics. Aird agreed to tutor the seventeen-year-old girl, and that is how the relationship between the two originated.

An important issue in this case was establishing whether or not a sexual relationship had occurred before the complainant turned eighteen as referred by the *Code*. Although Aird testified that the sexual contact did not begin until after the complainant had turned eighteen and after the tutoring sessions had finished, the judge rejected his evidence and accepted that of the victim. The fact that the complainant's mother and various friends could corroborate evidence that she had had sexual relations with Aird at the age of seventeen weighed against Aird. His appeal was ultimately rejected.

In terms of using section 153 of the *Code* to measure the nature and status of a relationship, it is important to keep in mind the section's underlying purpose, namely, to protect young people from exploitation within imbalanced relationships with adults. In keeping with Parliament's objective to protect the young and vulnerable, a few considerations have been established as significant factors when a decision regarding position of trust is being made. Specifically, these considerations are (1) the age difference between the accused and the young person; (2) the evolution of their relationship; (3) the status of the accused in relation to the young person; (4) the degree of control, influence, or persuasiveness exercised by the accused over the young person; and (5) the expectations of the parties affected, including the accused, the young person, and the young person's parents.

The difference between a position of trust and a position of authority is also of importance. Aird argued that he was not in a position of authority towards the complainant due to the fact that he had no direct authority over her grades or had the capability to take disciplinary action. This defence is flawed because if a person is not found to be in a position of authority, that person can still be in a position of trust. The two are related concepts but can be assessed separately in a legal setting. As explained further by Blair J in *R v PS*:[7]

> I take a "position of trust" to be somewhat different than a "position of authority". The latter invokes notions of power and the ability to hold in one's hands the future or destiny of the person who is the object of the

---

7   [1993] OJ No 704 at para 37 (Gen Div), aff'd [1994] OJ No 3775 (CA).

exercise of the authority. A position of trust may, but need not necessarily, incorporate those characteristics. It is founded on notions of safety and confidence and reliability that the special nature of the relationship will not be breached.

Ultimately, it was not argued that Aird was in a position of authority at the time of the relationship, but he was found to be in a position of trust. It was clearly apparent that given Aird's credentials and current practicum position in a classroom, the parents of the complainant had a great deal of confidence in the fact that he would provide a safe learning environment for their daughter. The complainant was also a young person at the time of the sexual relationship. She did not have sexual experience prior to these encounters, placing her in a vulnerable position. There was clearly an imbalance inherent in their relationship, unfairly taken advantage of by Aird to fulfill his personal desires.

C. ATTENTION TO THE NEED TO KEEP SCHOOLS SAFE

Protecting Our Students, which is known as the Robins Report,[8] is a significant piece of "legislation" which was established to further protect students from both violence and sexual abuse within schools. After the disturbing case of a Sault Ste Marie teacher, Kenneth DeLuca, who was charged with sexually assaulting thirteen different female students over a period of more than two decades, the government became proactive in wanting to ensure the safety of students. DeLuca seemingly got away with sexual assault crimes against various students, and the school board failed to take appropriate action to protect its students. The wide-scale injustices seen served to help change the way that school boards are lawfully expected to handle themselves when dealing with reported sexual abuse and allegations against teachers. More stringent regulations act as precautionary measures to help ensure that predators are not able to commit such terrible acts against children. Furthermore, subsequent amendments to the *Ontario College of Teachers Act, 1996*[9] were meant to make certain that students would be protected on an ongoing basis.

---

8   Sydney L Robins and Ontario Ministry of the Attorney General, *Protecting Our Students: A Review to Identify & Prevent Sexual Misconduct in Ontario Schools* (Toronto: Ministry of the Attorney General, 2000) [Robins Report].

9   SO 1996, c 12, as amended by the *Protecting Students Act, 2016*, SO 2016, c 24, also known as Bill 37, which came into force 5 December 2016.

Justice Robins prepared a draft of the comprehensive report in which he looked for ways to both "identify" and "prevent" the occurrence of sexual acts or violence against children. When the Report was submitted in its finality, it included more than a hundred recommendations that would serve to help the government keep schools safe. After its release, more intensive screening reports of teachers to be hired were put into place, and criminal record checks and more rigid guidelines concerning teacher transfers were implemented. The Robins Report also obligated school boards to notify the Ontario College of Teachers concerning any teacher who "is charged with an offence, disciplined, dismissed because of an offence or when a teacher resigns during an investigation regarding an offence." Certainly, the increased legal responsibility of school boards and teachers has changed the context of education in the twenty-first century.

Sexual crimes by individuals "in a relationship of authority, trust or dependency" against children are inconceivably malevolent acts.[10] Furthermore, as Kerans JA stated in *R v RPT*:

> This court has said that gross child abuse by somebody *in loco parentis* demands a denunciatory sentence, one which, as Laycraft J.A. said in *R. v. Beere*, (1982), 41 A.R. 249 (Alta. C.A.), at p. 254:
>
>> ". . . expresses society's abhorrence for the act and its need to reinforce societal values. Society must clearly state that those in a position of trust to children must not betray that trust; the integrity of the family unit must be supported."[11]

In *R v CP*, Carter J stated that

> [s]ociety places great trust upon its teachers. We are entitled to assume that teachers will be purely and absolutely professional in all their interactions with our children. We are devastated when this trust is broken.[12]

In a third case, LaForest J stated that teachers are inextricably linked to the integrity of the school system. Teachers occupy positions of trust and confidence and exert considerable influence over their students as a result of their positions. The conduct of a teacher bears directly upon the community's perception of the ability of the teacher to fulfill such a position

---

10   See *SL v RTM*, 2013 ONSC 1448.
11   1983 ABCA 175 at para 11.
12   2007 SKPC 150 at para 33.

of trust and influence, and upon the community's confidence in the public school system as a whole.[13]

During the late 1990s and into the twenty-first century, a better understanding of child abuse developed because of high-profile cases such as Mount Cashel and residential schools, and through government initiatives like the Badgley Report.[14] Justice Robins[15] hoped that his recommendations would go beyond just relationships to a larger strategy directed at a healthier school culture, free from violence, abuse, harassment, and discrimination. Justice Robins found that the extent of the sexual misconduct between teacher and student is not known, and many cases are not discovered by authorities or victims are too afraid or reluctant to come forward. He observed that there has become an unwritten rule of silence and denial of abuse in the system.

Justice Robins recommended deletion of the requirement that the suspected abuse be related to a "person in charge of a child." It should be clear that anyone employed or who volunteers in a position of trust and authority is a person in charge of those students. His report comments on the potential role of section 161(1)(b) of the *Code* in promoting children's safety. The section presents how people who commit crimes of sexual misconduct should be removed from their employment or from serving as volunteers if in a capacity that involves being in a position of trust or authority towards children.

Although consensual relationships by law and standards of teaching practice are prohibited, it has traditionally been seen as "less" heinous and "wrong."[16] For example, consider a case involving a popular high-school teacher, Leslie Merlino, who became especially close to one of her female students in 2006. The first illicit contact between the student and the teacher was described as "stroking of the hair."[17] During a school trip, the two females grew even more attached to each other. In October 2006, the police arrested Merlino and six months later she resigned. The Ontario

---

13   See *Ross v New Brunswick School District No 15*, [1996] 1 SCR 825 at para 43 [*Ross*].

14   Badgley Report, above note 3.

15   Robins Report, above note 8.

16   Stuart M Piddocke, Romulo Magsino, & Michael Manley-Casimir, *Teachers in Trouble: An Exploration of the Normative Character of Teaching* (Toronto: University of Toronto Press, 1997).

17   Bob Mitchell, "'Tragic' Affair Ends Teacher's Career" *The* [Toronto] *Star* (15 September 2009), online: www.thestar.com/news/gta/2009/09/15/tragic_affair_ends_teachers_career.html.

College of Teachers emphasized that Merlino was in a position of trust when she entered into and continued the inappropriate personal relationship.[18] Any sexual contact with a young person who is in a relationship of trust and dependence is considered sexual misconduct and exploitation. The hope is to protect impressionable students from sexual advances by those in positions of power. In this case, the law presumes that any sexual conduct — even if that context is consensual and voluntary — is sexual exploitation, and therefore consent is not a defence.

D. SEXUALLY ABUSIVE RELATIONSHIPS

1) Grooming

"Grooming" is a term used to describe "the process by which sex offenders carefully initiate and maintain sexually abusive relationships."[19] The abuser consciously makes connections with the victim and keeps their relationship a secret. There are a few stages to grooming, but the most important is the preparatory stage, in which the abuser separates the target from friends and family, and finds and preys on the young person's vulnerabilities, using bribery, rewards, love, and affection to foster and maintain the secrecy of the abusive relationship. Once this trust is formed, the abuser may test the victim's reaction to sex by "bringing up sexual matters in discussion . . . subtly increasing sexual touching. In this way, the offended attempts to normalize sex."[20]

In one case, Mary Kay Letourneau spoke to the judge at her sentencing, saying, "Your Honour . . . I did something that I had no right to do, morally or legally. It was wrong and I am sorry. I give you my word that it will not happen again. Please help me. Help us all."[21] She was convicted of second-degree child rape for having sex with a twelve-year-old student. She pleaded guilty and received jail time as a sex offender.

---

18   Ontario College of Teachers, *Professional Advisory: Professional Misconduct Related to Sexual Abuse and Sexual Misconduct* (2002), online: www.oct.ca/resources/advisories/professional-misconduct-related-to-sexual-abuse-and-sexual-misconduct. See also *Professional Advisory* dated 11 February 2011.

19   James L Knoll, "Teacher Sexual Misconduct: Grooming Patterns and Female Offenders" (2010) 19 *Journal of Child Sexual Abuse* at 371.

20   *Ibid* at 374.

21   Sheila Cavanagh, *Sexing the Teacher: School Sex Scandals and Queer Pedagogies* (Vancouver: UBC Press, 2007) at 31.

2) Predatory Behaviour

Predators do not act spontaneously. They will often put time and effort into planning their encounters and trying to keep them secret. Usually, predators continue the behaviour for a longer time, being "persistent and pervasive," using techniques of grooming to cultivate the child's trust and affection.[22] Unfortunately, there have been numerous cases of predators in an education context, and, in some cases, it takes years to catch them, if at all. Between 2000 and 2005, Mark Baggio groomed, solicited, and engaged in sexual relationships with two young females. He blatantly befriended them, engaging in inappropriate communications that increased in sexual nature from kissing and fondling to sexual intercourse.[23]

Fromuth and Holt studied the perception of teacher sexual misconduct in terms of the age of the student. They concluded that perceptions are important because they "have implications for the handling and even the reporting of these experiences." [24] Therefore, if a student–teacher relationship is not viewed negatively or not viewed as abuse, it may not be reported. If not reported, then teachers cannot be prosecuted. Fromuth and Holt have identified gender as being an important variable in the way sexual misconduct is perceived.[25] For example, the most interesting dyad is the female teacher–male student, which tends to be viewed less negatively than the male teacher–female student dyad.[26]

E. THE DUTY TO REPORT

In recent decades, society has undergone significant shifts towards improving child protection. The use of punitive discipline to control and

---

22 RJ Shoop, *Sexual Exploitation in Schools* (Thousand Oaks, CA: Corwin Press, 2004). See also Charol Shakeshaft, "Know the Warning Signs of Educator Sexual Misconduct" (2013) 94 *Phi Delta Kappan* 8.

23 *Ibid.*

24 Mary Ellen Fromuth & Aimee R Holt, "Perception of Teacher Sexual Misconduct by Age of Student" (2008) 17 *Journal of Child Sexual Abuse* 163 at 164; see also Sarah Sacheli, "Girls Thought Baggio Was Going to Marry Them" *The Windsor Star* (23 September 2008), online: www.windsorstar.com/girls+thought+baggio+going+marry+them/818245/story.html.

25 Fromuth & Holt, above note 24.

26 Shoop, above note 22. See also Mary Ellen Fromuth, Amber L Mackey, & Amy Wilson, "Effect of Student Vulnerability on Perceptions of Teacher-Student Sexual Involvement" (2010) 19 *Journal of Child Sexual Abuse* 419.

correct a child's behaviour is now widely accepted as abuse. In a 1981 article, Aaron pointed out that the "battered child syndrome" revealed the profound effects of physical and emotional abuse and how maltreatment severely impairs a child's development. As a result, medical and other professionals began to pay greater notice to the issue of child abuse. Aaron noted that "hundreds of articles appeared in medical, legal, social scientific, and lay literature. From 1961 to 1962 [alone], the volume of professional literature concerning child abuse multiplied 15 times."[27]

The correlation between child maltreatment and poor mental and physical health consequences prompted changes in legislation to establish laws to protect children. The legal framework today reflects our historical understanding that the rights of the child are synonymous with autonomy and participation in society.[28] With this sentiment, professionals who work with children are responsible for the children's best interests and their well-being. An essential element to child protection is the cognizant position of medical professionals, teachers, and other professionals who are required by law to know the rights of the child and report child neglect.

The *Child and Family Services Act*[29] was proclaimed in force 1 January 1985 with the goal to consolidate all previous legislation affecting children and provide clear directions and principles for child welfare under one Act.[30] The CFSA legislation focused on child abuse, the rights of the child, and child protection — all while preserving the family unit. It was about the vulnerability of children, ensuring that children are protected and the duties towards children in care. The first major changes to this legislation took place in 2017, with the passage of Bill 89.[31] On the one hand, the family unit is the optimal environment for child development, but child abuse that is suffered directly or witnessed in the home is the opposite of the typical care, development, and protection subsumed by parents or

---

27   Jody Aaron, "Civil Liability for Teachers' Negligent Failure to Report Suspected Child Abuse" (1981) 28 *Wayne Law Review* 183 at 184.

28   BC Hafen & JO Hafen, "Abandoning Children to Their Autonomy: The *United Nations Convention on the Rights of the Child*" (1996) 37 *Harvard International Law Journal* 449.

29   RSO 1990, c C.11, as amended [CFSA].

30   Colin B King et al, "Child Protection Legislation in Ontario: Past, Present, and Future?" (2003) 13 *Education & Law Journal* 105.

31   *Supporting Children, Youth and Families Act, 2017,* SO 2017, c 14.

guardians. CFSA section 72(1)[32] stipulates where a teacher or others have a duty to report, now under the *Child, Youth and Family Services Act, 2017*.[33]

In the summer of 2005, Leslie Welsh and Kristen Ross, both teachers at Adelaide McLaughlin Public School in Durham, Ontario, took two students on an overnight shopping trip. Signed consent forms were received from both the parents. It was not known to the parents that Welsh's husband would be staying in the hotel room as well. One of the students, under the age of sixteen at the time, later told Welsh and Ross that Welsh's husband had sexually touched her at the hotel.

The panel at the College of Teachers found that Ross did not report the student's sexual allegation the first time and again, the second time ten days following the initial disclosure. According to *Professionally Speaking*, "although Kristen Ross was charged with failing to report, contrary to the *Child and Family Services Act*, the Provincial Offences Court dismissed the charge and the Ontario Court of Justice upheld the decision on appeal." The conditions for Ross's professional misconduct in failing to report to the student's parents, Children's Aid Society, and school board were that she was "ordered to complete a course in professional ethics at her own expense within 60 days of the date of the order."[34]

On the other hand, Ross's colleague, Welsh, received a more significant reproach from the panel. The panel heard that Welsh had been sending inappropriate emails and letters to the student from 2003 to 2005. The communications from Welsh referred to the student as "my butterfly" or "my angel" and told the student she was her "special" or "best friend." In emails to the girl she wrote they were "kindred spirits."[35] Welsh told the panel she did not believe the student's allegations about her husband's sexual misconduct and, therefore, did not inform the student's parents, Children's Aid Society, or the school board. However, after the allegations were made, Welsh continued to send personal emails and letters stating, "Not laughing," "Feel your pain," "Let's carry on as we always have . . . no changes," "No more tears . . . life is too short," and "Deep breath . . . Smile . . . Hug . . . ."[36]

32   Aaron, above note 27.
33   SO 2017, c 14, Sch 1.
34   See the decision of the Discipline Committee (3 December 2009): *Ontario College of Teachers v Ross*, 2009 LNONCTD 50.
35   *Ibid.*
36   *Ibid.*

Although Welsh failed to report, she was not convicted by a Provincial Offences Court. This decision was upheld on appeal by the Ontario Court of Justice. In any event, Welsh was found guilty of professional misconduct, her qualifications were suspended for three months, and she was directed to complete a course in professional ethics sixty days after the date of her order at her own expense.[37] Welsh also stated in a letter to the student that she knew her communication with the student, if found out, would result in her losing her job.

In *R v Kaija*,[38] before Hornblower J, Kaija was charged with failure to report abuse. Kaija was a high-school teacher at St Clair High School, where he coached the senior boys' basketball team. In his own time, Kaija coached a boys' elementary school basketball team, the St Clair Mini-Colts. On the weekend of 20 February 2005 the Mini-Colts went to Peterborough for a tournament. Upon return, one of the mothers informed Kaija that her son had witnessed another coach of the Mini-Colts, Jim Miller, sexually assault another team player and also saw Miller masturbate in his bed. As a result of this information, Kaija called several meetings with the parents to discuss the allegations against Miller.

Kaija was charged with failing to report the alleged sexual assault to a Children's Aid Society as required by the *Child and Family Services Act*. Kaija had a reasonable suspicion that a child had been sexually assaulted, and he had failed to report that suspicion and further protect the child. The defence moved for a non-suit submitting, first, that there was no evidence that Kaija did not report to a Children's Aid Society, and second, that evidence of the sexual assault did not come to him in his capacity as a teacher in the course of exercising his professional duty.

During meetings with the parents, there was evidence that Kaija did not want to involve the police. Kaija told the parents if the police became involved he would disband the team. In addition, Kaija discharged Miller of his coaching position and took over his duties. There was a reasonable inference that Kaija dealt with the matter on his own and did not involve the police. Therefore, he was not involving the Children's Aid Society. The second ground was that there was no evidence that Kaija obtained the information regarding the sexual abuse while performing his professional duty. The principal, Mr Keane of St Clair High School, attested that Kaija's duties with the Mini-Colts were outside his duties as a high-school teacher.

---

37   *Ibid.*
38   2006 ONCJ 193.

On the other hand, the operation of the Mini-Colts gave the perception of being affiliated with the high school since it shared the same team name, the uniforms were identical, it was a feeder program into the high-school team, practices took place at the high school, the contact number for Kaija was the high-school number, and enrolment took place at St Clair High School. As a result, the parents of the Mini-Colts players believed that the operation of the basketball team was sanctioned by the school board and that it fell under Kaija's professional duties.

In *R v Newton-Thompson*,[39] the accused were charged with failing to report suspicion of harm to a child. The accused, the principal and vice-principal of the CW Jefferys Collegiate Institute, did not report their knowledge of a female student's sexual assault in 2006. In 2007, police found out about the assault and charged the accused with failing to report "forthwith" a suspicion of harm to a child, contrary to section 72(1) of the *Child and Family Services Act*.

The justice of the peace found that the charge was laid outside the six-month limitation period set out in section 76(1) of the *Provincial Offences Act*,[40] and, therefore, granted the motion for dismissal. The Crown applied before Croll J of the Superior Court, stating that the offence is a continuing offence until the report is made. However, Croll J agreed with the justice of the peace. The offence was not a continuing one.

1) Reasonable Cause

The standard of care is such that professionals have a responsibility to report suspected child abuse. Yet, "informants are not required to have reasonable cause to believe abuse has in fact occurred before making a report. They are, however, obliged to have reasonable cause to make a report to CPS [Child Protection Services]."[41] In *Young v Bella*, a jury found that there was not reasonable cause to assume that a social work student should be red-flagged as a potential child abuser due to a situation outlined in a term paper. It decided that the university had acted negligently by failing to review the validity of Young's term paper and, instead, taking actions based on speculation. The university argued that section 38(6) of the *Child*

---

39 2009 ONCA 449. See also Terri L Hilborn, "Reporting Suspected Child Abuse: Defining the Line between 'Reasonable Cause' and Conjecture between 'Reasonable Cause' and 'Conjecture and Speculation'" (2006) 16 *Education Law Journal* 133.
40 RSO 1990, c P.33.
41 *Young v Bella*, 2006 SCC 3 at para 34.

Welfare Act (NFLD) stipulates that information of child abuse must be reported; however, section 38(6) *also* states that reporting must not be done maliciously or without reasonable cause.[42] Lack of reasonable cause was the concern here.

Educators are in a unique position to influence the lives of children around them. Masten and Coatsworth[43] stated that the availability to a child of one adult with whom the child shares a positive relationship is a reported predictor of psychological resilience. Due to teachers' extensive and frequent interactions with children, arguably there should be increased efforts to improve teacher training to identify child abuse. In addition, the duty to report must be successfully integrated into the educational teacher training program. Any failure of teachers to report should not be out of fear of legal ramifications or the feeling that the child's case is not severe enough to report. The professional duty of a teacher is to protect children effectively. This law requires teachers to be knowledgeable of their duty to report child abuse to a Children's Aid Society.

F. THE DUTY OF CARE AND VICARIOUS LIABILITY

It is commonly understood that a teacher owes a student a duty of care. As to the standard of care, in *Thornton v School District No 57 (Prince George)*,[44] the Court held that it is that of a "reasonable" and careful parent, taking into account the judicial modification of the reasonable-and-careful parent test to allow for the larger-than-family size of the physical education class and the supraparental expertise commanded of [the teacher]. Furthermore, the Court held that permitting a student to participate in a physical activity is not negligent

> (a) if it is suitable to his age and condition (mental and physical); (b) if he is progressively trained and coached to do it properly and avoid the danger; (c) if the equipment is adequate and suitable arranged; and (d) if the performance, having regard to its inherently dangerous nature, is properly supervised.

---

42   RSN 1990, c C12.
43   Ann S Masten & J Douglas Coatsworth, "The Development of Competence in Favorable and Unfavorable Environments: Lessons from Research on Successful Children" (1998) 53 *American Psychologist* 205.
44   1978 CanLII 12 SCC.

This standard was adopted in *Myers (Next friend of) v Peel (County) Board of Education*[45] as a "statement . . . setting forth appropriate considerations." It was not, however, accepted as a "code."

1) Vicarious Liability of Employers

As to the issue of vicarious liability, in *Bazley v Curry*,[46] the Supreme Court of Canada stated that an employer may be vicariously liable (1) for acts of an employee which are authorized by the employer or (2) for unauthorized acts that are so closely connected with authorized acts that they may be regarded as modes of doing an authorized act. If the authorities do not clearly suggest a solution, the decision whether to impose vicarious liability must be determined in light of the broader policy rationale behind strict liability, being the provision of an adequate and just remedy and deterrence. These policy considerations are offset by the need to ensure that it is fair and just that liability be imposed on the employer. This determination will be made on the basis of the test set out by McLachlin J (as she then was) in *Bazley*.

Justice McLachlin further summarized the test as follows at paragraph 36:

> Underlying the cases holding employers vicariously liable for the unauthorized acts of employees in the idea that employers may justly be held liable where the act falls within the ambit of risk that the employer's enterprise creates or exacerbates. Similarly, the policy purposes underlying the imposition of vicarious liability on employers are served only where the wrong is so connected with the employment that it can be said that the employer has introduced the risk of wrong (and is thereby fairly and usefully charged with its management and minimization). The question in each case is whether there is a connection or nexus between the employment enterprise and that wrong that justifies imposition of vicarious liability on the employer for the wrong, in terms of fair allocation of the consequences of the risk and/or deterrence.

Justice McLachlin held that, in sexual abuse cases, providing an opportunity for the employee to be alone with children for extended periods of

45 [1981] 2 SCR 21 [*Myers*].
46 [1999] 2 SCR 534 [*Bazley*]. See also Jack H Berryman, "Duty of Care" *Professionally Speaking* (December 1998), online: http://professionallyspeaking.oct.ca/december_1998/duty.htm. Recently, our courts found board liability for failing to address allegations of bullying. See *Karam v Ottawa-Carleton District School Board*, [2014] OJ No 2966 (SCJ).

time, coupled with employment that places the employee in positions of intimacy and power over the child, would be sufficient to found vicarious liability.

In *Jacobi v Griffiths*,[47] the Supreme Court of Canada reviewed cases consistent with the application of vicarious liability. In *Bazley*,[48] the Court established the legal and public policy basis for the doctrine of vicarious liability. Justice McLachlin stated:

> In summary, the test for vicarious liability for an employee's sexual abuse of a client should focus on whether the employer's enterprise and empowerment of the employee materially increased the risk of the sexual assault and hence the harm.

The Supreme Court of Canada has, of course, revisited the issue of vicarious liability.[49] The Court confirmed the test for vicarious liability set out in *Bazley*. Liability will be imposed on an employer for an employee's wrongful acts where (1) the risks inherent in the employer's enterprise materialize and cause harm and (2) liability is both fair and useful.

In *John Doe v Bennett*,[50] the Supreme Court applied the principles established in *Bazley* and found a Roman Catholic Episcopal Corporation vicariously liable for the conduct of a priest. Bennett, who had served as a parish priest in geographically isolated communities in Newfoundland, had sexually assaulted a number of young boys over a long period of time. The Supreme Court confirmed the requirement of a strong causal link between the employment and the wrongful acts, and found that the link had been established in the circumstances. The emphasis is on the strength of the causal link between the employment and the wrongful act; the employment must materially enhance the risk of a wrongful act.

Where injury occurs in a school sports program, the basis of liability may include not only occupiers' liability, but also breach of a statutory duty under the applicable school or education act, or a tort framed in negligence based on the breach of the school's common law duty of care to protect students from reasonably foreseeable risk of harm.

As indicated, the law that must be applied in determining whether an employer will be held to be strictly or vicariously liable for the criminal or wrongful acts of an employee was set out by the Supreme Court of Canada

47 [1999] 2 SCR 570 [*Jacobi*].
48 Above note 46 at para 46.
49 *KLB v British Columbia*, 2003 SCC 51.
50 2004 SCC 17.

in a series of cases, starting with *Bazley*[51] and its companion case, *Jacobi*.[52] In *Bazley*, the Supreme Court of Canada approved the Salmond test (from Salmond and Heuston's *Treatise on Torts*)[53] as the appropriate test for determining whether an employer should be held vicariously liable for the misconduct of an employee. Under that test, an employer may be vicariously liable (1) for acts of an employee which are authorized by the employer, or (2) for unauthorized acts which are so closely connected with authorized acts that they may be regarded as modes of doing an authorized act.

Furthermore, liability will be imposed on an employer for an employee's wrongful acts where (1) the risks inherent in the employer's enterprise materialize and cause harm and (2) liability is both fair and useful. In *KLB v British Columbia*,[54] the Court held that to make out a successful claim for vicarious liability, plaintiffs must establish, first, that the relationship between the tortfeasor and the person against whom liability is sought is sufficiently close as to make a claim for vicarious liability appropriate; and second, that the tort is sufficiently connected to the tortfeasor's assigned tasks that the tort can be regarded as a materialization of the risks created by the enterprise.

In *SGH v Gorsline*,[55] a teacher who was also a track and field coach sexually assaulted a student. The teacher was held directly liable for the sexual assault and was ordered to pay damages to the student. The student brought an action for damages against the school board framed in negligence and vicarious liability. The action against the school board was dismissed, and the student appealed. The appellate court found that the trial judge was correct to conclude that the acts of the school teacher were not so closely connected to the authorized acts of the employers as to impose liability. The trial judge found that the board had not significantly contributed to the risk of child sexual abuse and, therefore, was not vicariously liable for the deliberate criminal activity of its employee. While the teacher's work provided an opportunity for the teacher to commit the offences and a measure of authority over the students, this was insufficient to impose vicarious liability. The incidental connection between the

---

51   Above note 46.
52   Above note 47.
53   Above note 46 at para 13, citing John Salmond & RFV Heuston, *Treatise on Torts*, 19th ed (London: Sweet and Maxwell, 1987).
54   Above note 49.
55   2004 ABCA 186.

board's activities of building schools, hiring teachers, and mandatory attendance was insufficient to trigger liability.

Although the trial judge recognized that this position provided more opportunity for Gorsline to be alone with the students, he concluded that Gorsline's duties did not amount to anything approaching the intimate contact referred to in *Bazley*. Although the board fostered special relationships between teachers and students, the evidence did not establish that these relationships were expected to have, or that the board tolerated, any element of intimacy.

The trial judge relied on the decision of the Supreme Court of Canada in *Myers*,[56] in which the Court held that "the standard of care to be exercised by school authorities in providing for the supervision and protection of students for whom they are responsible is that of the careful or prudent parent." The events in this case occurred in 1978–79 and had to be assessed in that context. The trial judge concluded that the board did not know, nor should it have known, of the defendant teacher's misconduct.

A second aspect of possible vicarious liability referred to by McLachlin J in *Bazley* has been called the "significant connection test." The test was restated by Cromwell JA (as he then was) in *BMG v Nova Scotia (Attorney General)*[57] in the following words:

> Where there is a significant connection between the creation or enhancement of a risk [by the employer's enterprise] and the wrong that accrues therefrom, even if unrelated to the employer's desires.

In *Ryabikhina v St Michael's Hospital*,[58] the plaintiff brought an action in defamation against a hospital and a nurse. The nurse had reported to the Children's Aid Society that the mother had failed to take her child to the emergency ward of the hospital after being advised to do so due to the child's persistent vomiting. However, section 72(7) of the *Child and Family Services Act*[59] provides that no action lies against a person providing information in compliance with the duty to report, unless the person does so maliciously or without reasonable grounds for the suspicion. There was no evidence that the report to the Society was made maliciously. The nurse had a duty under section 72 of the Act to communicate the information she had about the child. The Society had a duty to receive that information.

---

56 Above note 45. See Masten & Coatsworth, above note 43.
57 2007 NSCA 120 at para 58.
58 2011 ONSC 1882, supplementary reasons 2011 ONSC 2995; 2011 ONSC 1884.
59 Aaron, above note 27.

According to the public policy established in the *Criminal Code*, a young person under the age of eighteen cannot consent to sexual contact with a person in authority. This same public policy is applicable in a civil context. When considering a civil claim for battery in *Norberg v Wynrib*,[60] the Court stated it must look at the circumstances of each case to determine if there is an overwhelming imbalance of power in the relationship between the parties.

As to negligence, it is common ground that a school board owes a duty of care to the students. It is to protect the students for which it is responsible from unreasonable risk of harm from any of its members by providing supervision and protection such as that of the careful and prudent parent. This standard was set out by the Supreme Court of Canada in *Myers*.[61]

2) Parental Liability for Child's Actions

As to the liability of a parent for the actions of a child, in *Segstro (Guardian ad Litem of) v McLean (Guardian ad Litem of)*,[62] the court stated:

> . . . because parents are in a position to govern the child's behaviour they have a corresponding duty to use reasonable care to prevent foreseeable harm to others by proper supervision. Liability may arise for negligence in the exercise of that control should injury or loss occur (*Smith v. Leurs* (1945) 70 C.L.R. 256). Such liability is not strict.
>
> . . . Where it can be demonstrated that a child has a propensity to act destructively (*Thibodeau v. Cheff* (1911) 24 O.L.R. 214 (Div. Ct. App.)) then the duty to supervise (and to take other reasonable steps to avoid foreseeable loss) is heightened. At p. 221 the learned Judge stated that a parent is exposed to liability:
>
> . . . if he the [parent] knows of a child's frequent wrongdoing in a particular direction and, by his inaction (when he is able to restrain and confine the child), he indicated his willingness that the misconduct would be repeated.
>
> Special circumstances must be proved, however, and the parent is not accountable for every action of a child.
>
> To succeed a plaintiff must show (1) that the defendant child had a dangerous propensity; (2) that the parents knew of the propensity; (3) that the parents could reasonably anticipate another occurrence; (4) that

---

60   [1992] 2 SCR 226.

61   Above note 45. See Masten & Coatsworth, above note 43.

62   1990 CanLII 2320 (BCSC).

reasonable steps could have been taken to avoid a recurrence, and (5) that the parents failed to take such steps. (*Streifl v. Strotz et al* (1958) 11 D.L.R. (2d) 667 (B.C.S.C.)).

By analogy it is worthwhile looking at Ontario's *Parental Responsibility Act, 2000.*[63]

G. SEXUAL ASSAULT

In *AB v CD*,[64] a student who was in Grade 12 and approaching her eighteenth birthday had been sexually assaulted by her teacher. The student willingly participated in the sexual relationship for approximately four months, but by the end of the school year, she stopped the teacher from further inappropriate touching. The teacher was convicted under the *Criminal Code.* The court said that the plaintiff was entitled to damages from the teacher, but not from the school board. The board was found not to be negligent. The evidence did not establish that any omission by the board caused the sexual touching. To establish negligence, the plaintiff must establish, on a balance of probabilities, that the injury would not have occurred but for the negligence of the board.

1) Historic Claims

In another case, *WE v FE*,[65] a claim was brought against the Yukon commissioner and against a school principal. The plaintiff alleged that the principal at the elementary school he had attended almost thirty years earlier had sexually assaulted him. As to the allegations against the school principal, given the gravity of the allegation of misconduct, the court stated it must take great care in scrutinizing the evidence presented.[66] The court concluded that the plaintiff did not meet the test of the civil standard of proof, that is, on a balance of probabilities, that the abuse had occurred. The test is not whether the plaintiff honestly believed that he was sexually assaulted by the school principal, but whether he had proven to the standard that the law requires that he was sexually assaulted by the school principal.

63　SO 2000, c 4, as amended.

64　2011 BCSC 775.

65　2008 YKSC 40.

66　See *Continental Insurance Co v Dalton Cartage Co*, [1982] 1 SCR 164. See also *B(P) v E(RV)*, 2007 BCSC 1568.

In *TT v Spice*,[67] the plaintiff alleged that seventeen years earlier, he had been sexually assaulted by the defendant teacher. As a result of the alleged assault, he claimed to have suffered "serious, lasting and permanent personal injuries." The defendant acknowledged that the plaintiff was a student of his when the plaintiff was in Grades 8 and 9, but denied the allegation of sexual assault. The court stated that to succeed, the plaintiff needed to establish by a preponderance of probabilities that the conduct of which he complained did, in fact, occur by evidence that was clear, cogent, and convincing. The court was required to reach conclusions by assessing the respective credibility of the parties and applying the relevant onus and standard of proof.

In the Ontario case of *Sommerfield v Lombard Insurance Group*,[68] the court determined that an exemption clause did not apply and that the insurer for the teachers had a duty to defend a claim made against several teachers. The former student of the private school for boys brought an action against four teachers of the school, claiming that each teacher, independent of the others, abused him during the time he attended the school. The student alleged sexual battery and claimed that each teacher was professionally negligent for not reporting the sexual assaults of other teachers. A claim of professional negligence was not exempt from coverage under the insurance policy. The court was satisfied that the applicants had met the three-point test as set out in *Sansalone v Wawanesa Mutual Insurance Co*: (1) the plaintiff's allegation under the statement of claim, paragraph 14(h), of negligence and breach of fiduciary duty was properly pleaded; (2) the allegations were properly pleaded and the claim of negligence was not derivative to the claims of sexual abuse; and (3) the claims of negligence contained in paragraph 14(h) triggered the insurer's duty to defend.[69] The court made a declaration pursuant to rule 14.05(3) of the Ontario *Rules of Civil Procedure* that a duty to defend was owed pursuant to the policy of insurance.[70]

In *AP v MacDonald*,[71] the plaintiff was a student at the school where the defendant was a teacher. The plaintiff's statement of claim alleged that the teacher's conviction represented only a fraction of the sexual and physical assaults and batteries committed by the teacher against the plaintiff. No

---

67   2005 SKQB 169.
68   2004 CanLII 73245 (Ont SCJ).
69   2000 SCC 25.
70   RRO 1990, Reg 194.
71   2006 NLTD 24.

issue on the facts remained to be tried. The defendant was liable, and the only issue for trial was the quantum of damages resulting from the facts. Summary judgment was granted.

In *JN v GJK*,[72] the plaintiff brought a civil action alleging historical sexual assault when she was a student and the defendant was a teacher at her high school. The appellate court found that the defendant's behaviour in misleading the plaintiff as to the wrongfulness of his conduct and manipulating her into believing that it was her fault constituted a fraudulent concealment which overcame the ten-year limitation in section 3(1)(b) of the *Limitations Act* of Alberta.[73] The defendant teacher's appeal was dismissed. By analogy, see the Ontario *Limitations Act, 2002*.[74]

2) Third-Party Claims

In *DB v Parkland School Division No 63*,[75] a third-party claim brought by the board against the parents was dismissed. The decision was upheld by the Court of Appeal. A teacher with the board was convicted of sexually assaulting a student. The board served a third-party claim on the victim's parents, alleging that they were negligent and owed a duty of care to their daughter. The appellate court referred to an earlier decision of the Court of Appeal in *C(A) v S(HI)*.[76]

Parents, as original parties in court proceedings, are more likely to be found liable than when third-party claims have been brought against them. Claims have either been struck out entirely or failed at trial. While the courts held in *B(D) v C(M)*[77] and *C(A) v S(HI)*[78] that a board (when it was being sued in negligence) may well pursue a third-party claim against the parents of a child or children. The Board was not simply being sued on the basis of vicarious liability. If a Board were to be found liable it would likely assume the teacher's or employee's liability subject to any indemnification between the Board and that individual.

72   2004 ABCA 394.
73   RSA 2000, c L-12.
74   SO 2002, c 24, Schedule B. as amended.
75   2004 SKCA 113.
76   (1994), 123 Sask R 241 (CA).
77   2001 SKCA 9 at para 14.
78   Above note 76.

H. FREEDOM OF EXPRESSION AND DISCIPLINE

The Ontario College of Teachers mandates that the teaching profession be held to a higher standard than the general public.[79] As such, a teacher's conduct does not have to be criminal or even criminal-like to warrant disciplinary action. This obligation is closely tied to the integrity of the school system and the need to protect the vulnerability of students. Teachers occupy positions of trust and confidence. Further, they exert much influence over their students as a result of the students' perceptions of how well the teacher fulfills the position of trust and influence and the community's confidence in the public and private school systems as a whole.[80]

Teacher expression, such as posting on social media websites or discussing politics and public policy in the workplace, can have a profound effect on the employment relationship and the workplace. It even extends to a school board's ability to maintain a good reputation in the community and deliver education to its students. A school board's right to manage this kind of behaviour is balanced against a teacher's freedom of expression, which is not lightly outweighed. The right to freedom of expression, enshrined in section 2(b) of *the Canadian Charter of Rights and Freedoms*,[81] is liberally construed as one of Canada's most fundamental rights. All activities conveying or attempting to convey meaning are expression for the purposes of section 2(b). Freedom of expression is infringed where a party demonstrates that his or her conduct falls within the meaning of expression and that the purpose or the effect of the impugned government action is to restrict that expression. "Freedom" is the absence of coercion or constraint.[82] Acts of violence, however expressive, are excluded from the protected scope as set out in *Irwin Toy Ltd v Quebec (Attorney General)*.[83] Internet law in Canada protects privacy and personal information.[84]

---

79 Nick J Scarfo & Marvin A Zuker, *Inspiring the Future: A New Teacher's Guide to the Law*, 2d ed (Toronto: Carswell, 2017).

80 *Education Act*, above note 1. See also above note 2.

81 Part 1 of the *Constitution Act, 1982*, being Schedule B to the *Canada Act 1982* (UK), 1982, c 11 [*Charter*].

82 *Baier v Alberta*, [2007] 2 SCR 673 at para 25.

83 [1989] 1 SCR 927 at 968.

84 See *Jane Doe 464533 v ND*, 2016 ONSC 541; 2017 ONSC 127, and *Pritchard v Van Nes*, 2016 BCSC 686.

1) Just Cause Termination

The growth of social media has resulted in individuals having ready access to a variety of online forums where they can express their views and opinions.

The Newfoundland arbitration decision, *Communications, Energy and Paperworkers Union of Canada, Local 64 v Corner Brook Pulp and Paper Limited*,[85] makes it clear that using Facebook to post offensive or harassing comments about one's employer can have serious consequences for an employee. On 25 October 2012, Victoria Stokes, a forty-one-year-old employee with thirteen years of seniority, was terminated with just cause for posting commentary on Facebook which appeared to the employer to be "offensive, threatening, harassing in nature, disrespectful and insolent toward her Supervisors." At the time of Stokes's termination, she held the position of tallyman in the shipping department. The comments were posted by Stokes on her personal Facebook page three days after a safety incident occurred at the mill. Following the mill incident, Stokes's employer scheduled an incident investigation meeting. Unfortunately, the meeting was cancelled and rescheduled for the following day. However, prior to being informed about the meeting being rescheduled, Stokes posted a comment on her Facebook account which contained offensive and derogatory comments about the company's management. The post referenced two managers in particular and made specific reference to the mill incident The Facebook comment was brought to the attention of Chris Pembroke, the superintendent, by Stokes's co-worker on the same day it was posted. After reviewing and considering prior arbitration awards that discuss disciplinary penalties for social media posting, the arbitrator held that the employer had just cause to discharge Stokes for a number of reasons, including that the posting, written in an organized and structured manner, used threatening and offensive language.

In *Bell Technical Solutions v Communications, Energy and Paperworkers Union of Canada (Facebook Postings Grievance)*,[86] the arbitrator stated the following with respect to Facebook postings:

> It is well-established that inappropriate Facebook postings can result in discipline or discharge, depending upon the severity of the postings. The nature and frequency of the comments must be carefully considered to determine how insolent, insulting, insubordinate and/or damaging

---

85 2013 CanLII 87573 (NL LA).
86 [2012] OLAA No 481 at para 112.

they were to the individual(s) or the company. In some cases, the issue is whether the comments were so damaging or have so poisoned the workplace that it would no longer be possible for the employee to work harmoniously and productively with the other employees or for the company. Discharge may be imposed and appropriate when there is a serious breakdown in the employment relationship which would make reinstatement not possible.

While this decision, along with the one before it, depends on its specific fact situation, clearly postings that contain offensive comments about named individuals, severe threats, and derogatory comments about the employer can be grounds to discharge for cause.

The *Charter* does, however, protect the right of teachers to speak politically by enshrining and upholding the value of democracy. There has been debate, though, over the extent of protected teacher speech in the context of public schools. Teachers, as educators of children, hold positions of trust and confidence and can influence their students considerably. School boards have an obligation to ensure the operation of their schools and the education of their students. These important considerations are balanced against teachers' freedom of expression. The leading case on freedom of expression in the school board context is the Supreme Court of Canada decision in *Ross v New Brunswick School District No 15*.[87] A teacher made off-duty racist and discriminatory comments against members of the Jewish faith in a number of books and pamphlets, letters to a local newspaper, and a local television interview. A parent filed a human rights complaint against the teacher, which resulted in an order requiring the school board to remove him from his teaching position. Even worthless expression is, *prima facie*, protected, be they lies[88] or hate propaganda.[89]

The Supreme Court found that the teacher's comments fell within the meaning of expression in section 2(b) of the *Charter*; however, it found that the limits on his expression were justified under section 1, considering the educational and employment context of the teaching profession.

The Court emphasized that children are vulnerable to messages conveyed by teachers with much influence over them and are more likely to feel threatened and isolated by a teacher who makes comments that deni-

---

87 Above note 13 at para 42. Off-duty conduct continues to be grounds for teacher termination. See, for example, *Grand Erie District School Board v Ontario Secondary School Teachers' Federation, District 23*, 2016 CanLII 72391 (Ont LA).

88 *R v Zundel*, [1992] 2 SCR 731.

89 *R v Keegstra*, [1990] 3 SCR 697.

grate personal characteristics of a group to which they may belong. The Court stressed that a school board has a duty to ensure that the fulfillment of its public functions are undertaken in a manner that does not undermine public trust and confidence. A teacher's freedom of expression must be balanced against that duty: a duty to maintain a safe place for students and not have a negative impact on the school.

The teacher's comments had "poisoned" the educational environment. Teachers must be perceived to uphold the values, beliefs, and knowledge sought to be transmitted by the school system, which is linked to the system's integrity and the community's confidence in the system.

In the public school system context, harm is interpreted as the undermining of the ability of a teacher to fulfill his or her role as an educator and as a role model, of a school board's ability to operate and deliver education, and of the community's confidence in the public school system as a whole. Such harm is considered in the context of the vulnerability of students to messages from their teachers. Evidence of harm is not necessary and may be inferred, particularly from the community's perception of the ability of teachers and school boards to fulfill their roles.

2) The Right to Privacy

In *Jones v Tsige*,[90] the Ontario Court of Appeal reiterated that the tort of breach of privacy, or "intrusion upon seclusion," is a cause of action in Ontario. Recently the Superior Court of Ontario explicitly adopted a new privacy tort and acknowledged the harm that can result when the Internet is used as a means for predators and bullies to victimize others.[91] Simply by participating in social media, an employee does not sacrifice all reasonable expectations of privacy. It is, therefore, important to carefully weigh the extent to which a communication over social media was public, or intended to be public, in determining whether discipline is warranted.

Justice Sharpe, for the majority, made the following comment regarding the rationale for such a tort: "Technological change poses a novel threat to a right of privacy that has been protected for hundreds of years by the common law under the various guises and that, since 1982 and the

---

90   2012 ONCA 32.
91   *Jane Doe 464533 v ND*, 2016 ONSC 541.

Charter, has been recognized as a right that is integral to our social and political order"[92]

The important values of free speech, employees' reasonable expectations of privacy, and employers' duties to discipline employees progressively and consistently should remain central to the analysis in dealing with discipline stemming from social media. An employee's right to lead a free, private, independent life outside work should not be forgotten.

I. FACTORS IN DETERMINING DISCIPLINE

The penalty for misconduct must accord with the principles and objectives identified by the Supreme Court in *Toronto Board of Education v Ontario Secondary School Teachers' Federation, District 15*.[93] In that case, the Supreme Court identified various factors to be taken into account in deciding discipline for a teacher engaged in misconduct. Those factors were articulated in two earlier Supreme Court decisions.[94] In *Ross* and *Audet*, the Supreme Court considered the relationship between teachers and students in the context of the role of teachers in furthering educational goals and the potential for a teacher's conduct to undermine the education system in the eyes of the community.

In *Ross*, the Supreme Court concluded that a board having the requisite statutory power is entitled to discipline teachers found guilty of misconduct by removing them from the classroom. Public confidence in the education system is an appropriate purpose for taking disciplinary action. Justice La Forest discussed the role of teachers in the education system in this way:

> A school is a communication centre for a whole range of values and aspirations of a society. In large part, it defines the values that transcend society through the educational medium . . . .
>
> Teachers are inextricably linked to the integrity of the school system. Teachers occupy positions of trust and confidence, and exert considerable influence over their students as a result of their positions. The conduct of a teacher bears directly upon the community's perception of the ability of the teacher to fulfil such a position of trust and influence, and upon the community's confidence in the public school system as a whole . . . .

---

92   *Jones v Tsige*, above note 86 at para 68.
93   [1997] 1 SCR 487.
94   See *Ross*, above note 13; and *Audet*, above note 5.

By their conduct, teachers as "medium" must be perceived to uphold the values, beliefs and knowledge sought to be transmitted by the school system. The conduct of a teacher is evaluated on the basis of his or her position, rather than whether the conduct occurs within the classroom or beyond . . . .

I find the following passage from the British Columbia Court of Appeal's decision in *Abbotsford School District 34 Board of School Trustees v. Shewan* (1987), 21 B.C.L.R. (2d) 93, at p. 97, equally relevant in this regard:

> The reason why off-the-job conduct may amount to misconduct is that a teacher holds a position of trust, confidence and responsibility. If he or she acts in an improper way, on or off the job, there may be a loss of public confidence in the teacher and in the public school system, a loss of respect by students for the teacher involved, and other teachers generally, and there may be controversy within the school and within the community which disrupts the proper carrying on of the educational system.

It is on the basis of the position of trust and influence that we hold the teacher to high standards both on and off duty, and it is an erosion of these standards that may lead to a loss in the community of confidence in the public school system. I do not wish to be understood as advocating an approach that subjects the entire lives of teachers to inordinate scrutiny on the basis of more onerous moral standards of behaviour. This could lead to a substantial invasion of the privacy rights and fundamental freedoms of teachers. However, where a "poisoned" environment within the school system is traceable to the off-duty conduct of a teacher that is likely to produce a corresponding loss of confidence in the teacher and the system as a whole, then the off-duty conduct of the teacher is relevant.[95]

Abbotsford School District 34 Board of School Trustees v Shewan considered whether certain behaviour amounted to misconduct and, if so, what penalty was appropriate. A teacher submitted a partially nude photograph of his wife, also a teacher, for publication in a pornographic magazine. The school board became aware of the publication and suspended the teachers for six weeks for misconduct. On appeal to the Supreme Court of British Columbia,[96] Bouck J held that there was misconduct within the meaning of section 122(1)(a) of the *School Act*[97] but reduced the suspension

---

95   *Ross*, above note 13 at paras 44–45.

96   1986 CanLII 879 (BCSC).

97   RSBC 1979, c 375 [now RSBC 1996, c 412].

from six to four weeks. On further appeal,[98] the Court of Appeal held that in assessing whether the impugned acts of a teacher constitute misconduct, it is necessary to consider what standards the community sets for teachers. The teachers themselves must have realized that the community would not approve of their conduct:

> Their actions lowered the esteem in which they were held by the community including the students.[99]

In *Young v British Columbia College of Teachers*,[100] the BC Court of Appeal dealt with the issue of what penalty should be given to a teacher who became romantically involved with a student. The court acknowledged the seriousness of the matter but determined that imposition of the maximum sentence is "not the invariable" rule.[101]

The public interest in preventing harm to the school system takes priority over personal interests. Those who accept the responsibility of teaching undertake to conduct themselves in accordance with high standards. They violate those standards at the peril of their employment.

J. REGULATION OF PROFESSIONAL CONDUCT

Perceived to be in positions of trust, educators must ensure that they adhere to standards of professional conduct, such as those espoused by the 1996 *Ontario College of Teachers Act*.[102] When a breach of professional conduct occurs, public trust and justice must be served. The Ontario College of Teachers is the largest self-regulatory body representing the teaching profession in Canada. It is an independent body responsible for regulating the teaching profession in the province. The College has a duty to serve the public in three areas: teacher licensing, program accreditation, and member discipline.[103] Education in Ontario is publicly funded and teach-

---

98 (1987), 21 BCLR (2d) 93 (CA). Is there a nexus between suspension and termination? See, for example, *Edmonton School District No 7 v Dorval*, 2016 ABCA 8 [*Dorval*], and *Dowling v Ontario (Workplace Safety and Insurance Board)* (2004), 246 DLR (4th) 65 (Ont CA).

99 *Abbotsford School District 34 (Board of School Trustees) v Shewan*, 1986 CanLII 879 at para 87 (BCSC).

100 2001 BCCA 164.

101 *Ibid* at paras 16 & 17. See also *Dorval*, above note 98, and *Fernandes v Peel Educational & Tutorial Services Ltd (cob Mississauga Private School)*, 2016 ONCA 468.

102 Above note 9.

103 See Ontario College of Teachers, online: www.oct.ca/about-the-college.

ers are entrusted with the safety and well-being of their students; thus, the College must maintain that members are in good standing. Further, the College is committed to operating in an open and accountable manner to promote public trust and confidence in the teaching profession.[104]

> Society trusts teachers to be both guardians and purveyors of knowledge, truth, and virtue – this is the abstract idea behind the seriousness of breach of trust by educators. Though never far from the moral guardianship idea, trust also transcends this dimension.[105]

1) The LeSage Report: Assessment of the Process

The Ontario College of Teachers has been handling complaints and hearings since 1997. The quasi-judicial hearing process follows rules set out in the *Statutory Powers Procedures Act*[106] and the *Ontario College of Teachers Act, 1996*. When a complaint results in a referral to a disciplinary hearing by the investigation committee, a notice of hearing which contains charges of professional misconduct against the member is prepared. Behaviour that constitutes professional misconduct is listed in the Ontario Act's Regulation 437/97.[107]

In September 2011, the Ontario College of Teachers appointed the Honourable Patrick LeSage to review its investigation and disciplinary procedures and dispute resolution program. In June 2012, LeSage released a report that contained forty-nine recommendations.[108] The government first introduced Bill 103, the *Protecting Students Act*, in September 2013; however, the proposed bill died when the House was dissolved due to the election call in May 2014. Although the LeSage Report recommendations were directed at the Ontario College of Teachers, they were also relevant to the College of Early Childhood Educators. In August 2015, amendments to the *Early Childhood Educators Act* came into force to address recommendations coming out of the LeSage Report.[109] The *Protecting Students*

---

104 *Ibid.* See, for example, *Grogan v Ontario College of Teachers*, 2016 ONSC 6545
105 Scarfo & Zuker, above note 79 at 1.
106 RSO 1990, c S.22 and above note 9, respectively.
107 *Professional Misconduct*, O Reg 437/97.
108 Patrick J LeSage, *Review of the Ontario College of Teachers Intake, Investigation and Discipline Procedures and Outcomes, and the Dispute Resolution Program* (Toronto: Ontario College of Teachers, 2012) [LeSage Report].
109 The *Child Care Modernization Act*, 2014, SO 2014, c 11, which amended the *Early Childcare Educators Act, 2007*, came into force 31 August 2015.

Act[110] is intended to improve the investigation and disciplinary processes of the Ontario College of Teachers, reduce the potential of conflict of interest, and help protect students and children by

1) ensuring that a teacher's certificate is automatically revoked if he or she has been found guilty of sexual abuse or acts relating to child pornography

2) requiring employers to inform the College when they have restricted a teacher's duties or dismissed the teacher for misconduct

3) allowing the College to share information with the school board if the subject of a complaint poses an immediate risk to a child or student

4) requiring the College to publish all decisions from its discipline committee

5) setting clear rules for the use of dispute resolution

6) providing authority to the College to disclose information about members to the police and other regulators

7) improving timelines for the investigation and consideration of complaints

Three-member panels of publicly appointed and teacher-elected College members rule on each case. A panel can determine the appropriate penalty, which may range from a reprimand and direction to take counselling or direction to take counselling or courses, to losing one's licence to teach — either revocation of a member's certificate or suspension for a specified period up to twenty-four months.

A review of the cases published on the OCT website reveals how the process of handling professional misconduct is very time consuming and that, in its lack of clarity and transparency, it has a profound impact on the public's trust in the teaching profession. Furthermore, the cases demonstrate the need to place greater attention on the quality of the decision rendered. While most decisions require a member to physically appear before a registrar for verbal reprimanding and to agree to have his or her name and case published in the *Professionally Speaking* blue pages, the solutions prescribed for remediating the offending misconduct do not appear adequate. The goal of the OCT's quarterly published magazine, *Professionally Speaking*, is "to inform its members about the activities and decision of the College. The magazine provides a forum for discussion of issues relevant

---

110 Above note 9.

to the future of teaching and learning, teachers' professional learning and standard of practice."[111]

2) A Focus on a Positive School Environment

There is a clear link between a safe, positive, and non-discriminatory school climate and the academic and social progress of students. In 1996, the Supreme Court of Canada imposed a positive obligation on school boards to maintain a positive and non-discriminatory school environment in which students can flourish. In *Ross* it stated as follows:

> A school is a communication centre for a whole range of values and aspirations of a society. In large part, it defines the values that transcend society through the educational medium. The school is an arena for the exchange of ideas and must, therefore, be premised upon principles of tolerance and impartiality so that all persons within the school environment feel equally free to participate. As the Board of Inquiry stated, a school board has a duty to maintain a positive school environment for all persons served by it.[112]

The *Ross* case resulted in the sanctioning of a teacher for his out-of-class anti-Semitic comments. It sanctions putting limits on free speech and privacy — even outside the classroom — in order to maintain a positive and non-discriminatory school environment. Although the disciplinary proceedings against the teacher Malcolm Ross were found to infringe his *Charter* rights, they were held to be justified under section 1. The case emphasized the fiduciary, or trust, relationship between a teacher and a student, and the fact that the teacher is a role model for students, both in and outside the classroom. The focus on the fiduciary duties of teachers to act as trustees of vulnerable students accords with the need to be proactive with respect to maintaining safety, a positive environment, and protection from bullying and cyberbullying.[113] It is important for teachers to exercise their authority within the school in a way that is respectful of the rights of students, staff, and parents, but also in a way that is effective in promoting a positive school climate.

---

111 See *Professionally Speaking*, online: http://professionallyspeaking.oct.ca.
112 *Ross*, above note 13 at para 42.
113 See *Education Act*, above note 1, ss 300.4, 308, and 310.

3) Adherence to Professional and Ethical Standards

The Ontario College of Teachers is the province's professional body for the teaching profession and, as such, it explicitly requires teachers to adhere to professional and ethical standards, which include maintaining integrity and upholding moral standards. The *Ethical Standards for the Teaching Profession* in Ontario represent a vision of professional practice. At the heart of a strong and effective teaching profession is a commitment to students and their learning.

Members of the Ontario College of Teachers, in their position of trust, demonstrate responsibility in their relationships with students, parents, guardians, colleagues, educational partners, other professionals, the environment, and the public.

The purposes of the ethical standards for the teaching profession are as follows:

- to inspire members to reflect and uphold the honour and dignity of the teaching profession
- to identify the ethical responsibilities and commitments in the teaching profession
- to guide ethical decisions and actions in the teaching profession
- to promote public trust and confidence in the teaching profession[114]

It is expected that teachers will conduct themselves accordingly, and the position of the school boards in this regard is unwavering. Teachers must consider the impact of their actions both within the school and outside the school, and their behaviour in both areas must reflect the core values, morals, and ethics of the school board and of society, as well as the policies of the ministry of Education, their professional bodies, and their school boards.[115] According to Ontario's *Education Act*, section 264(1), the duties of a teacher include these:

(a) to teach diligently and faithfully the classes or subjects assigned to the teacher by the principal;
(b) to encourage the pupils in the pursuit of learning; and to teach morals;
(c) to inculcate by precept and example respect for religion and the principles of Judaeo-Christian morality and the highest regard for

---

114 Ontario College of Teachers, *Ethical Standards for the Teaching Profession*, online: www.oct.ca/public/professional-standards/ethical-standards.
115 Above note 9; see also Scarfo & Zuker, above note 79.

truth, justice, loyalty, love of country, humanity, benevolence, sobriety, industry, frugality, purity, temperance and all other virtues.

Additionally, under section 264(1), teachers are required

(d) to assist in developing co-operation and co-ordination of effort among the members of the staff of the school;

(e) to maintain, under the direction of the principal, proper order and discipline in the teacher's classroom and while on duty in the school and on the school ground.

K. AWARENESS OF PROFESSIONAL BOUNDARIES

1) Knowledge of Prohibited Teacher–Student Interactions

The *Ontario College of Teachers Act* contains and clarifies some offences with regard to prohibited teacher–student interaction, for example:

1. (1) "sexual abuse" of a student by a member means,

(a) sexual intercourse or other forms of physical sexual relations between the member and the student,

(b) touching, of a sexual nature, of the student by the member, or

(c) behaviour or remarks of a sexual nature by the member towards the student.

Section 1 of the *Professional Misconduct* regulation[116] identifies some other prohibited behaviours that relate to section 30(2) of the *Ontario College of Teachers Act*. Behaviours include the following set out in the above regulation:

5. Failing to maintain the standards of the profession.

6. Releasing or disclosing information about a student to a person other than the student or, if the student is a minor, the student's parent or guardian. The release or disclosure of information is not an act of professional misconduct if,

   i.   the student (or if the student is a minor, the student's parent or guardian) consents to the release or disclosure, or

   ii. if the release or disclosure is required or allowed by law.

7. 1. Abusing a student verbally.

---

116 Above note 107.

7.2 Abusing a student psychologically or emotionally.

7.3 Abusing a student sexually.

8. Practising or purporting to practise the profession while under the influence of any substance or while adversely affected by any dysfunction,
    i.   which the member knows or ought to know impairs the member's ability to practise, and
    ii. in respect of which treatment has previously been recommended, ordered or prescribed but the member has failed to follow the treatment. . . .

11. Failing to supervise adequately a person who is under the professional supervision of the member. . . .

14. Failing to comply with the Act, the regulations or the bylaws.

15. Failing to comply with the *Education Act* or the regulations made under that Act, if the member is subject to that Act. . . .

17. Contravening a law if the contravention has caused or may cause a student who is under the member's professional supervision to be put at or to remain at risk.

18. An act or omission that, having regard to all the circumstances, would reasonably be regarded by members as disgraceful, dishonourable or unprofessional.

19. Conduct unbecoming a member. . . .

27. Failing to comply with the member's duty under the *Child and Family Services Act*.

As a result of amendments made in December 2016, the Discipline Committee of the Ontario College of Teachers may make further orders relating to sexual abuse and child pornography.

2) Caution in Use of Electronic Communication and Social Media

The College has issued a professional advisory on the use of electronic communication and social media,[117] which states that while electronic

---

117 Ontario College of Teachers, *Professional Advisory — Use of Electronic Communication and Social Media* at 3, online: www.oct.ca/resources/advisories/use-of-electronic-communication-and-social-media.

communication and social media can foster and enhance education, misuse is an issue. Members are cautioned that even experienced teachers may inadvertently make mistakes.

> Maintaining professional boundaries in all forms of communication, technology-related or not, is vital to maintaining the public trust and appropriate professional relationships with students. Members must be aware of the numerous challenges and the ramifications associated with the use of electronic communication and social media.[118]

Ethical standards for teachers encompass care, respect, trust, and integrity, and there is an explicit stated expectation that members are to exert positive professional influence over students. While the College acknowledges that there is a distinction between teachers' private and professional lives, members are cautioned that because teaching is a public profession, a teacher's off-duty conduct does matter. Members are informed that the Supreme Court of Canada has rules that establish teachers' off-duty conduct, even when not directly related to students, can be relevant to their suitability to teach. Members should maintain professional conduct at all times, both in relation to their professional duties and also in their private lives. They are cautioned that any inappropriate use of electronic communication can lead to criminal charges or a civil action.

Members are also advised that inappropriate use of electronic communication and social media can result in their being disciplined and stripped of the licence to teach, and of being criminally charged or facing civil action.[119] Postings on Facebook and other social media sites deemed inappropriate by schools and school boards have increasingly been used as a basis on which to discipline teachers. Teachers must be careful to guide their behaviour while on the school grounds as well as outside of the school day.

3) Educator Privacy versus a Higher Standard of Conduct

Not only do school authorities have powers to search students' backpacks and lockers, but as custodians of school safety, principals have both the duty and the power to search the entire school building and its contents as well as any property issued to teachers by the board. The grounds for

---

118 *Ibid.*
119 *Ibid.*

search are, as with those for children, not as onerous for administrators as they are for police. Consideration of section 8 of the *Charter* and the common law, however, along with a review of school board policy and the guidelines of the principal's professional association, should be given in each unique circumstance.

The issue in *R v Cole*[120] was whether materials seized from a laptop that was issued by an employer could be used as evidence. In this case, a high-school teacher had been charged with possession of child pornography and unauthorized use of a computer, and the court considered whether these inappropriate images on an employee's workplace computer could properly be seized. The school board did have a policy that permitted teachers and other staff to use board-issued devices for personal purposes, which he did. The board also had a clear policy that these devices were subject to regular maintenance and review by board personnel. A technician, while performing maintenance activities on the teacher's laptop, found a hidden folder containing nude and partially nude photographs of an underage female student. The technician informed the principal, who then seized the computer, and school board technicians copied the temporary Internet files onto a second disc; these items were then given to the police. The police, without a warrant, reviewed their contents and then created a mirror image of the hard drive for forensic purposes.

At trial, the judge excluded all of the computer material pursuant to sections 8 and 24(2) of the *Charter*:

Section 8

Everyone has the right to be secure against unreasonable search or seizure . . .

Section 24(2)

Where, in proceedings under subsection (1), a court concludes that evidence was obtained in a manner that infringed or denied any rights or freedoms guaranteed by this Charter, the evidence shall be excluded if it is established that, having regard to all the circumstances, the admission of it in the proceedings would bring the administration of justice into disrepute.[121]

Some unique issues in this case included the fact that the laptop was protected by a personal password and exclusively used by the teacher, the fact that teachers were usually permitted personal use of school comput-

---

120 2012 SCC 53 [*Cole*].

121 *Charter*, above note 81.

ers, and that there was a school policy and procedures manual which prohibited having sexually explicit content on school computers and stating that all messages and data were considered the property of the school board. In this case, the Court considered the teachers were forewarned that the school and board would access private emails if inappropriate use of a laptop was suspected. Additionally, users had been advised that they should not assume that files stored on the network or hard drives were private.

In *Cole*[122] the Supreme Court of Canada extended the principle that Canadians may reasonably expect privacy in the information contained on their personal computers to work computers if personal use is permitted or reasonably expected. In respect of personal information stored on work-issued computers, the Court said that ownership of property and workplace policies can only "diminish" an individual's expectation of privacy in a work computer. These factors do not, in themselves, remove the expectation; "operational realities" of a workplace, policies, practices, and customers, among them, may only diminish an employee's expectation of privacy in personal information.

Teachers are cautioned that they can find themselves being investigated for seemingly private behaviour that occurs outside the school day, as well as for acts and interactions that occur during the course of their employment. They are advised to be acutely aware of this possibility. There is also a clear expectation that teachers will behave professionally and respect professional boundaries.

In summary, teachers are held to a higher standard of conduct due to their extended interaction with students and the community. Teacher misconduct is only one of many definable behaviours that may result in dismissal by boards and schools that accept a responsibility to protect students and provide a positive learning atmosphere in their schools. The high standards of the teaching profession must be met by all teachers.

---

122 Above note 120.

CHAPTER 8

Clicks and Stones
Cyberbullying in Canadian Schools

Eric M Roher[*]

A. INTRODUCTION

The issue of cyberbullying is now recognized as a severe and pervasive problem affecting Canadian schools. A 2010 cyberbullying research study led by Faye Mishna, Dean of the Faculty of Social Work of the University of Toronto, found that 49.5 percent of students surveyed had been victims of cyberbullying.[1] The majority of participants reported that they did not tell anybody about the bullying, nor did they take any measures in response to the bullying.[2] The study also indicated that just over one-third of participants indicated that they had bullied others online.[3]

Recent Canadian research indicates:

1) 47 percent of Canadian parents have a child who has been bullied.
2) Girls are more likely than boys to experience cyberbullying.
3) 73 percent of cyberbullying victims report receiving threatening or aggressive texts, emails, or instant messages.

---

[*]   The author wishes to thank Nevena Urosevic, Naveen Hassan, and Bethan Din-
       ning for their thorough and insightful research in the preparation of this chapter.
1   Faye Mishna et al, "Cyber Bullying Behaviors among Middle and High School
       Students" (2010) 80 *American Journal of Orthopsychiatry* 362 at 364 [Mishna et al,
       "Cyber Bullying Behaviors"].
2   *Ibid* at 365.
3   *Ibid*.

4) Cyberbullying is the number one form of low-level violence that occurs in Canadian schools.[4]

The Royal Canadian Mounted Police identify cyberbullying as using "communication technologies such as the Internet, social networking sites, websites, email, text messaging and instant messaging to repeatedly intimidate or harass others."[5] Cyberbullies hide behind computer, gaming, or telephone screens as they attempt to threaten, intimidate, or harass their victims. These individuals often believe that they are beyond the reach of the law and are not subject to school discipline.

A critical concern with cyberbullying is that it does not stop when the victim is out of sight of the bully. The bullies reach their victims at school, home, and at work. Unlike in years past when bullies had to be in the presence of their victims, the home is no longer a safety zone. With the prevalence of electronic devices, cyberbullies have access to their victims twenty-four hours a day, seven days a week.

Queen's University professor Dr Wendy Craig reported that students who are victims of bullying often experience headaches, trouble sleeping, anger, self-esteem issues, suicidal tendencies, peer conflict, substance abuse, and academic struggles.[6] Research indicates that suicide accounts for 24 percent of all deaths among fifteen to twenty-four-year-olds, making it the second leading cause of death for young Canadians.[7] Cyberbullying can be an important contributing factor to teenage suicide.

However, this conclusion is not limited to statistical data. It is reinforced through the increasing incidences of young students tragically taking their lives as a result of cyberbullying. For example, in January 2011, Nova Scotia student Jenna Bowers-Bryanton, an aspiring singer and songwriter, killed herself after months of bullying at school and online. Jamie Hubley, an Ottawa teen, also took his own life in October 2011 at the age of fifteen, after years of bullying at school and on the Internet. Amanda Todd, a Vancouver-area teenager who posted a story on YouTube about being cyberbullied, took her own life in 2012. Another recent example of the

---

4   Canadian Institutes of Health Research, "Canadian Bullying Statistics" (2012), online: www.cihr-irsc.gc.ca/e/45838.html.

5   Royal Canadian Mounted Police, "Bullying and Cyberbullying" (5 May 2016), online: www.rcmp-grc.gc.ca/cycp-cpcj/bull-inti/index-eng.htm.

6   Nova Scotia Task Force on Bullying and Cyberbullying, *Respectful and Responsible Relationships: There's No App for That* by A Wayne MacKay, Chair (29 February 2012) at 10 [Nova Scotia Cyberbullying Report].

7   *Ibid.*

vicious effects of cyberbullying is that of Rehtaeh Parsons, a seventeen-year-old, former Cole Harbour District High School student, whose death on 7 April 2013 has been attributed to online distribution of photos of an alleged gang rape that occurred seventeen months prior to her suicide. On a Facebook page set up as a tribute to her daughter, Parsons' mother blamed four boys who she claimed raped and released images of Rehtaeh, the constant "bullying and messaging and harassment," and the failure of the Canadian justice system or for her daughter's decision to commit suicide.

Stories such as these are the most blatant and tragic examples of cyberbullying. Many other victims suffer in silence or go unnoticed, continually living in fear and anguish. These recent tragedies, among others, speak to the need for parents, educators, schools, and school boards to work together and make a concerted effort to help keep the schools a safe and positive environment for all students.

B. UNDERSTANDING THE CYBERBULLYING PHENOMENON

Cyberbullying is a distinct form of bullying. Professor Wayne MacKay, in his Nova Scotia Task Force report on bullying and cyberbullying entitled *Respectful and Responsible Relationships: There's No App for That*, states that technology is changing how people interact and relate to each other.[8] Indeed, "young people have fewer inhibitions online and exhibit different personalities online."[9] One grade 11 student, describing teenage behaviour on Facebook, stated that they become "keyboard warriors."[10]

The cyberbullying paradox is that a young person can be completely isolated yet completely exposed and vulnerable at the same time. They can be isolated in the sense that the bullying can be easily hidden from their families and other important adults in their lives; this is due to the privacy technology affords individuals. However, at the very same time, they can generally not isolate themselves from the bullying because technology is not limited to space, and thus, the bullying can find its way into the very walls of the parental home or the teenager's bedroom. Essentially, this often adds to the anxiety and depression of students, as they feel that they cannot escape the bullying, even if they change locations physically.

8   *Ibid* at 7.
9   *Ibid.*
10 *Ibid.*

This problem is further amplified by the fact that most young people develop a certain dependency on their technological devices, taking them along with them everywhere they go. Dr Wendy Craig highlighted the unique defining characteristics of cyberbullying:[11]

1) anonymity
2) beyond supervision and detection
3) world-wide audience
4) sense of power
5) easy access to technology
6) physical distance from the victim (don't see them cry)
7) victim is always accessible online
8) easy to engage others in the bullying process

Furthermore, the impacts of bullying are far-reaching. According to a recently published Duke University Medical Center study, the impacts of bullying reached far into adulthood. Adults who were bullied as children have a higher prevalence of agoraphobia, generalized anxiety and panic disorder, antisocial personality disorder, depression, and suicidal thoughts.[12] Thus, the study finds that:

> Bullying is not just a harmless rite of passage or an inevitable part of growing up. Victims of bullying are at increased risk for emotional disorders in adulthood. Bullies/victims are at highest risk and are most likely to think about or plan suicide. These problems are associated with great emotional and financial costs to society.[13]

The study found that aggressors were also at a higher risk for psychiatric disorder.[14] Such studies recognize that the current reality surrounding cyberbullying is an "urgent call to action" and demonstrates a "need to address the problem of cyberbullying through a systemic approach, encompassing different levels of the system including peers, teachers,

---

11 *Ibid at* 85.
12 Duke Health, News Release, "Bullied Children Can Suffer Lasting Psychological Harm as Adults" (20 February 2013), online: corporate.dukehealth.org/news-listing/bullied-children-can-suffer-lasting-psychological-harm-adults [Duke Health News Release].
13 JAMA, News Release, "Study Examines Adult Psychiatric Outcomes of Childhood Bullying" (20 February 2013), online: media.jamanetwork.com/news-item/study-examines-adult-psychiatric-outcomes-of-childhood-bullying [JAMA News Release].
14 Duke Health News Release, above note 12.

school administrators, mental health professionals, law enforcement and parents."[15]

C. SOCIAL MEDIA APPLICATIONS

Facebook, the enormous, popular youth networking site, has attracted a remarkable amount of attention in recent years. It was launched in February of 2004 at Harvard University by a student named Mark Zuckerberg, now thirty-three years of age. The site allows users to chat, post photos and comments, as well as connect with fellow students with common interests through online groups. The site quickly grew, first to other universities and later to high schools. By the summer of 2006, it had grown to more than 30,000 educational institutions in the United States, Canada, and other English-speaking countries, with roughly eight million users.

In September of 2006, Facebook opened its virtual doors to the general public by permitting registrations from people in hundreds of geographic areas. The decision, which created some apprehension among the Facebook community, caused the site to explode in popularity. In March 2017, Facebook had an average of 1.28 billion daily active users.[16] The average user has 130 friends. More than 35 million users update their statuses each day. Facebook is the sixth most valuable public company in the world with a market value of approximately $325 billion.[17] Canada has the most active Facebook users; nineteen million Canadians access Facebook at least once a month, and fourteen million Canadians log in daily.[18] The recent backlash against Facebook in a school context has centred around two concerns: derogatory comments and creating a potentially disruptive environment in the school.

Other online social networking sites include Twitter, Snapchat, MySpace, YouTube, and Instagram. Twitter, which was founded in 2006, is an

---

15 Mishna et al, "Cyber Bullying Behaviors," above note 1 at 372–73.

16 Facebook Newsroom, "Stats" *Facebook Newsroom* (accessed 12 July 2017), online: newsroom.fb.com/company-info.

17 AES, "How Facebook Became an Advertising Behemoth" *The Economist* (8 April 2016), online: www.economist.com/blogs/economist-explains/2016/04/economist-explains-4.

18 Michael Oliveira, "10 Million Canadians Use Facebook on Mobile Daily" *The Globe and Mail* (19 February 2014), online: www.theglobeandmail.com/technology/10-million-canadians-use-facebook-on-mobile-daily/article16976434.

online messaging service that is a blend of instant messaging and blogging. In June 2016, Twitter had 328 million monthly active users.[19] There are 500 million tweets sent each day. A Twitter message contains no more than 140 characters, and 80 percent of active Twitter users are on mobile devices. Twitter users post messages about music, brands of coffee, and the sex lives of their pets, among other things. Comedian Jon Stewart has called this online networking service "inane chatter."[20]

Twitter is one of many social networking sites where students or school staff can be targeted with offensive, inflammatory, personal, or threatening comments. In addition, a person may use Twitter, based on the detailed and updated "tweets" provided by a user, to potentially stalk or harass that person.

Another popular messaging application that students have used to bully, threaten, or intimidate other students online is Snapchat. Snapchat is a photo messaging application developed by two Stanford students, Evan Spiegel and Robert Murphy. It was released in September 2011. Using the application, users can take photos, record videos, add text and drawings, and send them to a controlled list of recipients. These sent photographs and videos are known as "Snaps." Users set a time limit for how long recipients can view their Snaps. The range is from 1 to 10 seconds, after which they are hidden from the recipient's device and deleted from Snapchat's servers. In April 2016, Snapchat's users were sending eight billion photos and videos per day.[21] Snapchat has 100 million daily active users. The company has a current valuation of $16 billion.[22]

19   Twitter Usage, "Company Facts" (30 June 2016), online: https://about.twitter.com/company.
20   Joseph Galante & Ian King, "Hey, big biz, ur not 2 big 4 #tweets :-)" *The Globe and Mail* (6 April 2009), online: www.theglobeandmail.com/report-on-business/hey-big-biz-ur-not-2-big-4-tweets--/article1156317.
21   Kurt Wagner, "Snapchat Users Now Watch Eight Billion Videos Per Day" *Recode* (29 February 2016), online: recode.net/2016/02/29/snapchat-users-now-watch-eight-billion-videos-per-day.
22   Leslie Picker & Sarah Frier, "Snapchat Said to Be Valued at $16 Billion in New Fundraising" *Bloomberg* (29 May 2015), online: www.themoneystreet.com/snapchat-said-to-be-valued-at-16-billion-in-new-fundraising.

D. LEGAL RESPONSES TO CYBERBULLYING: *ACCEPTING SCHOOLS ACT, 2012*[23] AND POLICY/PROGRAM MEMORANDUM NO 144[24]

The common law in Canada clearly establishes that school authorities have a special duty of care towards students in their charge. This duty is imposed upon them by the unique nature of their work. Because parents are obligated to either send their children to school or provide home schooling, they are entitled to expect that schools will take reasonable measures to prevent reasonably foreseeable risks of harm in the school environment. Generally speaking, the standard of care owed by educators to students is that of a reasonably careful or prudent parent. This includes the duty to protect students from any reasonably foreseeable risk of harm.

As of 1 September 2012, Ontario became the third Canadian province to implement anti-bullying legislation through the *Accepting Schools Act, 2012*. This most recent amendment to the *Education Act*[25] defines bullying as aggressive and typically repeated behaviour by a pupil intended to have the effect of, or where the pupil ought to know the behaviour would likely have the effect of:

  (i)   causing harm, fear or distress to another individual, including physical, psychological, social or academic harm, harm to the individual's reputation or harm to the individual's property, or
  (ii) creating a negative environment at a school for another individual

(b) the behaviour occurs in a context where there is a real or perceived power imbalance between the pupil and the individual based on factors such as size, strength, age, intelligence, peer group power, economic status, social status, religion, ethnic origin, sexual orientation, family circumstances, gender, gender identity, gender expression, race, disability or the receipt of special education.[26]

Ministry policy also recognizes the role of technology in modern bullying and includes a specific reference to cyberbullying, defining it as:

---

23 Bill 13, *An Act to amend the Education Act with respect to bullying and other matters*, 1st Sess, 40th Leg, Ontario, 2011 (assented to 19 June 2012, SO 2012, c C.5).
24 Ontario, Ministry of Education, *Bullying Prevention and Intervention*, Policy/ Program Memorandum No 144 (5 December 2012) [PPM 144].
25 *Education Act*, RSO 1990, c E2.
26 *Ibid*, s 1(1).

1) creating a web page or a blog in which the creator assumes the identity of another person;

2) impersonating another person as the author of content or messages posted on the internet; and

3) communicating material electronically to more than one individual or posting material on a website that may be accessed by one or more individuals.[27]

Many of the recent amendments to the Ontario *Education Act* relate to a principal's authority to discipline students arising from bullying incidents. The duty to report and investigate bullying can be found under Part XII of the *Education Act*. In essence, it prescribes that any school board employee who becomes aware of bullying must report it to the principal. The principal, in turn, has a duty to investigate the matter. After the investigation, the principal is to communicate the results of the investigation to the school board employee unless the principal, in his/her discretion, believes that it would not be appropriate to do so.

Further amendments to the *Education Act* pertain to discipline for bullying and now include suspensions and even expulsions. Persistent or ongoing bullying now requires more serious disciplinary action, ranging from a suspension to expulsion, if the situation so warrants.

Program/Policy Memorandum No 144 on *Bullying Prevention and Intervention*, released by the Ontario Ministry of Education on 5 December 2012, supports the new changes to the *Education Act*. In the *Education Act*, bullying is to be prevented, in part, by developing strategies for promoting a positive school climate.[28] School climate is defined in PPM 144 as "the learning environment and relationships found within a . . . school community."[29] It elaborates on what a positive school climate entails:

> A positive school climate exists when all members of the school community feel safe, included, and accepted, and actively promote positive behaviours and interactions. Principles of equity and inclusive education are embedded in the learning environment to support a positive school climate and a culture of mutual respect. A positive school climate is a crucial component of bullying prevention.[30]

---

27 *Ibid*, s 1(1.0.0.2).
28 *Ibid*, ss 170(1)7.1 and 300.0.1.
29 PPM 144, above note 24 at 1.
30 *Ibid*.

PPM 144 further speaks to the issue of cyberbullying, stating the different forms such bullying may take. "Social aggression may also occur through the use of technology (e.g., spreading rumours, images, or hurtful comments through the use of email, cell phones, text messaging, Internet websites, social networking, or other technology)."[31] The increasing presence of cyberbullying issues and sanctions in law and policy is indicative of the growing recognition of the problem it poses and the need for it to be effectively addressed.

Ontario's *Provincial Code of Conduct*, ("PPM 128"), which was issued on 5 December 2012, establishes standards of behaviour on a province-wide basis. It provides that all members of the school community must treat one another with dignity and respect at all times, and especially when there is disagreement. It also states that all members of the school community must not engage in bullying behaviours.

Section 306 of the *Education Act* extends the right to suspend a student to include actions taken off school property and outside of school activities where the activity has an impact on the school climate. Permitting school administrators to discipline students for conduct that has an impact on the "climate of the school" will be useful in allowing them to address cyberbullying and online threats and intimidation which may take place off school property.

E. CANADIAN CASELAW

Two main Canadian cases which address the issue of cyberbullying in Canada are *RT v Durham Catholic District School Board*[32] and *AB v Bragg Communications Inc.*[33] *RT v Durham Catholic District School Board* is a case about a thirteen-year-old grade 8 female student, VK, who was involved in "conversations" on Facebook with another female student. VK informed the victim she was also a student in grade 8 at the school. In January 2008, VK wrote to the victim, making many statements that included the following:

U DON'T WANT ME TO GET MAD BECAUSE THEN ILL KILL YOU RIGHT IN UR SLEEP OR AT SCHOOL ON MONDAY.[34]

---

31 *Ibid* at 4.
32 2008 CFSRB 94 [RT].
33 2012 SCC 46 [Bragg].
34 RT, above note 32 at para 5.

In addition, VK wrote to the student, "I am gonna come to school on Monday and kick ur ass. im gonna kill u. ok? ok!"[35] On Facebook, VK not only used a similar name as the victim, but she used similar information when developing her profile. As such, VK was also contacting the victim's friends.

The victim's father came to the school to inform the vice-principal of his concerns regarding the threatening emails. He informed the vice-principal that he had already contacted the police and Facebook. The victim's father was concerned about his daughter's safety, as one message was a threat that she would be killed while attending an upcoming grade 8 trip. In addition, there was evidence that Facebook had closed VK's account three times, which she reopened.

In March 2008, VK was suspended by the school pending an investigation. In a proceeding before the school board's Expulsion Hearing Committee, the committee made the determination to expel VK from her school only. The mother of VK filed an appeal of this decision to the Child and Family Services Board. She sought to change the decision of the school board from an expulsion from the student's school to a non-expulsion.

In reviewing the evidence, the review board found that VK used Facebook to send emails to impersonate some students and to make death threats. In discussing whether the school climate had been affected, the review board noted that, after receiving these threatening emails, the victim had trouble sleeping, she felt isolated, she was afraid for herself and for her family, she was closing her blinds at home, and she was always watching over her shoulder.[36]

The review board held that VK's actions were of such a nature that it would be very detrimental to the school climate if she were permitted to return to the school.[37] Furthermore, the board held that her actions were deliberate and premeditated. The review board concluded that although the infraction did not occur at school or at a school-related activity, it had a negative impact on the school climate. It stated:

> The fear or significant harm generated by the Facebook communications and the subsequent knowledge that this was committed by one of the

---

35   *Ibid.*
36   *Ibid* at para 15.
37   *Ibid* at para 16.

pupils at the school leads the Board to find that the school climate was negatively impacted by the infraction.[38]

In considering the evidence, the review board upheld the decision of the school board to expel VK from the school.

The second and most recent case, delivered by the Supreme Court of Canada, is *AB v Bragg Communications Inc.* This case involves a fifteen-year-old Nova Scotia girl ("AB"), who commenced an action in defamation against the unknown creator of a Facebook profile purporting to be her own. It featured a picture of her, a slightly altered version of her name, as well as derogatory and sexually explicit comments about her appearance. Acting through her father as guardian, AB brought an application and made the following three requests of the Court:

1) an order requiring the Internet provider to disclose the identity of the individual(s) using the IP address from which the profile was published;
2) a publication ban in relation to the content of the profile; and
3) complete anonymity throughout the whole process.

Media outlets opposed the publication ban and the requests for anonymity on the basis that they unreasonably restricted the open court principle and freedom of the press. The trial and appeal courts both granted the order requiring the Internet provider to disclose the source of the Facebook profile. However, both courts denied the request for anonymity. They also denied the publication ban because they could not find sufficient evidence of specific and substantial harm to AB that would justify restricting access to media.

The Supreme Court of Canada (the "Court") overruled both prior court decisions with respect to anonymity. The Court held that AB should be entitled to proceed anonymously, but declined to order a publication ban on the non-identifying content of the fake Facebook profile on the basis that this information could not be connected to AB, and publishing it would not have a harmful impact.

In granting the request for anonymity, the Court held that although the principles of a free press and an open court have been promoted and protected in Canadian jurisprudence, the privacy and protection of children from cyberbullying were sufficiently compelling interests to justify restricting these principles. It likened these interests to the privacy and

---

38   *Ibid* at para 42.

safety interests of sexual assault complainants, which the Supreme Court of Canada has already upheld as a justified restriction on the freedom of the press principle.

In addressing the lower courts' failure to consider the objectively discernible harm to AB, the Court noted that in an application involving sexualized cyberbullying, there was no need for a child to demonstrate a particular vulnerability or harm resulting from cyberbullying, since the law attributes a heightened vulnerability to all children. It further noted that it is now "common sense" that children who have been subjected to bullying will suffer "inevitable harm."

Perhaps the most significant factor in the court's decision to grant AB's request for anonymity was the finding that bullied children who are not able to report bullying anonymously tend not to report bullying at all. The Court highlighted that the choice not to report bullying exacerbates the toxic long-term effects of bullying, which include loss of self-esteem, anxiety, fear, school drop-outs, and suicide attempts.

In this case, the Court created a precedent for allowing victims to report cyberbullying anonymously:

> In addition to the psychological harm of cyberbullying, we must consider the resulting inevitable harm to children — and the administration of justice — if they decline to take steps to protect themselves because of the risk of further harm from public disclosure.[39]

The Court's decision to grant AB anonymity affirms the fact that providing victims of cyberbullying with the legal mechanisms to seek out their bullies is a significant aspect of a holistic approach to combating bullying. However, it does not diminish from the importance of school administrators to continue to play a proactive role in preventing and addressing bullying by implementing anti-bullying policies and providing appropriate supports to both victims and the students who engaged in bullying.

F. THE AMERICAN EXPERIENCE

Courts in the United States are regularly called upon to adjudicate disputes involving restrictions on student expression or speech, and cases on cyberbullying are usually framed in those terms. The First Amendment to the US Constitution guarantees freedom of speech as well as freedom

---

39 *Bragg,* above note 33 at para 23.

of press. Caselaw addressing the issue of cyberbullying in recent years has had to balance those freedoms against the mental, physical, and emotional safety of persons targeted at the school.

The governing legal standard relating to cyberbullying in the school environment is that of the "substantial disruption" test. The test was first founded in the 1969 *Tinker v Des Moines Independent Community School District* case.[40] In *Tinker*, a number of students attended school wearing black armbands as a protest against the Vietnam War. They were suspended from school for violating a school district rule banning the wearing of armbands. The United States Supreme Court determined that the school's actions violated the students' right to freedom of speech.

> In order for the State in the person of school officials to justify prohibition of a particular expression of opinion, it must be able to show that its action was caused by something more than a mere desire to avoid discomfort and unpleasantness that always accompany an unpopular viewpoint. Certainly, where there is no finding and no showing that engaging in the forbidden conduct would "materially and substantially interfere with the requirements of appropriate discipline in the operation of the school," the prohibition cannot be sustained.[41]

The substantial disruption test has since been applied to cyberbullying cases to determine whether cyber expression has exceeded permissible limits within the school setting. According to the substantial disruption principle, off-campus cyberbullying or offensive cyber speech cannot be the basis of school discipline unless there is a substantial disruption on-site at school. While this standard is applied consistently across US circuit courts, its scope seems to vary among circuits.

1) Third Circuit: Circumscribing the Scope of Substantial Disruption

Two recent Third Circuit cases that circumscribed the scope of the substantial disruption test are *Layshock v Hermitage School District*[42] and *JS ex rel Snyder v Blue Mountain School District*.[43] *Layshock* and *JS* were essentially consolidated and decided simultaneously. In both cases, the court

---

40   393 US 503 (1969) [*Tinker*].
41   *Ibid* at 509.
42   593 F3d 249 (3d Cir 2010) [*Layshock*].
43   650 F3d 915 (3d Cir 2011) [*JS*].

protected the cyber speech in question and found that substantial disruption was not demonstrated.

In *Layshock*, a seventeen-year-old student created a fictitious profile of his principal on MySpace. It was created after school hours and off-campus at his grandmother's house; however, the page was accessed by Layshock and other students during school. The extent of the disruption reported by some of the teachers was comprised of students gathering together and commenting on the profile. The administration disciplined Layshock with a ten-day out-of-school suspension.

The facts in *JS* are very similar. A student was also suspended for creating a parody MySpace page of her middle school principal from her home computer on a weekend. The fake profile featured his picture along with profanities and other statements suggesting that he was a nymphomaniac and a pedophile. The school gave *JS* a ten-day suspension.

The full Third Circuit Court of Appeals heard the two cases together and ruled in favour of both Layshock and JS respectively. With respect to the facts in Layshock, the court pointed out that (1) Layshock did not create the profile at school, and (2) his speech did not cause a disruption at school. With regards to the first point, the court stated:

> It would be an unseemly and dangerous precedent to allow the state, in the guise of school authorities, to reach into a child's home and control his/her actions there to the same extent that it can control that child when he/she participates in school sponsored activities. Allowing the District to punish Justin for conduct he engaged in while at his grandmother's house using his grandmother's computer would create just such a precedent and we therefore conclude that the district court correctly ruled that the District's response to Justin's expressive conduct violated the First Amendment guarantee of free expression.[44]

In terms of the second point, the court clarified that a school district cannot punish a student merely because his or her speech reached inside the school. Rather, the speech must cause a substantial interference or at least a well-founded expectation of disruption.

In *JS*, the court highlighted that (1) JS created the profile at home; (2) she did not intend for the speech to reach the school and even took steps to make the profile private so it was not accessible to everyone; and (3) the school's response to the profile exacerbated rather than contained the disruption at school.

---

44 *Layshock*, above note 42 at 260.

The court availed itself of the *Tinker* test to analyze the case. It found that while the fake MySpace profile created by JS was vulgar and offensive and caused some "general rumblings,"[45] it did not cause the type of material and substantial disruption which would have justified the ten-day suspension of the student. Due to a filter on the school computer, the profile could not even be accessed at school. The court was silent on whether the *Tinker* test also applied to off-campus speech.

The message from these two Third Circuit cases is that students cannot be disciplined for out-of-school speech that does not cause a disruption — or a foreseeable disruption — in school. In coming to its conclusion and in light of the conflicting Second Circuit case of *Doninger v Niehoff*,[46] the court pointed out that JS intended the fake MySpace profile to remain a private joke and not to reach the school.

2) Second and Fourth Circuits: Broadening the Scope of Substantial Disruption

Two recent cases, one from the Second Circuit and the Fourth Circuit respectively, found that the cyberbullying or offensive cyber speech in question caused a substantial disruption in the school and was therefore not considered protected speech.

In *Kowalski v Berkeley County Schools*,[47] the court held that students could be disciplined for cyberbullying regardless of the location of the activity. It distinguished between students' First Amendment (freedom of speech) rights and adults' First Amendment rights, circumscribing the former in relation to the latter.

Kara Kowalski, a senior at Musselman High School created a MySpace page called "SASH" which stood for "Students Against Shay's Herpes" and targeted a student at the school. One of the students who joined in on the cyberbullying posted a photo of the student with red dots superimposed on her face, simulating herpes. Several students participated in the cyberbullying and filled the page with degrading comments on the targeted student.

Kowalski was suspended. In addition, Kowalski, who had been crowned "Queen of Charm" the previous year, was prohibited from crowning her

---

45   *JS*, above note 43 at 929.

46   642 F3d 334 (2d Cir 2011) [*Doninger*].

47   652 F3d 565 (4th Cir 2011) [*Kowalski*].

successor "Queen of Charm" in the annual Charm Review. She was also removed from the cheerleading squad. Kowalski felt that her discipline was excessive and that it made her feel isolated and depressed; however, the appeals court did not sympathize. Rather, it let her discipline stand.

The court found that even though Kowalski did not physically create the webpage at school, the *Tinker* standard could be applied. In applying the *Tinker* test, the court pointed to the fact that the material and substantial disruption test also included reasonably foreseeable substantial disruptions. As such, the court found that the creation of the SASH webpage created a reasonably foreseeable substantial disruption. Commenting on the case, the court stated that:

> Kowalski's role in the "S.A.S.H." webpage, which was used to ridicule and demean a fellow student, was particularly mean-spirited and hateful. The webpage called on classmates, in a pack, to target Shay N., knowing that it would be hurtful and damaging to her ability to sit with other students in class at Musselman High School and have a suitable learning experience . . . .
>
> . . . [E]very aspect of the webpage's design and implementation was school-related. Kowalski designed the website for "students" . . . . The victim understood the attack as school-related, filing her complaint with school authorities . . . .
>
> . . . [Kowalski] fails to see that such harassment and bullying is inappropriate and hurtful and that it must be taken seriously by school administrators in order to preserve an appropriate pedagogical environment. Indeed, school administrators are becoming increasingly alarmed by the phenomenon, and the events in this case are but one example of such bullying and school administrator's efforts to contain it . . . . [T]he Constitution is not written to hinder school administrators' good faith efforts to address the problem.[48]

This case addressed the specificity of a pedagogical environment, distinguishing student behaviour from adult behaviour, and confirming the importance of allowing administrators a certain amount of discretion to safeguard students and address bullying behaviour, which is felt at school. Kowalski also confirmed that it suffices for a material and substantial disruption to be foreseeable to justify discipline.

The Second Circuit case of *Doninger v Niehoff*,[49] decided slightly prior to Kowalski, came to the same conclusion. The case involved a student named

---

48 *Ibid* at 576–77.

49 *Doninger*, above note 46.

Avery in a Connecticut high school who was barred from the student government after she called the superintendent and principal "douchebags" in a LiveJournal blog post written while off-campus, that encouraged students to call an administrator and "piss her off more" because of delays in setting up the annual battle of the bands contest.

Drawing on the reasonable foreseeability aspect of the *Tinker* test, the three-judge panel found that Doninger's vulgar blog post was "potentially disruptive of student government functions."[50] The court further found that the district judge did not abuse his discretion in holding that the student's speech foreseeably created a risk of substantial disruption within the school environment.

While the court did mention that the "Supreme Court has yet to speak on the scope of a school's authority to regulate expression that, like Avery's, does not occur on school grounds or at a school-sponsored event,"[51] it did express its opinion that "a student may be disciplined for expressive conduct, even conduct occurring off school grounds, when this conduct 'would foreseeably create a risk of substantial disruption within the school environment'."[52]

Kowalski and *Doninger* broaden the scope of "substantial disruption" and emphasize that a "foreseeable risk" of such disruption suffices for the purposes of discipline. It is interesting to note the student/adult dichotomy present in the aforementioned American cases. While there is differentiation between student and adult free speech rights, this distinction does not seem to apply to victims of cyberbullying. In other words, courts are concerned with, and seem to apply the same standard to, adult victims of cyberbullying within the school environment (such as teachers or administrators) as to children. The cyberbullying standard in the United States applies to both students and staff.

All four cases, *Layshock, JS, Kowalski,* and *Doninger,* were appealed to the United States Supreme Court, but the Court declined to hear them. While all four cases apply the *Tinker* substantial disruption principle, different courts seem to be setting different threshold levels for the term "substantial," some finding substantial disruption more easily than others. As such, many are waiting for one such case to be received by the United

50   *Ibid* at 351.
51   *Ibid* at 346, citing *Doninger v Niehoff,* 527 F3d 41 at 48 (2d Cir 2008) [*Doninger II*].
52   *Doninger II, ibid,* (citing *Wisniewski v Board of Education,* 494 F3d 34 (2d Cir 2007)), cert denied, 128 S Ct 1741 (2008), aff'd *Doninger,* above note 46.

States Supreme Court to rule definitively on the issue. In the meantime, the *Tinker* standard stands, with varying degrees of court interpretation.

Zeno v Pine Plains Central School District[53] confirmed that schools can be held liable for monetary damages if they are deliberately indifferent to a student's harassment. Anthony Zeno transferred to Stissing Mountain High School after a move his family made from Long Island to Dutchess County, New York. Zeno is dark-skinned and biracial while Stissing is a predominantly white school. Almost immediately, and continuously over the next three-and-a-half years, Zeno was bullied, verbally and physically, by his classmates.

Zeno and his mother repeatedly reported the bullying incidents to various school and school district officials. The school district issued suspensions to students who bullied Zeno; in two cases, Zeno was granted Orders of Protection. Nonetheless, the bullying continued. School district officials were also contacted by the local Human Rights Commission, the local chapter of the National Association for the Advancement of Colored People, and Zeno's lawyer with various suggestions to address the bullying; however, none of the suggestions were implemented.

The bullying continued to escalate. Zeno did not have the required amount of credits to graduate with the rest of his class and decided to settle for a limited diploma, accepted only by some community colleges, rather than continue to endure the bullying.

Zeno brought a claim against the school district, which was first heard by the United States District Court for the Southern District of New York. The jury found in favour of Zeno and awarded him $1.25 million in damages. The district court granted the school district's post-trial motion for a new trial, subject to Zeno accepting a reduced award of $1 million. Zeno agreed to accept the reduced award and judgment was entered. The school district appealed.

The appeals court affirmed the verdict, finding that Zeno suffered "severe, pervasive, and objectively offensive"[54] harassment that discriminatorily deprived him of a "supportive, scholastic environment free of racism and harassment."[55] The bullying he experienced caused him to end his studies prematurely and earn an IEP diploma, thereby greatly limiting his future education and career prospects. The court found the school district's response to be slow, sloppy, and inadequate; it "amount[ed] to delib-

---

53 702 F3d 655 (2d Cir 2012).
54 *Ibid* at 665.
55 *Ibid* at 666.

erate indifference to discrimination."[56] The court reinforced the $1 million compensatory damages award to Zeno, concluding that the "harassment would have a profound and long-term impact on Anthony's life and his ability to earn a living.[57] According to Zeno, it is not enough for a school to respond to bullying; the response needs to be effective in order to be considered sufficient. Otherwise, a school can be found liable for substantial damages.

G. SEXTING AND TEENAGERS: OMG, WHAT R U THINKING?

Sexting is the practice of sending or posting sexually suggestive text messages and images (including nude or semi-nude photographs) via cellular telephone or over the Internet. Sexting has grown dramatically among young people across North America over the past few years. While sexting can and does occur between people of any age, there is real concern about teenagers who are engaging in this activity.

According to a 2008 study by the National Campaign to Prevent Teen and Unplanned Pregnancy, 19 percent of teens between the ages of thirteen and nineteen have sent or posted nude or semi-nude photos of themselves. Of the 22 percent of teen girls that reported having done so, 11 percent of these girls were between the ages of thirteen and sixteen. When asked whether they had seen nude or semi-nude photos that were not intended to be shared with them, 25 percent of teen girls and 33 percent of teen boys answered this question affirmatively.

In a Pew Research Center Internet survey conducted in December 2009, 15 percent of cellphone-owning teens ages twelve to seventeen said they have received sexually suggestive nude or nearly nude images of someone they know via text messaging on their cellphone. The research indicates that older teens are much more likely to send and receive these images; 8 percent of seventeen-year-olds with cellphones have sent a sexually-provocative image by text and 30 percent have received a nude or nearly nude image on their phone.

---

56   *Ibid* at 671.
57   *Ibid* at 672.

H. TEXTING AND TEEN SOCIAL LIFE

Texting has become a centrepiece in teen social life, and parents, educators, and advocates have grown increasingly concerned about the role of cellphones in the sexual lives of teens and young adults. In a 26 March 2011 article in *The New York Times*,[58] Kathy, a seventeen-year-old female student, indicated that at her school, if a student liked a boy and wanted to get his attention, "you know what you have to do." Saif, an eighteen-year-old student, described sexting as a way to express feelings. He said, "If a guy and a girl are in love, instead of saying it face to face, they can say it through technology."[59]

When asked, "Why do girls sext?," Zoe, an eighteen-year-old student, responded, "A freshman girl doesn't consciously want to be a slut but she wants to be liked and she likes attention from the older boys. They'll text her, 'Hey hottie' and it will progress from there."[60]

The world of teenagers is steeped in highly sexualized messages. Hit songs and music videos promote sexting. "Take a dirty picture for me" urge the pop stars Taio Cruz and Kesha in their recent duet "Dirty Picture." They say, "Send the dirty picture to me. Snap."[61] In a 2010 Super Bowl advertisement for Motorola, the actress Megan Fox takes a cellphone picture of herself in a bubble bath. "I wonder what would happen if I were to send this out?" she mused.[62]

"You can't expect teenagers not to do something they see happening all around them," said Susannah Stern, an associate professor at the University of San Diego who specializes in adolescence and technology.[63] "They're practicing to be a part of adult culture," Dr Stern observed. "And in 2011, that is a culture of sexualization and of putting yourself out there to validate who you are and that you matter."[64]

In January 2009, six teenagers (three females and three males, all under the age of eighteen) in Greensburg, Pennsylvania, were charged with child pornography for sending and receiving nude pictures of them-

---

58 Jan Hoffman, "What They're Saying about Sexting" *The New York Times* (26 March 2011), online: https://nyti.ms/2u9i0iC.

59 *Ibid.*

60 *Ibid.*

61 *Ibid.*

62 *Ibid.*

63 As quoted in Jan Hoffman, "A Girl's Nude Photo, and Altered Lives" *The New York Times* (26 March 2011), online: https://nyti.ms/2uamoOe.

64 *Ibid.*

selves via cellphone following the discovery of the images by a high school teacher.[65] In March 2009, a fourteen-year-old Florida boy was charged with transmitting pornography after he sent a photograph of his genitalia to a female classmate. The Florida boy explained that he did it because he was "bored."[66]

In Canada, it is not illegal for two teenagers under eighteen to carry naked photographs of one another, provided that it is for private viewing only. However, when a photograph is distributed, it becomes child pornography. In these circumstances, the charge is against the minor who distributed the photograph and not the minor who created it.

In a 2014 case from British Columbia, three teenaged boys pleaded guilty to criminal harassment for texting nude photos of girls aged thirteen to fifteen.[67] In exchange for their guilty pleas, the original charges of possession and distribution of child pornography were dropped. The court found that the boys were persistent and persuasive in their attempts to convince girls to send them images, although sometimes the girls provided the images more readily. The boys traded the images like "hockey cards," using social media. Similarly, two teenage Ontario boys were charged with possession and distribution of child pornography, resulting from a sexting incident involving a thirteen-year-old girl.[68]

In yet another case, a Toronto teen faced charges for allegedly trying to extort a girl using photos she sent him online. The young boy tried to use the photos to coerce the girl to send him a video of herself; when she refused, the boy used her email account to send the pictures to her email contacts. The boy was charged with "making, possession and distribution of child pornography, extortion, and threatening death."[69]

In January 2014, a seventeen-year-old girl from Victoria, British Columbia, was convicted of distribution and possession of child pornography and uttering threats. The young girl sent nude photos of her boyfriend's ex-girlfriend, also a teen, via text message and was found guilty on child

---

65 Anne Kingston, "The Sexting Scare" *Maclean's* (12 March 2009), online: www. macleans.ca/culture/the-sexting-scare [Kingston, "Sexting Scare"].

66 *Ibid.*

67 *R v SB*, 2014 BCPC 279.

68 Heather Rivers, "Charges Stem from 'Sexting' Incident" *Woodstock Sentinel Review* (17 March 2014), online: www.woodstocksentinelreview.com/2014/03/17/charges-stem-from-sexting-incident.

69 The Canadian Press, "Sexting Extortion: Toronto Boy Charged for Allegedly Trying to Extort Girl" *The Huffington Post* (18 October 2012), online: www. huffingtonpost.ca/2012/10/18/toronto-sexting-extortion_n_1983155.html.

pornography charges. The judge in the case found that the texts were meant to intimidate the victim and fell within the definition of child pornography.[70]

In *Jane Doe 464533 v ND*, released on 21 January 2016, Justice Stinson of the Ontario Superior Court presided over a motion for default judgment in what is likely the first case of civil tort liability for circulating intimate images online, known as "revenge porn."[71] The plaintiff had reluctantly sent an intimate video of herself to the defendant, her ex-boyfriend, on condition that it would be kept private. The defendant posted the video on a pornography website the same day. He also showed the video to a number of male friends. The defendant took down the video after three weeks, but the plaintiff suffered extreme anxiety, depression, and emotional upset as a result of the video being circulated. The plaintiff filed a motion for default judgment as the defendant had not defended the civil action.

In his judgment, Justice Stinson took judicial notice of "revenge porn," stating, "we now understand the devastating harm that can result from these acts, ranging from suicides by teenage victims to career-ending consequences when established persons are victimized." The court found $50,000 to be an appropriate award of general damages. It also awarded $25,000 each in aggravated and punitive damages respectively. The court granted injunctions for the defendant to destroy any intimate images he had of the plaintiff. In addition, the court barred the defendant from contacting the plaintiff or her family.

As pointed out by Jan Hoffman in *The New York Times*,[72] researchers have indicated that there may be a double standard between boys and girls. While a boy caught sending out a picture of himself may be regarded as a fool or even a boastful stud, girls, regardless of their bravado, are seen as having loose morals.

Danah Boyd, a senior social media researcher at Microsoft, has stated that photos of girls tend to go viral more often, because boys and girls will circulate girls' photos in part to shame them.[73] When photos go viral, it can have a devastating impact on the identity and reputation of the per-

---

70 "Sexting Teen Guilty of Distributing Child Porn" *CBC News* (10 January 2014), online: www.cbc.ca/1.2491605; Dirk Meissner, "Sexting BC Teen Found Guilty of Child Pornography" *CTV Vancouver News* (10 January 2014), online: http://ctv.news/gClrgDY.
71 2016 ONSC 541.
72 Hoffman, above note 58.
73 *Ibid.*

son. Circumstances when a sext goes viral could result in a deterioration of friendships, shunning, animosity, anger, name-calling, and fights. This conduct could cause fear, distress, and/or harm to the person's feelings, self-esteem, and reputation.

As noted in a recent article in *Macleans*, sexting is a reminder of how porous electronic communications can be.[74] Teenagers' casual willingness to provide explicit images of themselves heightens the risk of an incident they may regret. Educators should engage students in conversations about sexting. They should encourage students to take a strong stand against this conduct. It is important for schools to educate students, parents, and teachers about the seriousness of sexting. In this regard, students should be taught healthy relations strategies and communication skills. In particular, students and parents should recognize that the ease of distribution is so great over the Internet that a young person should assume that the photo or text message will not be seen only by the person he or she is sending it to. A valuable rule of thumb in sending any new media message — which would obviously include sexually explicit text messages or photos — is that "nothing is private." In this regard, students need to understand that if these images are never created, they cannot be distributed. Students should be taught how to manage their electronic reputations.

I. RETHINKING CYBERBULLYING LEGISLATION

In 2013, Nova Scotia became the first jurisdiction in Canada to implement legislation aimed at protecting victims of online harassment or "cyberbullying." On 11 December 2015, the Supreme Court of Nova Scotia struck down the *Cyber-safety Act* (the Act)[75] in *Crouch v Snell*, stating that it was contrary to the *Canadian Charter of Rights and Freedoms* and calling the legislation a "colossal failure."[76] The Act was proclaimed on 6 August 2013. It was drafted under heightened public scrutiny and in the months following the death of seventeen-year-old high-school student Rehtaeh Parsons who was bullied, attempted suicide, and subsequently died on 7 April 2013.[77]

---

74 Kingston, "Sexting Scare," above note 65.

75 *Cyber-safety Act*, SNS 2013, c 2.

76 2015 NSSC 340 at para 165 [*Crouch*].

77 Bethan Dinning, "Nova Scotia Court Strikes Down Cyber-Bullying Legislation" *BLG Education Law Newsletter* (Winter 2016) at 9, online: blg.com/en/News-And-Publications/Documents/Publication_4381_1033.pdf.

The Act was a multi-faceted attempt by the Government of Nova Scotia to make it easier for individuals to report bullying and to give the courts increased authority to protect victims of cyberbullying. The main provisions of the Act were as follows:

1) Greater powers and responsibilities to principals and school boards through amendments to the *Education Act*;
2) Parental responsibility for cyberbullying in some circumstances;
3) Creation of a cyber-investigative unit;
4) Victims of cyberbullying may apply for a protection order from the court, and
5) New statutory tort of cyberbullying which permits individuals to sue for damages or obtain an injunction.

In addition, the Act provided a broad definition of cyberbullying that included both adults and minors under nineteen years of age. The Act defined cyberbullying as:

> [A]ny electronic communication through the use of technology including, without limiting the generality of the foregoing, computers, other electronic devices, social networks, text messaging, instant messaging, websites and electronic mail, typically repeated or with continuing effect, that is intended or ought reasonably be expected to cause fear, intimidation, humiliation, distress or other damage or harm to another person's health, emotional well-being, self-esteem or reputation, and includes assisting or encouraging such communication in any way.[78]

Crouch v Snell involved a dispute between two former business partners. Giles Crouch claimed that Robert Snell had engaged in a "smear campaign" against him through email and social media following the breakdown of their business relationship. As a result, Crouch obtained a protection order under the Act against Snell that, among other things, restricted Snell from communicating with or about Crouch. Snell sought to have the order revoked and challenged the Act constitutionality in court.

In the decision, Justice Glen McDougall held that the Act violated the *Canadian Charter of Rights and Freedoms*, specifically the right to freedom of expression under section 2(b) and the right to life, liberty, and security of the person under section 7. The court also ruled that these infringements could not be defended as reasonable limits on *Charter* rights pursuant to section 1.

---

78   Above note 75, s 3(1)(b).

In light of the punishments available under the Act, including fines of up to $5,000 or imprisonment for a term up to six months, the court further held that the Act infringed on an individual's right to life, liberty, and security of the person. In addition, the court concluded that the Act was arbitrary, overbroad (in particular, in its definition of cyberbullying), and not procedurally fair. Therefore, the infringements on an individual's right to life, liberty, and security of the person could not be justified under the *Charter*.

In light of the above, the court concluded that, "The *Act* must be struck down in its entirety . . . . To temporarily suspend the declaration of validity would be to condone further infringements of *Charter*-protected rights and freedoms."[79] With this decision, Nova Scotia must completely reconsider its approach to cyberbullying. Justice Minister Diana Whalen has confirmed that the department is considering whether to appeal the decision, rewrite the law, or draft new legislation from scratch.[80] In the meantime, and as emphasized by the court in its decision, individuals who are confronted with cyberbullying will have to seek redress through traditional avenues, namely civil remedies for causes of action, such as defamation or applicable criminal charges.

The decision in *Crouch* will likely serve as a caution for other provinces looking to introduce legislation intended to protect individuals, in particular children, from online harassment and cyberbullying. This decision makes clear that courts will not uphold legislation that is far-reaching and overly broad, but rather will uphold the protections for freedom of expression and life, liberty, and security of the person afforded to individuals under the *Charter*.

J. *PROTECTING CANADIANS FROM ONLINE CRIME ACT*

The *Protecting Canadians from Online Crime Act* was introduced by Federal Justice Minister Peter MacKay on 20 November 2013. It received Royal Assent on 9 December 2014 and came into force on 9 March 2015.[81] The Act's full title is "An Act to Amend the Criminal Code, the Canada Evidence Act, the Competition Act and the Mutual Legal Assistance in Criminal Matters Act," but

---

79   *Crouch*, above note 76 at para 220.
80   Brett Ruskin, "Court Strikes Down Anti-Cyberbullying Law Created after Rehtaeh Parsons's Death" *CBC News* (11 December 2015), online: www.cbc.ca/beta/news/canada/nova-scotia/cyberbullying-law-struck-down-1.3360612.
81   SC 2014, c 31.

it is colloquially, and perhaps misleadingly, called the "cyberbullying bill." In the face of much criticism pertaining to the privacy concerns the new legislation raises and the increased investigative powers it grants police, the justice minister has insisted that the Act is in place to give police the tools they need to fight cyberbullying.[82]

The Act amends the *Criminal Code* in two ways, which are directly related to cyberbullying. First, it explicitly states that "communication," when it is an element of an offence, includes communication by means of telecommunication. Second, it makes the transmission of intimate images of a person without their knowledge or consent a crime:

> 162.1 (1) Everyone who knowingly publishes, distributes, transmits, sells, makes available or advertises an intimate image of a person knowing that the person depicted in the image did not give their consent to that conduct, or being reckless as to whether or not that person gave their consent to that conduct, is guilty . . . [of an offence].[83]

The *Criminal Code* defines "intimate image" as a "visual recording of a person made by any means including a photographic, film, or video recording, in which the person is nude, is exposing his or her genital organs or anal region or her breasts or is engaged in explicit sexual activity" in circumstances where they have a reasonable expectation of privacy.[84] Under the *Criminal Code*, distributing "intimate images" without consent is punishable with up to five years in jail.

The Act amends the *Criminal Code* to include a new offence of non-consensual distribution of intimate images as well as complementary amendments to authorize the removal of such images from the Internet. The Act also provides for the forfeiture of property used in the commission of the offence. In addition, the Act provides for a recognizance order to be issued to prevent the distribution of such images. Furthermore, the Act gives a court authority to restrict the use of a computer or the Internet by a convicted offender. The Act allows a judge to issue a peace bond limiting access to computers to anyone believed to be a risk to commit a new offence.

---

82 See Josh Wingrove, "Cyberbullying Bill C-13 Moves on Despite Supreme Court Decision" *The Globe and Mail* (1 October 2014), online: www.theglobeandmail. com/news/politics/cyberbullying-bill-c-13-moves-on-despite-supreme-court-decision/article20885941.

83 *Criminal Code*, RSC 1985, c C-46.

84 *Ibid.*

Computers and cellphones could be seized from an individual convicted of a cyberbullying offence.

While some legal experts welcome the increased attention cyber-bullying is receiving, the Act has received criticism for being too blunt an instrument to tackle the problem, especially when the offender is most likely a minor. The Act's narrow definition of cyberbullying has also been met with disapproval because it fails to consider the underlying and broader factors that contribute to bullying behaviour. Jane Bailey, a law professor at the University of Ottawa, said, "I would hate for the public to be misled into thinking that this is what will deal with cyberbullying, be-cause I think it's [only] a partial approach."[85] Professor Bailey stated that the problem with the new law is that "it focuses on criminal and punitive measures instead of the attitudes and actions of cyberbullies themselves."[86]

Shaheen Shariff, a professor at McGill University, argued that legis-lators need to have a better understanding of how people, and especially teenagers, view and use social media sites, such as Facebook.[87] Professor Shariff said that not all sexually suggestive images are posted without consent or with malicious intent. She asserted that there needs to be an acknowledgement that sexually provocative language that can seem de-rogatory and hurtful is often used affectionately between friends, or in hopes of getting admiration from peers. According to Professor Shariff, legislators need to have a "better understanding of how young people are thinking these days." She said, "This has become simply part of their com-munication, especially when they're teenagers."[88]

K. STEPS TO ADDRESS CYBERBULLYING

It is evident that cyberbullying is a serious problem that requires the watchful observation and proper intervention by school staff and parents alike. School administrators are encouraged to take appropriate and ef-fective steps to discipline bullies and protect students who are the subject of online bullying. Educators have an obligation to take these matters ser-iously and undertake a full and thorough investigation, where possible.

---

85 Andre Mayer, "Cyberbullying Bill Won't Stop Online Taunts, Critics Say" *CBC News* (27 November 2013), online: www.cbc.ca/1.2440785.

86 *Ibid.*

87 *Ibid.*

88 *Ibid.*

Parents and educators alike must be aware and sensitive to the fact that a substantial amount of interaction among today's youth occurs through electronic communication. Similarly, it is important to recognize that not all such communication is negative. Electronic devices, social media, and the Internet generally are tools that can be used to generate both positive or negative outcomes. Nonetheless, it is important that adults "differentiate technology use that is neutral or positive from technology use that is abusive or negative."[89]

Dr Wendy Craig made the following suggestions to school boards and administrators to reduce the presence of cyberbullying in schools:[90]

1) promote ethical behaviour online;
2) encourage empathy and common sense;
3) promote "netiquette" and cyber-kindness;
4) open dialogue on internet use;
5) inform about legal aspects of cyberbullying;
6) empower youth to be good cyber-citizens; and
7) educate about online safety and privacy conditions.

It is important for schools to educate students, parents, and teachers about the seriousness of cyberbullying. In this regard, students should be taught healthy relations strategies and communication skills. Schools should be encouraged to integrate curriculum-based anti-bullying programs into classrooms. Among other things, bullying prevention programs should encourage and reward fairness, equality, mutual respect, and co-operation. Such programs should focus on improving relations among members of the school community and creating a peaceful school culture.

It can be a hurtful and difficult challenge for students and parents to deal with the effects of cyberbullying after it has occurred. It also can be trying to get Internet service providers and mobile telecommunications service providers to respond and deal with a student's complaint about being cyberbullied.

Students should be encouraged not to give out or share their personal information number, email address, or passwords with others. Students should also be taught that if someone treats them rudely online, they should not respond. In addition, they should not erase or delete messages

---

89 Mishna et al, "Cyber Bullying Behaviors," above note 1 at 372.
90 Nova Scotia Cyberbullying Report, above note 6 at 91.

from cyberbullies. Where there is evidence of an email threat or harassment, the following information should be saved:

1) email addresses;
2) date and time received; and
3) copies of relevant email with full headers.

Students should be informed that they can report an email threat or harassment to their Internet service provider with the full headers displayed. The full header indicates every state of an email's journey. This information can assist a support team to track down where the email came from. In addition, where the conduct involves a criminal offence, such as a physical threat, the student and parents should inform their local police.

Where a school administrator is informed about an incident of cyberbullying, or has reason to believe that cyberbullying involving a student has taken place, he/she should conduct a thorough investigation. Such investigations may include:

1) meeting with the victim of the cyberbullying incident and his or her parents;
2) requesting copies of all relevant emails and/or the name of the chat room and date, time, and description of the chat;
3) trying to get as many details as possible;
4) exploring the identity of the alleged harasser (are there certain words or phrases in the email that are used by people that the student knows?);
5) asking the student if he or she knows or suspects whether there are other victims;
6) determining the history or background of events;
7) determining whether this was an isolated incident or an ongoing incident;
8) determining whether the student has any fear coming to school;
9) asking the student to prepare a written statement of the events that have transpired; and
10) interviewing any witnesses to the incidents or other students copies on emails and then interviewing the alleged harasser.

At the conclusion of all interviews, the school administrator must come to a conclusion about what actually occurred and who was at fault.

As part of the investigation of cyberbullying that has taken place off school premises, the school administrator must assess whether there is a sufficient impact on the climate of the school to impose school discipline. The school administrator will consider whether there is evidence of a disturbance in the school community, the creation of a poisonous environment, or conduct that negatively impacts the school climate.

Under the provisions of the Ontario *Education Act*, an initial determination will be made by the principal. The principal will have to determine, based on a balance of probabilities, whether the incident represents a contravention of provisions of the *Education Act* and/or breach of the board or school's code of conduct.

Students should be encouraged to speak out when they see someone being mean, threatening, or intimidating to another person online. Students should also be encouraged to report incidents of bullying or harassment to a person they trust, such as a parent, teacher, or principal. Principals should be able to access district-level support for any situation they feel is a threat to the safety of students, both inside and outside of school. Responding quickly and effectively to allegations of cyberbullying will serve to reduce a school board's legal liability and assist in the creation of a safe learning and teaching environment that promotes responsibility, respect, and civility.

In conclusion, cyberbullying is a real and extremely challenging issue for many of today's youth. Nonetheless, there are many tools that educators and administrators alike can use to reduce and counteract the presence of bullying within their schools. As found in the Duke Medical Study referred to above:

> Bullying can be easily assessed and monitored by health professionals and school personnel, and effective interventions that reduce victimization are available. Such interventions are likely to reduce human suffering and long-term health costs and provide a safer environment for children to grow up in.[91]

School administrators have a duty, to the extent possible, to take prompt and timely action to address and respond to allegations of online threats, intimidation, or harassment. Educators should encourage students to take a strong stand against cyberbullying. It should be clear that the school's code of conduct also applies to electronic communications.

Attempts by school administrators to block Facebook, Twitter, Snapchat, MySpace, YouTube, Instagram, or other social networking sites are not likely to succeed; these sites are simply the Internet generation's

---

91   Duke Health News Release, above note 12.

equivalent of the town hall or the school cafeteria — the place where people come together to exchange both ideas and gossip. An attempt by educators to block a particular site will likely not be successful, as there is a plethora of new social networking sites being introduced daily. School administrators should seize this opportunity to teach students about both the benefits and drawbacks of social media, while encouraging them to use the tools in positive and responsible ways.

CHAPTER 9

Special Education Law in Canada

Brenda Bowlby and Lauri Reesor[1]

A. INTRODUCTION

"Special education," from a pedagogical perspective, refers to the specialized programs, services, and instruction provided to students who, because of mental/cognitive or physical disabilities or both or because of a high level of giftedness, are otherwise unable to benefit from regular education to the same degree as most of their peers. These students are generally referred to as "students with special needs" or "exceptional students."

"Special education law" encompasses the statutory and regulatory laws (including ministerial[2] directives, orders, and guidelines) that govern the administration of special education within public education systems[3]

---

1 Lauri Reesor is a partner in the Ontario law firm Hicks Morley, and has a practice that involves extensive work with school boards on special education, human rights, and education law issues. Brenda Bowlby, who was a partner in the firm, retired in 2015 after 33 years of practice with the firm, having worked extensively with school boards on special education, human rights, and education law through her career.

2 Generally, the ministry or department responsible for education in each jurisdiction is called "the Ministry of Education," "the Department of Education," or "the Ministry of Learning," or has a name that includes education and other responsibilities, for example, Nova Scotia's Department of Education and Early Childhood Development. Our use of the phrase "ministerial" or "ministry" in this chapter is intended as a generic reference to all. The term "ministerial directives" will refer to ministerial directives, orders, and guidelines collectively.

3 The provision of education is a provincial matter under the *Constitution Act, 1867* (UK), 30 & 31 Vict, c 3, reprinted in RSC 1985, App II, No 5. Consequently, the provision of special education law is also a provincial or territorial responsibility.

and which define the legal rights of students with special needs as well as the legal rights of parents to be involved in and to challenge decisions regarding the special education provided to their children with special needs. These provisions taken together form a legal framework for the provision of special education.

In each jurisdiction, the legal framework under which special education is provided operates alongside other laws that impose legal principles that have an impact on the way students with disabilities are treated in the provision of education services. Foremost among these are laws that require equitable treatment of protected groups within society, including children with disabilities.[4] Key laws are the *Canadian Charter of Rights and Freedoms*[5] and local human rights statutes. Courts and tribunals have identified principles arising from the *Charter* and from human rights legislation that directly influence how special education is delivered in Canada.

In addition, the principles of common law — in particular, principles arising from the administrative law area of the common law — impose limits on the exercise of power by government and government agents and actors in order to prevent abuses of power and to ensure that citizens are treated fairly from a procedural perspective. These principles apply to school boards in the provision of special education to their exceptional pupils.

It is not possible in one chapter to provide a detailed review of the legal framework for special education in every jurisdiction in Canada. Therefore, we will focus on the common general procedural approaches emerging from these legal frameworks as well as significant differences, and provide examples from individual jurisdictions. We will review the impact that the *Charter* and the common law principles of administrative law have had on the provision of special education by governments and school boards. Finally, since there is an intersection between human rights and

---

4   While the *Universal Declaration of Human Rights*, GA Res 217(III), UNGAOR, 3d Sess, Supp No 13, UN Doc A/810 (1948) has undoubtedly had an influence on both the development of human rights laws in Canada and on the growth of special education to ensure accessibility of education to all, the focus of this chapter will be on Canadian laws. Numerous legal articles have been written about the impact of the *Universal Declaration of Human Rights* on human rights law in Canada; see, for example, William Schabas, "Canada and the Adoption of the *Universal Declaration of Human Rights*" (1998) 43 *McGill Law Journal* 403.

5   Section 2, Part I of the *Constitution Act, 1982*, being Schedule B to the *Canada Act 1982* (UK), 1982, c 11 [*Charter*].

special education, we will review the impact of human rights legislation on special education law in Canada.[6]

B. THE LEGAL FRAMEWORK FOR THE DELIVERY OF SPECIAL EDUCATION

The precise details of each jurisdiction's special education legal framework differ from province to province to territory. However, there are significant similarities in procedural approaches across Canada. This is not surprising, given that legal frameworks for special education are built around pedagogical principles, which are not limited by geographic boundaries except to the extent that any jurisdiction adopts a particular pedagogical approach and incorporates that approach into its laws. At the same time, there are some significant differences. The primary one relates to whether the approach is one of providing "special" education or "appropriate" education in an inclusive setting. Some jurisdictions focus on the formal identification of "exceptional" students, or students with special needs, and provide them with specific special education programs and services, which may involve withdrawal or special classrooms. Other jurisdictions focus on providing "appropriate" education that addresses all students' specific learning needs in a fully inclusive setting, including those that may require special services. However, even in the latter case, there are usually provisions to be found within the education legal framework regarding special education for students whose disabilities raise barriers for them beyond the norm in accessing education.

As noted above, in one chapter it is not possible to review in detail the legal framework for the delivery of special education in each province and territory. Therefore, we provide a broad brush overview of the common features and differences in the various provincial and territorial special education frameworks.

1) Access to Special Education

Virtually every Canadian jurisdiction recognizes, either expressly or inferentially, that access to special education by students with special needs

---

6   Other areas of education law, such as student discipline, also have implications for special education; beyond that, areas of law such as occupational health and safety are relevant for the staff who deliver special education. However, we do not have room in this chapter to discuss these areas.

is a right. This recognition is usually found in the primary education statute of the province or territory, although it may also be found in companion regulations made under that statute and ministerial directives of the particular jurisdiction. The threshold consideration is determining which students are eligible for special education supports. Generally, two approaches are found in Canadian jurisdictions.

a) Determining Access through a Focus on Exceptionalities

Some jurisdictions determine which students will receive special education supports by focusing on "exceptionalities"[7] or specific disabilities that interfere in the ability of students to learn. Examples of jurisdictions taking this approach include Ontario, British Columbia, Newfoundland and Labrador, Saskatchewan, and Alberta.

Ontario: The *Education Act* requires the minister to "ensure" that all "exceptional students" have access to "appropriate special programs and special education services." It defines "exceptional pupil" as "a pupil whose behavioural, communicational, intellectual, physical or multiple exceptionalities are such that he or she is considered to need placement in a special education program by a committee, established under subparagraph iii of paragraph 5 of subsection 11 (1), of the board."[8] Definitions of these "exceptionalities" are found in the ministry's *Special Education: A Guide for Administrators, 2001.*[9]

British Columbia: A ministerial order made under the BC *School Act* requires that a "student with special needs" be provided with "an educational program." It defines "student with special needs" as "a student who has a disability of an intellectual, physical, sensory, emotional or behavioural nature, has a learning disability or has exceptional gifts or talents."[10]

---

7   The term "exceptionality" in special education refers to defined categories of disabilities and giftedness, which is usually defined by criteria designed to identify students with very high levels of intellectual ability of a nature where the students require more than is available in the regular class in order to meet their educational potential.

8   *Education Act*, RSO 1990, c E.2, ss 1 and 8(3).

9   Ontario, Ministry of Education, *Special Education: A Guide for Administrators* (October 2001) at A-18, online: www.tncdsb.on.ca/new/resources/SPED%20A%20 Guide%20for%20Educators%2001.pdf.

10   BC Ministry of Education, *Special Needs Students Order*, Ministerial Order 150/89 (2015), as amended.

Newfoundland and Labrador: Ministerial policy provides that only students with a defined exceptionality may access special education services. Exceptionalities recognized include acquired brain injury, developmental delay, gifted and talented, hearing loss, medical condition, mental illness/mental health, neurodevelopmental and related disorders, intellectual disability, specific learning disorder, physical disability, speech and/or language disorder, and vision loss. With the exception of "gifted and talented," identification is based on diagnosis by a health-care professional of a disability that affects the student's educational performance.[11]

Saskatchewan: The *Education Act, 1995* states that special education services are to be provided to "students with intensive needs," defined as students assessed with "a capacity to learn that is compromised by a cognitive, social-emotional, behavioural or physical condition."[12] However, it should be noted that while the legislative framework remains unchanged, Saskatchewan has adopted a more inclusionary approach that focuses on the "strengths, abilities and needs of each individual student," while at the same time retaining, for students with intensive needs, the mechanisms for identification and provision of written "intervention plans" to address their special needs.[13]

Alberta: Alberta's *School Act* provides that a school board may determine that a student is in need of a special education program "by virtue of the student's behavioural, communicational, intellectual, learning or physical characteristics, or a combination of those characteristics," and that such students are "entitled" to access to a special education program.[14]

b) Determining Access through a Specific Learning Needs Focus

Other jurisdictions focus on the specific learning needs of students, without reference to specific disabilities, to identify which students require special education supports. These include Nova Scotia, Manitoba, and Québec.

---

11 Newfoundland and Labrador "Department of Education and Early Childhood Development Exceptionalities," online: www.ed.gov.nl.ca/edu/k12/studentsupportservices/exceptionalities.html.

12 SS 1995, c E-0.2, ss 146 and 178.

13 See online: www.saskatchewan.ca/residents/education-and-learning/prek-12-education-early-learning-and-schools/supporting-students-with-additional-needs.

14 RSA 2000, c S-3, s 47.

Nova Scotia: Under Nova Scotia's *Special Education Policy,* the determination of which students have entitlement to special education supports focuses on learning needs as opposed to criteria describing disabilities: "student with special needs" is defined as a student "who is identified by the school board as requiring additional program planning in the learning process to meet the student's needs."[15] However, the province does limit, by ministerial order, the use of special education funds only for students who have the following identified disabilities: "cognitive impairments; emotional/behavioural disorders; learning disabilities; physical disabilities and/or health impairments; speech impairments and/or communication disorders; sensory impairments — vision, hearing; multiple disabilities; [and] giftedness," while also stipulating that these descriptors are not to be used as "labels."[16]

Manitoba: Manitoba's "inclusive" approach to special education starts with a commitment to provide appropriate education programming to all students; it also requires "that a pupil be assessed as soon as reasonably practicable if he or she is having difficulty meeting expected learning outcomes," without reference to any disability.[17] The focus in this approach is on identifying student needs, although it recognizes that in assessing student needs, there will be "students with exceptional learning needs," who are defined as "those who require specialized services or programming when deemed necessary by the in-school team because of exceptional learning, social/emotional, behavioural, sensory, physical, cognitive/intellectual, communication, academic or special health-care needs that affect their ability to meet learning outcomes."[18]

Québec: Québec's ministère de l'Éducation issued its special education policy document, *Adapting Our Schools to the Needs of All Students,* in 2000. This policy emphasizes "prevention" by identifying and immediately addressing learning difficulties as they emerge. To that end, the concept of at-risk students was introduced, and the declaration of students as having

15   *Ministerial Education Act Regulations,* NS Reg 80/97, s 53(1)(a), as amended.
16   Nova Scotia Department of Education, *Special Education Policy* (Halifax: Department of Education, 2008) at 11, issued pursuant to the minister of education's powers under the *Education Act,* SNS 1995–96, c 1, s 145(1)(i), as amended.
17   *Appropriate Educational Programming Regulation,* Man Reg 155/2005.
18   Manitoba Education, Citizenship and Youth, *Appropriate Educational Programming in Manitoba: Standards for Student Services* (Winnipeg: Manitoba Education, Citizenship and Youth, 2006).

"social maladjustments or learning difficulties" or being handicapped in order to access special education supports was removed.

c) Jurisdictional Variations in the Identification of Exceptionalities

The actual process used to identify which students will have access to special education supports also differs somewhat from jurisdiction to jurisdiction. In some jurisdictions, there is a formal process in which the student is referred to a specially constituted group of educators and/ or health-care professionals who are charged with determining whether the student is exceptional or has special needs such that the student is in need of a placement where the student can receive special education services and programs. In other jurisdictions, the process for determining which students require special education services is much less formalized and is part of the ongoing assessments of learning needs by teachers and health-care professionals and those assessments inform the determinations made about the supports provided to students.

An example of a formal process for identification and placement is found in Ontario. This process involves a referral of the student by the principal of the student's school to a "committee" that decides if a student should be identified as exceptional and, if so, what the student's placement should be. This committee (usually many of them in each school board) is called the Identification, Placement and Review Committee, or IPRC. The process that must be followed by the IPRC is set out in a regulation,[19] which specifies the composition of the committee, the role of parents in the process, and the criteria and documents that the committee must and may consider. Principals are required to refer a student to an IPRC where a parent requests, and in the absence of a parental request, the principal "may" refer a student to the IPRC. If the IPRC decides that the student is "exceptional," it is required to categorize the nature of the student's exceptionality or exceptionalities, using definitions provided by the minister of Education that flesh out the broad categories mentioned in the definition above, and to recommend a placement. The IPRC may recommend special education programs and services to be provided to the student in the placement — and must do so if the parent requests — but it cannot order that these be provided. Finally, each student who has been identified must be reviewed annually by an IPRC, unless the student's parents waive the

---

19 *Identification and Placement of Exceptional Pupils*, O Reg 181/98, under Ontario *Education Act*, above note 8.

review. Built into this process is a two-step appeal process, described in Section B(3), below in this chapter.

At the other end of the spectrum from this very formalized approach for identifying students who are eligible for special education services is the much less formal process found in Manitoba. The approach set out in Manitoba's legislation and regulation[20] is to require principals to "ensure that a pupil is assessed as soon as reasonably practicable if he or she is having difficulty meeting the expected learning outcomes" of the provincially mandated curriculum.[21] If in-school personnel, including the student's teacher, resource teacher, and guidance counsellor, cannot assess why the student is having difficulty meeting the expected learning outcomes, or if they reach the opinion that differentiated instruction and adaptations will not be sufficient to assist the student in meeting those outcomes, then the principal must refer the student for a specialized assessment, to be conducted by a qualified practitioner. The practitioner may consider information from the student's file, which is obtained with the consent of parents.

The assessment is expected to identify what "other methods of differentiated instruction and adaptations," if any, can be put into place to help the student meet the expected learning outcomes. If the student cannot meet these, then the focus is on what can be done to help the student meet the approximate learning outcomes or to identify what learning outcomes the student can reasonably be expected to achieve. Students are not "formally" identified as exceptional or as having "special needs," let alone having their exceptionalities categorized. Rather, the system is based on the approach that differentiated instruction is required in every classroom in order for every student to meet learning outcomes. This approach, which applies to even regular students, recognizes that the needs of some students extend beyond the normal range of differentiation to different methods of instruction, adaptations, and even different learning outcomes.[22]

---

20   *The Public Schools Act*, CCSM c P250; Man Reg 155/2005, above note 17.
21   Man Reg 155/2005 *ibid*, s 4(1).
22   *Ibid*, s 4.

2) The Issue of Placement

In special education parlance, "placement" not only describes where a student with special needs receives the special education supports required but also encompasses the services and programming that the student receives. The spectrum of placements includes, very broadly, regular class full time with accommodations or supports; regular class with withdrawal for one-on-one assistance or withdrawal to a special class (where a particular program may be delivered) for less than half of the school day; special class with withdrawal to a regular class for less than half of the school day; full-time self-contained class; and a special school.

During the 1980s, as the delivery of legislated special education began to unfold in schools across Canada, the issue of placement was controversial, particularly for students with developmental delays, many of whom had previously been educated either in segregated schools or outside the regular school system entirely. Initially, these students tended to be placed in special (or self-contained) classes. The "mainstreaming" movement sought to have all students fully included and educated in regular classes. In Ontario, particularly, this issue ended up in litigation on a number of occasions before the Ontario Special Education Tribunal, Human Rights Boards of Inquiry, and in the courts. Ultimately, one case, *Eaton v Brant County Board of Education*,[23] reached the Supreme Court of Canada. The Court made clear in its decision that there is no "presumption" that a student with disabilities has the right to be placed in a regular class; instead, placement must be approached as an individualized determination, having regard to the restrictions arising from the student's disability and of the placement where the student can be provided with an equal opportunity to benefit from instruction. This approach starts with a consideration of whether that can be achieved in the regular class or whether the student will need to be placed in a setting, in part or in full, outside the regular class.

Currently, although some Canadian jurisdictions have endorsed a philosophy of "inclusive education,"[24] virtually all jurisdictions provide

---

23 [1997] 1 SCR 241 [*Eaton*]. This case will be further discussed in Section C, below in this chapter.

24 See, for example, Manitoba, *Appropriate Educational Programming in Manitoba*, above note 17; New Brunswick, Department of Education and Early Childhood Development, *Inclusive Education*, Policy 322; and Northwest Territories, Department of Education, Culture and Employment, *Ministerial Directive on Inclusive Schooling*, 2016. Newfoundland and Labrador's inclusive education policy is described online: www.ed.gov.nl.ca/edu/k12/inclusion.html.

a range of placements from full-time regular class to segregated, or special, class in recognition that some students may require intensive special education to meet their needs. Many jurisdictions have endorsed the principle of "least restrictive environment," or "LRE," meaning that students with disabilities should be removed from a regular education placement only to the degree or extent necessary to meet their educational needs.[25]

Virtually all jurisdictions require that each student with special needs be provided with an individual education plan which describes the student's strengths and weaknesses, goals for the student, and modifications of curriculum that the student will receive in the placement; lists any required services, programs, and accommodations to be provided to the student; and outlines how the student's progress will be measured.[26]

3) Parental Rights and Challenges

Most jurisdictions specifically provide parents with the right, usually found in education legislation or regulations, to be consulted about decisions to provide special education services and programs to their children, along with a right to challenge, at least to some degree, those decisions. However, there are differences from jurisdiction to jurisdiction in the types of challenges that can be made by parents.

Some jurisdictions provide that parents may request a review[27] or reconsideration[28] of a decision regarding the special education to be provid-

---

25 LRE is a core principle found in the US federal statute, *Individuals with Disabilities Education Act*, 104 Stat 1142.

26 The individual education plan is referred to by different names across Canada — for example, Individual Education Plan (Ontario, British Columbia, and Manitoba); Individualized Program Plan (Alberta and Nova Scotia); and Individual Support Services Plan (Newfoundland and Labrador and Nunavut). We will use the term "individual education plan," or "IEP," to reference all in this chapter.

27 For example, s 178.1 of the Saskatchewan *Education Act*, above note 12, provides that if parents disagree with the assessment of their child's special needs or the educational services that it is decided will be provided, they can ask the principal to review the assessment or decision. Failing resolution of the parents' concern by the principal, parents may request a review by the school board, which will appoint "a person" who was not part of the original decision-making process and who is acceptable to both the board and the parents, to conduct a review of the matter. There is no provision in the legislation that a hearing be conducted as part of the review.

28 Section 9 of the Québec *Education Act*, CQLR c I-13.3, provides that a student or parent affected by a decision of the school board may request the "council of

ed (or not) to their children, while other jurisdictions provide parents with a greater right to challenge by allowing them to appeal special education decisions. However, the nature of appeal processes differs from jurisdiction to jurisdiction: some jurisdictions provide that parents can "appeal" decisions of school administrators internally to more senior staff or to the school board itself.[29] In other jurisdictions, legislation or regulations provide for appeal processes leading to formal hearings before arm's-length adjudicators or tribunals.[30]

The scope of what can be challenged also differs from jurisdiction to jurisdiction. Some jurisdictions permit parents to challenge any decision that has a significant impact on their children's education, while other jurisdictions limit challenges to specific issues. For example, Ontario provides for parent appeals on identification and placement decisions, ultimately to a Special Education Tribunal,[31] but excludes special education programs and services from the subject-matter that can be appealed.[32] Further, in Ontario, while parent consultation is required in the creation of individual education plans (IEPs), school decisions regarding IEPs are not appealable.[33] In the Yukon, however, parents have a broad right of appeal to an Education Appeal Tribunal from any decisions regarding identification and virtually all aspects of the IEP, which sets out the goals, resources, methods, and strategies to be used in delivering the program as well as decisions regarding placement outside the regular class.[34]

---

commissioners," in other words, the elected or appointed individuals who administer the school board, to reconsider the decision.

29 For example, in Newfoundland and Labrador: *Schools Act, 1997*, SNL 1997, c S-12,2, s 22.

30 For example, in Ontario, a two-step appeal process is provided, first, under O Reg 181/98, above note 19, to a Special Education Appeal Board, which makes a recommendation to the school board which can be accepted or rejected by the board, and from there to a provincial Special Education Tribunal, which has the authority to make final and binding decisions: see Ontario *Education Act*, above note 8, s 57. The Yukon similarly provides for an appeal by parents in the *Education Act*, RSY 2002, c 61, s 16(2)(g): "the parents shall be provided with information concerning the right of appeal to the Education Appeal Tribunal."

31 Ontario *Education Act*, above note 8, s 57.

32 The Ontario Special Education Tribunal has, however, determined that, in the case of a regular class placement, "appropriate programs and services are interconnected with the issue of placement" and so are appealable: *I v Toronto District School Board*, 2005 ONSET 1 (CanLII).

33 See O Reg 181/98, above note 19.

34 Yukon *Education Act*, above note 30, s 17.

The common law provides no inherent right to parents to appeal to the courts special education decisions made by school boards or adjudicators/tribunals. However, courts do have the inherent jurisdiction to judicially review administrative decisions, including the decisions of school boards, in some circumstances. This topic is discussed in Section D, below in this chapter.

C. *CANADIAN CHARTER OF RIGHTS AND FREEDOMS* AND SPECIAL EDUCATION

The *Constitution Act, 1982* is the supreme law of Canada; it creates our nation's governmental structures, defines the areas of jurisdiction of the federal and provincial/territorial governments, and sets limits on the exercise of power by these governments, primarily through the *Charter*. Consequently, all government actors; the laws, policies, and rules that they create; and the decisions that they make are subject to the *Charter*.

Of prime importance for special education is the equality rights provision of the *Charter*, which states:

> 15. (1) Every individual is equal before and under the law and has the right to the equal protection and equal benefit of the law without discrimination and, in particular, without discrimination based on race, national or ethnic origin, colour, religion, sex, age or mental or physical disability.
>
> (2) Subsection (1) does not preclude any law, program or activity that has as its object the amelioration of conditions of disadvantaged individuals or groups including those that are disadvantaged because of race, national or ethnic origin, colour, religion, sex, age or mental or physical disability.[35]

Section 15 not only prohibits government action that is directly discriminatory of protected groups but also requires government to ensure that all citizens have an equal opportunity to benefit from the services offered by it.

In some cases, treating everyone in the same way can disadvantage certain groups or individuals because of a protected characteristic that they have. In education, this is particularly true for students with disabilities that give rise to cognitive, mental, or physical restrictions that interfere in the students' ability to access regular education. Consequently, in order to provide "equal benefit" of educational services to students with disabilities, governments must address the special needs of those chil-

---

35   Above note 5, s 15.

dren by providing educational services that offer an equal opportunity to those students to learn.

The impact of section 15 of the *Charter*, therefore, is to require that where a government provides educational services for the students who live within its jurisdiction, it must also address the needs of students with disabilities where those disabilities act as barriers to the students' ability to benefit from regular education as do their peers who do not have disabilities. In short, the provision of special education to students with special needs is required under section 15 of the *Charter* in order to fulfill their right to "equal benefit" of the education services.

The seminal Canadian judicial decision on special education is *Eaton*,[36] a decision of the Supreme Court of Canada involving section 15 of the *Charter*. This case involved a young student, Emily Eaton, who had significant physical and cognitive/developmental disabilities and who, up until Grade 2, had been placed in a regular classroom. The school board's Identification, Placement and Review Committee determined that her placement should be changed to a self-contained special education class, located in a regular school. Emily's parents wanted her education to continue in the regular classroom and appealed this decision to the Ontario Special Education Tribunal (OSET), which found that the appropriate special education placement for Emily was the self-contained special education class rather than a regular classroom. In making this determination, the Tribunal stated it had used the test of which placement was in Emily's best interests.

Emily's parents applied to the court for judicial review of the OSET decision, arguing, in part, that the decision violated Emily's section 15 *Charter* rights. The parents asserted that the "equal benefit" requirement of section 15 meant that Emily had a presumptive right to be educated in the regular classroom and that she could be removed from the regular classroom only if the school board could show it was not possible to educate her in that venue.

The Supreme Court disagreed with this argument and pointed out that for students with disabilities, "equal treatment" did not mean the same treatment but rather treatment that permits the same opportunities. The Court pointed out that placing a child in a self-contained class may be necessary for equal treatment in some cases:

---

36   Above note 23.

... segregation can be both protective of equality and violative of equality depending upon the person and the state of disability. In some cases, special education is a necessary adaptation of the mainstream world which enables some disabled pupils access to the learning environment they need in order to have an equal opportunity in education. While integration should be recognized as the norm of general application because of the benefits it generally provides, a presumption in favour of integrated schooling would work to the disadvantage of pupils who require special education in order to achieve equality. Schools focussed on the needs of the blind or deaf and special education for students with learning disabilities indicate the positive aspects of segregated education placement. Integration can be either a benefit or a burden depending on whether the individual can profit from the advantages that integration provides.[37]

The Supreme Court also addressed the role of parents and the educational decision makers, namely, teachers, professionals, schools, committees, and adjudicators/tribunals. It held that the best interests of the child, not parental wishes, must guide decisions:

We cannot forget, however, that for a child who is young or unable to communicate his or her needs or wishes, equality rights are being exercised on his or her behalf, usually by the child's parents. Moreover, the requirements for respecting these rights in this setting are decided by adults who have authority over this child. For this reason, the decision-making body must further ensure that its determination of the appropriate accommodation for an exceptional child be from a subjective, child-centred perspective, one which attempts to make equality meaningful from the child's point of view as opposed to that of the adults in his or her life. As a means of achieving this aim, it must also determine that the form of accommodation chosen is in the child's best interests. A decision-making body must determine whether the integrated setting can be adapted to meet the special needs of an exceptional child. Where this is not possible, that is, where aspects of the integrated setting which cannot reasonably be changed interfere with meeting the child's special needs, the principle of accommodation will require a special education placement outside of this setting.[38]

---

37   *Ibid* at para 69.
38   *Ibid* at para 77.

The Supreme Court made the point that for children with disabilities, the determination of whether they receive their education in a regular class or self-contained class should not be fettered by a presumption that they should be educated in a regular class. While a placement in the regular class will normally be considered first, because that is where most children are educated, the question should be where and how the child's special needs can be most effectively met, having regard to the best interests of the child. The Court also made clear that the wishes of parents are not paramount and cannot trump the best interests of the student[39] — which means that schools boards and schools must make decisions in the best interests of the student, even if parents disagree with those decisions.

The *Charter* also has been used by parents to challenge decisions made about where their children will be educated, to challenge the basis on which decisions regarding their children are made, and to argue that the failure by school boards to provide appropriate programs or services to their children violates their children's section 15 rights.

In *Wynberg v Ontario*,[40] parents tried to use section 15 to secure intensive behaviour intervention therapy as part of their children's special education program. The Ontario Court of Appeal made clear that in order for such a claim to succeed under section 15 of the *Charter*, the parents were required to establish that their children (all of whom had autism) were subject to differential treatment in comparison to the appropriate comparator group. In this case, the Court of Appeal found the appropriate comparator group to be other exceptional students who were receiving appropriate programs and services. It went on to say:

> To establish differential treatment, [the parents] are required to show that, unlike the comparator groups, they have been denied "appropriate" special education programs and services because they did not receive the particular intervention claimed. They can only do this if they show that the special education programs and services now available to them are not appropriate.[41]

The Court of Appeal rejected the parents' claim on the basis that evidence established that special education programs and services were available

---

39   *Ibid* at para 79.
40   (2006), 82 OR (3d) 561 (CA).
41   *Ibid* at para 136.

for their children in Ontario schools. There was no evidence to show that these alternative educational interventions were inappropriate to meet their children's special needs.

D. ADMINISTRATIVE LAW AND SPECIAL EDUCATION

Administrative law is that part of Canada's unwritten common law which governs the manner in which the administrative arms of government — that is, government actors and agencies, including school boards — make rules and decisions, and enforce or carry out their statutory and regulatory obligations (all of which may generally be referred to as "administrative actions"). There is an expectation that government actors not only will carry out their obligations in accordance with the legislation and regulations that govern their actions, but will refrain from taking actions beyond the authority that the legislation has conferred on them. In other words, government actors must act in accordance with the legislation and regulations that set out their powers and responsibilities, and they cannot take actions that are outside their powers and responsibilities. Doing so is referred to in administrative law as acting "*ultra vires*," or outside the decision maker's jurisdiction. Moreover, administrative actors are expected to act fairly in making decisions that might negatively affect individuals in their jurisdictions; decision makers must also use correct legal principles in reaching their decisions.

"Fairness" in administrative law gives rise to certain procedural rights when government actors make decisions. The extent of the procedural rights required in any case is dependent on the nature and gravity of the particular decision, with the result that the procedural elements required in any administrative decision making will vary through a range which starts, at the lowest end of the range, with a requirement that administrative decision-makers act in good faith and advise the individual to whom the decision relates what the decision is.

At the highest end of the range, an administrative decision-maker must provide to an individual affected by the decision a full hearing akin to a court hearing with the right to call and cross-examine witnesses. The range of fairness that can apply in decision making under the special education legislation is largely defined by the nature of the challenge that is permitted to a particular decision. Examples can be seen in various decisions required under the special education legislative framework in Ontario.

At the lower end of the range are situations where decisions that are less determinative of rights are made. For example, in Ontario, when schools create IEPs for students setting out how their needs will be met, parents may have the right to be "consulted" with respect to creation of the plan and its annual update. Parents may also make comments that must be considered by the principal, but they cannot be present during the school staff's discussions about the plan.[42]

The level of procedural fairness required in IPRC decisions, however, is somewhat higher: the regulation that sets up the IPRC process stipulates that parents have a right to attend IPRC meetings and to participate in all IPRC discussions about their child.[43] They cannot, however, call or cross-examine witnesses or make opening or closing arguments. If parents disagree with the IPRC decision, they have the right to appeal, in which case, increasing levels of procedural rights are required in the two levels of appeal, including the right to a full hearing before a Special Education Tribunal.[44]

Almost at the highest end of the range of administrative fairness are appeals of school board decisions to an administrative adjudicator, such as the OSET. Where legislation requires an appeal to be held by a tribunal or third-party adjudicator, generally a hearing must have a level of procedural fairness almost akin to that found in a court hearing. If, in the particular jurisdiction, there has been enacted a statute which governs the conduct of hearings required under statutes, that statute will set out procedures that must be complied with[45] along with, or instead of, common law principles of fairness. If a tribunal has been created by statute to hear the appeal, the tribunal may also establish its own procedures.

Where legislation provides to parents an opportunity to challenge school board decisions on special education for their children by way of review or request for reconsideration, this provision does not usually carry with it an expectation that a hearing will be held. Rather, what will be required, subject to what legislation or regulations might otherwise provide, is that the review or reconsideration of the decision be conducted

---

42 O Reg 181/98, above note 19, s 6(2).

43 *Ibid*, s 5(1).

44 OSET, *Rules of Procedure*, online: www.sjto.gov.on.ca/documents/oset/Rules%20 of%20Procedure.html.

45 For example, in Ontario, an appeal to the OSET requires a hearing, the procedure for which is governed by the *Statutory Powers Procedure Act*, RSO 1990, c S.22.

fairly, that the parent's reasons and arguments for the request be considered, and that the parent be provided with the decision.

The expectations that administrative law imposes on government actors — to carry out their functions as stipulated by legislation or regulation and to do so in accordance with applicable legal principles, including acting fairly — are enforceable in the superior courts of each jurisdiction in Canada by way of an application for judicial review of the administrative action in question.

Where a court finds government action to have run afoul of applicable administrative law principles, the court may "quash" the offending administrative action, which renders the challenged decision to be a nullity. The court may send the matter back to the decision maker with a direction that the matter be redecided in accordance with proper principles. In some cases, the issue that arises is whether the administrative decision-maker has failed to take an action when required to do so, in which case, if the court agrees, it may issue a *mandamus* order directing the decision maker to take action.

Generally, the court will not substitute its own decision for that of the government actor since the role of the court is not to make the decision but to ensure that the decision maker complies with applicable procedural requirements and the limits of his or her authority. It is important to underline that a judicial review is not an appeal and a court conducting a judicial review will not second-guess the correctness of a decision maker's decision, so long as the decision is made in accordance with applicable legal principles and is within the decision maker's prescribed statutory or regulatory authority.

Before an individual can challenge government action by judicial review, the individual must have "standing," which means that the individual must be affected in a real way by the administrative action that the individual wishes the court to review.[46] Normally, the parents of a child, or minor, who may have been impacted by the administrative action of a school board, will be accorded standing to act on behalf of the child as the child's "litigation guardian." In most education statutes, parents are given rights in the special education process which makes a finding of "litigation guardian" unnecessary.

---

46 An individual will be accorded "standing," or permitted by the court to challenge administrative action, only if the individual has a stake in the outcome of the administrative action or decision.

An example of a parent using judicial review to challenge the decision of a school board is found in *Bonnah (Litigation guardian of) v Ottawa-Carleton District School Board*.[47] This case arose in circumstances where the parents had appealed an IPRC decision to change the placement of their son Zachary Bonnah, a decision that would result in his move to a new school. The regulations dealing with IPRC decisions provide that where parents appeal the IPRC's decision, the child cannot be put in the new placement determined by the IPRC without parental consent; consequently, the existing placement is "stayed" until the appeal process is completed.

Meanwhile, Zachary's disabilities caused him to engage in behaviours that were potentially physically harmful to other students and to staff, prompting the principal of Zachary's school to determine that, pursuant to Ontario's *Education Act*, section 265(m),[48] Zachary's continued presence in the school would be harmful to the mental or physical well-being of other students. As a result, section 265(m) required that the principal exclude Zachary from the school. The school board then proceeded to direct that Zachary attend the new placement that had been determined by the IPRC, which was the determination that his parents were appealing. The parents commenced a judicial review application seeking to quash the school board's direction that Zachary attend the new placement. The application was unsuccessful in the first instance and was appealed by the parents to the Ontario Court of Appeal. The Court of Appeal quashed the school board's decision, finding that the school board had exceeded its authority when it removed Zachary from his existing placement and put him into the very placement that was the subject of the parents' appeal, thereby acting contrary to the stay of placement provision in the regulation.

The Court of Appeal went on to note, however, that the stay of placement did not preclude the principal from excluding Zachary under section 265(m). Rather than proceeding to transfer Zachary, the school board should have offered a new placement for Zachary and if the parents rejected this, then Zachary would remain out of school pending the outcome of the OSET hearing.

---

47 (2003), 64 OR (3d) 454 (CA).

48 Above note 8, s 265: "(1) It is the duty of a principal of a school, in addition to the principal's duties as a teacher, . . . (m) subject to an appeal to the board, to refuse to admit to the school or classroom a person whose presence in the school or classroom would in the principal's judgment be detrimental to the physical or mental well-being of the pupils."

Judicial review has been used most frequently in special education cases involving the decisions of administrative tribunals.[49] For example, the *Eaton* case, referred to above,[50] originated in an OSET decision which was judicially reviewed based on the parent's claim (among others) that the Tribunal had failed to apply the principles of section 15 of the *Charter* correctly.

In other jurisdictions, human rights tribunal decisions on special education cases have been challenged by way of judicial review; for example, a recent significant case decided by the Supreme Court of Canada came from British Columbia. *Moore v British Columbia (Education)*[51] started as a human rights complaint to the BC Human Rights Tribunal, which upheld the complaint that Jeffrey Moore had been discriminated against when the programs that he needed to address his dyslexia had been cancelled and no alternative program put into place.

As a result, Jeffrey's father had been advised by school staff to enrol Jeffrey in a private school that did offer the program in question. In this case (discussed in more detail in Section F, below in this chapter), the government made an application for judicial review to the court on the basis that the Human Rights Tribunal had made errors of law.

Although the BC Supreme Court granted the judicial review, a decision that was upheld by the BC Court of Appeal, the Supreme Court of Canada subsequently found that the Human Rights Tribunal had made no such errors and restored its decision. Throughout, the issue was not whether the Human Rights Tribunal's decision was correct — since correctness is not considered in a judicial review — but rather, whether the decision was within the Tribunal's authority to make and whether the Tribunal applied correct legal principles in doing so.

---

49 Most jurisdictions have now codified the right to challenge administrative action in statutes and regulations that outline the procedures to be followed in initiating an application for judicial review to the courts.

50 See text accompanying notes 36–39.

51 2012 SCC 61 [*Moore*].

E. THE INTERSECTION OF HUMAN RIGHTS LAW AND SPECIAL EDUCATION

As noted above, the special education legal framework operates alongside laws that require equitable treatment of protected groups within society, including children with disabilities. Foremost among these laws is human rights legislation. Education has long been recognized as a "service" that is protected by human rights legislation,[52] and special education has been recognized as the means by which accommodations are determined and implemented for students with disabilities that create barriers for those students in accessing educational services.[53]

In Ontario, for example, the Human Rights Tribunal of Ontario has found that the special education system established by that province's *Education Act* and the Ontario *Human Rights Code*[54] serve a common purpose with respect to the accommodation of students with disabilities. The Tribunal specifically found that at its centre, the purpose of special education is to ensure that exceptional students "are able to receive the benefits of education available to others" and that "special education is all about finding the appropriate accommodation for students with disabilities."[55]

The processes established in each jurisdiction for identifying students with special needs and providing them with special education services and programs that meet their needs can assist school boards in demonstrating that they have met both the substantive and procedural aspects of their duty to accommodate under human rights legislation. However, the mere existence of a special statutory scheme pertaining to special education in a jurisdiction will not insulate a school board in that jurisdiction from scrutiny under human rights legislation by human rights tribunals.

---

52 For example, see the Ontario *Human Rights Code*, RSO 1990, c H.19, as amended at s 1: "Every person has a right to equal treatment with respect to services, goods and facilities, without discrimination because of race, ancestry, place of origin, colour, ethnic origin, citizenship, creed, sex, sexual orientation, gender identity, gender expression, age, marital status, family status or disability."

53 In Manitoba, in fact, school boards are specifically directed to have regard to the province's human rights legislation, including a requirement that they establish written human diversity policies that have regard for the principles of the *Human Rights Code* and that such policies promote a "safe and inclusive learning environment": *The Public Schools Act*, above note 20, ss 41(1)(b.4), 41(1.6), & 41(1.7).

54 Above note 52.

55 *Campbell (Litigation guardian of) v Toronto District School Board*, 2008 HRTO 62 at para 42.

Those tribunals have very broad jurisdiction to review the actions of a school board when parents allege that their children have not been properly accommodated as required by provincial or territorial human rights legislation.

1) Principles Underlying the Duty to Accommodate

Through the years, Canadian courts and human rights tribunals have outlined the common principles that underlie the duty to accommodate arising from human rights legislation. More than thirty years ago, the Supreme Court of Canada first recognized that a duty to accommodate[56] arises in situations where an individual is precluded from participating in an activity or exercising a right enjoyed by others because of a factor that is a protected ground under human rights legislation.

In the case of a student with disabilities who is precluded by reason of those disabilities from having meaningful access to education in the same way as the student's peers, human rights legislation in every Canadian jurisdiction imposes an obligation on school boards to provide appropriate accommodation(s) that will permit meaningful access, unless doing so would give rise to undue hardship.[57] In the context of human rights, appropriate accommodations are the special education services, programs, and accommodations that will provide to a student with disabilities an equal opportunity to access regular education. If a student is unable to access regular education because of intellectual disabilities, the duty to accommodate may require the school board to modify educational goals so that the student will have an equal opportunity to reach his or her maximum potential: the goal of education for all students.

It is also important to note that, especially in the case of disability, the duty to accommodate must be approached as an individualized process. The Supreme Court of Canada has stated:

> The importance of the individualized nature of the accommodation process cannot be minimized. The scope of the duty to accommodate varies according to the characteristics of each enterprise, the specific needs of

---

56 *Ontario Human Rights Commission and O'Malley v Simpsons-Sears Ltd*, [1985] 2 SCR 536.

57 "Undue hardship" can include disadvantage to other students: see *Lewis v York Region Board of Education* (1996), 27 CHRR D/261 (Ont Bd Inq).

each employee and the specific circumstances in which the decision is to be made . . . . Reasonable accommodation is thus incompatible with the mechanical application of a general standard.[58]

This focus resonates with one of the fundamental principles of special education, namely, that the needs of the student must be assessed and addressed on an individualized basis (which is underlined by the preparation of an individual education plan for each student entitled to special education).

The duty to accommodate, however, is not unlimited. A school board has a duty to provide accommodation only to the point where providing the accommodation would be an undue hardship for the accommodation provider.[59] It is critical to note that "undue hardship" cannot be speculative; that is, a school board must be able to demonstrate through concrete or tangible evidence that hardship is probable in order to justify why the accommodation cannot be provided. Arguments based on impressionistic evidence or possibilities will not succeed.[60]

Courts have set out criteria that will be considered where an "undue hardship" argument is made. For example, to support an argument that providing an accommodation would be an undue hardship based on financial constraints, the school board would have to provide evidence that it considered (1) the cost of the accommodation as compared to its budgetary constraints and funding; (2) the availability of alternatives to manage or reduce the cost; and (3) the impact that absorbing the cost would have on the viability of the program or on programs or resources available to other students.

Similarly, where a school board seeks to ground an argument of undue hardship on safety concerns for the student or other staff and students, the school board must be able to prove that it considered the magnitude of the risk, who bears it (whether the accommodated student alone bears the risk or whether the risk will be imposed on other students, staff, administration, or the general public), and the availability of measures to reduce or spread the risk. Where straightforward safeguards, including, among other things, the training of staff, providing additional staff, and implementing

---

58 *McGill University Health Care Centre (Montreal General Hospital) v Syndicat des employés de l'Hôpital général de Montréal*, [2007] 1 SCR 161 at para 22.

59 *Hydro-Québec v Syndicat des employées de techniques professionnelles et de bureau d'Hydro-Québec, section locale 2000 (SCFP-FTQ)*, [2008] 2 SCR 561.

60 See, for example, *Council of Canadians with Disabilities v VIA Rail Canada Inc*, [2007] 1 SCR 650.

behavioural and safety plans, can be put in place, it will be difficult to argue undue hardship.

2) The Procedural Aspect of Accommodation

As noted above, the intersection between human rights law and special education is readily apparent. The IPRC and IEP process (or similar process, depending on the jurisdiction) lends itself naturally to assisting school boards in meeting their obligations under the relevant provincial or territorial human rights legislation. In fact, engaging in the identification, placement, and IEP process (or equivalent) may be considered an essential tool in demonstrating that the school board has carried out both its substantive and procedural accommodation obligations under human rights legislation. The substantive aspect of accommodation is the actual provision of the accommodation. The procedural aspect of accommodation is the process followed in arriving at the decision regarding whether or not the accommodation can be provided and, if so, what the appropriate accommodation will be.

In providing accommodation, a service provider is obliged to follow a procedure which ensures:

1) that the service provider makes appropriate requests for information regarding the restrictions or limitations arising from the disability that is to be accommodated (in order to understand the accommodations that are required);
2) that appropriate consideration is given to this information;
3) that the individual seeking accommodation (or, in the case of a student, the student's parents) has an opportunity to provide input;
4) that all possible accommodations are considered;
5) that the service provider chooses reasonable and appropriate accommodations.

These procedural requirements generally coincide with the procedures provided for under the various special education schemes across Canada. In these schemes, the needs of students with disabilities are assessed and decisions are made regarding appropriate educational services, programs, and accommodations, in consultation with parents and then in completing the student's individual education plan. Therefore, following normal special education procedures will generally meet the procedural aspect of providing human rights accommodation.

F. THE OVERLAP BETWEEN SPECIAL EDUCATION AND HUMAN RIGHTS OBLIGATIONS

Increasingly, parents are turning to human rights tribunals to enforce complaints relating to the special education provided (or not provided) to their children. The issue of the scope of a school board's duty to accommodate in special education and undue hardship was the focus of the Supreme Court of Canada decision in *Moore*.[61] At issue in *Moore* was the school board's closure, due to financial constraints, of a program that provided intensive remediation for students with certain types of learning disabilities. The student had been recommended for intensive remediation in this program by the board's own psychologist. After the board closed the program, the parents were advised that the school board would no longer be providing the program at any of its schools. The principal of the student's school and the psychologist agreed that the student needed the special program and told the parents that they would have to seek out the program from a private school. The student was effectively left without any option within the public education system.

The Supreme Court made clear that the issue in the case was accommodation in education and that what was required by way of accommodation was to provide meaningful access to education for the student; this accommodation had been provided through the special education program that was cancelled. The Court reviewed other educational programs that had *not* been cut by the board in dealing with its financial constraints, as well as the programs that had been cut, and found that the cuts made by the board were disproportionate in their negative impact on exceptional students, given that other discretionary programs (such as outdoor education) continued to operate while programs, such as that required by the student to have meaningful access to education, were cancelled.

The *Moore* decision emphasizes the necessity for school boards to look critically at cost reduction alternatives as well as to review the potential consequences and impact on students with special needs before making any decisions that would result in a reduction in programming or services for exceptional students. The defence of undue hardship will not be available to a school board in the absence of proof that it considered these issues, had no reasonable alternative available but to cut the services

---

61   Discussed in Section D, above in this chapter.

to students with special needs, and had no means to provide alternative equally effective services or programs in lieu of the eliminated services.

The issue of meaningful access to education within the human rights framework was also central in a 2013 decision of the Human Rights Tribunal of Ontario, *RB (Next friend of) v Keewatin-Patricia District School Board.*[62] The decision addressed issues of accommodation in dealing with students who have significant behavioural issues. It picked up on issues and key themes arising out of the *Moore* decision. The case dealt with a decision by the school, contrary to parental wishes, to reduce the amount of educational assistant (EA) support for a student with significant behavioural issues. The Tribunal found that the school's decision was made without sufficient consideration of what impact the reduction would have on the student's behaviour.

Shortly after the reduction in EA support, the student's behavioural issues became more serious and increasingly violent; ultimately, these behavioural issues resulted in the exclusion of the student. Complicating the challenges faced by the school in addressing the behavioural issues associated with the student's disability was the fact that an already difficult relationship between the parent and the school deteriorated to the point where a communication ban was imposed on the parent. A trespass notice was also issued to the parent, following an alleged threat.

Most significantly, the *Keewatin-Patricia District School Board* decision has highlighted that where a school board fails to deliver on the mandate and objectives of public education to a student with disabilities with the result that the student is denied meaningful access to education, a finding of *prima facie* discrimination will be made. Special education is the method by which a student is given meaningful access to education, and before a school board reduces the special education services that form part of the student's placement, the school board must demonstrate that the student no longer needs the support, that it is in the student's best interests to reduce the support (for example, to avoid over-reliance on EA assistance), or that the reduction is required to avoid an undue hardship. Moreover, the Tribunal made clear that an objective assessment must be undertaken on the impact of a proposed reduction of a service or program on the student *prior* to effecting the change. The Tribunal's decision also indicates that the procedural aspect of the school board's duty to accommodate requires

---

62 2013 HRTO 1436, reconsideration denied 2013 HRTO 1920 [*Keewatin-Patricia District School Board*].

that open communication with the parents be maintained; doing so includes facilitating meetings with the parents and — in a case such as this where the student's psychological status was in question — the relevant medical team to ensure that the student's individual needs are taken into account in discussing the accommodation and special education supports to be provided. The Tribunal underlined that a difficult relationship with the parents cannot interfere with the school board's duty to accommodate and provide meaningful access to education for the student.

The intersection between a school board's accommodation obligations under human rights legislation and a school board's provision of special education programming and services is inevitable and should not be viewed as separate processes. Rather, the special education identification, placement, and programming processes for exceptional students should all be utilized with a view to providing meaningful access to education for each student whose disabilities interfere in the student's ability to access regular education. Doing so will assist the school board in defending against any potential complaint under human rights legislation.

CHAPTER 10

Copyright and Canadian Schools

Margaret Ann Wilkinson

A. INTRODUCTION

Historically, copyright did not seem to have a direct effect upon those who were teaching and administering (or, indeed, studying) in Canada's schools: books were provided through school libraries and then loaned to students, or textbooks were owned by school boards and loaned to students for use in a given course or, in some cases, personal copies were loaned to the classroom or the students by the teachers who owned them. It was the publishers who were involved with copyright in the materials contained in the books, and in purchasing from reputable publishers, distributors, or bookstores in Canada, the schools, the teachers, the students, and the school administrators could rely on all copyright concerns having been dealt with. They were, therefore, concerned not with copyright in the material contained in the books, but with the private property interests in the books themselves, the artifacts that contained the information: Who owned *this* copy of the book? Who had borrowed a given copy from the owner?

All this changed with the introduction into schools of duplicating machines such as the Gestetner and, subsequently, the photocopier: now those working or studying in schools could make their own copies of materials. This capability brought Canadian schools, at least theoretically, face to face with copyright because copying is one of those acts, which, absent an applicable exception under the *Copyright Act*,[1] only the copyright holder has the right to do. Nonetheless, Canadian schools, by and large,

---

1   RSC 1985, c C-42.

288 / Margaret Ann Wilkinson

felt little pressure from copyright holders in the early days of machine copying. Music teachers were among those who felt the effects of copyright: when orchestral, band, or choral scores were borrowed (or rented) from music distributors, the distributors specified that all parts received (whether for sopranos or tenors, violins or violas, flutes, or percussion) had to be returned (and, typically, all notes made on the scores by budding musicians had to be erased). As other technology was developed, those acquiring audiovisual materials for use in schools became accustomed to distributors placing limitations that specified who would be allowed to watch the film, for example, and where it could be shown (for example, only in classrooms). This, too, was copyright in action. As the digital age of telecommunications advanced, educators continued to reveal themselves as early technology adopters, and each technology advance and its adoption has brought the school community more in contact with copyright law.

Canada's copyright law is the sole responsibility of the federal government,[2] which has chosen to legislate virtually all law governing copyright within one statute: the *Copyright Act*.[3] The concept of copyright is an old one, in existence since the eighteenth century and affecting Canada since it was colonized. However, in light of continuous technological change since the eighteenth century, the concepts included in the *Copyright Act* have been continuously evolving and expanding. Since the nineteenth century, Canada has been involved in international treaties designed to create links between nation states and common approaches among member states to providing protection under the copyright legislation of the various states.

Indeed, in 1948, just like education,[4] copyright was instantiated by the United Nations in the *Universal Declaration of Human Rights*, which stated, "Everyone has the right to the protection of the moral and material interests resulting from any scientific, literary or artistic production of which he is the author."[5] And, in 2013, Canada's Supreme Court confirmed, in a

---

2   *Constitution Act, 1867* (UK), 30 & 31 Vict, c 3, s 91(23), reprinted in RSC 1985, App II, No 5 (copyrights).

3   Above note 1, s 89.

4   See, most particularly, the *Universal Declaration of Human Rights*, GA Res 217(III), UNGAOR, 3d Sess, Supp No 13, UN Doc A/810 (1948), art 26, which addresses education.

5   *Ibid*, art 27(2). The World Intellectual Property Organization (WIPO) is now the home of the original eighteenth-century copyright treaty (the *Berne Convention*),

case involving a creator's copyright interest in a cartoon, that copyrights have status as human rights:

> [c]opyright infringement is a violation of s. 6 of the [Québec] *Charter*, which provides that "[e]very person has a right to the peaceful enjoyment and free disposition of property, except to the extent provided by law" . . . . Additionally, the infringement of copyright in this case interfered with Robinson's personal rights to inviolability and to dignity, recognized by ss. 1 and 4 of the [Québec] *Charter*.[6]

In the late twentieth century, copyright, as well as remaining the subject of a number of public international law treaties, became the subject of an increasing number of international trade agreements: the largest and chief of these is the *Trade-Related Aspects of Intellectual Property Rights Agreement*, or *TRIPS Agreement*.[7] Since 1967, a new approach has become entrenched among nations when making changes to their national copyright law: the "three-step test"[8] requires a country defending a provision in its own copyright legislation (against a challenge from another nation in a given international trade situation) to show that any exception provided in the defending country's legislation to the rights of copyright holders is (1) a special case, (2) a case which does not conflict with the rights holders' normal exploitation of the work, and (3) a case which does not unreasonably prejudice the legitimate interest of the rights holders.

In light of these international expressions of protection for copyright, Canada's federal government is not free to do as it likes, having regard only to the Canadian political landscape, in terms of legislating in the area of copyright: it needs to have regard for its international treaty commitments. Nor can any province try to use any area of provincial constitutional competence (e.g., education) to legislate anything that constitutionally falls

---

as well as subsequent public international legal treaties involving copyright; it is now a UN body.

6   *Cinar Corp v Robinson*, 2013 SCC 73 at para 114 [*Robinson*].

7   33 ILM 1197 (1994) [*TRIPS Agreement*].

8   The three-step test was first introduced in connection with the reproduction right in copyright in the 1967 revision of the *Berne Convention*. It now governs copyright exceptions generally, appearing not only in the *Berne Convention* but also in the *WIPO Copyright Treaty* and the *WIPO Performances and Phonograms Treaty*. In addition, on the international trade side, it appears in both the *North American Free Trade Agreement*, 32 ILM 289 (1993), and in the *TRIPS Agreement*, above note 7.

within the area of copyright.[9] In this light, it is instructive to note that the *Accessibility for Ontarians with Disabilities Act, 2005*,[10] for example, cannot require organizations to ignore copyright in pursuit of the objects of that legislation. Thus, in the regulations to that statute,[11] "Libraries of educational and training institutions"[12] are required to make materials available for persons with disabilities; however, this should not be interpreted to mean that such institutions should make material accessible in violation of the *Copyright Act*.[13]

B. PERTINENT CHANGES TO THE *COPYRIGHT ACT* SINCE 2012

1) Legal Protection for Technological Protection Measures

In 2012, Parliament made a number of changes to Canada's *Copyright Act*.[14] One major change now included in the *Copyright Act* in consequence makes it illegal in Canada to circumvent a digital lock, or a technological protection measure (TPM).[15] Parliament defines a technological protection measure as

> any effective technology, device or component that . . .
> (a) controls access to a work, . . . [to a recorded performance] or to a
>   sound recording . . . [that is being made available under the author-
>   ity of the copyright holder]

---

9   For the purposes of this chapter, it will be assumed that that which is contained within the *Copyright Act* is copyright. There is, however, scholarly debate about whether a number of the newer elements of the *Copyright Act* should be considered "copyright." Suffice it to point out here that copyright is not defined in the *Constitution Act, 1867* — and there is no universally accepted definition for it that can definitively rule, for example, the moral rights in or out of it, or the protection of digital locks or management information in software in or out of it.

10 SO 2005, c 11 [AODA].

11 O Reg 191/11: *Integrated Accessibility Standards*, under the AODA, above note 10.

12 *Ibid*, s 18.

13 The provisions of the *Copyright Act* in respect of persons with disabilities will be discussed in Section I(4), below in this chapter.

14 *Copyright Modernization Act*, SC 2012, c 20.

15 *Copyright Act*, above note 1, s 41.1(1)(a). Theoretical questions can be asked about whether technological protection measures, as well as the related digital rights management measures, are "copyright" at all, but, regardless, measures of both kinds are now regulated under the *Copyright Act*. "Rights management information in electronic form," usually referred to as digital rights management, or DRM, information, cannot be altered or removed by a user: see s 41.22.

as well as any effective technology, device or component that

(b) restricts the doing of any act . . . [which is controlled by a copyright holder or for which the rightsholder is entitled to remuneration]"[16]

The TPM provisions prohibit circumvention of a digital lock no matter whether the information "behind" the lock, to which anyone seeks access, is merely data or facts and thus not itself subject to copyright, or whether one is seeking access to works or other subject-matter that would have been subject to copyright protections at one time but are now too old for such protections to apply, or whether the works or other subject-matter "behind" the technological protection measures are actually in copyright.[17]

There are six statutory exceptions allowing circumvention. Three circumstances in which individuals can "go behind" a digital lock seem particularly relevant to schools:

1) in order to allow interoperability between programs where a person owns or has a licence for the program and circumvents its techno-logical protection measure[18]
2) in order to take measures connected with protecting personal data[19]
3) in order to make alternative format copies for people with perceptual disabilities.[20]

The other three exceptions seem less likely to arise in school situations: (1) for encryption research,[21] (2) for law enforcement,[22] and (3) for verifying a computer security system.[23]

It is particularly important to note that the exceptions to copyright infringement that allow users to take certain actions with respect to

---

16   *Ibid*, s 41.
17   Although the *Copyright Act, ibid*, now defines TPMs in terms of works, perform-ers' performances, and sound recordings (which are subject to copyright as defined in the Act), how can a user ever know whether the information behind the lock is actually *not* works, performers' performances, and sound recordings covered by the Act when there is no exception in the Act to allow anyone to circumvent a digital lock in order to check?
18   *Ibid*, s 41.12.
19   *Ibid*, s 41.14(1).
20   *Ibid*, s 41.16(1).
21   *Ibid*, s 41.13.
22   *Ibid*, s 41.11.
23   *Ibid*, s 41.15.

copyrighted works — users' rights such as fair dealing, for instance[24] — do *not* apply in the context of technological protection measures.

Canada's *Copyright Act* still sets out the law concerning all the rights that a copyright holder holds — and in what — and provides a number of exceptions to the rights of copyright holders that users of information can rely upon. However, as of 2012, if information has been protected by a digital lock, and none of the six specific exceptions provided in connection with digital locks (set out above) apply, an individual cannot go behind the digital lock. To do so will be circumvention of that lock and, under the *Copyright Act*, is illegal (regardless of that individual's right to use a particular copyrighted work, performers' performance, or sound recording that may lie behind the digital lock).

The enforcement of the new anti-circumvention provisions in the *Copyright Act* is not about infringement of copyright; it is, instead, solely about digital locks. The possible penalties for circumvention of the locks are

(a) on conviction on indictment, . . . a fine not exceeding $1,000,000 or . . . imprisonment for a term not exceeding five years or . . . both; or

(b) on summary conviction, . . . a fine not exceeding $25,000 or imprisonment for a term not exceeding six months or . . . both[25]

and, as well, all the remedies available for copyright infringement.[26]

2) The "Notice and Notice" Regime and Schools

A second change to the *Copyright Act*, passed in 2012 but originally delayed in implementation,[27] imposes a new role for Internet service providers in Canada's new "Notice and Notice" regime.[28] These provisions came into

---

24 This is discussed in much greater depth in Section I, below in this chapter.

25 Above note 1, s 42(3.1), for "libraries, archives and museums" and "educational institutions" as defined in the *Copyright Act*.

26 See *ibid*, s 41.1(2).

27 Although the legislation permits the government to create regulations, in the end, after consultation and submission by interested parties, the government decided to bring "into force these provisions after determining that the regime will function without regulations, as the elements of the legislation are sufficient": *Copyright Modernization Act: Order Fixing the Day that is Six Months after the Day on which this Order is published as the Day on which Certain Provisions of the Copyright Act Come into Force*, SI/2014-58, (2014) C Gaz II, 140, Explanatory Note.

28 Typically contrasted with the "Notice and Take-Down" regime of the United States.

force 1 January 2015[29] and apply to probably most schools and school-related institutions. The organizations affected are Internet service providers, defined in the Act as those that provide

> the means, in the course of providing services related to the operation of the internet, or another digital network, of telecommunication through which the electronic location that is the subject of the claim of infringement is connected to the Internet or another digital network.[30]

This definition could well include schools operating websites, where students and staff hold individual accounts through which they access the Internet, and thus, can upload content to the Internet. If a school or other education organization falls within this legal definition, it is responsible, if a copyright holder or its representative sends it a notice claiming infringement, for passing on that notice to the provider of the claimed infringing content[31] (in this example, the school's staff member or student). Failure to follow through on this statutory responsibility could be expensive for educators: a court can award between $5,000 and $10,000 in statutory damages against an Internet service provider.[32]

C. COPYRIGHT LAW AS IT APPLIES TO MATERIALS USED IN CANADIAN SCHOOLS

Consideration of copyright in Canadian schools must focus first on the fact that copyright exists in nearly every resource found or used in school. By operation of the Canadian *Copyright Act*, copyright interests arise in every original work,[33] sound recording,[34] performer's performance,[35] and broadcast[36] that is created in Canada. Various international treaties and agreements ensure that virtually every other jurisdiction on Earth has legislated that copyright shall arise in all original works, sound recordings, and performers' performances created in those places, as well.[37] It is helpful

29 *Copyright Act*, above note 1, ss 41.25, 41.26, and 41.27(3).
30 *Ibid*, s 41.25(1).
31 *Ibid*, s 41.26(2).
32 *Ibid*, s 41.26(3).
33 *Ibid*, s 5.
34 *Ibid*, s 18.
35 *Ibid*, s 15.
36 *Ibid*, s 21.
37 For further discussion, see Margaret Ann Wilkinson, "Filtering the Flow from the Fountains of Knowledge: Access and Copyright in Education and Libraries"

to those working in Canadian schools that Canada has entered into these same international agreements: these make it possible for Canada's *Copyright Act* to govern the actions of anyone using information in Canada, in any way, no matter where in the world that information may have come from.[38] The fact that a book is published in France is immaterial to the way Canadian teachers should treat it in terms of copyright; the fact that an Internet posting has been made in the United Kingdom is similarly immaterial to the way a principal in a Canadian school should deal with it in terms of respect for copyright.[39]

The term "work" as used in the *Copyright Act* includes not only printed materials such as books (including encyclopedias, dictionaries, and yearbooks[40]) and articles, but also newspapers and magazines,[41] paintings, drawings, maps, charts,[42] tables,[43] plans, photographs, engravings, sculptures, works of artistic craftsmanship,[44] works of choreography,[45] musical compositions (with or without words),[46] computer programs,[47] models of buildings and structures (and the buildings and structures themselves),[48] "plastic works relative to geography, topography, architecture or science,"[49] and publicly delivered addresses, speeches, and sermons.[50] In all cases, copyright covers both paper-based and digital works.

---

in Michael Geist, ed, *In the Public Interest: The Future of Canadian Copyright Law* (Toronto: Irwin Law, 2005) 331.

38 See above note 1, s 5.

39 It is very important for those working in the Canadian school system to recognize that only the *Copyright Act* of Canada applies to their actions and that, although there are certain similarities in the law of copyright as legislated by different nations, there are also differences. In particular, sources written from an American perspective, or the perspective of any other country's law, are not reliable when considering the law of copyright applicable to Canadian school situations.

40 Above note 1, s 2 (collective work (a)).

41 *Ibid* (collective work (b)).

42 *Ibid* (artistic work).

43 *Ibid* (literary work).

44 *Ibid* (artistic work).

45 *Ibid* (choreographic work).

46 *Ibid* (musical work).

47 *Ibid* (computer program).

48 *Ibid* (architectural work).

49 *Ibid* (every original literary, dramatic, musical or artistic work).

50 *Ibid* (lecture).

Copyright arises in the normal course in all works prepared or published or owned by Canadian governments; however, for works prepared or published by provincial, territorial, or federal government bodies, the period of copyright is reduced to fifty years from the year of publication.[51] Since 1997, the federal government has permitted free use of its primary legal materials.[52] Some resources used in some Canadian schools are "out of" copyright; however, these materials are rare since copyright exists in any work throughout the lifetime of its author[53] and for fifty years thereafter,[54] and in sound recordings, broadcasts, and performers' performances simply for fifty years.[55]

Other countries have longer periods of protection for copyright. For example, the United States has enacted a period of protection based upon the life of the author plus seventy-five years. Nonetheless, these longer periods in other countries are irrelevant for anyone in Canadian schools. As discussed above, only Canadian law is applicable to uses of materials in Canadian schools and, therefore, only the period of copyright provided under the Canadian *Copyright Act* is ever relevant.

---

51 *Ibid*, s 12. In this, Canadian law differs radically from American law, which generally holds that state and federal governments cannot hold copyright in works created by them. Note that copyright in Canadian municipal government works is not affected by s 12 and therefore lasts for the same period as for other works, generally for the life of the author plus fifty years.

52 See *Reproduction of Federal Law Order*, SI/97-5: no charge or permission is necessary provided that due diligence is exercised to ensure the accuracy of reproduction and that the reproduction is not represented as an official version. Between 2010 and 2013, the federal government posted a statement that permissions were not required for personal, non-commercial reproduction of any materials for which it held copyright, and, where permissions were required, they were to be handled through Publishing and Depository Services. This entire 2010–2013 policy has now been rescinded, and users are advised to contact individually whatever department or agency created the information in order to request the requisite permissions.

53 "Author," as used in the *Copyright Act*, above note 1, is understood to include such terms as artist, composer, photographer, and creator.

54 This is a short-hand statement of the period of protection: the fifty-year period actually begins after the end of the year of the author's death. See *Copyright Act*, above note 1, s 6.

55 After the end of the calendar year of the first fixation of a sound recording, the first broadcast, the first fixation of a performance in a recording or, if not fixed in a recording, the first performance; see *Copyright Act*, *ibid*, s 23).

Before 2012, Canadian law had, in various ways at various times, created shorter periods of copyright protection in photographs than existed for other works. But the *Copyright Modernization Act* changed the *Copyright Act* so that, currently, *all* works, including photographs, enjoy the same period of protection, that is, the life of the author or photographer plus fifty years.[56]

---

56 Prior to 1997, s 10 of the *Copyright Act*, above note 1, made special provisions for a short term of copyright in photographs: see, for example, *North American Free Trade Agreement Implementation Act*, SC 1993, c 44, s 60(1). See also *An Act to amend the Copyright Act*, SC 1997, c 24, s 7 and s 54(1) [1997 Act]. The 1997 Act did away with the special shorter provisions for photographs in the case of those taken by natural persons, leaving the period of protection for them to be the normal one for works, life plus fifty years. There seem to have been some erroneous interpretations made then that the new longer "life of the author plus fifty years" period of protection for photos taken by persons, rather than corporations, did not apply to all photographs taken by persons then alive or dead within the then past fifty years, but only to those photographs in which copyrights still existed under the old shorter periods of protection for all photographs legislated before 1997. The basis for this belief appears to have been s 54(1) in the 1997 Act, which declared that the new period for personal photographers applied to photographs in which copyright subsisted on the date on which that section came into effect. However, suggesting that a photograph by a personal photographer could not be "caught" by the 1997 amendment (and given life and fifty years) ignored the proper interpretation of "subsist," a word denoting that something simply exists (*Oxford English Dictionary Online*). In fact, Dennistoun JA held years ago, about "subsist," that "copyright . . . is a proprietary right which arises from authorship alone. It is sometimes called 'automatic copyright,' for without any act beyond the creation of a . . . work it is acquired by the author" in *Gribble v Manitoba Free Press Ltd*, [1931] 3 WWR 571 at para 37 (Man CA). The 2012 *Copyright Modernization Act*, above note 14, s 6, did away with the special provisions in s 10 entirely: the special short term of copyright for photographs where the "author" was a corporation has also now been removed. As in the case of the 1997 amendments, a transitional provision, s 59(1), provided in 2012 that the repeal of s 10 does not revive copyright in any photograph in which copyright had expired. However, due to the definition of "subsist," the verb used to describe the existence of all rights in all works as the *Copyright Act* now stands, if the author is living or has died within the last fifty years, the photograph is protected by s 6. Further support for this perspective is found in the parliamentary debates and the Summary and Preamble to the 2012 amendments, where it is clear that the government's intent was to ensure all photos enjoy "life + 50." So, the conclusion is that the period of protection for a photograph is no more complex than it is for any other work in Canada: all photographs are in copyright in Canada if the photographers are living or their photographers have died within the past fifty calendar years.

If a work or other subject-matter is out of copyright because copyright has expired, then the *Copyright Act* does not apply to it, and schools and those working or studying within them are free to use such materials as they see fit. However, it may be difficult to prove that these materials are out of copyright if they are packaged "behind" technological protection measures or have digital rights management (DRM) protection. Theoretically, the TPM and DRM provisions of the *Copyright Act* apply only in respect of material in copyright, but there is no provision for breaking a lock to ascertain if the material being protected is, in fact, out of copyright.

D. WHAT IS COPYRIGHT AND WHO HOLDS IT?

Copyright is not a "thing": it is a series of rights which the *Copyright Act* creates. There is a very short set of rights given to a performer to control certain further uses of a performance;[57] to a maker of a sound recording to control certain further uses of the sound recording;[58] and to a broadcaster in connection with further uses of a broadcast.[59]

The *Copyright Act* creates a much larger set of rights in the owner of copyright in a work than it creates in connection with performances, sound recordings, or broadcasts. The rights that arise upon creation of an original work are all originally given by the *Copyright Act* to the "author" of the work, unless the author creates the work as part of her or his employment.[60] Teachers and others employed by schools or boards of education in Canada do not own copyright in the works created by them during employment (unless their employment contracts explicitly say otherwise): their employers own copyright.[61] On the other hand, unless

---

See Margaret Ann Wilkinson & Tierney GB Deluzio, "The Term of Copyright Protection in Photographs" (2015) 31 *Canadian Intellectual Property Review* 95.

57 See again *Copyright Act*, above note 1, s 15.

58 *Ibid*, s 18.

59 *Ibid*, s 21.

60 *Ibid*, ss 13(1) and (3). There is a difference here between Canadian and American copyright law: under American law, a larger group of creators is excluded from original copyright ownership because in the United States, all "works made for hire" are owned by those hiring, whereas in Canada, unless the hiring will make an individual an employee under the employment law of Canada's various provinces and territories, the individual will retain original copyright ownership.

61 The situation is different in the case of university professors in Canada. The Canadian courts in copyright cases have considered professors, rather than their universities, to initially own copyright in the works they have created. See,

the rights are specifically contracted away, teachers and other employees do own the rights to performances and sound recordings made by them.[62]

One interesting users' right is now embedded in the *Copyright Act*:

   (1)   It is not an infringement of copyright . . .

   (f)   for an individual to use for private or non-commercial purposes, or permit the use for those purposes, a photograph or portrait that was commissioned by the individual for personal purposes and made for valuable consideration, unless the individual and the owner of the copyright in the photograph or portrait have agreed otherwise.[63]

Unfortunately, it does not apply to institutional or corporate users and does not apply to anything other than personal uses, so it would not apply to the use of photographs commissioned by the school or another educational entity. If the school or educational entity wants to control use of photographs it commissions, such control must be negotiated into the contract for the taking of the photos.

It is also important to recognize that students are not legally part of the organizations in which they are educated; they are customers or clients of their schools. Therefore, each student will own copyright in the original works created during her or his education: each drawing, model, writing assignment, computer program, photograph, and so on.[64] No school, no teacher, no other educator, or anyone other than the student, has any right to use a student's original work in any way that is protected by copyright without the permission of that student.[65]

One expression of the set of rights that comprise the copyright in a work is "the right to . . . reproduce the work or any substantial part thereof . . . to perform the work or any substantial part thereof in public or, if the work

---

for example, *Dolmage v Erskine*, [2003] OJ No 161 (SCJ). As is discussed further in Section G(3), below in this chapter, the "open access" movement has been created through the philanthropy of copyright holders; no employee of a school can contribute works to an open access website or other project, since no employee owns copyright in her or his works created through that employment.

62   See, in this connection, *Copyright Act*, above note 1, s 16.

63   *Ibid*, s 32.2(1); the commissioned photographs provision was newly enacted in 2012.

64   See, for example, *Boudreau v Lin* (1997), 150 DLR (4th) 324 (Ont Ct J Gen Div), involving a university student and his professor (and, ultimately, their university).

65   Because of students' ages, permissions may have to be sought from adults responsible for them.

is unpublished, to publish the work or any substantial part thereof . . . ."[66] The term "substantial part" is not further defined in the *Copyright Act*, but Canadian courts have repeatedly indicated that the amount meant by this concept cannot be determined purely by counting pages or words: the determination must include qualitative factors.[67] The rights include controlling the posting of works to the Internet,[68] the translating of works,[69] converting dramatic works into non-dramatic works[70] and vice versa,[71] recording or filming works,[72] and publicly exhibiting an artistic work that has been created since 7 June 1988 (except for purposes of selling or renting).[73] Each one of these individual rights that are part of the copyright in a work can be sold separately or given away freely by the original owner of copyright in a given work and can again be freely re-sold or gifted by the subsequent owner or owners (quite apart from any other copyright rights that arose in that same work).[74] Indeed, the owner of the reproduction right in a Canadian book, for example, can sell part of that right — for example, the English language rights in Canada — to one entity and another part — for example, the French language rights in Canada — to another; or the French language translation rights to a Canadian children's story originally written in English to one publisher in France and another in Haiti; or the film rights to a book to one filmmaker targeting the children's market and a different one focused on the adult market.[75]

---

66 *Copyright Act*, above note 1, s 3. In s 2.2(1), "publication" is defined to include "(a)(i) making copies of a work available to the public . . . but does not include (c) the performance in public, or the communication to the public by telecommunication, of a . . . work or a sound recording, or (d) the exhibit in public of an artistic work."

67 See, for example, *Cie générale des établissements Michelin-Michelin & Cie v CAW Canada* (1996), [1997] 2 FC 306 at 343 (TD).

68 *Copyright Act*, above note 1, s 3(1)(f): "to communicate the work to the public by telecommunication."

69 *Ibid*, s 3(1)(a).

70 *Ibid*, s 3(1)(b).

71 *Ibid*, s 3(1)(c).

72 *Ibid*, ss 3(1)(d) & 3(1)(e); and if someone in a school were to film a performance of a work by students (with permission of the owner of the performance rights in that work), for example, there would be new performance rights created in and held by the student performers. See also s 15, discussed above.

73 *Ibid*, s 3(1)(g).

74 *Ibid*, s 13(4).

75 *Ibid*.

It is important to remember that where the ownership lies at any given time in respect of any work or any aspect of the copyright associated with a given work is a completely separate question from the question "how long does copyright last?" The period of copyright in a work is always determined with reference to the lifetime of the individual who created the work (the author), whether or not that person ever had any ownership interest in the copyright. Although the school board may own copyright in all the works created by its teachers, the period that copyright will last in a work created by a given teacher within that board will be the lifetime of that teacher plus fifty years. If boards, for example, want to prolong the periods of the copyright monopolies they hold in works created by their teachers, they should do all that they can to contribute to long lifetimes for their teachers!

E. THE MORAL RIGHTS OF CREATORS

Even though school employers, absent contracts to the contrary, own copyright in their employees' works, they are not completely free to deal in any way with works created by their employees. The individual employees who created the works have certain rights under the *Copyright Act* which are separate from the copyright rights and which cannot be sold or transferred by the authors of works: these are termed "moral rights."[76] Indeed, all authors hold moral rights in works in Canada, and, as well, since 2012, performers hold moral rights in their performances made since 7 November 2012.[77]

The creator of a work or performer of a performance has the right, where reasonable in the circumstances, to have her or his name associated with the work, or to insist upon a pseudonym or anonymity.[78] The creator also has the right to insist that a work is not distorted, mutilated, or otherwise modified to the prejudice of her or his honour or reputation.[79] Note, however, that this right does not give the creator any right to insist

---

76 It should be noted that the law in Canada differs markedly in this respect from the law in the United States, where moral rights protection has been legislated to apply in only certain very specific and relatively rare circumstances.

77 *Copyright Act*, above note 1, ss 17.1 & 17.2. The majority of the *Copyright Modernization Act*, above note 14, came into effect on that day.

78 *Copyright Act*, above note 1, s 14.1(1). This is often referred to as the "paternity right."

79 *Ibid*, s 28.2(1)(a). This right is often referred to as the "right to integrity." If the work is a painting, sculpture, or engraving, distorting, mutilating, or modifying

that the work not be destroyed. Finally, there is a uniquely clear protection given to allow the creator to insist that the work not — to the prejudice of the creator's honour or reputation — be "used in association with a product, service, cause or institution."[80]

In Canada, these rights last as long as the copyrights — or, as they are known in distinction to the moral rights, the "economic rights" — last: for the life of the author plus fifty years in the case of works[81] and simply fifty years for a performance.[82] After the death of the author or performer, the moral rights can be exercised by the heirs of the author or performer as established by will or under provincial or territorial intestacy legislation where there is no will.[83] However, although these rights cannot be sold or transferred in the same ways as the economic rights can be dealt with,[84] they can be waived, in whole or in part, by the author or heirs.[85] If a waiver is made to an owner or licensee of the economic rights, anyone authorized by that owner or licensee can assume that the moral rights have been waived unless the original waiver expressly limited its effect with respect to subsequent economic rights owners or assignees.[86]

It may be helpful to bear in mind that students will have both economic rights and moral rights in school performances. By contrast, while teachers or other employees will always hold the moral rights in such performances, they will hold the economic copyright in such performances only if they have specifically reserved the economic right as part of the contract of employment.[87]

---

it is alone enough to be an infringement of the right to integrity: the artist need not separately establish that their honour or reputation was prejudiced (s 28.2).

80 *Ibid*, s 28.2(1)(b). This right has been called the "right of association."

81 *Ibid*, s 14.2.

82 *Ibid*, ss 17.2 and 23.

83 See, further, *ibid*, ss 14.2(2) & 14.2(3) (author's rights) and ss 17(2) & 17(3) (performer's rights).

84 See, especially, *ibid*, s 14.1(3).

85 *Ibid*, s 14.1(2).

86 *Ibid*, s 14.1(4)

87 As the *Copyright Act* specifically permits an individual to do under s 16.

F. THE CHALLENGE OF DETERMINING WHO OWNS COPYRIGHT

1) A National Register

From the perspective of those seeking to make uses of works and other subject-matter in copyright, it is unfortunate that, while there is a register of copyrights in Canada (the Canadian Copyrights Database),[88] it is not definitive[89] and cannot necessarily be relied upon to indicate where the rights to make a particular use of a work or other subject-matter lie. It is becoming increasingly useful to search the register in Canada because successive revisions to the *Copyright Act* have added incentives to make it advantageous for copyright holders to register their interests.[90] The register, however, cannot reveal where the moral rights interests lie.

2) Contracts

In the absence of an entry on the register, someone wishing to make use of a work is not guaranteed a publicly available way to search out the appropriate economic rights holder. As discussed above, the economic rights in copyright can be transferred, in whole or in part, at any time, by contract — and contracts are most often kept entirely confidential between the parties. Moreover, it is possible for a rights holder to give another either an exclusive licence, making the person receiving the licence the only person in Canada entitled to deal further with that right, or a non-exclusive licence, making that second person only one of the persons in Canada entitled to deal further with that right. While this can be confusing to an individual searching out permission to make a given use of a work, it can also be helpful because, in the second situation, of non-exclusive licences, if the first non-exclusive licensee does not give the person seeking permission

---

88   Accessed from the Canadian Intellectual Property Office home page, under "Copyright" and then "Search." See www.cipo.ic.gc.ca/eic/site/cipointernet-internetopic.nsf/eng/Home.

89   Because, as discussed above, copyright arises upon creation of the work or other subject-matter and does not require registration to exist. Logically, then, the register cannot be expected to provide a record of all copyright interests.

90   See *Copyright Act*, above note 1, s 39 (2), which, in cases where the copyright is registered, removes the limitation of remedies to an injunction and not damages when the defendant is not aware of the copyright or had no reasonable grounds to suspect copyright subsisted.

the right to the use being sought, a second non-exclusive licensee might — and any permission from a non-exclusive licensee will make the use permissible and non-infringing.

When the showing of films outside commercial movie houses became commercially viable, schools began to make widespread use of such material, and distribution companies catering to schools in Canada came into being. Typically, any given film would be made available to schools in Canada exclusively through one distribution company, and schools and boards entered into contracts to allow the films to be shown to student audiences. Locating a copyright holder and understanding what specific interests that copyright holder controls is often not a straightforward matter: frequently, it is sensible to ask the copyright holder, through whom you are seeking to make a use, to provide a warranty that they can indeed give the permission sought.

G. INTERMEDIARIES BETWEEN COPYRIGHT OWNERS AND USERS

Publishers, distributors, and collectives are all organizations that act as intermediaries between copyright owners and those who wish to make various uses of works and other copyright subject-matter.[91] These intermediaries can deal with the copyright interests in a work, sound recording, performance, or broadcast only to the extent they have acquired a right to do so from the original copyright holders.

1) Publishers and Distributors

Because of the expenses involved with publishing in pre-digital times, publishers used to demand and receive from authors a complete transfer of all copyright interests in a work in exchange for publishing the work. Therefore, it was often the case that those seeking to make any subsequent use of a work needed only to ask the work's publisher, for better (if the publisher permitted the requested use, for free or for an affordable fee), or for worse (if the publisher refused the requested use or priced the use out of reach of the requester). In present times, however, it is becoming rare for an author to transfer the entirety of the copyright in a work to a publisher.

---

91 The *Copyright Act, ibid*, refers to performers' performances, sound recordings, and broadcasts as "other subject-matter."

For this reason, it has become necessary to ask whether a publisher holds the right to give permission for particular uses of published works.

In certain contexts, such as audiovisual materials, access to materials in order to make certain uses of them has come, over time, to lie in the hands of a number of distribution companies. The National Film Board, for example, distributes its own productions.[92]

2) Collective Societies

Prior to 1988, Canadian copyright law recognized the right of certain groups of rights holders to join together and offer certain uses of certain types of works and other subject-matter to the public at set rates. These rates were monitored by a board established under the *Copyright Act*. However, most holders of economic rights in copyright were unable to function in this way for fear of violating Canada's *Competition Act*,[93] which prohibits price-fixing across industries. Since 1988, however, the *Copyright Act* has virtually exempted collective societies from the purview of the *Competition Act* and has defined a "collective society" as

> [a] society, association or corporation that carries on the business of collective administration of copyright . . . for the benefit of those who, by assignment, grant or license, appointment of it as their agent or otherwise, authorize it to act on their behalf in relation to that collective administration, and
>
> (a) operates a licensing scheme, applicable in relation to a repertoire of works . . . of more than one author . . . pursuant to which the [collective] sets out classes of uses that it agrees to authorize under this Act, and the royalties and terms and conditions on which it agrees [to do so], or
>
> (b) carries on the business of collecting and distributing royalties . . . payable pursuant to this Act.[94]

---

92 "Any form of reproduction, in whole or in part, by any method, known or not yet known, is strictly prohibited without prior written authorization from the NFB." See National Film Board, "Intellectual Property Rights," online: help.nfb.ca/important-notices/#campus-limitations.

93 It may be noted that the commissioner of competition appointed under the *Competition Act*, RSC 1985, c C-34, retains some residual authority under the *Copyright Act* over activities of the Copyright Board: see *Copyright Act*, above note 1, ss 70.5 & 70.6.

94 *Ibid*, s 2 (collective society).

This, in turn, has led to an entirely new set of entities with whom schools and school boards (or their provincial governments) have come to do business in terms of obtaining permission for uses to be made of copyright materials in schools. The Canadian collectives have been formed mostly by the owners of four rights: (1) rights over production and reproduction, (2) rights over performance of the work in public, (3) rights over converting an artistic work into a dramatic one by performance, and (4) rights over communicating works by telecommunication.[95]

Access Copyright (originally known as Cancopy) began, immediately after 1988, to negotiate on behalf of English language authors and owners of copyright interests in the reproduction of print works. It obtained its first blanket schools licence in 1991 with the Ontario Ministry of Education for which it received $2 million.[96] Copibec (originally UNEQ) negotiated on behalf of French language authors.[97] By private arrangement between the two collectives, Access Copyright has come to administer all the rights for works in both languages in the territories and every province except Québec, while Copibec has come to administer in Québec all the rights for works in both languages. Eventually, by the end of the twentieth century, all publicly funded schools in Canada and many privately funded schools were covered by blanket licences (for the uses covered by these two collectives) negotiated between their governing bodies and one of these two collectives.[98]

95 See Margaret Ann Wilkinson, "Copyright, Collectives, and Contracts: New Math for Educational Institutions and Libraries" in Michael Geist, ed, *From "Radical Extremism" to "Balanced Copyright": Canadian Copyright and the Digital Agenda* (Toronto: Irwin Law, 2010) 503 at 511 (Figure 1 and surrounding text) [Wilkinson, "Copyright, Collectives, and Contracts"].

96 Margaret Ann Wilkinson, "Conflicting Values in Coping with Copyright" (1992) 49 *Canadian Library Journal* 251.

97 Each collective represented the rights of those holding rights to reproduce works in Canada: those represented could include those who held rights to works created or published in Canada or created or published elsewhere. No rights holder who is eligible to be represented by these Canadian collectives is required to be so represented, a key difference between the Canadian system and the collective system in Europe. Moreover, Access Copyright, for example, does not hold exclusive rights to the works it represents, so Access Copyright is not the only source available for those seeking permissions to use such rights. Although both Access Copyright and Copibec are Canadian entities, much of the revenue collected by each flows out of Canada to rights holders located in other jurisdictions.

98 The Council of Ministers of Education, Canada (CMEC) stepped in for all the provinces (except Québec) and successfully negotiated a single "Pan-Canadian

It is very important to note, however, that these collectives do not have exclusive arrangements with their publisher and author members. While it is possible to get permissions from these collectives for uses of works, it is also possible to get permissions for uses directly from the publishers or authors who hold the rights; indeed, in some cases, permissions can be obtained from other organizations to whom the authors or publishers have given the right to deal with reproduction rights in Canada. For instance, in a good many cases, the Copyright Clearance Center in the United States is also now able to give these Canadian use permissions.

The *Copyright Act* permits most collective societies with which Canadian schools do business either to enter into agreements with users or file proposed tariffs with the Copyright Board.[99] In 2004, Access Copyright filed a "game-changing" tariff with the board, affecting all public schools except those in Québec and intended to govern the period 2005–2009.[100] Access Copyright then similarly sought tariffs from the Copyright Board for uses made by all provincial and territorial governments; a tariff was issued 23 May 2015.[101] It was followed by tariffs to govern uses by post-secondary institutions (the latest in this series is meant to govern uses for the per-

---

Schools Copyright" licence agreement with Access Copyright for 1999–2004. For details about the CMEC and its activities in copyright, see John Tooth, "Copyright for Schools and School Libraries" (2014) 60 *Feliciter* 7 at 7 and n 1. Access Copyright and Copibec had privately negotiated between themselves that Copibec would represent reproduction rights in both the English and French repertoires within Québec while Access Copyright would represent the English and French repertoires throughout the rest of the provinces and territories.

99 *Copyright Act*, above note 1, s 70.12. There are roughly thirty-five collective societies, representing different rights that copyright holders hold under the *Copyright Act*. See Copyright Board of Canada, "Copyright Collective Societies," online: www.cb-cda.gc.ca/societies-societes/index-e.html. Some of them must apply to the board for tariffs: see s 67.1 respecting collective societies for the performance of music and sound recordings (e.g., SOCAN). Unlike Access Copyright and Copibec, they do not have the alternative of licensing directly with users. There are also many rights under the *Copyright Act* in respect of which the holders have not formed collectives.

100 "Statement of Royalties to Be Collected by Access Copyright for the Reprographic Reproduction, in Canada, of Works in Its Repertoire," Supplement to C Gaz I, 1 (27 June 2009), online: www.cb-cda.gc.ca/tariffs-tarifs/certified-homologues/2009/20090626-b.pdf.

101 "Statement of Royalties to Be Collected by Access Copyright for the Reprographic Reproduction, in Canada, of Works in Its Repertoire Provincial and Territorial Governments (2005–2014) Supplement to C Gaz I, 1 (23 May 2015). A further application for a tariff for 2015–2018 has also been filed; see "Statement of Royalties to

iod 2011–2017).[102] In the summer of 2014, Copibec took the step of applying to the Copyright Board for a tariff with respect to Québec's universities,[103] but it has not yet taken this step with respect to Québec schools.

The CMEC and Access Copyright were engaged in litigation over the proposed 2005–2009 school tariff for a number of years, and the tariff was not actually imposed (retroactively) until 2009.[104] This tariff established a model for calculating copying in institutions that still forms the basis for the Copyright Board's approach to tariffs for the print industry.[105] This school tariff was then extended until 31 December 2012.[106] By this time, Access Copyright was deriving $18 million annually from this relationship with Canadian schools.[107]

For a period, before mid-February 2016, the CMEC and Access Copyright did not have any legal relationship (neither a licence nor a tariff). The CMEC had decided that schools in Canada do not make any uses for which such a relationship would be required.[108] However, on 20 February 2016, the Copyright Board issued a statement of royalties pertaining to elementary and

Be Collected by Access Copyright for the Reprographic Reproduction, in Canada, of Works in Its Repertoire" Supplement to C Gaz I, 1 (10 May 2014).

102 Access Copyright — Post-Secondary Educational Institutions Tariff (2011–2013 and 2014–2017), online: www.cb-cda.gc.ca/home-accueil-e.html#decisionsadvisement. Listed with "Decisions under Advisement" by the board as of 28 July 2017.

103 Copyright Board, "Statement of Proposed Royalties to Be Collected by Quebec Reproduction Rights Collective Administration Society (COPIBEC) for the Reproduction and Authorization to Reproduce, in Canada, for the Years 2015–2019, the Works in Its Repertoire by Universities and Persons Acting under Their Authority" Supplement to C Gaz I, 1 (28 June 2014).

104 See detail in above note 100. This tariff was eventually replaced, in a recalculation by the Copyright Board to reduce the amount of the tariff, as ordered by the Supreme Court in *Alberta (Education) v Canadian Copyright Licensing Agency (Access Copyright)*, 2012 SCC 37. The replacement tariff can be found in Copyright Board, "Statement of Royalties to Be Collected by Access Copyright for the Reprographic Reproduction, in Canada, of Works in Its Repertoire: Educational Institutions, 2005–2009" Supplement to C Gaz I, 3 (19 January 2013), online: www. cb-cda.gc.ca/tariffs-tarifs/certified-homologues/2013/tariff-19012013.pdf.

105 See, in particular, Figure 2 and surrounding explanatory text, in Wilkinson, "Copyright, Collectives and Contracts," above note 95 at 518.

106 Tooth, above note 98 at 7.

107 *Ibid*.

108 The CMEC has caused a booklet to be distributed to teachers and school library staff across Canada: Wanda Noel & Jordan Snell, *Copyright Matters! Some Key Questions & Answers for Schools*, 4th ed (Toronto: CMEC, 2016), online: http://cmec. ca/Publications/Lists/Publications/Attachments/291/Copyright_Matters.pdf.

secondary schools, 2010–2015.[109] Neither party involved in this tariff proceeding was happy with either the outcome or the reasons given for it.[110] For Access Copyright, its perception that the Board's value placed on the copyright interests held by its members was low would appear more widely consequential because Access Copyright has been seeking tariffs not only from schools but also from a range of other parties.[111] If the position of the CMEC, namely, that schools do not make uses covered by the tariff, were accurate, then this tariff decision was irrelevant to those working in education. One consequence of the CMEC position that it had severed all ties with Access Copyright and that schools and their boards are not affected by the issuance of the February 2016 tariff seems to be that Canadians schools, except those in Québec, would no longer need to comply with the *Copyright Act* requirement that a specifically regulated poster be placed beside each school printer and each photocopier.[112]

---

109 See "Statement of Royalties to Be Collected by Access Copyright for the Reprographic Reproduction, in Canada, of Works in Its Repertoire Elementary and Secondary Schools (2010–2015)" Supplement to C Gaz I, 1 (20 February 2016), online: www.cb-cda.gc.ca/tariffs-tarifs/certified-homologues/2016/TAR-2016-02-20.pdf.

110 See "Reproduction of Literary Works, 2010–2015: Reasons for Decision" (19 February 2016) (Vancise, Majeau, & Landry JJ), online: www.cb-cda.gc.ca/decisions/2016/DEC-K-122010-2015-19-02-06.pdf.

111 See above note 101.

112 The need for the prescribed sign is set out in the *Copyright Act*, above note 1, s 30.3(1)(c), but then negated by s 30.3(2) where there is no relationship with Access Copyright. The prescribed sign (*Exceptions for Educational Institutions, Libraries, Archives and Museums Regulations*, SOR/99-325, s 8) reads:

WARNING!
Works protected by copyright may be copied on this photocopier only if authorized by
(a) the *Copyright Act* for the purpose of fair dealing or under specific exceptions set out in that Act;
(b) the copyright owner; or
(c) a licence agreement between this institution and a collective society or a tariff, if any.

For details of authorized copying, please consult the licence agreement or the applicable tariff, if any, and other relevant information available from a staff member.

The Copyright Act provides for civil and criminal remedies for infringement of copyright.

As is discussed further below, however, it remains prudent for schools to post signs that mimic the sign posted by the Great Hall Library of the Law Society of Upper Canada and approved by the Supreme Court:[113]

> The copyright law of Canada governs the making of photocopies or other reproductions of copyright material. Certain copying may be an infringement of the copyright law. This library is not responsible for infringing copies made by the users of these machines.

As will be further discussed below in light of the recent decision of the Federal Court in *Access Copyright v York University*,[114] it is open to Access Copyright to sue school boards or other entities within school administrations, except in Québec, for photocopying without observing the conditions of the tariff. Moreover, one problem for the school community that arises from the moves by Access Copyright and Copibec into the tariff environment, rather than continuing the previous licensing environment, is that the Copyright Board has no power to include, in a tariff, indemnification of the school community for lawsuits that may arise from copyright holders not covered by the tariff.[115] Such an indemnification clause was an important part, from the point of view of educators, of the previous licences negotiated with Access Copyright and Copibec,[116] although, as of

---

113 See *CCH Canadian Ltd v Law Society of Upper Canada*, 2004 SCC 13 at para 39 [*CCH v LSUC*]. Note that this author believes that the appropriate sign to post is one mirroring, as closely as possible, that used by the Great Library and approved verbatim by the Supreme Court, rather than using the CMEC fair dealing guidelines which John Tooth advocates posting (Tooth, above note 98 at 8). This author advocates avoiding the posting of the CMEC guidelines precisely because, as Tooth himself points out, *ibid*, those fair dealing guidelines are "virtually identical to those of the ACCC [now Colleges and Institutes Canada] and the AUCC [now Universities Canada]." The guidelines promulgated by the AUCC lie at the heart of the lawsuit, described below (at text accompanying notes 123, 174, 175, 183, and 188), which was brought by Access Copyright against York University.

114 *Canadian Copyright Licensing Agency v York University*, 2017 FC 669 [*Access Copyright*].

115 Noted by Daniel Gervais, "A Uniquely Canadian Institution: The Copyright Board of Canada" in Ysolde Gendreau, ed, *An Emerging Intellectual Property Paradigm: Perspectives from Canada* (Cheltenham, UK: Edward Elgar, 2008) at 220.

116 For evidence provided by the ministers of Education to the Copyright Board, see "Reprographic Reproduction 2005–2009: Reasons for the Decision Certifying Access Copyright Tariff for Educational Institutions" (26 June 2009) at para 182 (Vancise, Bertrand-Venne, & Charron JJ), online: www.cb-cda.gc.ca/decisions/2009/Access-Copyright-2005-2009-Schools.pdf.

2009, such clauses had apparently never been invoked, at least in Access Copyright agreements.[117]

3) Open Source Sites

Understanding the ubiquity of copyright and the multiplicity of rights and interests that can be involved in terms of copyright in any given work, as discussed above, is critical to understanding the role and limitations inherent in the open access movement. Finding a work in an open access source does not mean that that work is free from copyright. If the person who has made the work available to the open access distributor legally held the copyright interests he or she purported to be dealing with when making the work so available,[118] finding a work in an open access repository means that certain permissions to use the work, under certain conditions, are being given to the user.[119] If the rightful owner of the copyright interest involved is not the person (individual or corporate body) who made work available to the open access repository, then the rightful owner can sue for the subsequent copyright-protected uses. For instance, if a teacher posted a presentation she or he made to an open access site when, by operation of the *Copyright Act*, the school board (as employer) is owner of all the copyright interests in the presentation (though the teacher owns the moral rights), a subsequent user of the open access site would not be protected, by the permissions to use indicated in the open access site, from a copyright infringement lawsuit. Or, if a professor assigned all her or his copyright interest in a chapter to the book's publisher, but also placed a copy of the chapter in an open access repository to be available to the public, the publisher could sue the open access repository for making the chapter available or sue any users who made subsequent uses that infringed the publisher's copyright, or both.

To be protected, at least to some extent, from this kind of problem, users of open source sites would want to have a warranty from the creators of the site that they had the appropriate copyright permissions to make the works available for the uses they purport to permit. A warranty

---

117   *Ibid* at para 181: information provided by Access Copyright to the Copyright Board.
118   See again the discussion on ownership of copyright above, at text accompanying notes 60 to 75.
119   See the succinct discussion of types of open access in Bobby Glushko & Rex Shoyama, "Unpacking Open Access: A Theoretical Framework for Understanding Open Access Initiatives" (Spring 2015) 61 *Feliciter* 8.

does not stop the rightful holder of the rights from suing the subsequent user, but, if the subsequent user is found to be infringing, it does permit the user at least some recovery from the person providing the warranty.

Open source is a way copyright holders who retain at least some copyright interests in their works or other subject-matter can philanthropically grant certain permissions (within their retained interests) for certain uses of those works to all users or users of certain classes.[120] It is always *very* important to check the terms of use of the site and then recognize and remember the limitations and conditions frequently, if not almost invariably, placed upon all subsequent uses of a work or other subject-matter obtained open source.

4) Software Licences

Software is protected by copyright.[121] Typically, in the licence terms that connect users with their use of various software packages or services, there are terms dealing with copyright. These terms will cover use of the software, certainly, but oftentimes also deal with the ongoing copyright interests in data entered into that software which constitute copyrighted works or other subject-matter.[122]

It is important to consider any terms that relate to copyright in works or other subject-matter entered into a system by the user before making the decision to purchase any particular package or service. If the user has transferred copyright to material entered into the system to the vendor of the system (generally through the terms of use provisions) and then tries to use that material independently, the user or the employer, or both may find themselves facing a lawsuit for infringement, contract violation, or both, or simply cut off from use of the software, along with loss of access to its content. Use of one popular software website for doing genealogical research,

---

120 See, further, Margaret Ann Wilkinson, "Access to Digital Information: Gift or Right?" in Mark Perry & Brian Fitzgerald, eds, *Knowledge Policy for the 21st Century: A Legal Perspective* (Toronto: Irwin Law, 2011) at 314–19 and 336–39, especially, online: www.irwinlaw.com/content_commons/knowledge_policy_for_the_21st_century.

121 The *Copyright Act*, above note 1, s 2, defines "computer programs" as "literary works." Software can also carry patent protection if it is part of a registered Canadian patent for an "invention" as defined under the *Patent Act*, RSC 1985, c P-4.

122 Data that does not amount to a work or other subject-matter as defined in the *Copyright Act*, above note 1, is not subject to copyright.

for example, appears to prohibit the user from downloading, into an independent database, information which she or he has personally entered into the website database.[123]

Figure 11.1 Participants in the Canadian education copyright environment

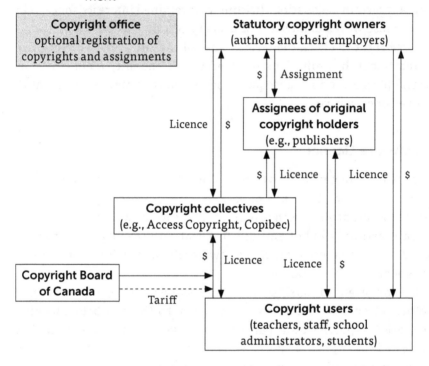

H. THE PENALTIES ASSOCIATED WITH INFRINGEMENT OF COPYRIGHT

If an employee of a school, a school board, or any educational institution uses material in a way that infringes another's copyright interest, the employee and the employer can be sued. This reality was brought home to those working in the university sector by the launching of two lawsuits: one by Access Copyright against York University and named individuals[124]

---

123   The term, which the author has seen, provides: "You may not create and/or publish your own database that features substantial parts of this Website."

124   *Access Copyright*, above note 114 (Statement of Claim), online: www.scribd.com/doc/134926954/AC-v-York-Statement-of-Claim-T-578-13-Doc1. Not only is York University named but also Firoza Elavia, Viviana Patroni, Bernard Hung-Kay Luk, Ann Porter, and Jonathan Nitzan, all of whom are professors at the university.

and a second by Copibec against Université Laval.[125] As of the time of writing, none of the allegations made in the second of these lawsuits, the one involving Copibec and Laval University, has been decided by a court of law. Being sued, of course, does not make Laval University (or another individual, institution, or corporation that is sued) liable — only the court deciding the lawsuit can do that. One the other hand, on 12 July 2017, Justice Phelan of the Federal Court released his decision, favouring Access Copyright, in *Access Copyright*.[126]

At issue in the lawsuit brought by Access Copyright against York University was whether York University was infringing copyrights represented

---

York University countered with a Statement of Defence and Counterclaim, online: www.scribd.com/doc/165933322/AC-v-York-U-Defence-and-Counterclaim, to which Access Copyright responded with a Reply and Defence to Counterclaim, online: www.scribd.com/doc/174602529/AC-Reply-and-Defence-to-Cc-Oct-4-2013. The CMEC sought leave to intervene in this action, but the motion was denied on 1 April 2014, although the CMEC was permitted to reapply at a later stage, should it so wish. On 30 July 2014, Prothonotary Aalto decided to grant York University's application for the case to be bifurcated (essentially, split into two parts). The decision is discussed further below.

125 This second lawsuit was announced as launched in the Québec Superior Court by Société québécoise de gestion collective des droits de reproduction, operating as Copibec, and framed as an application for a class action lawsuit to be brought against Laval "on behalf of authors and publishers from Quebec, the rest of Canada and other countries around the world." See "Copibec: $4 Million Class Action Lawsuit against Université Laval for Copyright Infringement" *Market Wired* (10 November 2014), online: www.marketwired.com/press-release/copibec-4-million-class-action-lawsuit-against-universite-laval-copyright-infringement-1966249.htm. The first step for Copibec in this action required the courts to certify the action as a class action. This was denied by the Québec Superior Court; see *Société québécoise de gestion collective des droits de reproduction (Copibec) c Université Laval*, 2016 QCCS 900. An appeal to the Court of Appeal from this decision was filed by Copibec, but Laval succeeded in having it rejected by the appeal court; see *Société québécoise de gestion collective des droits de reproduction (Copibec) c Université Laval*, 2016 QCCA 955. Further proceedings taken by Copibec in the matter were heard by the Québec Court of Appeal on 23 November 2016 and a decision allowing Copibec to continue the action as a class action against Laval was released by that court on 8 February 2017 (see *Société québécoise de gestion collective des droits de reproduction (Copibec) c Université Laval*, 2017 QCCA 199). Copibec's interpretation of the litigation can be seen, online: www.copibec.qc.ca/fr-ca/accueil/apropos/bulletin/bulletin_juin2016.aspx.

126 Above note 114. Under the *Federal Courts Rules*, York University, which lost, has until the end of September 2017 to appeal to the Federal Court of Appeal: see *Federal Courts Act*, RSC 1985, c F-7, s 27. See also note 144 below.

by Access Copyright. Determining this question involved consideration of two issues: first, what was the effect of the fact that the Copyright Board of Canada, at the request of Access Copyright, had, at the end of 2010, issued an "Interim Tariff" for Post-Secondary Educational Institutions intended to be effective during the period 2011–2013;[127] and second, did York University have viable "fair dealing" rights that shielded it from Access Copyright's claimed infringement? Justice Phelan decided against York University on both of these points. More will be said about each aspect of the judgment in a later discussion below.

Where schools are involved in uses of copyrighted material from other countries, the Canadian government has just increased the penalties for infringement,[128] but has not disturbed some existing rights to import works:

> . . . it is lawful for a person ["person" meaning an individual or an institution]
>
> (a) to import for their own use not more than two copies of a work or other subject-matter made with the consent of the owner of the copyright in the country where it was made; . . .
>
> (c) at any time before copies of a work or other subject-matter are made in Canada, to import any copies, except copies of a book [where only one copy may be imported, subsection (d)], made with the consent of the owner of the copyright in the country where the copies were made, that are required for the use of a library . . . or educational institution [both only as defined in the Act]; . . .
>
> (e) to import copies, made with the consent of the owner of copyright in the country where they were made, of any used books, except

---

127 See *Access Copyright Interim Post-Secondary Educational Institution Tariff, 2011–2013*, online: www.cb-cda.gc.ca/tariffs-tarifs/proposed-proposes/2010/interim_tariff.pdf [*Access Copyright Tariff*].

128 The *Combating Counterfeit Products Act*, SC 2014, c 32, also known as an *Act to Amend the Copyright Act and the Trade-marks Act*, passed into law in December 2014. At time of writing, amendments made to the criminal offence provisions of the *Copyright Act* were in force. The amendments also include expansion of the secondary infringement provisions (*Copyright Act*, above note 1, s 27(2)) in terms of exportation (*ibid*, s 27(2.11)), but there is also an explicit exception which indicates that this new provision does not apply to copies made pursuant to the limitations and exceptions under the Act or, where "made outside Canada, that would have been made under such a limitation or exception had it been made in Canada" (*ibid*, s 27(2.12)).

textbooks for use within an educational institution in a course of instruction.[129]

One specific defence to infringement that the *Copyright Act* makes available is that of incidental use:

> It is not an infringement . . . to incidentally and not deliberately
> (a) include a work or other subject-matter in another work or other subject-matter; or
> (b) do any act in relation to a work or other subject-matter that is incidentally and not deliberately included in another work or other subject-matter.[130]

Thus, presumably, a teacher would not infringe, in taking a photograph of a student speaking at an assembly, by unintentionally capturing, in the photo, a painting donated to the school that was hanging on a wall in the background.[131]

Where a contract is in place governing the conduct of the school or educational body with respect to certain material, violating the terms of the agreement can lead to lawsuits for breach of contract or copyright infringement or both. In addition to creating other problems, breaching the contract can put the school or educational body at risk of losing access to the material.

I. HOW TO MAKE NON-INFRINGING USES OF WORKS AND OTHER SUBJECT-MATTER IN COPYRIGHT

There are a number of different ways to avoid infringing the rights of copyright holders:[132]

---

129 *Copyright Act, ibid*, s 45(1).

130 *Ibid*, s 30.7.

131 There are no reports of court cases decided to date that involve this defence, which was added in 1997, although it was mentioned by the Supreme Court in *Canadian Broadcasting Corp v SODRAC 2003 Inc*, 2015 SCC 57 at para 54; however, the broadcast in that case was not considered incidental and so the defence was not relevant to the outcome of the case.

132 Although you may satisfy your moral rights obligations under the *Copyright Act*, above note 1, by acknowledging the source and author when you use a work or source, or a performer when you use a performer's performance, such acknowledgements are not a defence to infringement of the copyrights.

1) Where your use is covered by a tariff ordered by the Copyright Board in respect of an institution such as yours, you can make use of a work or other subject-matter represented by that collective in the ways permitted under the tariff.

2) Where there is in place a licence that covers the use you intend to make (a blanket licence from the appropriate collective, or a licence given through an open access source, or a specific licence you have sought and received from the copyright holder), you can make the use licensed.[133]

3) If you have written permission[134] from the relevant copyright holder, you can make the use.

4) Where the *Copyright Act* permits you to make the use you intend, you can make the use.

5) You can make use of a different source to meet the information need at hand: this source would be one for which you do have permission or can otherwise legally make the use.

Choosing any one of the options set out above, other than the fourth, may well involve cost: the fourth choice, on the other hand, when a statutorily permitted use applies in your situation in respect of the particular resource and the use of it you seek, is free. However, determining whether the fourth choice is legally available to you can be challenging.

It must be noted, in this connection, that access to the statutory fair dealing right is not available if you are using material you have acquired within the context of an ongoing licence. It also bears reminding that statutory fair dealing rights do not override the TPM and DRM provisions of the *Copyright Act*.

Licensed access, unlike access acquired through the statutory users' rights, can (1) include provisions that deal with technological protection measures and digital rights management; (2) mimic the statutory users' rights provisions; and (3) provide indemnification provisions to schools and school organizations. Typically, a licence involving digital materials

---

133 If you are unable to locate the relevant copyright holder, the Canadian *Copyright Act* contains a unique provision under which you may apply to the Copyright Board for a licence that will allow you to make the use you request (for whatever fee may be set by the board). See *Copyright Act*, above note 1, s 77.

134 Licences under the *Copyright Act*, *ibid*, are required to be in writing, as outlined in s 13(4), and you will wish to have evidence of permissions received, even if you received them merely by requesting them and not by entering into a contract for them. It is best to get both permissions and licences in writing.

provides DRM access to those materials, deals with permissions for certain uses of the copyrighted material, deals with patent issues that arise (often, for example, in terms of the technology of accessing the databases involved), and deals with TPM and DRM issues as well. Indeed, frequently, especially where Canadian vendors are involved, even though the moral rights cannot be transferred from authors, the vendor's licence offering will also provide that authors of the works and performances involved have waived their moral rights. Contracts override the *Copyright Act*.[135] The only way users' rights will apply to uses governed by a contract will be because the parties have agreed to have them apply and have written them into the language of the contract.

Language taken from the users' rights provisions of the Canadian *Copyright Act*, the American fair use provisions, or any other statute can be embedded in such contracts. How much such language and from where it is taken is all a matter of contract negotiation. Contracts also specify what jurisdiction's law applies to them; for example, a contract concluded in Canada between Canadian parties may still specify that the law of the state of Delaware will apply to it, and then the Canadian courts will apply the law of Delaware to interpretation of that contract. A vendor can refuse to agree to having Canadian law govern the contract, even if the two parties have agreed to embed wording in the contract that mirrors the Canadian fair dealing provisions. Even if Canadian law is to apply to the contract and the Canadian fair dealing provisions were drafted into it, if that drafting took place prior to 2012 when "education" was added as an element of the fair dealing category, the contract may not include education as an element of fair dealing. To the extent this represents the licences in place in your organization, these changes to the *Copyright Act*

---

135 This is a choice made by Parliament: it is possible to have statutes override contracts — many examples exist in provincial landlord-and-tenant statutes where contract provisions that contravene the tenant protections in the statute are rendered null and void. See, for example, *Residential Tenancies Act, 2006*, SO 2006, c 17, s 3(1): "This Act . . . applies with respect to rental units in residential complexes, despite any other Act and despite any agreement or waiver to the contrary." The same type of override is present in other statutes, such as the *Construction Lien Act*, RSO 1990, c C.30, s 4: "An agreement by any person who supplies services or materials to an improvement in this Act does not apply to the person or that the remedies provided by it are not available for the benefit of the person is void." See also s 5(1): "Every contract or subcontract related to an improvement is deemed to be amended in so far as is necessary to be in conformity with this Act." There is no such override to a contract in the *Copyright Act*, above note 1.

and subsequent court decisions about them will not directly affect your licensed collection. Getting users' rights fully into a contract becomes a matter to be negotiated and could cost an educational organization.

This situation involving the primacy of contracts over copyright leads to the following result: if the materials consist entirely of works represented by Access Copyright, but your access to these materials is licensed directly from vendors and not from Access Copyright,[136] you will not have to get a blanket licence from Access Copyright or to accede to a tariff ordered by the Copyright Board on application by Access Copyright and targeting institutions such as yours. What is more, you will not be able to rely upon the users' rights provisions of the *Copyright Act* except to the extent you have been able to negotiate them into your contracts with vendors. Your use of all materials will depend completely upon what has been negotiated into the contracts. You will, however, have to be careful about the moral rights interests in the materials you are using, unless the contract has given you assurance that all the relevant authors have waived their moral rights.

York University was one of a number of post-secondary institutions that chose not to comply with the terms of the Interim Tariff issued by the Copyright Board on 13 December 2010 — terms that would have required York University to pay to Access Copyright certain sums as required by the tariff.[137] In terms that have come into widespread use across the post-secondary community in Canada during this past decade, York styled itself as an "opt-out"[138] institution, indicating that it had chosen to "opt out" of the tariff processes Access Copyright chose to pursue before the Copyright Board of Canada.[139] In the case of York, amongst other practices, as Justice Phelan later found, opting out meant that "some [York University] instructors went to a non-[Access Copyright] licensed print shop, Keele

---

136 However, you must have evidence to show that your institution has licences and permissions from others: in the *Access Copyright* case, above note 114, Justice Phelan found that York had not satisfied its evidentiary burden in this regard because it did not produce clear complete evidence about those other relationships (see para 287).

137 *Access Copyright Tariff*, above note 127.

138 This label was recognized by Justice Phelan in *Access* Copyright, above note 114 at para 50.

139 York had sent Access Copyright a notice indicating that it was opting out as of 31 August 2011: see *Access Copyright, ibid* at para 171.

Copy Centre, for which no sanctions were imposed by the York administration"[140] to get coursepacks produced for their students.

Justice Phelan decided that York University had no option to "opt out" of the Interim Tariff ordered by the Copyright Board and was bound by its terms from 1 September 2011 until 31 December 2013.[141] He found that York University professors who copied material subject to the tariff "triggered obligations [for York] under the Interim Tariff"[142] because these actions "were so closely connected to the professors' authorized employment activities as to render York vicariously responsible."[143]

The decision currently has important implications for schools across Canada because it declares that there are only two options open to institutions whose uses of materials go farther than the users' rights exceptions to the rights of copyright holders extend: either to abide by a tariff ordered by the Copyright Board or, where a collective is able, and has chosen to offer a licence, to license permissions for uses.[144] There is no legally recognized status of "opt out" for institutions. This will be important to schools because, at the time of writing, there is a tariff in place for uses made that were represented by Access Copyright for all schools except those in Québec for the years 2010–2015[145] and a further such tariff proposed by Access

---

140 *Ibid* at para 48.

141 *Ibid* at paras 7–13.

142 *Ibid* at para 241.

143 *Ibid* at para 243.

144 York University has announced its intention to appeal this decision to the Federal Court of Appeal (see online: http://news.yorku.ca/2017/07/31/york-university-appeal-recent-copyright-decision. If York University is successful on appeal, then the decision of the Federal Court of Appeal in the matter will replace this judgment as authority in these areas. Unless and until an appeal is successfully made — or there is another Canadian case decided at this same level of court — this Federal Court judgment represents *the* Canadian law in this area. A *Copyright Act* review is required to begin in fall 2017 (see *Copyright Act*, above note 1, s 92) and, as a result of that review, it is possible that Parliament may decide to amend the *Copyright Act* such that the decision of Justice Phelan in this case does not apply to the law going forward from the point of amendment of the statute.

145 "Statement of Royalties to Be Collected by Access Copyright for the Reprographic Reproduction, in Canada, of Works in Its Repertoire — Elementary and Secondary Schools (2010–2015)," above note 109. This Tariff was remitted back to the Copyright Board on 27 January 2017 for reconsideration of the impact of coding errors on Access Copyright's repertoire: see notice, online: www.cb-cda.gc.ca/tariffs-tarifs/certified-homologues/reprographic-reprographie-e.html.

Copyright for the years 2016–2019 pending before the Copyright Board.[146] Currently in Canadian law, the only valid reason for not paying for uses according to a tariff or a licence is to have a users' right to make those uses. The most important "users' right" in the Canadian *Copyright Act* is that of fair dealing.[147]

1) Fair Dealing — An Expanded Definition

The Canadian *Copyright Act* has been aptly described as

> a balance between promoting the public interest in the encouragement and dissemination of works of the arts and intellect and obtaining a just reward for the creator (or, more accurately, to prevent someone other than the creator from appropriating whatever benefits may be generated).[148]

While the *Copyright Act* creates the frameworks of economic and moral rights described above, it also sets out a series of what has been described by the Supreme Court as "users' rights."[149] These rights are legislated exceptions to the rights of the holders of economic rights under the *Copyright Act*.[150] They have been described as key to promoting the public interest in copyright in Canada.[151] It must, however, be borne in mind that, in libraries, at least, up to 95 percent of current collections are held under licence and have not been purchased outright, and, therefore, in respect of that 95 percent, the users have no direct access to their statutory fair dealing rights: the fair dealing rights can be realized only to the extent they have been embedded in the licences involved.

As a practical matter, where anyone acting within the education sector is acting within the context of a users' right, no holder of a copyright

---

146 "Statement of Royalties to Be Collected by Access Copyright for the Reprographic Reproduction, in Canada, of Works in Its Repertoire — Educational Institutions (2016–2019)" (9 May 2015) Supplement to C Gaz I, 1, online: www.cb-cda.gc.ca/tariffs-tarifs/proposed-proposes/2015/reprography2016-2019.pdf.

147 *CCH v LSUC*, above note 113 at para 48.

148 Justice Binnie, speaking for majority of the Supreme Court, in *Théberge v Galerie d'Art du Petit Champlain Inc*, 2002 SCC 34 at para 30.

149 See McLachlin CJ writing for a unanimous Supreme Court in *CCH v Law Society*, above note 113 at para 48 (quoted below).

150 It must be noted again here that they do not apply to the moral rights.

151 Victoria Owen, "Who Safeguards the Public Interest in Copyright in Canada?" (2012) 59 *Journal of the Copyright Society of the USA* 803.

interest connected with that use can successfully sue that individual or institution.

Of the users' rights legislated into the *Copyright Act*, the "fair dealing" exception may well be the most important to the life of the school community in Canada today: in the revisions to the *Copyright Act* of 2012, the fair dealing provisions were significantly enlarged by the addition of the word "education."[152] No definition of "education" has been provided in the *Copyright Act*,[153] and the Supreme Court has not opined on its meaning.[154] Canadian law presumes the word "education" in the *Copyright Act* to have a meaning, but, unless and until the courts opine on its meaning,[155] there is no way of knowing for certain what that meaning is.

---

152 *Copyright Act*, above note 1, s 29. The *Copyright Modernization Act*, above note 14, also added "parody" and "satire" to this section (s 29). The section continues to include "research" and "private study." The *Copyright Act*, s 29.1 states that "criticism" and "review" constitute fair dealing, but adds certain criteria that must be met in order for these uses to constitute fair dealing. The *Copyright Act*, s 29.2 similarly creates conditions under which "news reporting" will be considered fair dealing.

153 See Wilkinson, "Copyright, Collectives, and Contracts," above note 95 at 526–29, on broad definitions of "education" in other areas of Canadian law. On the other hand, the rules of statutory interpretation suggest that the term "education" interpreted in the context of the *Copyright Act*, above note 1, should probably not "rob" the context of "educational institution" in the same Act, and the associated exceptions and limitations in the Act, of all meaning. This is particularly so when Parliament added "education" to fair dealing while at the same time making amendments to the rights of "educational institutions." This might leave "education" in the *Copyright Act* to be interpreted more narrowly than in other contexts in Canadian law.

154 The Supreme Court's decision in *Alberta (Education) v Canadian Copyright Licensing Agency (Access Copyright)*, 2012 SCC 37 [*Alberta*], released in the summer of 2012 when the *Copyright Modernization Act* which added "education" to fair dealing in the *Copyright Act* was pending, dealt only with the *Copyright Act* as it stood when the facts of the *Alberta* litigation arose.

155 The Copyright Board's decision, "Collective Administration in Relation to Rights under Sections 3, 15, 18, and 21, Statement of Royalties to be Collected by Access Copyright for the Reprographic Reproduction, in Canada, of Works in Its Repertoire [Provincial and Territorial Governments — 2005–2014]" (22 May 2015), online: www.cb-cda.gc.ca/decisions/2015/DEC-2015-03-22.pdf, opined (at para 252) that it did not have to decide what the scope of "education" in s 29 of the Act is. Similarly, Justice Phelan, in *Access Copyright*, above note 114, simply found that York's dealings with copyrighted material fell within the enumerated activities of "education, research, and private study" without proposing any definition of "education" in this context: see paras 15, 256, and 267.

Any lawyer or political scientist or educator will be simply making an educated guess because no opinion can anticipate the decision of the courts.

Even before the addition of "education" to fair dealing, the Chief Justice had written:

> [t]he fair dealing exception, like other exceptions in the *Copyright Act*, is a users' right. In order to maintain the proper balance between the rights of a copyright owner and users' interests, it must not be interpreted restrictively.[156]

However, establishing that use of a work or other subject-matter is for a purpose set out in the fair dealing sections of the *Copyright Act* is not *carte blanche* to assume that the use lies within users' rights.

The Supreme Court has established a set of criteria that must be considered, based on the facts of each particular case, in order to establish whether a particular use lies within users' rights. It must be noted, however, that it was not users of the Great Library who were being sued, but rather the Law Society of Upper Canada, which owned and operated the Great Library. The users' rights at issue were those that could have been claimed by the users of the Great Library; the Law Society was able to exercise the defence of fair dealing only because the Supreme Court recognized that "[a]lthough the retrieval and photocopying of legal works are not research in and of themselves, they are necessary conditions of research and thus part of the research process."[157] In other words, the institution of the Law Society, through its Great Library, could act as an agent for its users and, through its users' uses, claim fair dealing itself. On the other hand, when York University sought to establish that its uses were fair, Justice Phelan, in his recent decision finding against York, stated that "the question is the fairness of the goal of allowing students to access required course materials for education."[158] He found that "York created the Guidelines and operated under them primarily to obtain for free that which [it] had previously paid for."[159] This, he found, was not within fair dealing.

The set of factors set out by the Chief Justice is routinely reproduced simply as a list of the headings used by the Chief Justice to organize the judgment in which she described them. But such a brief listing oversimplifies the factors to be considered, and, in this brevity, can even be mislead-

---

156 *CCH v LSUC*, above note 113 at para 48.
157 *Ibid* at para 64.
158 *Access Copyright*, above note 114 at para 270.
159 *Ibid* at para 272.

ing about the ways in which the factors are to be considered in evaluating whether a use is fair. The Supreme Court decision that first explained the factors has a structure to its discussion of fair dealing which has often been overlooked by later commentators: first, the Chief Justice set out "The Law,"[160] and then she wrote the section "Application to the Facts."[161] Only reading the two sections together can give the complete guidance to users, including teachers, school staff, and education administrators, that was intended by the Supreme Court. The Chief Justice indicated, "courts should attempt to make an objective assessment of the user/defendant's real purpose or motive in using the copyrighted work."[162] For instance, in her judgment the Chief Justice held that a use can be fair dealing even though it occurs in a commercial context, but wrote, in the Law section of her judgment, that "some dealings, even if for an allowable purpose, may be more or less fair than others; research done for commercial purposes may not be as fair as research done for charitable purposes."[163]

Nonetheless, the lawsuit in that case had arisen out of the context of the commercial practice of law and, in the second part of her consideration of fair dealing, "Application to the Facts." The Chief Justice held that the Law Society of Upper Canada had satisfied this part of the analysis of fair dealing through its posting of an access policy.[164]

In a subsequent case involving commercial entities, the Supreme Court held that the fact the transaction involved is commercial from the sellers' point of view (potential customers previewing music) does not mean that it is to be characterized as commercial from the users' point of view. The users' point of view is the relevant perspective for the courts.[165]

Then, in a later case, the Supreme Court expanded upon this concept of looking at each situation objectively in light of its own unique factual situation:

> If, as in the "course pack" cases [from New Zealand and United Kingdom courts], the copier hides behind the shield of the users' allowable

---

160 *CCH v LSUC*, above note 113 at paras 48–60.

161 *Ibid* at paras 61–73.

162 *Ibid* at para 54.

163 *Ibid*.

164 *Ibid* at para 66. That policy was quoted in full by the Chief Justice in para 61 of the judgment and should serve as a model for all schools and school administrations in Canada.

165 *Society of Composers, Authors and Music Publishers of Canada v Bell Canada*, 2012 SCC 36 at para 30 [*SOCAN v Bell*].

purpose in order to engage in a separate purpose that tends to make the dealing unfair, that separate purpose will . . . be relevant to the fairness analysis.[166]

The first factor listed by the Chief Justice to be considered in assessing whether a dealing is fair is the *purpose of the dealing*, but we now know that the answer is more complicated than simply finding the purpose listed in section 29, 29.1, or 29.2 of the *Copyright Act*. We must make an objective assessment of the real purpose or motive of the user *and* we must assess whether, though the dealing is for an allowable purpose, it is more or less fair.[167] At the same time, we need to understand that use for a commercial purpose will tend to be unfair but, still, may not be. Then, having made that determination, we must still consider the facts before us in light of the other five factors.

The second factor is the *character of the dealing*. Here again, the Chief Justice did not describe the assessment in absolute terms:[168] a single copy may be fair (but not necessarily), and multiple copies made and widely distributed would tend to be unfair (but, again, not necessarily). A copy destroyed after use may have been made more fairly, but, again, not necessarily. The "custom or practice in a particular trade or industry" may be relevant: for instance, publishing "study notes" is unfair (not falling within the fair dealing category of criticism), but literary criticism textbooks are fair. In his recent judgment, Justice Phelan found "wide-ranging, large volume copying tends toward unfairness"[169] and that "the copying at issue [in *CCH v LSUC*] was . . . not the mass copying of portions of books, texts, articles, entire artistic works, or portions of collections, nor was it the multiple copyright of those materials into coursepacks or digital formats [that occurred at York]."[170]

The third factor is the *amount of the dealing*; however, the Supreme Court in *Society of Composers, Authors and Music Publishers of Canada v Bell Canada* states that this is *not* where facts determining that the taking

---

166 *Alberta*, above note 154 at para 22.

167 In his recent decision in *Access Copyright*, Justice Phelan found that York had established that its use met this first criteria, although it was not a strong factor in his decision. See *Access Copyright*, above note 114 at para 275: "the goal of the dealing is mixed and is a factor to be considered [but] is not a strong factor in the fairness analysis."

168 *CCH v LSUC*, above note 113 at para 55.

169 *Access Copyright*, above note 114 at paras 18 & 276–89.

170 *Ibid* at para 261.

has been small and no copy has been kept by the user should be assessed. These should be assessed as part of the "quantification of the aggregate dissemination" which is part of the second factor (the character of the dealing, just discussed).[171] In terms of the amount of the dealing, two perspectives should be considered: "[b]oth the amount of the dealing and importance of the work."[172] This third aspect of the evaluation of fair dealing seems to have been quite misunderstood by commentators, authors, and users since the judgment in *CCH v LSUC* was issued in 2004. For instance, there are no percentages involved in assessing whether a dealing is fair under the Canadian *Copyright Act*. Percentages are relevant in Australia, where the Australian *Copyright Act*, section 40(5), establishes that copying over 10 percent of editions, works, or adaptations not divided into chapters will not be fair dealing in Australia.[173] This point has been judicially established recently by Justice Phelan who found that York University had not established fairness, either quantitatively[174] or qualitatively:[175]

> the [York University] Guidelines set . . . fixed and arbitrary limits on copying (thresholds) without addressing what makes these limits fair . . . . There is no explanation why 10% or a single article or any other limitation [in the York Guidelines] is *fair.*[176]

The Supreme Court has clarified in *SOCAN v Bell* that this factor should be assessed based on the individual use, the proportion of the excerpt in relation to the whole work, and not on the amount of the dealing in the aggregate.[177] In *CCH v LSUC*, the Chief Justice specifically indicated that "[i]t may be possible to deal fairly with a whole work."[178] The Chief Justice mentioned examples[179] of probable fair dealing with a whole work, including use of a whole academic article for research or private study, and use of a whole judicial decision for research or private study. On the other hand,

---

171 *SOCAN v Bell*, above note 165 at para 42.
172 *CCH v LSUC*, above note 113 at para 56.
173 Australian *Copyright Act 1968* (No 63, 1968).
174 *Access Copyright*, above note 114 at paras 291–95.
175 *Ibid* at paras 296–317.
176 *Ibid* at paras 20–21 [emphasis in original]; see also paras 295 and 306. York was unsuccessful on this factor "almost completely both quantitatively and qualitatively. In the context of this case, this is a critical factor which establishes that there is nothing fair about the amount of the dealing" (para 318).
177 *SOCAN v Bell*, above note 165 at para 41.
178 *CCH v LSUC*, above note 113 at para 56.
179 *Ibid.*

use of a whole work of literature for criticism would probably not be fair dealing.[180] The question of the amount is inextricably connected with the fact that, in Canada, copyright subsists only in "the whole or any substantial part" of a work.[181] In 2013, the Supreme Court held that substantiality must be assessed using a qualitative and holistic approach (not a quantitative one), from the perspective of the "intended audience for the works at issue" and placing the trial judge in the position of "someone reasonably versed in the relevant art or technology."[182]

The fourth factor is whether there are *alternatives to the dealing*, meaning, whether there is a non-copyrighted equivalent that could be used. Is the dealing reasonably necessary to achieve the ultimate purpose?[183] In the 2012 *Alberta* decision, the Supreme Court was aware that teachers were copying to supplement textbooks already purchased for each student when it held that "buying books for each student is not a realistic alternative to teachers copying short excerpts to supplement student textbooks."[184] A court could arrive at an entirely different decision in terms of the applicability of fair dealing if schools do not purchase a textbook for each student in a given class and, instead, turn only to copying even short excerpts from textbooks — that is, a different decision even for only short excerpts from textbooks in a case where each student is not already in possession of a purchased textbook on that subject. In *Access Copyright*, Justice Phelan distinguished the situation at York from that in K-12 classrooms:

> It is one thing for a teacher to have the school librarian run off some copies of a book or article in order to supplement school texts, and it is quite another for York to produce coursepacks and materials for distribution through LMSs [learning management systems], which stand in place of course textbooks, through copying on a massive scale.[185]

---

180 *Ibid.* The Chief Justice, in her Application to the Facts section, wrote that this third factor, like the first two, was satisfied in the case through the Law Society's Great Library access policy (see para 68).

181 *Copyright Act*, above note 1, s 3.

182 *Robinson*, above note 6 at para 51. This decision was released after the *Copyright Modernization Act* had come into force and modified the *Copyright Act*; however, it arose from facts that occurred before those amendments to the *Copyright Act* and therefore the Court made its decision without reference to any of the amendments.

183 *CCH v LSUC*, above note 113 at para 57.

184 *Alberta*, above note 154 at para 32.

185 *Access Copyright*, above note 114 at para 324.

He found that York had failed to establish that there were no alternatives to its dealing, finding "the justification of cheaper access cannot be a determinative factor,"[186] although he did find, with respect to the whole question of alternatives, that "with the mix of factors and the weighing thereof, this factor favours York but not as strongly as it has argued."[187] He thought teaching without textbooks at the university level could be achieved fairly but that "York has not actively engaged in the consideration of alternatives [to the textbook] which exist or are in development"[188] since "[t]here are alternatives — these include using custom book services, purchasing individual chapters or articles from the publisher, or purchasing more of the necessary books and articles. There is just no reasonable *free* alternative to copying."[189]

In considering whether the dealing was reasonably necessary to achieve the ultimate purpose, the Supreme Court found in *CCH v LSUC* that, since the Great Library was situated in Toronto and the Law Society's members worked and lived in every part of Ontario, "patrons . . . cannot reasonably be expected to always conduct their research on-site."[190]

Factor five involves consideration of the *nature of the work*.[191] Evaluation of this factor, like the evaluation of the preceding four, involves a nuanced understanding of the facts surrounding a use.[192] On the one hand, "if a work has not been published, the dealing may be more fair in that its

---

186 *Ibid* at para 24. See also paras 319–31.

187 *Ibid* at para 331.

188 *Ibid* at para 329.

189 *Ibid* at para 330 [emphasis in the original].

190 *CCH v LSUC*, above note 113 at para 69. See also paras 60 and 70 for consideration of this factor. It may be noted that this is one of two factors in respect of which the Chief Justice found the Law Society's Great Library access policy irrelevant. (The other is the sixth, discussed below.)

191 This factor, in *Access Copyright*, above note 114 at para 388, was found to be non-determinative but nonetheless "tends toward the negative end of the fairness spectrum" in the case: see also paras 332–38.

192 It may be noted that, here again, as with respect to the first three factors, the Great Library's access policy was held by the Chief Justice to satisfy this factor of the test for fair dealing. See *CCH v LSUC*, above note 113 at para 71. The Great Library's policy limited itself to research, private study, criticism, review, or use in legal proceedings (see para 61 which sets out the full policy). The Chief Justice cited with approval the judgment of Linden JA, in the court below, where he said, "It is generally in the public interest that access to judicial decisions and other legal resources not be unjustifiably restrained" (quoted by the Chief Justice at para 71).

reproduction with acknowledgement could lead to wider public dissemination."[193] And, even if a work or other subject-matter has been made widely available, that "does not necessarily correlate to whether it is widely disseminated. Unless a potential customer can locate and identify a work he or she wants to buy, the work will not be disseminated."[194] On the other hand, if the unpublished work is confidential, the dealing may be unfair.[195]

The sixth and final factor is the *effect of the dealing on the work*: "if the reproduced work is likely to compete with the market for the original work, this may suggest the dealing is not fair."[196] In *CCH v LSUC*, the Chief Justice found that "no evidence was tendered to show that the market for the publishers' works had decreased as a result of these copies."[197] While the court recognized that the burden of proof for establishing the fair dealing defence lay with the user, the Law Society lacked access to evidence about publishers' markets and "it would have been in the publishers' interest to tender it at trial."[198] In the *Alberta* case, Access Copyright did adduce evidence that textbook sales had shrunk 30 percent over twenty years, but the court found there was no evidence directly linking this to teachers' photocopying. The evidence of loss of sales could be equally linked to other factors such as adoption of semester teaching, a decrease in registrations, longer lifespans of textbooks, increased use of the Internet and other electronic tools, and more resource-based learning.[199] On the other hand, in the recent decision in *Access Copyright*, Justice Phelan found that Access Copyright had met its burden to establish that York University's policy and practices did have an effect on the market for the copyright holders' works[200] (though he did recognize that this factor was not the most important factor to a court considering fair dealing[201]). He recognized that

> much of Access's evidence of impacts on the market was general in nature, [but held that] it establishes that the likelihood of impacts from

---

193 *CCH v LSUC, ibid* at para 58.

194 *SOCAN v Bell*, above note 165 at para 47.

195 *CCH v LSUC*, above note 113 at para 58.

196 *Ibid* at para 59.

197 *Ibid* at para 72. In respect of this factor, as in respect of the fourth factor, the Supreme Court did not find relevant evidence in the Great Library's access policy.

198 *Ibid.*

199 *Alberta*, above note 154 at para 33.

200 See *Access Copyright*, above note 114 at paras 26 and 339–55.

201 *Ibid* at para 340.

York's own Guidelines will be similar. This is sensible given the massive amounts of copying at issue, the history of the payments to Access prior to York opting out of the Interim Tariff, and the size of York as the second largest university in Ontario.[202]

2) Institutional Policies and Their Relationship with Fair Dealing

Given the weight accorded by the Supreme Court to the access policy of the Law Society of Upper Canada's Great Library in the reasons for judgment in the landmark case involving that library, it has been tempting to look for the development of policies as an integral part of accessing the users' rights provisions of the *Copyright Act*. Indeed, in recent years, Universities Canada (formerly the AUCC) developed and promulgated a model policy,[203] as then did both Colleges and Institutes Canada (formerly the ACCC)[204] and the CMEC.[205] One reason for tempering this enthusiasm to develop national, provincial, or sectoral approaches to policy building is that the Supreme Court stated clearly "[p]ersons or institutions relying on . . . fair dealing . . . need only prove . . . *their own* practices and policies were re-search-based [referring to section 29 as it then was, before the addition of "education"] and fair."[206] Copyright law is not negligence law: in negligence (a branch of tort law), evidence that an individual has met the standard of a competent professional, which means that the individual has not been negligent, can mean pointing to the standard expected of similar professionals. In that context, evidence of sectoral, regional, national, or even international standards and policies to which the individual adheres can be very helpful to a professional, though even in that setting, where a statute states a rule, evidence of customary practice will not exonerate someone who breaks that rule.[207] Courts have not permitted evidence of custom

---

202 *Ibid* at para 352.

203 Association of Universities and Colleges of Canada, "Fair Dealing Policy," online: www.scribd.com/doc/45806217/Fair-Dealing-Policy-With-Intro-December-22-2010.

204 Colleges and Institutes Canada, "Fair Dealing Policy," online: library.nic.bc.ca/research/PDFs/FAIR_DEALING_POLICY_FINAL.pdf.

205 Council of Ministers of Education, Canada, "Fair Dealings Guidelines," online: cmec.ca/docs/copyright/Fair_Dealing_Guidelines_EN.pdf.

206 *CCH v LSUC*, above note 113 at para 63 [emphasis added].

207 *Drewry v Towns* (1951), 2 WWR (NS) 217 (Man QB).

to establish a defence to allegations of copyright infringement.[208] The use of policy evidence in *CCH v LSUC* was to an entirely different purpose: the Great Library's policy evidence assisted the Law Society in establishing evidence of its institutional general practices, its good management practices, rather than having "to adduce evidence that every patron uses the material provided for in a fair dealing manner."[209] The Supreme Court found

> [t]he Access Policy places appropriate limits on the type of copying the Law Society will do. It states that not all requests will be honoured. If a request does not appear to be for [an allowable] purpose . . . the copy will not be made. If a question arises as to whether the stated purpose is legitimate, the Reference Librarian will review the matter. The Access Policy limits the amount of work that will be copied, and the Reference Librarian reviews requests that exceed what might typically be considered reasonable and has the right to refuse to fulfill a request.[210]

The Law Society of Upper Canada continues to post the same notice.[211] The word "photocopy" does not appear anywhere in the notice. The language is about copying and is completely format neutral. The verb "provides" is used in connection with copying and seems completely consistent with the digital electronic environment as well as with the analog fax environment in which its language was tested by the Supreme Court. The audience for the policy is the Great Library's users, not those who worked within the Great Library and Law Society. The AUCC Guidelines model (from which York University created its own Guidelines), for instance, appeared to address a different audience: the university itself (see, for instance, guideline #9 which begins "University staff shall use . . .").[212] In *Access Copyright*, Justice Phelan found "York's own Fair Dealing Guidelines are not fair in

208 *Gribble v Manitoba Free Press Ltd*, above note 56. Use as a defence to infringement would be an entirely different use of custom than was allowed for establishing copyright ownership in the Supreme Court decision in *Robertson v Thomson Corp*, 2006 SCC 43.
209 *CCH v LSUC*, above note 113 at para 63.
210 *Ibid* at para 73.
211 See The Law Society of Upper Canada, "Access to the Law Policy and Guidelines," online: www.lsuc.on.ca/For-Lawyers/Manage-Your-Practice/Research/Access-to-the-Law-Policy-and-Guidelines.
212 Above note 203.

either their terms of their application."[213] He noted, citing to the decision in *CCH v LSUC*,[214] that

[t]he fairness assessment looks at the text of the policies, the rationale for the policies, and the practical or real dealing by the users of the owners' works. Both the Guidelines themselves and the practices under the Guidelines must be fair.[215]

He found that the York Guidelines specifically differed from those of the Law Society in the following ways:

One important distinction is that the copying done at the [LSUC] Great Library was for others, not for the Library itself. In York's situation, the copying and the Guidelines served York's interests and the interests of its faculty and students. There is an objectivity in *CCH* which is absent in York's case.[216]

. . . [T]he manner in which [the Law Society's] Access Law Policy was implemented and practiced is markedly different from the York Guidelines. These differences included:
- Copying at a single location under the supervision and control of research librarians in the Great Library contrasted with no effective supervision, control, or other method of "gatekeeping" at York;
- A policy strictly applied and enforced by librarians [at the Law Society] versus virtually no enforcement of the Guidelines by anyone in authority at York;
- Single copies made versus multiple copies;
- A large amount of *ad hoc* or situational copying for users at the Great Library contrasted with the mass systematic and systemic copying at York; and,
- An absence of negative impacts on publishers in *CCH* as contrasted with the negative impacts on creators and publishers caused or at least significantly contributed to by York.[217]

213 *Access Copyright*, above note 114 at para 14.
214 *CCH v LSUC*, above note 113 at para 63.
215 *Access Copyright*, above note 114 at para 255.
216 *Ibid* at para 260.
217 *Ibid* at para 262.

3) "Educational Institutions"

In addition to the users' right of fair dealing, there is a separate set of users' rights legislated for "educational institutions" (as these are defined by the statute) and a further set legislated for "libraries, archives and museums." Libraries operating within educational institutions have access to *both* these special sets of users' rights, which, in certain cases, may lead schools or other parts of education administrations to consider locating certain activities within their libraries. However, whereas all schools and school administrations in Canada, and the teachers and administrators working within them, have access to the fair dealing users' rights, not all have access to the rights given to educational institutions. That is because the concept of an "educational institution" has been given a specific definition in the context of the *Copyright Act*: one that excludes many schools and school administrations in Canada. For purposes of discussing schools, the relevant parts of the *Copyright* Act define "educational institution"[218] as

(a)   a non-profit institution licensed or recognized by or under an Act of Parliament or the legislature of a province to provide pre-school, elementary, secondary, or post-secondary education, [and] . . .

(c)   a department or agency of any order of government, or any non-profit body, that controls or supervises education or training referred to in paragraph (a).

The key is that, to be educational institutions under the *Copyright Act*, preschools, elementary schools, and secondary schools must be owned by institutions that have been founded as non-profit. It is not a question of the profitability of the school or whether or not school fees are charged; it is a question of how the institution providing the education was founded to operate.[219]

---

218   Above note 1, s 2 (educational institution).

219   The Chestnut Woods School of Montessori Education, which ceased operation, but had operated in St Catharines, Ontario, is listed as having been owned by Tammy A Hoffman-Purdie and D Purdie and not by a corporation and therefore could not have been established as a non-profit organization. This may be contrasted with Counterpoint Academy Inc, which has also ceased operation, in this case in Ottawa, but is listed as having been owned by Laura Tilson-Non-Profit Organization. See #16 and #20, respectively, on Ontario Ministry of Education, "Private Elementary and Secondary Schools, Schools that have ceased operation, For school year 2013–2014," online: www.edu.gov.on.ca/eng/general/elemsec/privsch/closed.html.

Even for schools and school administrations lying within the statutory definition of "educational institution," it is very important to realize that the exceptions legislated for educational institutions do not limit the activities of those schools and educational bodies covered by that definition to only those limitations and exceptions provided for such institutions. This is clear because, in the context of libraries (which have a similar set of special exceptions for "libraries, archives and museums"), the Supreme Court declared that

> [A] library can always attempt to prove that its dealings with a copyrighted work are fair under s. 29 of the *Copyright Act*. It is only if a library were unable to make out the fair dealing exception under s. 29 that it would need to turn to s. 30.2 of the *Copyright Act* to prove that it qualified for the library exception.[220]

The users' rights given specifically to educational institutions as of 1997 begin at section 29.4 of the *Copyright Act* and continue through to section 30. In 2012, the exception for reproducing a work in order to display it for instruction was updated to reflect technology such as Smart Boards (section 29.4(1)); however, it remains limited by section 29.4(3), except in the case of manual reproduction, to cases where the work is not "commercially available."[221]

In 2012, the *Copyright Modernization Act* introduced a series of further new amendments to the *Copyright Act* for the benefit of educational institutions that were intended to create a framework for distance education (see section 30.01). These exceptions are hedged with limitations and conditions. For example, the ability to communicate a "Lesson" (defined in section 30.01(1)) by telecommunication is bounded by conditions (including, for example, provisions that the "public" to whom communication is to be made can consist only of students enrolled in the course and others acting under the authority of the school (section 30.01(3)) and that any fixation of the "lesson" has to be destroyed within thirty days of the end of the course (section 30.01(6)). The right to make a work available through the Internet available to students is similarly qualified (section 30.04).

---

220 *CCH v LSUC*, above note 113 at para 49.

221 "Commercially available" is defined in s 2 of the *Copyright Act*, above note 1. See Rob Tiessen, "The Definition of 'Commercially Available'" (2013) 59 *Feliciter* 14 at 14.

4) Copyright and Accommodating Persons with Disabilities in Schools

Canada's *Copyright Act* contains a newly updated users' rights section for persons with perceptual disabilities and those acting in their interest, from which all schools and school organizations (not just the defined "educational institutions") can benefit:

> 32 (1) It is not an infringement of copyright for a person with a perceptual disability, for a person acting at the request of such a person or for a non-profit organization acting for the benefit of such a person to
>
> (a) reproduce a literary, musical, artistic or dramatic work, other than a cinematographic work, in a format specially designed for persons with a perceptual disability;
>
> (a.1) fix a performer's performance of a literary, musical, artistic or dramatic work, other than a cinematographic work, in a format specially designed for persons with a perceptual disability;
>
> (a.2) reproduce a sound recording, or a fixation of a performer's performance referred to in paragraph (a.1), in a format specially designed for persons with a perceptual disability;
>
> (b) translate, adapt or reproduce in sign language a literary or dramatic work, other than a cinematographic work, in a format specially designed for persons with a perceptual disability;
>
> (b.1) provide a person with a perceptual disability with, or provide such a person with access to, a work or other subject-matter to which any of paragraphs (a) to (b) applies, in a format specially designed for persons with a perceptual disability, and do any other act that is necessary for that purpose; or
>
> (c) perform in public a literary or dramatic work, other than a cinematographic work, in sign language, either live or in a format specially designed for persons with a perceptual disability.
>
> *Limitation*
>
> (2) Subsection (1) does not apply if the work or other subject-matter is *commercially available*, within the meaning of paragraph (a) of the definition commercially available in section 2, in a format specially designed to meet the needs of the person with a perceptual disability referred to in that subsection.[222]

The concept of "perceptual disability" is defined in section 2 of the Act as

---

a disability that prevents or inhibits a person from reading or hearing a literary, musical, dramatic, or artistic work in its original format, and includes such a disability resulting from

(a) severe or total impairment of sight or hearing or the inability to focus or move one's eyes,

(b) the inability to hold or manipulate a book, or

(c) an impairment relating to comprehension.

The *Copyright Act* now also contains a section (section 32.01) setting out a detailed users' right whereby a non-profit organization can make and send a work (but not a cinematographic work, such as a film, or a large print book) outside Canada to another non-profit organization for use by people with print disabilities. The work's author must be a Canadian citizen or permanent resident or a resident of the other country; further, the work cannot be sent if it is known or reasonably ought to be known that such a work is already available commercially in that other country. Whereas the older section, quoted above, deals with "perceptual disability," this new section deals with "print disability." In section 32.01(8), it defines "print disability" in exactly the way that "perceptual disability" is defined — except that "or hearing" is omitted.

These users' rights in the *Copyright Act* are coming under increasing scrutiny as provincial governments become active in creating legislation about accessibility for people with disabilities: Ontario has had such legislation for a number of years now,[223] Manitoba has had legislation since 5 December 2013,[224] and Nova Scotia since 27 April 2017.[225]

Ontario's enactment is designed to achieve accessibility for persons with a disability, which is defined in section 2 as

(a) any degree of physical disability, infirmity, malformation or disfigurement that is caused by bodily injury, birth defect or illness and, without limiting the generality of the foregoing, includes diabetes mellitus, epilepsy, a brain injury, any degree of paralysis, amputation, lack of physical coordination, blindness or visual impediment, deafness or hearing impediment, muteness or speech impediment, or physical reliance on a guide dog or other animal or on a wheelchair or other remedial appliance or device,

(b) a condition of mental impairment or a development disability,

---

223 AODA, above note 10.
224 *The Accessibility for Manitobans Act*, CCSM c A1.7.
225 *Accessibility Act*, SNS 2017, c 2.

(c) a learning disability, or a dysfunction in one or more of the processes involved in understanding or using the symbols of spoken language,

(d) a mental disorder, or

(e) an injury or disability for which benefits were claimed or received under the insurance plan established under the *Workplace Safety and Insurance Act, 1997*; ("handicap").

It can be seen from the example of the definition of "disability" in the Ontario statute that the scope of this provincial legislation is much wider than the users' rights provided under the federal *Copyright Act* (described above).

Internationally, a copyright process to give users' rights to a wider range of persons with disabilities is underway. The issue of extending users' rights to more than persons who are blind, visually impaired, or print disabled is being debated at the United Nations level. The World Intellectual Property Organization, or WIPO, has as an agenda item before its Standing Committee on Copyright and Related Rights: "Educational and Research Institutions and Persons with Other Disabilities."[226] However, no consensus among nations on this point has yet emerged.[227]

The same standing committee, several years ago, did give birth to the first international copyright treaty about users' rights: the *Marrakesh Treaty to Facilitate Access to Published Works for Persons who are Blind, Visually Impaired, or otherwise Print Disabled*.[228] This treaty required twenty countries to ratify or accede to it in order to come into effect. Canada did not initially sign the treaty, but became the twentieth to accede, thus bringing it into effect. Although Canadians are not directly governed by inter-

---

226 AODA, above note 10, s 2. See, generally, World Intellectual Property Organization, "Standing Committee on Copyright and Related Rights (SCCR)," online: www.wipo.int/meetings/en/topic.jsp?group_id=62.

227 At the most recent session of the SCCR, May 2017, the nation states did not coalesce around a committee-wide statement of the outcomes of the meeting, which indicates the SCCR did not even form a consensus about what transpired during its deliberations. Instead, future meetings of the SCCR will have to rely on a "Summary by the Chair." Even in this summary, the only future action on "Limitations and Exceptions for Educational and Research Institutions and Persons with Other Disabilities" recorded was to maintain the item on the agenda for the next meeting. This indicates there is no current progress internationally toward any consensus about this topic. See online: www.wipo.int/meetings/en/doc_details.jsp?doc_id=372036.

228 The *Marrakesh Treaty* was adopted by WIPO 27 June 2013, with more than eighty signatories. Canada had helped achieve the language that enabled nation states to adopt the treaty.

national treaties, Canada and its provinces are internationally obliged to enact, in Canadian law, provisions consistent with Canada's treaty obligations. Canadians are then bound to obey the Canadian laws. The current state of the *Copyright Act* satisfies our new international commitment to the *Marrakesh Treaty*.

To the extent that schools and school administrations are working to achieve the goals of provincial disabilities legislation, and those goals involve activities that fall within the sphere of copyright, schools and school administrations must comply with the *Copyright Act*. In other words, they can fully exploit the users' rights given them in the *Copyright Act*, sections 32 and 32.01 (and any other users' rights sections of the *Copyright Act* that schools find relevant to meeting these needs); however, meeting the information needs of people with disabilities other than through those users' rights sections will require that schools and school administrations meet people's other needs while respecting the copyright interests inherent in the materials being dealt with: permissions must be acquired, whether through the philanthropy of the rights holders or through the purchase (of licences) by schools or school administrations.[229] To the extent that provincial legislation conflicts with copyright, it will be *ultra vires* the province and not enforceable because, as discussed at the outset of this chapter, copyright has been given exclusively, under the *Constitution Act, 1867*, to the federal government.

---

229 In this connection, the following chapter may be of interest: Wilkinson, "Access to Digital Information: Gift or Right?," above note 120. See also Meaghan Shannon, *A Comparison of Ontario's Accessibility for Ontarians with Disabilities Act and the Canadian Copyright Act: Compliance, Enforcement, Risks, and the Implications for Ontario Community Colleges* (MSL Thesis, Western University Faculty of Law, 2016), online: http://ir.lib.uwo.ca/mslp/2.

Contributors

Brenda Bowlby was a member of Hicks Morley, an employment, labour, and education law firm, until she retired from the partnership in 2015 after thirty-three years. Her practice involved representing school boards, and she built the firm's special education practice, appearing before the Ontario Special Education Tribunal on numerous occasions and representing school boards in significant court cases and Human Rights Tribunal cases involving special education issues. Among the cases she has argued is *Eaton v Brant County Board of Education* (starting with the Special Education Tribunal of Ontario and concluding in the Supreme Court of Canada), which remains Canada's leading case on special education law. She is a co-author of *An Educator's Guide to Special Education* and *An Educator's Guide to Human Rights Law*, both in their second editions.

Nora M Findlay, PhD, has recently retired after serving more than twenty-five years as an educator and school-based administrator in Saskatchewan. She is a recipient of a SSHRC (Social Sciences and Humanities Research Council) doctoral fellowship and a CAPSLE (Canadian Association for the Practical Study of Law in Education) fellowship. She has also received a High Commendation Award from the UCEA (University Council for Educational Administration) Centre for the Study of Leadership and Ethics for her doctoral dissertation. Nora has published in a number of periodicals, including the *Education & Law Journal* and *Educational Administration Quarterly*, contributed policy analyses to *CAPSLE Comments*, and co-authored several book chapters on education law. Her scholarly interests include school law, student rights, school safety, Indigenous education, educational administration, and school leadership.

Frank Peters came to Canada as a teacher. He initially taught in northern Alberta in Fort Chipewyan and later served as a principal with Fort McMurray Catholic Schools. A faculty member at the University of Alberta for over three decades, he served in such roles as associate dean in the Faculty of Education and associate chair and graduate coordinator in the Department of Educational Policy Studies until retiring in 2014. His major areas of expertise relate to educational governance and education and law. He has also taught courses in both the theory and practice of educational leadership and educational change. For almost twenty years he coordinated a required course he co-developed in the bachelor of education degree program dealing with ethics and law in education. He has been privileged to supervise about twenty-five doctoral students. Among his ongoing interests are the challenges teachers will face in dealing with increasingly diverse classrooms in a context of limited resources and greater demands for "tangible" results.

Lauri Reesor is a partner at Hicks Morley and chair of the firm's Human Rights practice group. In her thriving management-side labour and employment practice, Lauri places particular focus on human rights litigation, class action litigation, and labour arbitrations. She has also developed a niche expertise in education law practice, including a concentration in special education law. Lauri is a strong advocate, regularly appearing on behalf of employers, school boards, and other service providers at all levels of court, at the Human Rights Tribunal of Ontario, the Special Education Tribunal, the Child and Family Services Review Board, and the Pay Equity Hearings Tribunal, and before labour arbitrators. Lauri is a frequent speaker at conferences on key labour and employment issues as they relate to human rights accommodation and special education law.

Eric M Roher is national leader of the Education Focus Group and partner at Borden Ladner Gervais LLP. He practises in the areas of education law, labour relations, and employment law. He advises a range of public- and private-sector employers, as well as school boards and independent schools. He also represents clients before administrative tribunals and labour relations boards, including the Human Rights Tribunal of Ontario, the Ontario Labour Relations Board, the Ontario College of Teachers, and the Workplace Safety and Insurance Board. Eric is an adjunct professor at the University of Toronto Faculty of Law where he teaches a course on education law. His work has appeared in a wide variety of publications, including the *Education & Law Journal, Principal Connections, The Register*, and *CAPSLE Comments*.

Theresa Shanahan was called to the bar of Ontario in 1990, practising law for several years before obtaining a PhD in education. She is an associate professor and former associate dean in the Faculty of Education at York University, and is a member of the Graduate Program in Public Policy, Administration and Law. Her research is broadly focused on education law and education policy (K–12 and post-secondary), legal education, professionalism, and university governance and decision making. She is co-editor of *The Handbook of Canadian Higher Education Law*; *The Development of Post-secondary Education Systems in Canada: A Comparison between British Columbia, Ontario and Québec*; and *Making Policy in Turbulent Times: Challenges and Prospects for Higher Education*. Current research projects include educators' ethical decision making and their understanding of professionalism (with Sarah Barrett); and risk management in the legal framework for student discipline and school safety in Canadian education. Among the courses she has taught are Foundations of Education, Human Rights and Education, Theory into Practice in Education, Inquiries into Schooling, Changing Currents in Postsecondary Education, Policy Issues in Postsecondary Education, and the Sociology of Professional Education.

Nadya Tymochenko, a partner at Miller Thomson LLP, oversees the firm's Education Law Industry Group. Nadya works for publicly funded school boards, private schools, and colleges. She advises clients on governance matters, including the roles, duties, and liabilities of trustees and senior administrators, access to information and protection of privacy, school closings, school councils, and risk management, as well as student matters, which include special education, human rights, student discipline, and health and safety issues. She also advises school boards on their labour and employment issues, such as collective agreement interpretation, employee discipline and terminations, grievance arbitrations, Ontario Labour Board matters, employment agreements, employee accommodation, human rights, and employee health and safety. Nadya is a frequent presenter at conferences, including those of the Canadian Association for the Practical Study of Law in Education, the Ontario Council of Administrators of Special Education, and the Ontario Bar Association. She is the co-author of *An Educator's Guide to Managing Sexual Misconduct in Schools* and *An Educator's Guide to Parental Harassment* and also the co-editor of *An Educator's Guide to the Health and Safety of Students*.

Dr. Shirley Van Nuland is an associate dean of Education and associate professor in the Faculty of Education at the University of Ontario Institute of Technology. She brings more than twenty-five years of teaching experience to the university gleaned from her roles as teacher and principal in Ontario's elementary and secondary school systems and as an education officer with the Ontario Ministry of Education. Her work has been recognized through the Chancellor's Award for Excellence in Teaching from Nipissing University, the Service Award from the Canadian Association for Foundations of Education (CAFE), and the Publication Award from CAFE. Among the courses Shirley teaches are "Education Law, Policy, and Ethics," and Foundations of Education. Her research interests include standards of practice, ethical standards, and codes of conduct as these intersect in the lives of teachers and students.

Dr. Margaret Ann Wilkinson, trained as a lawyer and as a librarian, is a member of the Law Society of Upper Canada. She has practised law and is currently a faculty member at Western University, where she is also affiliated with graduate programs in both Law and Health Information Science. Awarded the Ontario Library Association's Les Fowlie Intellectual Freedom Award, she publishes on copyright, moral rights, patent, personal data protection, privacy, confidentiality, and professional ethics. She is the author of "Copyright, Collectives, and Contracts: New Math for Educational Institutions and Libraries," which appears in *"Radical Extremism" to "Balanced Copyright,"* edited by Michael Geist, and a co-author of *Canadian Intellectual Property Law: Cases and Materials*, 2d ed (2017). Her research is funded by the Social Sciences and Humanities Research Council.

Dr. David C Young is an associate professor in the Faculty of Education at St Francis Xavier University in Antigonish, Nova Scotia, where he also serves as the chair of the Department of Curriculum and Leadership. His research is focused on the broad topic of educational administration and policy. More particularly, his current writing deals with issues pertaining to law and education. His work has appeared in a wide variety of publications, including *CAPSLE Comments*, the *Education & Law Journal*, the *Canadian Journal of Educational Administration and Policy*, and the *Journal of Educational Administration and Foundations*. He is also co-editor of *Teaching Online: Stories from Within* (2014). Among the courses he has taught are Psychological Foundations of Education, Educating Exceptional Students, Social Foundations of Education, Educational Policy, Educational Research, School Administration, Inclusive Schools, and Education Law.

Marvin Zuker was appointed a Judge of the Ontario Court of Justice in 1978. He retired in December 2016. He holds the rank of Associate Professor at the Ontario Institute for Studies in Education, University of Toronto, where he has taught since 1982. Justice Zuker has written extensively in the areas of family, civil, and education law. He is the author and co-author of numerous books on education and on the rights of women and children. Titles include *Children's Law Handbook*, third edition, with Lynn Kirwin; *Education Law*, fourth edition, with Anthony Brown; *Sexual Misconduct in Education*, second edition, with Grant Bowers and Rena Knox; and *Canadian Women and the Law* and *The Law Is Not for Women*, both with June Callwood.

Table of Cases

Index

Hentze (Guardian ad litem of) v Campbell River School District No 72, 157
higher, emergence of, 179–83
in loco parentis, 157–59, 185, 187–88
Madsen v Mission School District No 75, 160
Myers (Next friend of) v Peel County Board of Education, 156
parens patriae, 158–59
R v Ogg-Moss, 158
sports and physical education, higher standard for, 179–82
Ethical Standards for the Teaching Profession, 220

Fabrique Act, The, 30
Facebook, 76–78, 101, 222–23, 229, 231–32
Fair dealing
alternatives to the dealing, 326
amount of dealing, 324, 325
Access Copyright v York University, 309, 312–14, 318–19, 322–25, 326–30
Application to the Facts section of SCC decision, 323
blanket licences, 305, 316
CCH v LSUC, 325–26, 327–28, 330–31
character of dealing, 324
Colleges and Institutes Canada, 329
contracts and licences, 302–3, 315, 316
Copyright Act, 316, 320–29, 332–33
Copyright Board tariffs, 316–17, 318–20
DRM protection, 316–17
educational institutions, users' rights for, 332–33
effect of the dealing on the work, 328
incidental use, 315
institutional policies and, 329–31
moral rights of creators, 317, 318
nature of the work, 327–28
non-infringing uses of works, 315–20
permissions, 316
purpose of the dealing, 324
Society of Composers, Authors and Music Publishers of Canada v Bell Canada, 324–25
TPM provisions, 316–17
Universities Canada, 329
users' rights provision, 317–18, 320, 329
waived rights, 317
whole work, use of, 325–26

Field trips
Bain v (Guardian ad litem of) v Calgary Board of Education, 175
definition of, 175–76
educational purpose, 176
emergency plans, 176
field trips, 175–79
itineraries, diversion from, 175, 176
medical emergencies, 177–78
planning considerations, 176
standard of care extension, 175
transportation, 178–79
Freedom of expression
Bethel School District No 403 v Fraser (No 84-1667), 130–31
Charter rights, 123–26, 133, 135, 150, 210, 219
Hazelwood School District v Kuhlmeier, 131–32, 135
Lutes (Litigation Guardian of) v Prairie View School Division No 74, 132–33
material disruption and/or substantial disorder, 130
off-campus communication, 133–36
Pridgen v University of Calgary, 133–36
privacy, educators' right to, 213–14, 223–25
Ross v New Brunswick School District No 15, 210, 219
Tinker v Des Moines Independent Community School District, 129, 131–32, 135
French language education
Arsenault-Cameron v Prince Edward Island, 118–19
Catholic French language schools, 117
Charter rights and, 117
Mahe v Alberta, 119–20
Ontario and, 117
right to, 117–20
Funding
Catholic schools, public funding of, 40–41, 86, 121–24
current funding structures, issues with, 124
equal allocation frameworks, 46, 47
fair funding structure, attempts to establish, 39, 46–47
other denominations, no public funding for, 122